AN UNFORMED MAP

THEORY IN FORMS
A series edited by Nancy Rose Hunt, Achille Mbembe, and Todd Meyers

"	"	384	W. Ralston 2871
"	"	385	C.E.C. Sorensen 8191
"	"	386	Lt N. Macbeth: Appn Appt
"	"	387	Office Accommodation f Govt Depts in Lagos
"	"	388	A Peters 6033
"	"	389	S.A. Parker 10429 WAF
"	"	390	General Revision of Sal in Civil Service
"	"	391	Bukuru-Ropp Road
"	"	392	Sgt Smitherman 7388
"	"	393	Non Ferrous Metals Ind Act 1918

AN UNFORMED MAP

Geographies of Belonging between Africa and the Caribbean

PHILIP JANZEN

Duke University Press   *Durham and London*   2025

© 2025 DUKE UNIVERSITY PRESS. All rights reserved

Project Editor: Ihsan Taylor
Designed by Courtney Leigh Richardson
Typeset in Garamond Premier Pro by Westchester Publishing Services

Library of Congress Cataloging-in-Publication Data
Names: Janzen, Philip, [date] author.
Title: An unformed map : geographies of belonging between Africa and the Caribbean / Philip Janzen.
Other titles: Theory in forms.
Description: Durham : Duke University Press, 2025. | Series: Theory in forms | Includes bibliographical references and index.
Identifiers: LCCN 2024044750 (print)
LCCN 2024044751 (ebook)
ISBN 9781478031925 (paperback)
ISBN 9781478028697 (hardcover)
ISBN 9781478060901 (ebook)
Subjects: LCSH: Colonial administrators—Africa. | Caribbean Area—Colonial influence. | Great Britain—Colonies—America—Historiography. | Great Britain—Colonies—Africa—Historiography. | France—Colonies—America—Historiography. | France—Colonies—Africa—Historiography.
Classification: LCC JV412 .J36 2025 (print) | LCC JV412 (ebook) | DDC 325.4072/2—dc23/eng/20250225
LC record available at https://lccn.loc.gov/2024044750
LC ebook record available at https://lccn.loc.gov/2024044751

Cover art: Collage of images: children at a schoolhouse in Jamaica, ca. 1904 (Library of Congress); pages from the 1919 Nigeria Register of Correspondence (National Archives of the United Kingdom); police station, prison, and Wesleyan Church, from "Kumasi Town Layout," ca. 1920 (Basel Mission Archives); Félix Eboué (*left*) and Charles de Gaulle in Chad, 1940 (Library of Congress); Christ Church in Cape Coast, 1901 (National Archives of the United Kingdom). (*Background*) Adobe Stock.

Excerpts from *All God's Children Need Traveling Shoes* by Maya Angelou, copyright © 1986 by Caged Bird Legacy LLC. Used by permission of Random House, an imprint and division of Penguin Random House LLC. All rights reserved. Reproduced with permission of the Licensor through PLSclear.

For Rachel

Et mon originale géographie aussi ; la carte du monde faite à mon usage, non pas teinte aux arbitraires couleurs des savants, mais à la géométrie de mon sang répandu.
—AIMÉ CÉSAIRE, *Cahier d'un retour au pays natal* (1939)

It was a rupture in history, a rupture in the quality of being. It was also a physical rupture, a rupture of geography.
—DIONNE BRAND, *A Map to the Door of No Return: Notes to Belonging* (2001)

Contents

Acknowledgments
xi

INTRODUCTION
Fault Lines
1

1
FROM THE CARIBBEAN TO AFRICA
15

2
MIDDLE PASSAGES
31

3
FRAGMENTS AND PHOTOGRAPHS
53

4
BURIED VOCABULARIES
73

5
INTIMATE GEOGRAPHIES
105

6
OLD TALK
133

7
POETRY AND PERIPHERIES
155

EPILOGUE
179

Notes   Bibliography   Index
183   225   247

Acknowledgments

This book began as a seminar paper in my first semester of graduate school at the University of Wisconsin-Madison. Florence Bernault mentioned the names of Félix Eboué and René Maran, wrote down a few bibliographic references, and suggested that I write a paper about their experiences in Central Africa. It was not a very good paper, but I kept pulling the thread long after the seminar ended. Since then, I am amazed at where these stories have taken me. The transformation of that paper into this book, however, was possible only because of a network of family, friends, teachers, colleagues, archivists, and editors.

The main reason I ended up in Wisconsin was Meredith Terretta, who introduced me to the work of Aimé Césaire in Ottawa. She has been opening doors for me and pushing me through them ever since. In Madison, I was fortunate to have Jim Sweet as an adviser. Partway through that first semester, he intervened in a critical moment, and at many other junctures he offered valuable guidance. His encouragement, generosity, and hospitality have been relentless since our first meeting. In addition to Jim and Florence, I am grateful to my other teachers at Wisconsin, whose insights have left a mark on my scholarship: Neil Kodesh, Emily Callaci, Claire Wendland, and the late Teju Olaniyan. My thanks also to Greg Mann, who joined my committee, read carefully, and offered many detailed and helpful suggestions.

I met a lot of good friends in Madison who introduced me to the strange customs of a strange land. Thank you especially to Athan Biss, Jake Blanc, Sean Bloch, Dave Bresnahan, Pirate John Coakley, Ben Cross, Geneviève Dorais, Nikki Eggers, Lindsay Ehrisman, Lacy Ferrell, Sarah Hardin, Hermann von Hesse, Patrick Kelly, Chris Kirchglaser, Maura Kudronowicz, Dave Murdock, Janey Myers, Julia Nicols-Corry, Patrick Otim, Jillian Slaight, Derek Taira, Caitlin Tyler-Richards, and Brooke Ward. And the ODR at Tenney Park.

The research for this book took me to West Africa, the Caribbean, and Europe, and I was the very fortunate recipient of funding from the Social Sciences and Humanities Research Council of Canada, the Social Science Research Council, the American Council of Learned Societies, the Mellon Foundation, and the Department of History and African Studies Program at Wisconsin. A special mention also to my Larry Nafziger postdoctoral fellowship in Ottawa.

Along the way, many people helped me find beds and food, secure visas, and locate documents. In Ghana, I relied endlessly on the acumen of Bright Botwe and Godsway Doe-Fiawornu. Auntie and Uncle Quaynor were gracious guides and hosts. For other advice and camaraderie, I depended on Carina Ray, Clifford Campbell, Lacy Ferrell, Mathieu Humbert, and Alison Okuda. In Nigeria, I owe a lot to Philip Olayoku, ever-insightful scholar and Liverpool fan. Olutayo Adesina, Lisa Lindsay, Sara Katz, Sam Daly, and Mutiat Oladejo provided all the necessary research tips. Ade, Hassan Nafisat, and the rest of the archivists at the National Archives and at the Kenneth Dike Library in Ibadan were instrumental. A chance encounter with Niyi Osundare at the University of Ibadan was a highlight. In Sénégal, Mariétou Diop and Abdoulaye Sow were vital to the success of my research. Bienvenu Kabou and the indomitable Pierrot introduced me to "Dakar by night."

In Trinidad and Tobago, Rita Pemberton arranged everything for me. I am grateful to Lorraine Nero, Glenroy Taitt, and Darron Small at the Alma Jordan Library. It was a true honor to meet Dr. Margaret Rouse-Jones. And Mikhail Nicholson had the foresight to send me to Charlotteville. In Martinique, Charles Scheel made the research possible. He and Patty repeatedly opened up their home and served regular doses of *boudin créole*. Thank you also to Kesewa John, Frédéric Kouby, Malik Noël-Ferdinand, Jessica Saint-Louis, and Dominique Taffin. And a special thanks to Wyck Jean-Louis for sharing stories about her grandfather.

In the United Kingdom, Jeff Green and Marika Sherwood told me where to go and how to find what I needed. Nishant Batsha and Ebony Jones offered crucial respite from the archives. Mary and Patrick McBrearty were warm hosts and served the finest breakfast spread in London. Thank you also to Rhoda Boateng, Leslie James, Paul Johnson, and Lucy McCann. In France, Marie-Andrée Durand undertook many hours of extra work on my behalf. For hospitality and friendship, thank you to Nate Marvin, Brett Reilly, Chantal Ndami, Sébastien Akira-Alix, and Marc Botzung and the Spiritain priests. My thanks also to Bernard Michel. Other archivists and librarians who deserve a special mention are Richelle Mackenzie, Nina Meyer, Patrick Moser, Alexia Turpin, and Anne Welschen.

Much of the writing and revision of *An Unformed Map* happened at the University of Florida (UF), where it has been a great privilege to work with Nancy Hunt. In addition to being an extraordinary scholar, she has supported me—and this book—since I arrived in Gainesville. I have also benefited enormously from the wisdom and wit of Luise White, and I am looking forward to sending in this manuscript so that we can hit a new stop on the L. W. Burger Tour.

My office at UF is located in the Center for African Studies, and it is a pleasure to work down the hall from Brenda Chalfin, Abdoulaye Kane, Miles Larmer, Todd Leedy, Agnes Leslie, Renata Serra, and Alioune Sow. Leo Villalón, another colleague in African Studies, made an important intervention several years ago, for which I will always be indebted. Over in the Department of History, I am lucky to work alongside many wonderful colleagues, especially the other "junior" hires who arrived around the same time: Seth Bernstein, Fernanda Bretones, Sandy Chang, Max Deardorff, James Gerien-Chen, Anton Matytsin, Lauren Pearlman, Heather Vrana (who helped secure some last-minute images!), and Ben Wise. Two friends in Gainesville have been particularly instrumental and loyal: Ethan Frey and Ben Lemmond.

I am also grateful to my faculty mentor, Jon Sensbach, who, with the help of Bill Link, arranged a manuscript workshop in 2022. Brent Hayes Edwards and Judith Byfield went above and beyond, offering many pages of detailed suggestions and questions. I still don't think I have responded well enough to their feedback, but this was the best I could do. At a different workshop, this one organized by Nancy Hunt, Stephan Palmié and Leah Rosenberg offered creative and insightful advice on chapter 3. Jeffrey Ahlman, Florence Bernault, Marcel Diki-Kidiri, James Essegbey, Charles Scheel, and David Schoenbrun all read parts of this book on very short notice, and I remain indebted to each of them. And for their help with translations from Fante, Ga, Banda, and Sango, my thanks to Seth Nii Moi Allotey, Marcel Diki-Kidiri, James Essegbey, Efua Osam, and Hermann von Hesse. French translations are mine, unless indicated otherwise.

Many others have read proposals, answered long emails, and offered encouragement from afar. I am especially grateful to Jean Allman, Karin Barber, Lotfi Ben Rejeb, Andrea Ceriana Mayneri, Kwame Dawes, Alex Gil, Tamara Giles-Vernick, Andy Ivaska, John Janzen, Alex Lichtenstein, Dan Magaziner, Minkah Makalani, Michelle Moyd, Rachel Nolan, Carina Ray, Terry Rey, Casey Schmitt, Lorelle Semley, and Robert Trent Vinson.

At Duke University Press, it has been a privilege to work with Elizabeth Ault, Ben Kossak, and Ihsan Taylor. I had no idea making a book entailed so much more than writing. I thank them for their patience, guidance, and many reassurances.

My thanks also to the anonymous reviewers for their questions and comments and for engaging with my arguments and ideas. A subvention from the UF College of Liberal Arts and Sciences and Center for the Humanities and the Public Sphere (Rothman Endowment) helped to cover the costs of the images and index.

My greatest debts are to my friends and family back home. To Lucas "No Big" Di Lenardo, Gabe "Drift Away" Menard, and Darren "Boost Your Packets" MacLure, thank you for your humor and spitefulness and for reminding me who I am. To Mike Dixon and the Rockers, thank you for coaching me and welcoming me. And to Ghenette Houston, a second older sister; Brian Ladd, premier photographer of large baseball bats in Alberta; Jane Willms, in contention for the most thoughtful listener in the world; Ben Willms, authority of the pinball underworld; Paul Siebert, chef extraordinaire; Moira Toomey, also in contention for the most thoughtful listener in the world; David Siebert, a secretly brilliant historian; Ally Siebert, who likes to eat half-clementines; Steve Houston, guardian and regaler of Saskatchewan lore; Gloria Houston, who has always known my favorite foods; Donovan Friesen, the man behind the CKCU microphone; and Eric and Susan Rupp, my greatest musical supporters—thank you for many years of friendship. It means more than you will ever know.

To my mother and father, Marlene Toews Janzen and William Janzen, thank you for believing in me, for teaching me how to read and write, for teaching me how to use libraries, for teaching me the importance of history, and for many other lessons about life. I am profoundly grateful to have such loving parents. To my sister, Rebecca, thank you for candid advice and for setting an example that I can't ever seem to catch up to. To Clara Toews and Sol Janzen, thank you for always being there for your nephew. To Gord and Ann, thank you for welcoming me into your family. And to Rachel, my incredible wife, what can I say? You have been with me every step of the way. I am sure you are sick of hearing about "the lives and ideas of a group of people from the Caribbean who . . . ," but you have always listened. Thank you for your love and kindness and for your sparkling sense of humor. You bring a smile to my face every day. I cannot imagine my life without you.

Introduction

FAULT LINES

The sound of wind came first. It careened down from the Blue Mountains and rushed unsteadily through the streets, swirling around trees, scraping across corrugated iron roofs, and rattling shutters. Then, at half past three, the ground began to tremble. For thirty seconds, the city shook. Brick walls crumbled, houses collapsed, tram lines twisted, and water pipes burst open. Stone and splintered wood piled into the streets. Telegraph poles swayed and fell, their wires tangling in the debris. As the tremors eased, desperate voices called out through the rubble, piercing the abrupt stillness. By evening, fires had engulfed the remains of Jamaica's capital and clouds of yellow-gray dust filled the air, floating eerily over the city. Not a building was left untouched. More than eight hundred people lost their lives.[1]

The next morning, January 15, 1907, Kingston lay in ruin. The streets, overcome by the wreckage, were impassable. Familiar landmarks, such as the Colonial Bank, the Jamaica Club, and the Parish Church were unrecognizable. Most

FIGURE 1.1. The Parish Church in Kingston, Jamaica, after the 1907 earthquake. *A Visit to Jamaica in 1907*, University of Florida Manuscript Collections.

people sought refuge at the Race Course at the north end of the city, taking shelter in circus tents and hoping to reunite with family and friends. Some found solace listening to sermons and singing hymns. All were overcome by the scale of destruction, and in the days that followed, they began tending to the difficult tasks of honoring the dead and rebuilding their home.

News of the earthquake spread quickly around the world. When the first reports arrived in southern Nigeria, five thousand miles away, a young teacher named Lebert Josiah Veitch was devastated. Veitch was from the north coast of Jamaica, from the parish of St. Ann, and he had studied and taught in Kingston for nearly a decade. In January 1905, however, he had taken a position at a British colonial school in Bonny, near the mouth of the Niger River. As Veitch read about the effects of the earthquake, the Atlantic Ocean's expanse loomed. "A quivering blow as of a giant's fist smashing the lower side of the earth's crust," read the Reuters news telegram printed in *The Lagos Standard*. "Provisions are needed most urgently."[2] Worried and helpless, Veitch turned to a friend, Dandeson Coates Crowther, the archdeacon of the Niger Delta Pastorate.[3]

Crowther, the youngest son of Samuel Ajayi Crowther, had formed the Pastorate in 1892 with other Saro returnees in reaction to the exclusionary racism of the Anglican-run Church Missionary Society.[4] In April 1907, a few months after the earthquake, the Pastorate was celebrating its fifteenth anniversary, and Crowther invited Veitch to give an address. Veitch's evocative description of conditions in Jamaica left the audience in "sobs and tears." Crowther then passed a resolution expressing "sympathy" with the people of Jamaica and called for the contribution of "adequate funds for their relief."[5] By the end of June, *The Daily Gleaner* in Kingston happily reported that Crowther's resolution, combined with Veitch's "stirring appeal," had raised more than £28.[6]

Compared with the total extent of the damage, this was a tiny sum, but its significance was more than material. For more than two centuries, the Niger Delta had been a hub of the transatlantic slave trade, a site where European empires had fractured history, and these ruptures echoed into the twentieth century. On colonial maps and in colonial archives, always centered in Europe, Jamaica and Nigeria were partitioned, pushed to the margins, linked only by their shared status as colonies of the British Empire. By coming together to support the rebuilding of Kingston, however, Crowther and Veitch asserted a common cause, transcending the naturalized fault lines that divided Africa and the Caribbean.

This book is about moments of disjuncture and the creation of new geographies. It is also about the forms of colonial archives and the challenges of writing history across imperial boundaries. At the center of this study are the lives and ideas of Caribbean people who, like Veitch, joined the British and French colonial administrations in Africa. While Veitch's story is in some ways exceptional, his path from Jamaica to Nigeria was not unique. Between 1880 and 1940, more than five hundred others from the Caribbean followed this path.[7] Typically two or three generations removed from slavery, Caribbean administrators grew up in colonial societies, saw themselves as British and French, and tended to look down on Africans as uncivilized and inferior. Once in Africa, however, they were doubly marginalized—excluded by their European colleagues and unwelcome among Africans. The effects of this middle position were profound. How did Caribbean administrators reckon with assimilation, racism, and dislocation? And what do the traces they left behind reveal about the designs of colonial archives and the distortions of colonial knowledge production?[8] *An Unformed Map* responds to these questions by examining the uneven intellectual trajectories of Caribbean administrators in Africa. As they learned African languages, collaborated with African intellectuals, and engaged with African cultures and histories, many began to rethink their positions in the British and French empires. I argue that such exchanges generated new geographies of belonging, foundations from which others could imagine new political horizons. Moreover, by weaving together a range of unconventional sources, methods, and narrative forms, this book offers a model for writing history in the face of archival fragmentation.

> So looking through a map
> of the islands, you see
> rocks, history's hot
> lies, rot-
> ting hulls, cannon
> wheels, the sun's
> slums: if you hate
> us. Jewels,
> if there is delight
> in your eyes.
> The light
> shimmers on water,
> the cunning
> coral keeps it
> blue.[9]

Archives and Methods

An Unformed Map follows a wave of research on African diasporic exchanges in the first half of the twentieth century.[10] Typically centered in "Black London" and "Paris Noir," this vibrant field of study analyzes how cosmopolitan settings in Europe facilitated relationships between Africans, Antilleans, and African Americans that were not possible anywhere else. These "Black Atlantic" histories emphasize the importance of translation, cultural production, and intimate, everyday interactions in the creation of political and cultural networks. Much of this scholarship also highlights the irony that the capitals of the British and French empires acted as seedbeds for the rise of anticolonial movements that profoundly altered the meanings of empire, nation, and citizenship.

Individually, these are important works, but taken in the aggregate, the focus on London and Paris reinscribes an imperial geography of "centers" and "peripheries," a map of rocks and hot lies. This staging of history, buttressed by the national archives of former empires and typically segregated between British and French, forecloses opportunities to consider people and their ideas from beyond a colony-metropole nexus.[11] In these asymmetrical narratives, the histories—and historiographies—of people from Africa, the Caribbean, and "elsewhere" are fragmented by the methodological nationalism of European-based periodizations and analytical categories. What emerges as coherent takes form only in relation to the metropole, with sprinklings of "local color."[12] Rendered invisible, meanwhile, are the many histories that were not circumscribed by imperial boundaries.[13]

The trajectories of Caribbean administrators in Africa starkly reveal the limits of such approaches. They also illuminate a method for composing "Black Atlantic" histories that move across different geographies.[14] When I began research on this project as a graduate student, I followed the existing scholarship to the colonial archives of the United Kingdom and France—after all, Caribbean administrators were civil servants.[15] I did find relevant sources, including government correspondence, annual reports, and personnel files. Yet the forms of these archives—their colonial logics, geographical divisions, and conceit of totality—limited the kinds of questions I could ask. In these archives, Africans and African-descended peoples became legible as historical actors only when they fell within the purview of the British and French empires as "colonial migrants."[16] For those who produced these records, the classificatory infrastructures of empire made exchanges like those between Veitch and Crowther unthinkable.[17]

In an attempt to move beyond these limitations, I began to follow the paths that Caribbean administrators followed themselves, paths that led away from the conventional fieldwork patterns of Ghana–United Kingdom and

Martinique–France.[18] Over the course of two years of multi-sited research in Africa and the Caribbean, I gradually assembled a unique, transatlantic archive—colonial reports mixed with newspapers, political pamphlets, private correspondence, ethnographic notebooks, novels, handwritten dictionaries, and a suitcase full of poems. By "reading across" these seemingly disparate sources, I saw how Caribbean administrators overcame divisions of language and geography, creating new connections between Africa and the Caribbean. In short, by following their boundary-crossing examples, I uncovered histories made incommensurable by the design of colonial archives.[19]

After completing my research, however, I struggled to find a suitable model for bringing my sources together. In the end, I produced a dissertation that was constrained by a biographical mode of intellectual history, one that reified the categories and cartographies of empire. When I began revising that work and writing this book, I became increasingly frustrated with these shortcomings. The British and French empires had fragmented the lives of people such as Lebert Veitch and Dandeson Crowther and then reproduced this fragmentation in the colonial archives that recorded their stories. Yet Veitch and Crowther, along with many others, had transcended these doubled fragmentations, leaving traces of extra-imperial networks of belonging across the Atlantic. How could I assemble my sources into narratives that would reflect both the disjunctures of empires *and* the moments of connection that emerged outside their grasp? And how could I historicize the effects of colonial archives without reproducing their forms?

It had not been enough, I realized, to shift away geographically from London and Paris and toward obscure archives not found on the old maps of colony-metropole research itineraries. More important was to move away from the epistemologies of empire that have undergirded much scholarship on Africa and the Caribbean over the past century.[20] Indeed, the conventions of academic history writing prescribe boundaries of knowledge production in the same manner as colonial archives.[21] The result is an institutionalized fragmentation of forms and methods under the guise of "disciplinarity," a broken geography of inquiry.[22] Seeking a new framework to bring together my disjointed sources, I turned to the writings of Caribbean intellectuals and found inspiration in the figure of scattered islands.

> Looking through a map
> of the Antilles, you see how time
> has trapped
> its humble servants here. De-
> scendants of the slave do not

lie in the lap
of the more fortunate
gods. The rat
in the warehouse is as much king
as the sugar he plunders.
But if your eyes
are kinder, you will observe
butterflies
how they fly higher
and higher before their hope dries
with endeavour
and they fall among flies.²³

Form and Fragmentation

Earthquakes, like the one that hit Jamaica in 1907, have played a central role in Caribbean history. The archipelago itself was shaped—and continues to be shaped—by tectonic shifts thousands of feet below sea level. No less significant have been the seismic changes wrought by European imperialism: the genocides of Indigenous peoples, the enslavement of Africans, the creation of plantation societies, the importation of indentured laborers from Asia, underdevelopment, and neocolonialism. The reverberations of these geological and imperial ruptures have imposed new political, cultural, and economic geographies on the Caribbean.²⁴ They have also produced a view of the region as fragmented—islands separated not only by water, but also by history, language, nation, race, and other factors.

Caribbean intellectuals have long questioned such representations, however, asserting the region instead as a space of relation. Sylvia Wynter, for example, contrasts the "alienation" of the plantation with the "folk culture" of the plot, or provision grounds. The plantation and its heirs, she writes, have used "the myth of history" to maintain their power, while the plot, with "its own history," is a space that offers "other possibilities" and connections, a "social order" outside of the plantation system.²⁵ Édouard Glissant similarly questions the dominant narratives of a fragmented Caribbean, suggesting that the "subterranean convergences" of the region challenge a "linear, hierarchical vision of a single History."²⁶ Unlike the Mediterranean, Glissant writes, "a sea that concentrates," the Caribbean Sea "explodes the scattered lands into an arc."²⁷ George Lamming, meanwhile, sees the islands of the Caribbean as a "continuous family of mountains" that "broke and fell beneath the sea." "Long submerged," he writes, these mountains "left an archipelago of peaks like a swarm of green children patiently awaiting its return."[28] And Daniel Maximin describes the Caribbean as a "rosary of islands," a space whose "open insularity" has generated an "archipelagic consciousness."[29]

An earlier variation on these powerful ideas comes from Aimé Césaire's landmark poem *Cahier d'un retour au pays natal*. In a frequently cited passage, Césaire describes the ruptures of the Caribbean:

> Iles cicatrices des eaux
> Iles évidences de blessures
> Iles miettes
> Iles informes
>
> Islands scars of the waters
> Islands evidence of wounds
> Islands crumbs
> Islands unformed[30]

For Césaire, these islands are "scars" and "crumbs," disjointed by time and space. They are also "evidence" of a brutal history that has left the Caribbean divided and wounded. A few lines later, however, Césaire asserts that these fragmented islands are also potent sources for imagining a new formation:

> Raison rétive tu ne m'empêcheras pas de lancer
> absurde sur les eaux au gré des courants de ma soif
> votre forme, îles difformes,
> votre fin, mon défi.
>
> Mulish reason you will not prevent me from casting
> absurd upon the waters at the mercy of the currents of my thirst
> your form, deformed islands,
> your end, my challenge.[31]

Even "mulish reason," Césaire declares, will not prevent him from pursuing his "challenge": finding coherence in these crumbs, "casting" these fragments together, and transforming the colonized, "deformed" geography of the Caribbean into an arc.

Particularly striking in Césaire's reflections on form and fragmentation is the word "*informes*," a French adjective that evokes a dizzying spiral of meanings. Most dictionaries translate *informe* as "shapeless," "formless," or "without form," the latter recalling its use at the beginning of the book of Genesis: "La terre était informe et vide." In their 1983 English translation of the *Cahier*, however, Clayton Eshleman and Annette Smith translated "*informes*" as "unformed."[32] This peculiar, though productive, translation pulls the adjective in multiple directions simultaneously. On one hand, *unformed* looks backward, to something that once had form but was rendered shapeless. Yet *unformed* also gestures to the future, anticipating the possibility of a new form only beginning to take shape. This translation thus contains both incomplete destruction and inchoate creation, past and future circulating within each other, new forms emerging from the decomposition of older ones. In the context of Césaire's poem, "Islands unformed" suggests both the breaking down of a perspective that sees the Caribbean as fragmented islands and, at the same time, the possibility of joining those islands together into a new, cohesive form.

Césaire's decision to use *informe* also connects this passage with the thinking of French philosopher Georges Bataille. In 1929, two years before Césaire arrived in Paris as a scholarship student from Martinique, Bataille launched *Documents*. This short-lived publication about archaeology, art, and ethnography brought together intellectuals such as Michael Leiris, Marcel Griaule, and Carl Einstein.[33] Rather than reproducing the forms of other art journals, Bataille and his collaborators attempted to unsettle oppositions such as high/low and modern/primitive with ironic and often provocative juxtapositions of image and text. As Leiris later wrote, *Documents* was "a war machine against received ideas."[34] One recurring feature of the journal was the lively "Dictionnaire Critique," and in the December 1929 issue, Bataille offered a definition for *informe*, quoted here in part:

> Un dictionnaire commencerait à partir du moment où il ne donnerait plus le sens mais les besognes des mots. Ainsi *informe* n'est pas seulement un adjectif ayant tel sens mais un terme qui servent à déclasser, exigeant généralement que chaque chose ait sa forme.[35]

> A dictionary would begin as of the moment when it no longer provided the meanings of words but their tasks. In this way *formless* is not only an adjective having such and such a meaning, but a term serving to declassify, requiring in general that every thing should have a form.[36]

In Bataille's rendering, the "task" of *informe* was to "declassify" the enclosures of form. Much like *Documents* itself, Bataille used *informe* to challenge naturalized categories and structures and to disrupt their power to exclude and delegitimize. Later in the entry he also referred derisively to the forms that "*les hommes académiques*" imposed on their objects of study. Yet Bataille's paradoxical definition—or, rather, "negation of definition"—also allowed for other possibilities of representation: *informe* "requir[ed]" the generation of form.[37]

There are clear resonances of this potent ambiguity in Césaire's usage of *informe*, with its tensions between destruction and creation. It seems unlikely that Césaire had any direct connections with Bataille, though it is possible that Césaire read *Documents*—he was an admirer of Leo Frobenius, who contributed to the journal.[38] Whatever the case, the multiple versions of the *Cahier* reveal that Césaire had a careful relationship with the word. "*Iles informes*," and the surrounding section, did not appear in the original version of the poem, published in *Volontés* in 1939.[39] Nor did this section appear in either of the 1947 revisions.[40] Rather, Césaire added this conspicuous fragment toward the end of the 1956 edition published by Présence Africaine.[41] Perhaps as he prepared this "édition définitive" in the wake of the disappointments of departmentalization, he found refuge in a word that conjured a new geography, one that disrupted and unsettled the legacies of French colonialism in the Caribbean.[42] For Césaire, this unformed geography may not have been within reach politically, but poetically it was within his grasp.[43]

There is an echo of Césaire's *informe* in the thinking of Kamau Brathwaite. In a 1992 essay, "Caliban's Garden," Brathwaite recalled a transformative childhood experience in Barbados. Walking along the beach near Bridgetown, Brathwaite had a "vision" of the "sweep of islands" between Florida and Venezuela:

> I also began to recognise that these broken islands were the sunken tops of a mountain range that had been there a million years before. That in addition to the death of the Amer-Indians I was also witnessing the echo of an earlier catastrophe. That the islands had been part of a mainland. That we once had been whole—and that what we now had between each other was holes. But that whole and hole, those two types of things should somehow come together. That was a challenge I knew I had to be able to span. To find the rhythm.[44]

Brathwaite's "challenge," much like Césaire's "*défi*," was to span the "holes"—or "scars"—of the Caribbean Sea, to disrupt the impositions of colonial forms. Looking through a map of the Antilles, there were only dots, a mountain range *unformed* into "broken islands." In the spaces between, however, there was possibility, a plural unity that might come to be, as yet *unformed*. This "challenge" is a thread that runs through many of Brathwaite's other works, both academic and poetic.[45] Whether writing about African cultures in the Americas or about the effects of colonialism in the Caribbean, he sought to "find the rhythm," to bridge the "holes" with the "whole," to join the fragments with form. As he noted in the famous one-sentence conclusion of his 1974 essay on creolization, "The unity is submarine."[46]

A year later, in 1975, Brathwaite used this same phrase—"the unity is submarine"—at the beginning of an essay titled "Caribbean Man in Space and Time."[47] Reviewing the state of scholarship on the Caribbean, Brathwaite, like Wynter, criticized the focus on the plantation as the "main unit of study," a unit that derived from the plantation system itself.[48] In its place, Brathwaite advocated for new attention to culture, "creative arts," oral sources, and the plural processes of creolization. He also called for a "multi-dimensional model" as an alternative unit of Caribbean study. This model, he explained, would attend to "interaction between inner and outer plantation, inner and outer metropole, and the lateral and diagonal relationships between these."[49] At the end of the essay, Brathwaite closed with a variation on his aphorism: "The unit is submarine." Kelly Baker Josephs suggests that this "repetition-with-a-difference" may have been Brathwaite's subtle way of emphasizing the importance of searching for new, submerged units of study. For Brathwaite, it was imperative to trace "lateral and diagonal relationships" beyond the plantation, even if they at first appeared unformed in the sky-blue frame of the map.[50]

The layered meanings, translations, and genealogies of *informe*, articulated through the poetics of Césaire and Brathwaite, provide a conceptual language for writing the scattered histories of Caribbean administrators in Africa. This language, with its residue of dissolution, carries the colonial logics that produced my fragmented archive—the plantation, the holes, the broken islands, the hot lies, the imposition of a linear, hierarchical History. At the same time, the futurity implicit in this language holds possibilities for disrupting colonial logics and casting these fragments together in new forms—the plot, the whole, the arc, the continuous family of mountains, the rosary of islands. *An Unformed Map* embraces the productive ambiguity of this language. By tracing the submarine convergences of an unformed archive, this study uncovers how Caribbean administrators in Africa transcended the fault lines of empire and created new geographies of belonging.

> Looking through a map
> of the islands, you see
> that history teaches
> that when hope
> splinters, when the pieces
> of broken glass lie
> in the sunlight,
> when only lust rules
> the night, when the dust

is not swept out
of the houses,
when men make noises
louder than the sea's
voices; then the rope
will never unravel
its knots, the branding
iron's travelling flame that teaches
us pain, will never be
extinguished. The islands' jewels:
Saba, Barbuda, dry flat-
tened Antigua, will remain rocks,
dots, in the sky-blue frame
of the map.⁵¹

Narratives

In the chapters that follow, I draw on the conceptual language of *informe* to assemble my disjointed sources, making narrative form—and fragmentation—an integral part of my arguments. To this end, I pay close attention to composition, structure, staging, vocabulary, and tone.⁵² I also inflect the text with images, "temporal distortions," and extracts of letters, fiction, and poetry to represent the contingencies and confluences in the lives of Caribbean administrators.⁵³ Finally, to disrupt the artificial divisions of academic disciplines, I blend methods from history, literary studies, human geography, linguistic anthropology, and ethnography.⁵⁴

In chapter 1, I examine the economic and ideological factors that prompted Caribbean people to join the British and French colonial administrations in Africa. Following the tone of my sources, I present this historical context in the constrained idiom of the colonial archive, looking through a map of the islands. Chapter 2 continues in this stilted, conventional manner, drawing mainly on the petitions of René Maran in Oubangui-Chari and Cunliffe Hoyte in the Gold Coast. I use their particular experiences to describe the general in-betweenness of Caribbean administrators in Africa, especially their fraught relationships with Africans and Europeans. These petitions, however, also show how Maran and Hoyte began to question the contradictions of colonial categories, and I mirror this shift in my prose, using termites, metaphorically, to disrupt the yellowing mustiness of *sentiments distingués* and humble, obedient servants.

Chapter 3, the turning point, begins with a series of "orchestrated fragments."[55] In my analysis of these fragments, I suggest that the scopic metaphors that prevail in scholarship on colonialism only serve the illusion of archival plenitude. Then, using the story of Francis Simmons, I narrate my own frustrations with the seductive forms of colonial archives. The chapter closes with examples of Caribbean administrators creating new geographical alignments amid exclusion and alienation. The remaining four chapters follow this example, assembling disparate sources with new methodological alignments in four detailed case studies of African-Caribbean exchanges.

Chapters 4 and 5 focus on translation, examining how learning African languages changed the intellectual trajectories of David McNeil-Stewart of Trinidad and Félix Eboué of French Guiana. Chapter 4 examines how McNeil-Stewart's study of Fante, Twi, and Ewe in the Gold Coast allowed him to develop close relationships with leaders in Kumasi and Keta, including leaders of the African Methodist Episcopal Zion Church. I also speculate on the ways he may have translated Trinidad in West Africa as he reflected on the linguistic connections between Akan languages and the Creole he grew up speaking in Belmont. The chapter ends with McNeil-Stewart's son, Kenneth, and his place in the burgeoning print culture of 1930s Accra.

In chapter 5, I explore Eboué's understudied ethnographic work from Central Africa and his intimate networks in Oubangui-Chari. More specifically, I use his dictionary and collection of Banda folktales to uncover his relationships with interpreters and colonial-appointed chiefs. I also chart his development of a "*géographie cordiale*" with figures such as Fily Dabo Sissoko as he moved back and forth across the Atlantic in the later stages of his career. Finally, I consider how, after his death, Eboué's ethnographic fictions transformed him into a Pan-African symbol.

Chapter 6 turns to the social and political networks of three teachers who worked in the Gold Coast and Nigeria: Joseph Britton of British Guiana, Edith Goring of Barbados, and Lebert Veitch of Jamaica. I focus in particular on their relationships with their students, some of whom became leading figures of West African nationalism in the mid-twentieth century. Rather than narrating the stories of Britton, Goring, and Veitch chronologically, however, according to the forms of the archives that hold their stories, I have assembled them in a series of layered, interconnected recollections.

Finally, in chapter 7, I turn to the remarkable case of Henri Jean-Louis Baghio'o, a lawyer from Guadeloupe who worked as a judge in French Congo from 1923 to 1925. Using Jean-Louis's suitcase of poetry, I trace his journeys across the geographies and temporalities of decolonization, from 1950s Algeria to nineteenth-century Guadeloupe to sixteenth-century Mali. Written mostly in rhyming stanzas, the poems highlight a trajectory from civil servant to devout anticolonialist. The poems also draw together a network of politicians and activists that Jean-Louis encountered in Congo, Cameroon, and Sénégal and around the Caribbean. Ultimately, by articulating these sources and methods in creative dialogue, this study destabilizes the optic of empire and challenges the structures of colonial knowledge production, opening new possibilities for gathering the fragments of scattered histories.

In Book Three of *Omeros*, Derek Walcott describes Achille's dreamlike voyage from St. Lucia to Africa. Winding his way up a river in a pirogue, he arrives at a settlement of "peaked huts," where he meets his father, Afolabe.[56] Pointing to their hearts, they introduce themselves, but Achille cannot remember the name his father gave him. Nor can his father, even as he tries to explain its importance. A sound is "missing," and the fault lines of "the deaf sea" come to the surface.[57] They are separated by language, slavery, empire, and three centuries. Achille is "only the ghost / of a name."[58] As he finds his way back to St. Lucia, Walcott describes the transformations of the Middle Passage: "Each man" became "the nameless freight of himself," leaving "their remembered / shadows to the firelight."[59]

Like Achille, Caribbean administrators had to reckon with missing sounds, forgotten shadows, and lost meanings. Not African, but not British or French either, they moved along the slippages in-between. At times, eager to assert their imperial identities, they reinforced the geographies of empire. At other times, they found themselves isolated and betrayed, embodying the contradictions of colonialism. In these spaces of exclusion, however, there germinated new geographies of belonging, grounded not in particular imperial territories but in the networks they formed across the deaf sea, the traces of an unformed map.

Geography, as Katherine McKittrick writes, may appear "static" but is always "alterable terrain."[60] Caribbean administrators understood this as well as anyone. Their mobility, facilitated by the British and French empires, also allowed them to subvert imperial forms. As they cut across the Atlantic, their trajectories became transversals, evading, disrupting, and undoing colonial divisions of space.[61] At the same time, they were assembling new connections beyond the sky-blue frame of the map. By forging ties across disjuncture, they conjugated the tensions and multiple temporalities of *informe* into action, creating a transatlantic nexus between Africa and the Caribbean.

I

From the Caribbean to Africa

I was trying to put together the fragments of my early education; trying to recall when I had first heard the word Africa, what emotions it had registered. —GEORGE LAMMING, *The Pleasures of Exile* (1960)

In the Antilles, the black schoolboy who is constantly asked to recite "our ancestors the Gauls" identifies himself with the explorer, the civilizing colonizer, the white man who brings truth to the savages. —FRANTZ FANON, *Black Skin, White Masks* (1952)

On November 5, 1901, a post office worker in British Guiana wrote to the governor and requested a promotion and transfer to "any part of the African Colonies or Protectorates."[1] John Barbour-James had never left British Guiana, much less the Caribbean. Born in Epsom in 1867, he had grown up under the hard blue sky of the Corentyne coast, where gaulins and white cranes flew over rice fields, swamps, and courida trees, where the sound of the surf echoed

FIGURE 1.1. Post Office Square, Water Street, Georgetown, British Guiana, ca. 1900. Photographs and Prints Division, Schomburg Center for Research in Black Culture, New York Public Library.

in rhythm with indifferent cycles of drought and flood, and where, on Sunday mornings, he and his older brother had followed their parents to the nearby Anglican church. When he was old enough, he was sent by his father, a farmer and teacher, to the Congregational School in Hopetown, where he learned to read and write with words that had come to the Caribbean on ships from across the sea. Now thirty-four, Barbour-James had a stable position at the post office in Belfield and was a lay reader at Christ Church in Georgetown. He was also married, with four children and a fifth on the way. Only Barbour-James knew his precise motivations for requesting a transfer to Africa, but it was clear that he was looking for a change.[2]

After two weeks passed with no response from the governor, Alexander Swettenham, Barbour-James wrote again and reiterated his desire for a transfer to "some part of His Imperial Majesty's African possessions."[3] Prompted by Barbour-James's persistence, Swettenham sent the application on to the Colonial Office in London. In his accompanying letter, however, he noted that

Barbour-James was "a native of British Guiana, of coloured parentage" and thus "scarcely of the class to be made a District Commissioner."[4] When the application arrived in London, the Colonial Office had similar concerns. One official stated plainly: "I do not like importing coloured men into West Africa."[5]

Several months later, in March 1902, Barbour-James sent a third letter to Swettenham, this time to convey his support for the British Boer War effort.[6] Writing on behalf of an "Association of loyal Negro subjects" who were willing to "render any help required for the service of Our Empire," Barbour-James expressed his hope that a British victory would bring "far-reaching and beneficial results . . . for the native Races." He also urged the British to consider "the interest of these Natives" and referred to them as his "kinsmen." Swettenham sent the letter on to London, as well as to Alfred Milner, the High Commissioner for Southern Africa.[7] Perhaps swayed by Barbour-James's expressions of loyalty, the Colonial Office acquiesced to his earlier request for a transfer and appointed him to the Gold Coast as a district postmaster.[8] Soon after, Barbour-James boarded a steamship and embarked on his journey to West Africa, leaving behind his wife, Caroline, and their children.[9]

These three letters illuminate the main factors that motivated people from the Caribbean to join the British and French colonial administrations in Africa. Barbour-James was eager to escape the constraints of life in the Caribbean, he was devoted to the British Empire, and he claimed a sense of paternalistic kinship with Africans. His desire for a transfer to "some part of His Imperial Majesty's African possessions" may have been geographically vague, but in ideological terms it could not have been more specific. For Barbour-James, as for many others in the Caribbean at the turn of the twentieth century, imperial and diasporic visions of Africa were deeply entangled. There was no sharp distinction between Africa as a space of empire and as an imagined diasporic homeland.[10] Before delving further into these intellectual entanglements, however, this chapter turns back to the nineteenth-century Caribbean to explain the economic and ideological factors that led Barbour-James and people like him across the Atlantic.

Islands Ruled by Sugar Cane

Despite the promises of abolition, British and French Caribbean colonies in the second half of the nineteenth century were saturated with the economic, political, and racial legacies of slavery.[11] These legacies varied around the Caribbean due to differences in demographics, geography, economic structures, and imperial power, yet there were also similarities. Above all, economic activity remained tied to plantations. Small groups of white elites controlled the political institutions,

FIGURE 1.2. Workers in a tobacco field in Montpelier, Jamaica, ca. 1900. Library of Congress, 96511801, Strohmeyer and Wyman.

financial resources, and land, and they maintained an exploitative labor structure by imposing low wages, high rents, tenancy and vagrancy laws, pass systems, sharecropping, and poll taxes. Planter-controlled governments, meanwhile, passed restrictive laws on land transactions that barred group purchases and established minimum acreage requirements. This prevented workers and peasants from pooling their resources and buying smaller portions of land.[12] Such measures ensured the continued stratification of Caribbean colonies. Former slaves had little choice but to continue working on plantations as poorly paid laborers in conditions not unlike slavery.[13]

To be sure, some people found ways to buy property, especially in larger colonies where there was more available land. Others grouped together to establish small farms and villages or resorted to squatting on abandoned and uncultivated fields. Missionary societies also sometimes bought land and redistributed it to former slaves. In general, however, the economic patterns of slave societies endured. In 1848 Barbados, for example, African-descended people owned less than 1 percent of the agricultural land, even though 90 percent of the island's laborers worked in agriculture.[14] Those who sought refuge in towns were no better off. Poverty, malnutrition, and crowded, squalid living conditions bred illness, epidemics, and high infant mortality. In 1890s Grenada, for example, almost half of all children born to poor mothers died before age one. Between 1896 and 1897 in Jamaica, meanwhile, 17.5 percent of all children died before age one, and 26.8 percent died before age five. And in rural Martinique, the infant mortality rate was 23 percent as late as 1952.[15]

White politicians and landowners also preserved their power by importing indentured laborers. This was particularly significant later in the nineteenth century, when sugar prices went into steady decline due to increased global competition and new processing technologies. Between 1838 and 1917, nearly 500,000 indentured laborers from India arrived in the British Caribbean—mainly in British Guiana, Trinidad, and Jamaica. Forty-five thousand, meanwhile, arrived in Guadeloupe and Martinique.[16] The British and French also brought indentured laborers to the Caribbean from China and West Africa.[17] This influx of workers allowed plantation owners to keep wages low and strip workers of their bargaining power. Arrivals from India and China also dramatically altered the social and racial landscapes of the Caribbean.[18]

Economic conditions for freed slaves and their descendants remained grim for the remainder of the nineteenth century and into the twentieth century. Coupled with persistent racial discrimination, the strains on daily life led to a series of uprisings across the Caribbean: the Morant Bay Rebellion in Jamaica in October 1865; the Insurrection du Sud in Martinique in September 1870; the Confederation Riots in Barbados in April 1876; the April 1899 fires and 1900 strikes in Guadeloupe; and the Water Riots in Trinidad in March 1903, among others.[19] These eruptions revealed deep discontent and desire for change, but they also revealed the willingness of the British and French colonial states to suppress dissent with brutal violence. In short, emancipation did little to change the basic economic and political realities of Caribbean society. Power remained with white elites, and they used this power to sustain their profits. In these circumstances, many people turned to migration to support themselves and their families. Some traveled to other British and French colonies in the Caribbean, as well as to the Dominican Republic, Cuba, Costa Rica, Panama, and the United States.[20] Others, such as John Barbour-James, migrated to West and Central Africa.

In addition to these economic factors, a sense of attachment with the British and French empires also motivated people from the Caribbean to take up colonial appointments in Africa. At the turn of the twentieth century, imperial culture in the Caribbean was pervasive. Imperial institutions and practices informed language, religion, social customs, and even architecture. Most important for reinforcing imperial culture was education. Missionaries and churches had spearheaded education systems in the Caribbean, but government schools gradually took over. By the 1870s and 1880s, the British and French colonies in the Caribbean made primary school free and compulsory.

Education held the potential for social mobility, but it also reinforced existing hierarchies. For one thing, there was far more funding for prisons and police than for education, and so schools for working-class children and those in rural areas were often inadequate and inaccessible.[21] In Trinidad, for instance, in 1900, one-third of children did not receive any formal education.[22] There was better access in the French Caribbean, but even then most students completed only primary school.[23] Secondary schools came with costly fees, and scholarships were rare. The tiny minority that continued on to secondary schooling in the Caribbean was mostly white or mixed-race. Some secondary schools in Jamaica simply denied admission to Black students.[24]

For those who did attend colonial schools, the curriculums followed European models and celebrated imperial culture. Teachers were usually from the Caribbean but trained within similar contours, often under European teachers. Students thus learned the languages, literatures, histories, and geographies of Europe rather than of the Caribbean.[25] Léon-Gontran Damas, for example, born in French Guiana in 1912, later recalled this peculiar dynamic: "The textbooks, one must remember, were destined solely for use by the metropolitans. I can distinctly remember that in my class . . . we were more familiar with the names of plants growing in France than with those growing at home."[26]

In this form, education was a powerful tool for assimilation, and schools presented the British and French empires as benevolent communities to which young students were fortunate to belong. In British colonies, children sang "Rule Britannia" on Empire Day, while in the French Caribbean, students learned to recite "Nos ancêtres les Gaulois." C. L. R. James, born in Trinidad in 1903, later described the debilitating effects of colonial education:

> It was only long years after that I understood the limitation on spirit, vision, and self-respect which was imposed on us by the fact that our masters, our curriculum, our code of morals, *everything* began from the basis that Britain was the source of all light and leading, and our business was to admire, wonder, imitate, learn; our criterion of success was to have succeeded in approaching that distant ideal—to attain it was, of course impossible. . . . [I]t was the beacon that beckoned me on.[27]

FIGURE 1.3. Children reciting at a schoolhouse in Jamaica, ca. 1904. Library of Congress, 2003680329, H. C. White Co.

The assimilative nature of colonial education, along with other circulations of imperial culture, led people in the Caribbean to "deny themselves as a collectivity" and to think of themselves as "British" and "French," not as "West Indian," "Antillais," "Trinidadian," or "Martiniquais," and certainly not as "Black."[28] Reflecting on his childhood in 1930s Kingston, Stuart Hall noted that "the word 'black' had never been uttered in my household or anywhere in Jamaica in my hearing, in my entire youth and adolescence—though there were all kinds of other ways of naming."[29]

The uneven reach of Caribbean education in the late nineteenth and early twentieth centuries also generated a small but significant middle class. As the Guyanese historian Walter Rodney later wrote: "The rise of the middle class can only be effectively chronicled and analyzed in relationship to the schools."[30] Of key importance for this emerging social group was literacy, the ability to speak "proper" English and French, and the command of British and French imperial culture. Class lines were also linked closely with racial lines, resulting in a tripartite division of Caribbean societies. The white minority remained the elite upper class, while those in the middle class, often mixed-race, used "other ways of naming" to distinguish themselves from the workers and peasants of the lower classes. Colonial education systems thus created an intermediary group between the descendants of former slaveholders and former slaves. This group was made up of people who usually had some property and who worked as teachers, journalists, printers, pharmacists, postmasters, doctors, solicitors and barristers, and clerks. Many also became civil servants.

In the late nineteenth- and early twentieth-century Caribbean, joining the colonial civil service offered the opportunity to leave behind the world of plantation labor and fashion a middle-class British or French identity. Most who joined the civil service remained in the Caribbean, but some also worked in Europe, South Asia, and even the South Pacific.[31] Others, such as John Barbour-James, sought appointments in Africa. "All of the students in my class had but one idea," recalled Aimé Césaire, born in Martinique in 1913. "Pass the exam. . . . Go to France and obtain a position in Africa, in Sénégal or elsewhere."[32] This attraction to Africa points to another factor that motivated people in the Caribbean to cross the Atlantic. In addition to dire economic circumstances and the spread of imperial culture, Caribbean administrators were guided by their ideas about Africa and Africans, perceptions shaped by the mixing of their colonial educations and diasporic imaginations.

A Sound That Is Missing

"About Africa, at the time, I had two ideas," recalled Vivian Renwick. "First that the place was very unhealthy and second that it was covered with dense forests from which lions and tigers occasionally emerged to take their toll of unwary human beings."[33] In May 1915, Renwick was a foreman in the Trinidad Agriculture Department, and when his supervisor offered him a three-year appointment in Nigeria, his imagination took hold. Likely influenced by his education at St. Mary's College in Port of Spain, Renwick also worried that West Africa would be "inhabited by savage and hostile tribes."[34] Nevertheless, inspired by a "spirit of adventure," he accepted the job offer and soon after left Trinidad for Nigeria.

Renwick's ideas about Africa and Africans were common in the early twentieth-century Caribbean, and they reveal the power of colonial knowledge production. In such monolithic renderings, "Africa" was primitive and unhealthy,

FIGURE 1.4. Rue du Pavé, Fort-de-France, Martinique, ca. 1902. Library of Congress, 2021635733, H. C. White Co.

a place of wild animals, jungles, and mystery. Africans, meanwhile, were portrayed as savages—backward, superstitious, and lazy.[35] Renwick's ancestors had come to the Caribbean from Africa, but this history was warped and fractured by school curriculums and class politics. Most people in the Caribbean considered themselves utterly distinct from Africans. In Jamaica, for instance, identifiers such as "African," "Negro," "Congolese," and "Black" were pejorative, even though 90 percent of the population was of African descent.[36] Édouard Glissant similarly notes that in Martinique "the word African or Negro represented an insult."[37] And as C. L. R. James wrote in 1932, "In the West Indies to-day there are no native peoples in the sense that there are natives in Africa."[38]

Such thinking was not all-encompassing, however, and African cultures remained an important influence in the early twentieth-century Caribbean.

Renwick himself noted that he worked with an "old man...who, rumour said, had come from the Congo." Renwick described this man, known as "John Congo," as "a reticent fellow who kept his history and his knowledge to himself" and who "had been domiciled in Trinidad such a long time that he had probably forgotten all about his native land."[39] Renwick may have mentioned John Congo simply to set himself apart, but this was not a unique situation. Africans had continued arriving in British and French Caribbean colonies as indentured laborers well into the 1860s, and at the time of Renwick's birth in Port of Spain in 1892, there were two thousand Africans living in Trinidad.[40]

African languages, customs, and institutions underwent significant changes over the nineteenth century, but their durability into the twentieth century indicates their importance.[41] The presence of "Aradas," "Mandingoes," "Houssas," "Karamenties," "Eboes," "Congoes," and "Yorubas" in Caribbean societies had significant effects.[42] For example, even as Christianity generally abounded, Africans and their descendants grafted Christian beliefs onto African religions and rituals, such as with Myal and Revival Zion in nineteenth-century Jamaica.[43] In rural areas of the Caribbean, meanwhile, healers such as obeah men and *quimboiseurs* relied on African-based healing practices.[44] In Martinique and Guadeloupe, one of the popular dances of the late nineteenth century was the *calenda*, likely a diluted version of *calundu* or *kilundu*, a healing ritual and form of ancestor worship from Central Africa.[45] In late 1860s Trinidad, a group of Radas from Dahomey established a vodun healing community in Belmont, a neighborhood of Port of Spain. They named their settlement Dangbwe, in honor of the serpent deity of Ouidah, and newspapers reported that members of the community cured smallpox "on African principles."[46] And in Guadeloupe, several African communities still existed in the early twentieth century, including groups that sang songs in Kikongo.[47] The Caribbean middle class may have been eager to distinguish themselves from Africans, and especially from African religions, but these influences were significant, especially when mediated by personal connections and family memories.[48]

Combined with colonial renderings of "the dark continent," the legacies of African cultures in the Caribbean fostered a sense of paternalistic kinship toward Africans. In some cases, such attitudes also motivated Caribbean people to join the British and French colonial administrations in Africa. For instance, Félix Eboué of Cayenne, French Guiana, who worked in Central Africa for more than two decades, was the grandson of freed slaves. His parents, Yves Urbain Eboué and Aurélie Léveillé, were both grandchildren of enslaved Africans who had arrived in French Guiana from West Africa in the early nineteenth century. According to Eboué's biographer, Brian Weinstein, the family "kept cowrie shells as a souvenir of Africa [and] believed that their ancestors came from a royal African lineage and that traders with whom they had been dealing kidnapped them from the river village where they lived."[49] Eboué's mother spoke to her children in Creole and told them Guianese riddles and folktales, while Eboué's paternal grandmother, Marie-Gabrielle Eboué, shared stories about her experiences with slavery. These influences created a powerful image of Africa in a young Eboué. As he later declared, "Africa, cradle of my ancestors, had always exercised a profound attraction over me."[50]

Cunliffe Malcolm Hoyte of Trinidad, who went to the Gold Coast as a sanitary inspector in 1910, came from a family that traced similar traditions. According to Hoyte's nephew, Ralph Hoyte Jr., their ancestors were enslaved in West Africa and brought to Barbados. Subsequent generations moved to British Guiana and then to Trinidad, where they settled in Belmont. Hoyte Jr. notes that the family referred to Cunliffe as "Dhani" because "the African families who lived in Belmont had a custom. They gave their first born boy an African name."[51] It is unclear how Hoyte's parents chose this name or what language it comes from, but the fact that such an "African" custom existed highlights the extent to which ideas about Africa proliferated in the Caribbean outside the realm of imperial culture. This intellectual context undoubtedly inspired interest and curiosity about Africa in Hoyte and others.[52]

Henri Jean-Louis of Guadeloupe, meanwhile, who worked as a judge in Brazzaville in the 1920s, believed he was part of a lineage from Timbuktu. Specifically, he claimed to be the descendant of "Mohamed Baghio'o," the "Pasha Cheikh" of Timbuktu in the fifteenth century.[53] According to Jean-Louis, slave traders kidnapped descendants of Baghio'o and sold them away to the Caribbean. This history remained alive to Jean-Louis, and in a later memoir he recalled his appointment to Brazzaville as "one of my most cherished dreams" and as an "opportunity to return to the land of my ancestors."[54] Noting that the "emotion was still strong," he described his memories of traveling to Africa for the first time:

> The blood coursing through my veins push[ed] me in search of a distant fatherland . . . beyond the great blue spaces, a continent call[ed] me. . . . I had desired it since childhood, and there I was approaching it, cautiously, with the obscure premonition of mysterious depths. . . . That trip uncovered an echo that rose inside of me, it resounded throughout my body and called all my being to exaltation. . . . My heart beat as strongly as it had at age 20.[55]

For Jean-Louis, the appeal of taking up a position in his "distant fatherland" was informed by both family memories and colonial renderings of a "mysterious" continent. As with many others in the early twentieth-century Caribbean, a singular, timeless "Africa" overshadowed the violent realities unfolding on the other side of the Atlantic. These realities, however, were also a key factor in bringing people such as Jean-Louis to Africa. The British and French needed personnel to expand their authority, and for some colonial officials the Caribbean came to represent an ideal source for recruitment.

Colonial Imperatives

In November 1901, at the same time that John Barbour-James submitted his application for a transfer from British Guiana to "any part of the African Colonies or Protectorates," the British began a war against the Aro in southeastern Nigeria. They claimed their purpose was to put a stop to Aro slave trading and introduce "civilization," but the war also allowed the British to expand their monopoly over trade operations in the region.[56] In many other parts of Africa, the British and French were consolidating their power in a similar manner, and in the wake of military campaigns, they needed personnel to establish colonial governments.[57] Hiring Europeans was not always a viable option because they required high salaries, regular vacation leave, and pensions. They also often struggled with tropical illnesses. British and French officials thus relied increasingly on Africans to fill positions as clerks, interpreters, and laborers.[58] They were reluctant to promote Africans to senior positions, however, believing Africans to be incapable or to require too much training.

Seeking a solution to this dilemma, some colonial officials turned to the Caribbean. At the core of this initiative were ideas about race and civilization that prevailed in the late nineteenth and early twentieth centuries. For one thing, the British and French believed that administrators from the Caribbean, who had more familiarity with colonial infrastructure, could provide the same quality of work as Europeans but could be paid lower salaries. As one British official put it in 1917: "These West Indian people do good work for small pay."[59] Colonial officials also believed that, unlike Europeans, Caribbean administrators would not get sick in Africa because of their familiarity with tropical climates. Such thinking endured even as many Caribbean administrators became ill in Africa and had to return to the Caribbean. "There is no reason to suppose that a negro from the West Indies will not enjoy the same health in West Africa as a native of the Coast," declared one official in the Gold Coast.[60] In French colonies in Africa, meanwhile, this thinking was so pervasive that some Caribbean administrators used it to their advantage to secure appointments and promotions.[61]

Beyond ideas about cost and health, some colonial officials also subscribed to theories about the "providential design" of the transatlantic slave trade. In the early nineteenth century, a number of antislavery advocates in the northern United States began suggesting that God had preordained the slave trade so that enslaved Africans and their descendants could learn under a "superior" race and then one day return to Africa to "redeem" and "civilize" the continent.[62] This ideology drove emigration initiatives such as the American Colonization Society and other efforts to resettle freed slaves in Africa, from which colonial officials took inspiration.[63]

In 1894, for example, Ernest Ingham, the Anglican bishop of Sierra Leone, proposed a recruitment trip to the Caribbean to recruit West Indian missionaries. Ingham was born in Bermuda to a white, aristocratic family, and the governor of Sierra Leone, Frederic Cardew, heartily endorsed Ingham's proposal:

> I believe the repatriation of West Indian Africans in the Protectorate even in the small numbers which may be expected under the Bishop's scheme will have a beneficial and civilizing effect on the aboriginal natives and that better results may be expected from their efforts than from those of a like number of Sierra Leone natives, the mass of whom it appears to me, if I may judge from the tone of the public press, have not that sympathy for their fellows in the interior which is required for civilizing as well as christianizing work.[64]

Cardew, and others in the colonial government, evidently believed that African-descended people in the Caribbean would be effective "civilizers." The following June, Ingham arrived in the Caribbean and traveled to Barbados, Antigua, Jamaica, and Bermuda. When he returned to Sierra Leone later that year, he published a brief pamphlet summarizing his experiences. Declaring the journey a success, Ingham claimed to have found many people eager to migrate to West Africa and noted that, with their "unique educational advantages," West Indians could turn Africa into "a nursery and seed-plot." The pamphlet also revealed Ingham's belief in providential design:

> After generations of bondage in the West Indies, these Africans are now in a position of comfort, knowledge, and independence that, but for this bondage, never could have been theirs. The opening up of their own land as the coming continent very nearly coincides with the period of their emancipation. Can this be accidental? Is God's hand not in it? We verily believe that it is, and that He will be with every effort to draw the attention of the best of these people to their own fatherland; that He will in

His own time and way draw many over there to share in its uplifting, and that by these and other means some will actually be led to repatriate themselves.[65]

Ingham urged the British to recruit "Negro evangelists and teachers" and claimed that "these are the people who will understand Equitorial [*sic*] Africa and Africans better than the Anglo Saxon." For Ingham, Cardew, and others in the British administration, West Indians were not only qualified, but destined, to help "civilize" Africans. Ingham's tour of the Caribbean did not lead to widespread "repatriation," but his brand of thinking was influential. Five years after Ingham's return to Sierra Leone, Cardew began his own recruitment campaign of railway workers from the Caribbean.[66]

Ideas about providential design were also prevalent among nineteenth-century French intellectuals. Jacques-François Roger, for instance, argued that the transatlantic slave trade had exposed Africans and their descendants in the Americas to "Western" skills and knowledge and that they should return to Africa to apply what they had learned to support the "regeneration" of the continent.[67] Like their British counterparts, French colonial officials looked to the Caribbean to fill recruitment gaps. They saw Antilleans as more "French" than Africans and thus as more competent administrators.[68] French officials also expressed regard for the supposed affinity between Antilleans and Africans, making frequent allusions in reports to the unique capabilities of Caribbean administrators for "understanding the native."[69]

Notions of providential design also took hold among the descendants of freed slaves, including prominent nineteenth-century thinkers such as Edward W. Blyden.[70] Born in St. Thomas in the Danish West Indies in 1832, Blyden advocated for the mass migration of African-descended peoples in the Americas to Africa, and he followed this path himself, settling in Liberia in 1850. Once in Africa, he continued to write about the importance of "return migration" for the future of the continent. In an 1862 essay, for example, he declared: "We call it, then, a providential interposition, that while the owners of the soil have been abroad, passing through the fearful ordeal of a most grinding oppression, the land, though entirely unprotected, has lain uninvaded. We regard it as a providential call to Africans every where to 'go up and possess the land.'"[71] While Blyden was later adamant that Africans should lead such initiatives instead of returnees from the United States or the Caribbean, his extensive writings influenced some of those from the Caribbean who joined colonial governments in Africa.[72]

Conclusion

How and why did Caribbean people join the British and French colonial administrations in Africa? Bleak economic circumstances motivated Caribbean people to migrate in search of financial security, while colonial education led the emerging middle class to seek ways of asserting their British and French imperial identities. Caribbean administrators were also attracted by the idea of "Africa"—their personal connections, sometimes mediated by colonial ideology, fostered a sense of paternalistic kinship with Africans. European colonial officials, meanwhile, believed Caribbean administrators could provide "European"-level services at a lower cost, would be more resistant to illness, and were uniquely qualified, even destined, to participate in the "civilizing" mission.

Between 1880 and 1940, more than five hundred people from the Caribbean migrated to Africa to join the British and French administrations. Yet their expectations for life in African colonies were often misguided. Firmly stuck between their African pasts and colonial aspirations, how would Caribbean administrators respond to the realities of life in Africa? How would they reckon with the inconsistencies and contradictions of their positions as colonized colonizers? And how would they make sense of their fraught relationships with Africans and Europeans as they navigated the incongruencies of race, nation, and empire?

2
―――

Middle Passages

The native of the West Indies occupied an intermediate position between the European and the native of West Africa. —LEWIS HARCOURT, SECRETARY OF STATE FOR THE COLONIES, 1914

The West Indian has not proved to be so much superior to the West African and I do not think any distinction should be made. —EDWARD BLAND, GENERAL MANAGER, NIGERIAN RAILWAY, 1918

The whites generally believe that the prestige of the conquering race is damaged by giving important positions to *hommes de couleur* in the colonies; as strange as it seems, the natives do not tolerate being placed under their authority. —MARCEL DE COPPET, GOVERNOR OF DAHOMEY, 1933

"With a French heart, I feel that I am in the land of my ancestors," wrote René Maran in February 1910.[1] "Ancestors that I disapprove of because I do not share their primitive mentality or their tastes, but they are nonetheless my ancestors." Maran had just arrived in Bangui, the small capital of Oubangui-Chari, but his feelings of dislocation were familiar. Born on a boat between French Guiana and Martinique, he had spent much of his childhood at a boarding school in France, separated from his family.[2] His father, the son of freed slaves from French Guiana, worked for the colonial government in Central Africa, and his parents returned to France only every few years. "My holidays were spent between the four solitary walls of a school," he recalled.[3] A few years after graduating, Maran followed his father's path into the colonial civil service, and in January 1910 the Ministère des Colonies sent him to Oubangui-Chari.[4]

Maran's sense of dislocation in Bangui was reinforced when he began his appointment as police commissioner. In September 1910, he had to settle a dispute between a Portuguese merchant named Sampayo and one of his "boys," who claimed that he had not been paid. When Maran called Sampayo to the police station and demanded that he pay what was due, the merchant became indignant. He claimed that Maran was taking the African man's side because of "atavism" and that it was "hardly a surprise" that Maran was "protecting the natives" because he himself was "only half-civilized."[5] Maran submitted a report about Sampayo's insults, but the head of the *circonscription* (district) refused to take action. "Our authority with regard to foreigners would be too greatly reduced," he explained.[6]

Most Caribbean administrators in West and Central Africa faced similar circumstances. They grew up in colonial societies, saw themselves as "British" and "French," and felt that they were part of the British and French empires. They also tended to look down on Africans, even as they were attracted by the notion of an African homeland. Once in Africa, however, these ideas collided with the racial and hierarchical dynamics of African colonies. Europeans treated Caribbean administrators as colonial subjects, sometimes particularizing them as "West Indians" and "Antillais" and at other times folding them together with Africans as "natives" and "*indigènes*."[7] Africans, meanwhile, derided Caribbean administrators as Europeanized lackeys. Isolated on two fronts, Caribbean administrators moved uneasily between categories, intrusive shadows blurring divides between European and African, "colonizer" and "colonized."

This chapter generalizes the middle positions of Caribbean administrators in Africa with six portraits from the lives of René Maran and Cunliffe Hoyte. While limited to Oubangui-Chari and the Gold Coast between 1910 and 1918, the chapter gives texture to the experiences of Caribbean administrators in other parts of the continent—their tense relationships with Africans and Europeans, and their feelings of superiority, ambiguity, and alienation. I also consider how Maran and Hoyte used petitions to challenge the inconsistencies of colonial categories. As they navigated the contradictions of colonial politics, I argue, their conceptions of empire and imperial belonging began to shift.

Les deux partis le rejetaient

When Maran arrived in Bangui in 1910, the region was reeling from more than forty years of upheaval and violence.[8] In the 1870s, slave raiders from Wadai to the north and Khartoum to the northeast began encroaching on the territory that became the French colony of Oubangui-Chari. These expanding raids spurred mass migrations to the southwest, toward the Oubangui and Chari rivers. While some people benefited from the slave trade, most were displaced, and those who were not enslaved found refuge in small, scattered settlements. Slave raiding intensified over the next few decades, only slowing by the first decade of the twentieth century with the arrival of the French, who exerted their power in the region with a series of military conquests and treaties. The French also began dividing land between concessionary companies who had a singular purpose: extracting profit.[9] These companies relied on ruthless violence to coerce Africans into building roads and railways, working as porters, and harvesting rubber, palm oil, and other resources. This forced labor was simply slavery by another name.[10] The French also began imposing taxes, usually payable in rubber or ivory. And, to solidify their control over African labor, the French initiated a policy of *regroupement*, the relocation of small villages to larger settlements connected by roads to centralized political and economic networks.[11]

Administrators such as Maran were directly involved in consolidating colonial power in Central Africa. In a letter from September 1910, for example, he described his daily routine as a police commissioner in Bangui:

> For the last two months I have been waking up at 4 in the morning and it is only at 11 o'clock at night, completely tired, that I get back to my bed.... I am forever running around, sweating, laughing, panting, cursing, shouting, and grumbling. I cannot stay put. I climb stairs two by two and descend them in fours. I dash out in the paths of the bush; the city avenues see me fly by like a meteor.... I survey the marketplace, the different public roadworks; I settle disputes; I dispatch legal documents. What do you want? One is a police commissioner or one is not.[12]

A year later, in June 1911, Maran was assigned to a post in Diouma, nearly three hundred miles north of Bangui, and he wrote that he was excited to be leaving the "unsanitary town" for the "pure delights" of the "*brousse.*"[13] By October 1912, he had moved south again to Grimari, about 150 miles northeast of

FIGURE 2.1. René Maran (center), with two men in Oubangui-Chari, ca. 1915. © Fonds Familial René Maran. All rights reserved. Reproduced with permission.

Bangui, and in a letter to his friend Paul Manoel Gahisto, he described his activities: "Soon I will be leaving on a tour. I will have 20 militia men with me and will be out for 15 days. The tour is directed against a langouassi, named Zayba, a resistant chief that I want to submit to reason." In the same letter, Maran casually reported the collection of rubber in Grimari: "Yesterday five or six merchants came ... and took the 8 tonnes of rubber brought here by the 66 chiefs in the subdivision."[14] This offhand accounting masked the coercion and violence intrinsic to rubber collection. Similarly, in an August 1913 letter to Léon Bocquet, he took a similar tone to describe his plan to "force the inhabitants [of a nearby village] to plant manioc, peanuts, and potatoes."[15] And in April 1914, in another letter to Gahisto, Maran explained that "the natives of the region" were "not accommodating" and that he would "amuse [him]self by trying to subjugate them."[16] When things did not go according to plan, he relied on the *indigénat* to impose short but arbitrary prison sentences.[17]

Maran's commitment to the *mission civilisatrice* was often indistinguishable from that of his superiors in the Ministère des Colonies. In a February 1915 letter, for example, he expressed his enthusiastic belief in the importance of French incursions in Central Africa: "These tribes (*peuplades*), still mostly cannibalistic, would forget quickly. Without the cats, the mice would quickly return to their old erring ways. It would be miserable to have to restart what has already been done, and done well."[18] In other letters, however, he noted the destruction of colonization: "It is a colony of plunder. The Pizarro brothers would have lessons to learn from here."[19] Moreover, the racism Maran encountered at the hands of Europeans weighed heavily. There was no question about his middle position in Central Africa. As his friend Paul Tuffrau later wrote, describing the difficulties of Maran's predicament: "Despite his completely European culture and his loyalty to the service, he was, in the eyes of most colonialists, nothing but a *sale nègre*, and in the eyes of the natives, a turncoat. The two sides rejected him."[20]

Charybdis and Scylla

Cunliffe Hoyte boarded the *Magdalena* in Trinidad in April 1910 with a sense of uncertain anticipation. Born in Belmont, he was a respected teacher at the Government Training School in Port of Spain, inclined toward biology, but he had long been eager for an appointment to West Africa. To that end, he had attended a series of lectures in 1909 on "tropical sanitation" and then passed an examination to work as a sanitary inspector in Port of Spain.[21] The timing was fortuitous. There were already West Indians working for colonial governments in West Africa, and John Rodger, the governor of the Gold Coast, was specifically seeking sanitary inspectors from the Caribbean. According to Rodger, it was "impossible" to find or train adequate sanitary inspectors in West Africa.[22] After arriving in England at the end of April, Hoyte signed a three-year agreement, and then boarded the *Falaba* in Liverpool, bound for Cape Coast.[23]

Hoyte's journey from Trinidad to the Gold Coast was a reversal of the transatlantic slave trade routes that had shaped the Caribbean and West Africa since the sixteenth century. In the Gold Coast, European demand for slave labor had generated enormous wealth for the tiny minority of Africans who controlled the trade and contributed to the development of powerful political federations such as the Asante state. Yet this demand had also destabilized existing social and political structures by reorienting the economy around slavery. What had once been a marginal feature of society, one that sometimes offered possibilities for assimilation, was transformed into an economic necessity. In some cases, slave trading was a means for survival. In the early nineteenth century, however, after the British ended their direct involvement in the slave trade, the Gold Coast economy began a shift toward "legitimate" trade.[24] Of primary importance were products such as palm oil, gold, and kola nuts. This transition reduced the number of captives leaving West Africa for the Americas, but it actually increased—and transformed—slavery in the Gold Coast. To ensure continued profits, farmers and merchants relied on various forms of unfree labor to plant and harvest their products and bring them to markets. Later in the nineteenth century, the British used the prevalence of slavery in the Gold Coast to justify their incursions into the interior. By 1900, the British had displaced the power of the Asante state and consolidated their control over the political and economic networks of the region.

When Hoyte arrived in the Gold Coast in May 1910, there were already West Indians in the colony. Most worked as police officers or prison guards or for the railway, and their presence fueled resentment among Africans whom the British had passed over for positions with the colonial government.[25] In July 1907, for example, an anonymous letter writer from Sekondi sent a complaint to *The Gold Coast Leader*. Using the pseudonym "Railway," the letter writer argued that West Indians knew "next to nothing," that they were no more skilled than Africans, and that their higher salaries were a "burden to the revenue of the colony." Railway demanded that the government "put a stop to this wholesale importation of West Indians" and stated emphatically that "as Asia is for the Asiatics so is Africa for Africans."[26] For West Indians, such antipathy made clear that few Africans viewed them as exiled kin. "Africa for Africans" was a rallying cry for unity against European imperialism in Africa, popularized first by Martin Delany in the 1850s and then by Edward Blyden, among others.[27] Yet Railway used the phrase for different ends. Instead of rejecting the presence of Europeans in Africa, the letter called for the expulsion of *all* foreigners, including—perhaps especially—West Indians. By invoking the phrase in this context, Railway subverted a call for racial solidarity with an appeal to nativism and unity within—instead of beyond—circumscribed geographical boundaries.

Hoyte faced similar opposition, not only because of his West Indian background, but also because sanitation work was, in his words, "very unpopular."[28] Sanitary inspectors were a symbol of the imposition of an imperial order, especially after the outbreak of plague in Accra in 1908 and the subsequent efforts to build a segregated area for Europeans. Hoyte worked mainly in Accra and the surrounding area conducting house inspections, examining animals at the government slaughterhouse, attempting to limit the spread of yellow fever, collecting parasitic worms and mosquito larvae for laboratory observations, and training other sanitary inspectors.[29] He also organized a mosquito brigade, a culvert-clearing gang, and a refuse-collecting gang. In all cases, Hoyte met resentment from Africans. In fact, the 1911 Gold Coast Medical and Sanitary Report noted "an undoubted tendency on the part of the natives to regard a Sanitary Inspector as a malignant type of Police officer."[30]

FIGURE 2.2. Jamestown Union Anniversary, Accra, ca. 1917. Basel Mission Archives, D-30.01.043, Grace Photo Studio.

Like Maran, Hoyte encountered discrimination at the hands of the colonial government. His annual salary, for instance, was £160, slightly more than half the rate of European sanitary inspectors, whose annual salaries were on a scale between £250 and £310.³¹ Hoyte left the Gold Coast on leave in 1913, but when he returned, his feelings of alienation only worsened, so in March and July 1915, he wrote two lengthy petitions describing his predicament.³² He claimed, for example, that after returning to the Gold Coast in December 1913, he received "treatment" from "certain senior officers" that was "distinctly aggressive and offensive" and "highly tinctured with racial prejudice." He added that this made him feel "humiliated and degraded," that this "ill-treatment" seemed "pre-meditated," and that when he had raised concern he was "threatened." Hoyte also raised objections about working extra hours "during my leisure . . . without any remuneration whatever" and declared that "this mode of distribution of labour in which I do all the work and others draw all the pay is far from encouraging." Finally, Hoyte was frustrated about a lack of promotion: "The very books and measures I introduced for junior officers are now thrust into my hands. I am ... now instructed with my own instructions." The department, he claimed, was "obstructing and then blocking" his opportunities for advancement, something that was "discouraging in the extreme."[33]

In addition to listing these grievances, Hoyte explained the difficulties he encountered as a West Indian in the Gold Coast. He began by describing his motivations for coming to West Africa and claimed a genuine commitment to the "civilizing" mission of the colonial government: "In the first place I wanted to please; I wanted to get on; I wanted to demonstrate my capacity for work—good, solid, lasting work; I wanted to help; for Kipling had said 'Take up the White man's burden—Ye dare not stoop to less.'" Hoyte was under no illusion that he was a "White man," and this was partly an effort to present himself as a loyal British subject, yet his allusion to Kipling also expressed the betrayal he felt as a West Indian working for the British administration in the Gold Coast. While he was growing up in Trinidad, the language of the British Empire had taught Hoyte that he was British, and when he arrived in the Gold Coast, he carried those ideas with him. As historian Winston James writes, young people in the British Caribbean were "taught that they were British and came to think of themselves as such ... with genuine pride."[34] In fact, Hoyte closed his July petition by praising the "spirit of magnanimity" that "characterised" British rule in Trinidad, his "native land." After five years in the Gold Coast, however, his ideas about the British Empire were starting to shift. His colleagues and superiors excluded and mistreated him, making clear that they did not see him as an equal. Meanwhile, he also continued to encounter hostility from Africans, and he likened his position to that of Odysseus. Using a formal third-person tense, he wrote that he felt caught "between the Charybdis of bitter public feeling on one side and the Scylla of studied ill-treatment from the Department he served so faithfully in the past, and to which he is still giving his best services under the circumstances, on the other." Hoyte, and other West Indians in West Africa, moved and lived along this perilous strait, unsure of where they belonged.

Rongés par les termites

In J—1915, Maran was heading to France on leave. The route from Oubangui-Chari to the coast went through the Belgian Congo, and when he arrived in Thysville (present-day Mbanza-Ngungu), he stopped at the Hotel Alimentation du Bas-Congo (ABC). The *propriétaire*, however, refused to give him a

FIGURE 2.3. The Hotel ABC in Thysville, Belgian Congo, ca. 1915. RMCA Collection, Tervuren, AP.0.2.6684. All rights reserved.

room because "*nègres*" were not accepted.[35] In a letter of complaint to the lieutenant-governor of Moyen-Congo, Maran described the "comical" events that ensued. First, Maran produced his passport and other forms of identification to prove that he was "not a native." He then pointed out that his name was already in the hotel registers because he had stayed at the Hotel ABC in Thysville in December 1909, August 1911, and April 1912.[36] All the more "vexing," Maran explained, was that the previous night he had stayed at the Hotel ABC in Léopoldville without any issues and that this same thing had "happened twice during previous journeys." While he did eventually secure a room, Maran expressed concern that this pattern could become "more common" in the French colonies of Central Africa, and he urged the lieutenant-governor to help him and other "*fonctionnaires de couleur*" to avoid such "regrettable incidents."

This episode demonstrates how Caribbean administrators deftly manipulated the contradictions of colonial and racial categories. The hotel manager had made race the basis for exclusion, refusing to give Maran a room "under the pretext that '*nègres*' were not accepted at the hotel [*sous prétexte que les 'nègres' n'y étaient pas acceptés*]." Knowing that he had no recourse for challenging the manager's decision on these grounds, Maran used his passport to change the category of exclusion to "native." In other words, he substituted the language of race for the dichotomized language of colonial ideology: European/native. He knew that he could not claim to be "European," but with his passport and other colonial documents, he could offer "sufficient proof" that he was "not a native [*preuves suffisantes que je n'étais pas un indigène*]." The daily realities of colonial situations revealed the porous nature of these categories, but they still held power. In fact, Maran made this binary ideal work to his advantage. By proving that he was "not an *indigène*," he was also making an implicit claim to belonging among Europeans, a claim that ultimately convinced the hotel manager to relent and give him a room.

In his letter to the lieutenant-governor, Maran took the argument a step further by referring to himself and other Caribbean administrators as "*fonctionnaires de couleur*." By qualifying a colonial category (*fonctionnaire*) with a racial designation (*de couleur*), Maran was defying the operational logics that governed life in African colonies.[37] His letter did not displace these logics; nor did the letter change the racist thinking of Europeans in Central Africa. Yet these subtle linguistic shifts nonetheless point to the incoherence of colonial categories and demonstrate how Maran and other Caribbean administrators used this incoherence for their own ends as they grappled with the challenges of living in-between.

Maran's letter is also a revealing reflection of his impossible position. On one hand, he was a colonial administrator, and he saw himself as French, as part of the French Empire. Yet as a "*fonctionnaire de couleur*" in Central Africa, his capacity to belong to that empire, to be a part of the French nation, was always dependent on context. He could "prove" with his French passport that he was "not a native," but at the Hotel ABC in Thysville, and for many of his colleagues and superiors, he was still an "*indigène*" or a "*nègre*" because of his appearance. Yet Maran also did not belong—nor did he want to belong—among the *indigènes*. In a sardonic tone near the end of the letter, he noted: "When I return to the colony..., I may be forced to go outside the urban perimeter to sleep in a '*case indigène*'—if they are willing to offer me one, that is." Situations such as this one left Maran and other Caribbean administrators with a keen awareness of where they did not belong but with little understanding of where they did.

When Maran's letter arrived at the office of the lieutenant-governor in Brazzaville in June 1915, a clerk typed a copy and filed it with related correspondence, where it remained for almost forty years. Then, in 1952, a colonial official in Brazzaville named André Fraisse found the letter and added it to a series of files he collected on Maran's encounters with racism in Central Africa. By this time, Maran was a well-known author, and Fraisse, who had previously worked in Southeast Asia, was a friend of Maran's. He brought the files back to France, and today, these "Documents sur René Maran (le conflit du Blanc et du Noir)" are part of the Fonds André Fraisse at France's Archives Nationales d'Outre-Mer in Aix-en-Provence. In an introductory note at the beginning of the collection, Fraisse wrote that the material documented Maran's *"humiliations raciales"* in Afrique Équatoriale Française (AEF), a *"pays très raciste."* There is also a brief comment at the end of the note about the state of the collection, sitting between ellipses: "... *Ces feuilles, rongés par les termites, que j'ai pu sauver* ... [These pages, gnawed away by termites, that I was able to save]."

Paper was critical to colonial power—treaties, taxation, court proceedings, contracts with *compagnies concessionaires*, export agreements. Even in the case at hand, Maran's passport and other identification documents were essential to the perpetuation of colonial categories. Yet as the case also reveals, the fictions behind such categories could not withstand the realities of colonial situations, much like paper itself, which could not hold up to the realities of humidity and termites in Brazzaville. Maran's termite-eaten letter, then, offers an oblique metaphor for his position in Central Africa. Even as he relied on such categories, he disrupted them, revealed their limitations, and gnawed away at their fictions. Now housed in the temperature-controlled Archives Nationales d'Outre-Mer, however, the metaphor folds back in on itself. The fragments of Maran's letter sit in a state of arrested decay, in a site where the old narratives of empire comfortably perpetuate themselves, free from the effects of colonization in Central Africa.

Dictation

Not long after arriving in the Gold Coast, Hoyte began studying Ga. "It would be an advantage," noted his supervisor, "if he could speak the language."[38] In January 1915, Hoyte passed the lower standard examination and then, a year later, passed the higher standard examination.[39] On the latter, he scored 81 out of 100 for dictation, 91 out of 100 for translation, 95 out of 100 for conversation, and 89 out of 100 for interpretation.[40] In the sections on conversation and interpretation, the content centered on sanitary work, as examiners were supposed to use questions "connected with the candidate's official business." For the dictation section, however, the examiner chose a passage titled "Ga Maji Ablema Saji (The History of Ga Towns)." As he read it aloud, Hoyte transcribed:

> Nēkē nū ne̱ ni mibagha ehe sane ne̱, gbalo̱ le̱ ghami ake̱ edše nšo̱ mli ni ebabo̱ ade ke̱ ewokumēi fiā šikome, ni ame̱yo nšo̱ ne̱ nā. No mli le̱ moko moko be̱ bie̱ ši nme̱ne̱ nme̱ne̱ Gâmēi ni yo̱ ne̱ kosebii dšiame̱ ni kose hû ame̱yo̱. Nēkē nū ne̱ ke̱ ewekumēi yaā wuo. Gbî ne̱ ēhe̱ ye̱ nšo̱nā, ni le̱le̱ ko

damo ši ni emli gbomēi le šele ake eba; ni ekwo ahîma kete ebadšieame keba šikpon. Nū le, egbei dši Lakote Aduaoši. Gbomêi ni yo lele le mli le, ~~okesi~~ Okēši blofomēi dšiame ni ekele hî ši. No se Kinkâ ke Osu ke Nliši blofomēi hû babea. Amefiā ame hâle wolo ake šikpon ne enôn, koni lele fiā lele ni aabadamo ši le, eke wolo le atšôame koni ame wo le nyômo, edša ke šikpon ne enôn. Na kai mēi ni yo sa le hāle ni eke ame ake wodši ne aafite, si amefele ye šika-tšo he, koni eke ye odasi ake šikpon le enôn. Ni amefe nakai.[41]

This thing that I'm going to tell you, was told to me by a prophet that he came from the sea and settled with his family along the shore. At that time nobody lived here and until modern times the Ga people who lived here were villagers and they lived in the bush. This man and his relatives were fishermen. On that day, while he was catching fish, a boat docked and the people in it called him to come over; he got into his canoe and got the men onto land. The man's name is Lakote Aduaoshi. The men in the boat were Portuguese white men and they stayed with him. Later, the Dutch and Danes and English white men also came. They all gave him a document indicating his ownership of the land, so that he could claim revenue from any ship that stopped over by showing the documents to them because he owned the land. He told those people who gave him [the documents] that since the documents might get damaged, they should mark the agreement on a golden stick [*šika-tšo*] so he could use that as evidence that the land belonged to him. And they did just that.[42]

This passage describes the settlement of the coastal region that is now Accra by Lakote Aduaoshi. It also highlights several important themes in Ga history: migration as a pillar of Ga identity, in this case from the sea; the transition from farming to sea fishing; the development of trade relationships with the Portuguese, Dutch, Danish, and English; and the emergence of urban centers—Kinka, Osu, and Nleshi—as the foundation for Accra.[43] The passage also describes the introduction of European ideas about land and wealth. The Ga word *wolo*, meaning paper or document, is used twice and is made essential to the notion of ownership. In fact, Lakote Aduaoshi was so concerned about preserving these European documents that he suggested their agreement be marked on a "*šika-tšo*," a golden staff or stick, so he could show it to other ships and earn revenue from trade.

This particular version of Lakote Aduaoshi's story was recorded by Johannes Zimmermann, a German missionary with the Basel Mission in his 1858 book *A Grammatical Sketch and Vocabulary of the Akra- or Gā-Language*.[44] Another

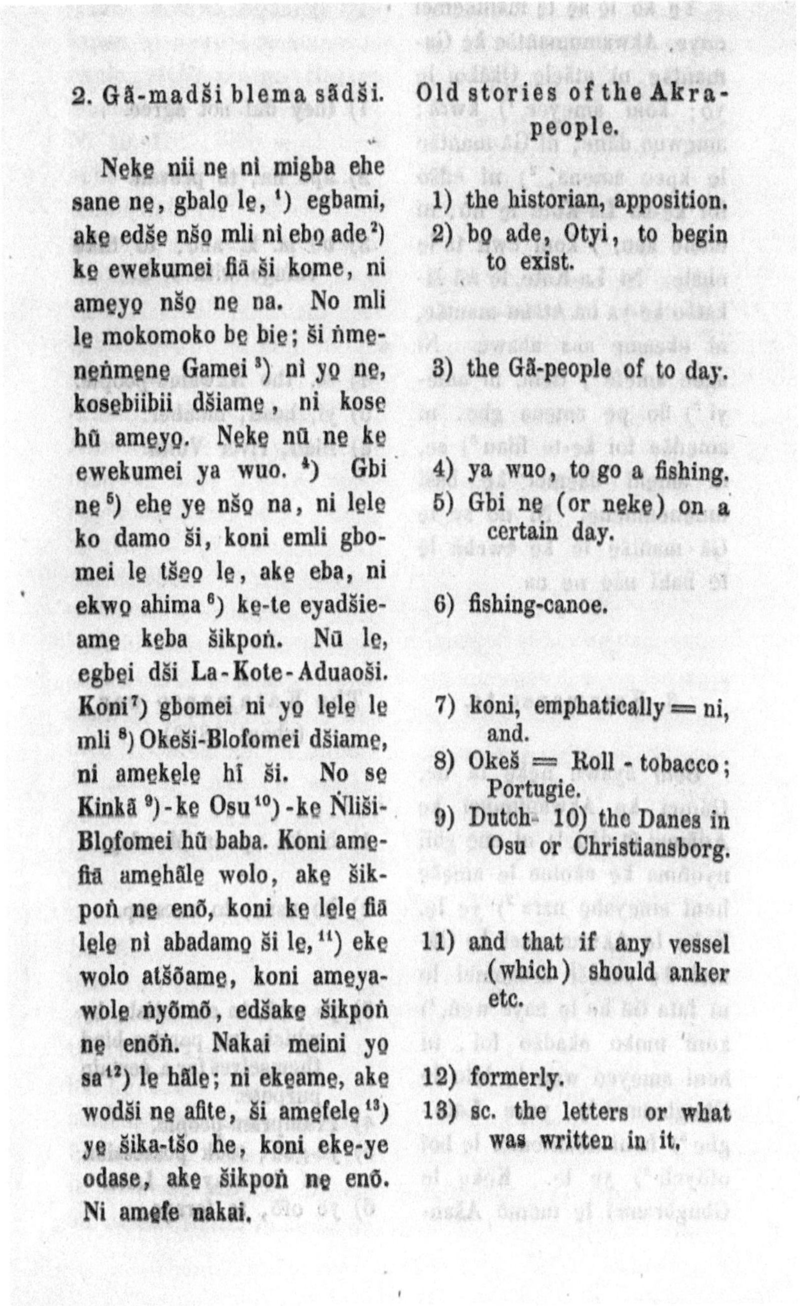

2. Gã-madši blema sãdši.

Nekę nii nę ni migba ehe sane nę, gbalǫ lę, ¹) egbami, akę edšę nšǫ mli ni ebǫ ade²) kę ewekumei fiã ši kome, ni amęyǫ nšǫ nę na. No mli le mokomoko bę bię; ši ṅmęneṅmęnę Gamei³) ni yǫ nę, kosębiibii dšiamę, ni kose hũ amęyǫ. Nekę nũ nę ke ewekumei ya wuo. ⁴) Gbi nę⁵) ehę yę nšǫ na, ni lęlę ko damo ši, koni emli gbomei lę tšęǫ lę, akę eba, ni ekwǫ ahima⁶) kę-te eyadšieamę kęba šikpoṅ. Nũ lę, egbęi dši La-Kote-Aduaoši. Koni⁷) gbomei ni yǫ lęlę lę mli⁸) Okeši-Blofomei dšiamę, ni amękęlę hĩ ši. No sę Kinkã⁹)-kę Osu¹⁰)-kę Ṅliši-Blofomei hũ baba. Koni amęfiã amęhãlę wolo, akę šikpoṅ nę enõ, koni kę lęlę fiã lęlę ni abadamǫ ši lę,¹¹) ekę wolo atšõamę, koni amęyawolę nyõmõ, edšakę šikpoṅ nę enõṅ. Nakai meini yǫ sa¹²) lę hãlę; ni ekęamę, akę wodši nę afite, ši amęfelę¹³) yę šika-tšo he, koni ekę-ye odase, akę šikpoṅ nę enõ. Ni amęfe nakai.

Old stories of the Akra-people.

1) the historian, apposition.
2) bǫ ade, Otyi, to begin to exist.

3) the Gã-people of to day.

4) ya wuo, to go a fishing.
5) Gbi nę (or nekę) on a certain day.

6) fishing-canoe.

7) koni, emphatically = ni, and.
8) Okeš = Roll-tobacco; Portugie.
9) Dutch- 10) the Danes in Osu or Christiansborg.

11) and that if any vessel (which) should anker etc.

12) formerly.
13) sc. the letters or what was written in it.

FIGURE 2.4. The story of Lakote Aduaoshi as it appears in Johannes Zimmerman's *Grammatical Sketch and Vocabulary of the Akra- or Gā-Language* (1858). Munich Digitization Center, BSB10589247.

version of the story appeared in Carl C. Reindorf's 1895 *History of the Gold Coast and Asante*. Reindorf, born just east of Accra with Danish and Ga ancestry, was at one point Zimmerman's student before becoming a major scholar and pastor in his own right. While Reindorf did not reproduce the entire narrative, he did note that Lakote Aduaoshi (spelled as "Aduawushi") was "on the coast with his people before the Akras moved thither."[45] Reindorf also claimed that it was the brother of Lakote, "Lẹteboi," who was "acknowledged by the Dutch government, by an instrument drawn, which was afterwards carved on the silver-handed cane of the priest of Nai, as the king of Akra in 1734."[46] The slight differences between the two versions of the story are a reflection of the layered histories of language and power embedded in written documents in the Gold Coast, such as Lakote Aduaoshi's *wolo*, Lẹteboi's instrument, the books of Zimmerman and Reindorf, and even Hoyte's language exam.

What did Hoyte make of this story? He was only transcribing a dictation of the text, so it is difficult to know. Yet given his interest in history, poetry, and Greek mythology, he was likely already familiar with the works of Zimmerman and Reindorf. In fact, Hoyte's examiner read the dictation word for word from Zimmerman's book.[47] Beyond this recognition, Hoyte may have considered how exchanges such as those between Lakote Aduaoshi and European traders had led to the rise of the transatlantic slave trade in West Africa. There is no explicit mention of slavery in Zimmerman's short text, but he does use the word *nyomo*, meaning revenue, wages, or debt, a word that is linked semantically with *nyon*, or slave.[48] *Nyon* carried—and still carries—a negative connotation, even as other terms for unfree labor were more prominent, such as *tsulo* (servant), *awoba* (pawn), and *odonko* (a slave from the region north of Asante).[49] As Hoyte wandered Accra looking for mosquito larvae and enforcing sanitation laws, he would have been exposed to the complex legacies of slavery in the Gold Coast. In such moments, he may have reflected on how the transatlantic slave trade had not only displaced millions to the Caribbean but had also transformed the societies and economies of West Africa.

Hoyte also may have identified the continuities between this passage and the incursions of the British colonial state in the early twentieth century. Lakote Aduaoshi had used *wolo* to assert his power in trade relationships with ships that came along the coast. By 1916, however, much of the economic power in the old Ga towns of Accra resided with European firms, and the British relied on new forms of *wolo* to control trade, land, and wealth.[50] In the course of his daily routines, Hoyte encountered people who had to pay colonial taxes, adhere to colonial laws, make sense of colonial land ordinances, and follow the regulations of colonial sanitary inspectors. As a colonial official who was also a descendant of enslaved Africans, Hoyte was doubly implicated in this evolution of African-European exchanges between the sixteenth and twentieth centuries.

When Hoyte took his Ga higher standard examination in January 1916, he had still not received any official responses to his petitions from March and July 1915. In fact, internally, Hoyte's superiors had mocked his "imaginary grievances" and characterized his "ideas of persecution" as "idiotic and childish."[51] Meanwhile, Hoyte still encountered resentment in his daily work. In October 1916, for example, a letter in *The Gold Coast Leader* asked: "What are the use of the West Indian sanitary inspectors?" There were only two West Indian sanitary inspectors in the Gold Coast at the time, so this criticism was targeted. The letter writer also noted that Hoyte and his colleague from Trinidad, David McNeil-Stewart, were "bent only on filling their pockets with high wages and do not seem to care about the work they were sent out for."[52] Given Hoyte's continued marginalization between Africans and Europeans, learning Ga perhaps created a space to think more critically about the longer history of European imperialism in Africa and the Caribbean. It may have also allowed Hoyte to reflect on how this history had dictated his own trajectory from Port of Spain to Accra.

Bounjouvouko

Between 1917 and 1918, Maran accompanied the French doctor Eugène Jamot on an inoculation campaign against sleeping sickness in Kémo-Gribingui, a district in central Oubangui-Chari.[53] At the end of November 1917, Maran, Jamot, and a group of African porters arrived in Kandjian, a Banda village. According to the village chief, Doungouyolo, Maran called everyone together, but when two village headmen, Mayo and Gripendé, did not obey these orders in the way Maran wanted, he began beating them. Another headman, Badingouanzé, tried to explain himself, but Maran punched him and continued hitting him "until he was tired."[54] The inoculation campaign then proceeded north toward Fort-Crampel, and Doungouyolo appointed his brother Mongo to help supervise the porters. They passed through Dékoa and arrived in Fort-Crampel in March 1918. Upon arrival, a number of the men, including Mongo, complained that they were thirsty and headed to the Gribingui River to rest. Maran, however, wanted to make an account of supplies. When the porters did not immediately assemble, he began beating a man named Oroumbia, who later stated that Maran had kicked him in the kidneys and left him with swollen eyes and a bloody nose.[55] Maran then started beating Mongo and broke his ribs. Doungouyolo claimed that when Mongo arrived back home, he "slept for one month" and then died. In June 1918, Doungouyolo reported Mongo's death to Jean Bonneveau, the head of the Gribingui district, and a series of witnesses, including Mayo, Gripendé, Bandingouanzé, Oroumbia and others who were part of the expedition, corroborated the story.[56]

A year later, in June 1919, the tribunal in Bangui condemned Maran to a fine of fifty francs *"avec sursis"* for "committing violent and unlawful acts against the person named Mongo."[57] In August, a Commission d'Enquête confirmed the ruling. Maran then sent a letter to the head of the commission giving his version of events.[58] He admitted to resorting to violence and stated: "It is possible that I hit a native who responded to the name of Mongo." Yet Maran also claimed that the demands of the administration had created an "impossible" situation. The porters did not have adequate food or opportunities to rest, but he had to keep the convoy running or his superiors would accuse him of "negligence." He had asked for other men to help manage the nearly six hundred porters, but French officials did not give him any further support. In these circumstances, Maran explained, he had "no other means available" and so resorted to "showing [his] strength."[59] In a personal letter from the time, meanwhile, he condemned these colonial imperatives: "We are doing the work of slave traders (*négriers*)."[60]

In a 1952 letter to André Fraisse, Maran added more detail, explaining that one of his subordinates was actually responsible for the beatings, but that he had taken the blame to save the subordinate from Bonneveau.[61] Bonneveau, Maran claimed, was a "sadist" who had coordinated the witness declarations and the trial against him. In the same letter, Maran also noted that this was not the first time Bonneveau had sought to undermine him. Earlier on during the Jamot campaign, while he was giving instructions to a group of porters, Bonneveau had told the porters that they did not need to "obey" Maran because he was a *"sale nègre"* like them.[62] In the letter to Fraisse, Maran described his position: "What would you have done in my place, if you had heard the natives under your control saying amongst each other, in their language: 'You know, don't bother obeying what he just told us ... because the main commander just told me that this *nègre* does not have authority over a *nègre* like me.'"[63] Maran's letters from his time with the Jamot expedition hint at similar incidents. For example, he described a M. Baudon who "publicly reprimanded me as, pardon the expression, one does not berate a boy," in the presence of "a thousand natives" during a meeting of village chiefs.[64] In another letter, Maran succinctly summarized his position in relation to his European colleagues: *"Noir je suis, boy on voulait que je devinsse."*[65]

Maran's correspondence also includes the terminology that Africans used to describe him. In Oubangui-Chari, he explained, Africans sometimes referred to him as the "*boy du commandant*," implying that he was little more than a lackey of the French administration. On other occasions, Africans referred to Maran as a "*bounjouvouko*."[66] In Sango, the main trade language along the Oubangui River, the word *vuko* means the color black, while *bounjou* referred to the French, or Europeans more generally.[67] Maran, who knew some Sango, explained that Sango-speakers typically used *bounjouvouko* to describe Africans who worked as clerks for the administration.[68] Turned on Maran, however, the term was a more potent slur. It designated him as not quite French or African, but a mix of the two—and inferior to both. Elsewhere in the same letter, Maran described the toll of this double-edged mistreatment: "For five years, at every occasion, people have not stopped humiliating me, slandering me, denigrating me, despising me . . . because I am a *nègre*."[69]

Maran's sense of marginalization eventually led to his much publicized departure from Central Africa. In July 1921, Albin Michel published Maran's first novel, *Batouala: Véritable roman nègre*. The novel was about life in a Banda village and centered on an aging chief named Batouala; his rival, a younger man named Bissibingui; and one of Batouala's wives, Yassiguindja. What sparked controversy, however, was the novel's preface, in which Maran made forceful criticisms of colonial rule. "Civilization, civilization, pride of the Europeans and mass grave of innocents," he wrote. "You build your kingdom on corpses. . . . You are not a torch light, but an inferno. All that you touch, you consume."[70] Despite this strong language, Maran was no anticolonialist and he made these criticisms alongside a commitment to colonial reform. His critics overlooked this fact, however, and when the book won the Prix Goncourt in December 1921, a scandal erupted in France.[71] The press denounced *Batouala*, as did members of the French Chamber of Deputies, and Maran, now in Chad, became persona non grata. He even began to fear for his life and asked to return to France through Nigeria instead of through Brazzaville. "This route," Maran wrote in March 1923, "is the only one that will guarantee my safety."[72] Several months later, he resigned, and with the help of his friend Félix Eboué and two *députés* from Guadeloupe, Gratien Candace and Achille René-Boisneuf, Maran was able to leave Chad via Nigeria. He arrived back in France in August 1923.[73]

Right, Justice, and Liberty

In August 1916, Hoyte had still not received any responses to his two petitions from March and July 1915, so he wrote to the governor and colonial secretary inquiring about his concerns.[74] This time, he did receive a response. Alexander Slater, the colonial secretary in Accra, instructed Hoyte's supervisors to inform him that the government had given his petitions "the fullest consideration" but that there was "no higher appointment for which he [was] eligible." Slater added that Hoyte's complaints had diminished his chances for promotion: "His attitude towards the Government of which he is a servant does not encourage the hope that his claims to any such higher appointment will be very strong." Finally, Slater directed Hoyte's supervisors to "suitably rebuke" him for "firing off letters direct to the Governor and Colonial Secretary."[75] Absent in the response was any reference to Hoyte's complaints about racism.

Undeterred, Hoyte wrote a third petition while on leave in Edinburgh the following year. This time, he wrote directly to the undersecretary of state for the colonies in London.[76] Referring to himself in the third person, he declared: "The treatment he has received is so foreign to all those recognized principles of Right, Justice, and Liberty, which are the hall-mark of British rule and upon which our Empire is founded and preserved." Yet Hoyte also noted that he felt "encouraged" that his concerns would eventually be redressed because "the present war is being waged for the identical purpose of securing and preserving Right, Justice and Liberty for an ill-treated people whom our Empire had contracted to protect."[77] Elsewhere in the petition, he reiterated his grievances about racism and promotions and then took direct aim at the inconsistent treatment of Caribbean administrators. In the Gold Coast, Hoyte explained, the government recognized "two classes of officers, viz., European and Native." He then explained that he was often asked to "perform the duties" of a "European Sanitary Inspector" but was always "denied the privilege of acting for a European." Instead, he was "classed with the Native Staff" and treated and paid like "a Native."[78] Yet here, too, Hoyte claimed that he encountered discrimination because he was "not allowed the privilege of a native to draw the Ashanti Consolidated Allowance." Hoyte was thus caught between two polarized categories, and like Maran, he was acutely aware of the contradictions of these categories. Quoting from the General Orders of the Gold Coast and the West African Pensions Law, he claimed that he was "a European" because "neither of his parents were born in West Africa."[79] Hoyte was well aware that he was not "a European," just as he was well aware that he was not a "White man." Yet his detailed understanding of British colonial laws allowed him to claim status as a "European."

Upon receiving Hoyte's petition, the Secretary of State for the Colonies asked Hugh Clifford, the Gold Coast governor, for his "observations." Clifford wrote back describing Hoyte as an "able but ill-balanced West Indian official" and derided the petition as "a farrago of insinuations" and an "exhibition of insubordination." As for Hoyte's claim to being "European," Clifford described it as "ingenious but unconvincing." In closing, Clifford warned that if Hoyte continued to "air imaginary grievances," he would "ask that he may be retired."[80]

Hoyte surely expected the Gold Coast government to reject his claim to being "European," but his intellectual move was still significant. By claiming to be a "European" and invoking the "recognized principles" of "Right, Justice, and Liberty," he defied a pattern of inconsistent categorization and made a direct challenge to the racist thinking that governed the deployment of these categories and principles. Hoyte had grown up in a stratified colonial society in Trinidad and by 1917 had spent seven years living and working in the Gold Coast, where he found himself isolated between Africans and Europeans. During this time, he had also become aware of the incongruencies between race, nation, and empire and learned how the British relied on racial categories to impose their power—whether in Port of Spain, Accra, or Edinburgh. Had Hoyte remained in Trinidad, he might not have realized this broader trend, but by traveling to different parts of the British Empire, he learned to recognize the falsity of its categories and "principles." His petitions were outward expressions of this awareness: he pointed out the contradictions of monolithic categories such as "African," "West Indian," and "European," and he questioned the hypocrisy of a racist empire that claimed to be built on—and to be spreading—the principles of "Right, Justice, and Liberty."

Near the end of Hoyte's July 1915 petition to the Gold Coast governor, he had quoted a passage from a critical review of Machiavelli, written by Thomas Babington Macaulay in 1827: "He alone reads history aright, who, observing how powerfully circumstances influence the feelings and opinions of men, how often vices pass into virtues, and paradoxes into axioms, learns to distinguish what is accidental and transitory in human nature, from what is essential and immutable."[81] Hoyte claimed that he had cited the passage to inspire the governor to treat his case with "the sober judgement of an unprejudiced mind."[82] Yet for Hoyte there were deeper resonances in Macaulay's statement. His experiences with assimilation, migration, and racism allowed him to recognize that what was "transitory" about the British Empire were the shifting boundaries around who counted as "British"—whether in the Caribbean, Europe, or West Africa. He also realized that what was "essential and immutable" were the racial demarcations that undergirded the empire and dictated the contours of these shifting boundaries. Hoyte never completely repudiated the British Empire—in fact, he remained part of the Gold Coast administration until his retirement in 1939, after which he remained in West Africa.[83] Nonetheless, with his petitions he exposed the arbitrary nature of colonial categories and articulated the alienation felt by many other Caribbean administrators in Africa.

Conclusion

Caribbean administrators grew up in colonial societies where the influence of imperial culture led many to think of themselves as "British" and "French" and as civilizationally superior to Africans. Once in Africa, however, the realities of daily life upended these assumptions. The rigid boundaries of racial categories superseded the malleable lines of "British" and "French" identities and determined where Caribbean administrators lived, where they were posted, whether or not they were promoted, and how much they were paid. Africans, meanwhile, typically resented the presence of Caribbean administrators. They derided them as lackeys who enforced colonial laws, participated in colonial violence, and espoused paternalistic attitudes. Such experiences made Maran, Hoyte, and others keenly aware of the language of racial difference, the hollowness of imperial belonging, and the profound effects of living in-between.

That colonial rule in West and Central Africa necessitated such incongruities is familiar scholarly territory. Historians and anthropologists have long pointed to tensions, contradictions, and incoherence to challenge monolithic readings of empires.[84] This important work, mostly stemming from the "rise" of colonial studies in the 1990s, has broken down binary categories such as colonizer/colonized, modern/traditional, and resistance/collaboration.[85] In their place, scholars have crafted narratives that highlight "agency," "negotiations," and "claims-making" and that foreground the uneven flows of power across a range of colonial situations—from the work culture of coal miners in southeastern Nigeria, to the struggles of production and reproduction among Asante women in Ghana, to the demands of railway workers in Sénégal, and so on.[86]

When I first started tracing the lives of Maran, Hoyte, and other Caribbean administrators in colonial archives, it was easy to see how their stories fit into such narratives. I could readily emphasize, as I have in this chapter, how they used petitions to negotiate and disrupt colonial categories such as "European" and "Native," prying open the "fissures within systems of control and constraint."[87] Indeed, there were dozens of examples to choose from in personnel files, annual reports, official correspondence, and endless folders of colonial *affaires*. Yet as I gathered more information about Maran, Hoyte, and others, it became clear that the complexities of their lives and ideas "exceed[ed] the explanatory power" of these now-conventional narratives of colonialism in Africa.[88] It also became clear that the forms of these narratives had emerged from the forms of colonial archives. As several scholars have argued, the determination to show how Africans and other colonized peoples made claims on colonial categories can reinforce the "false universalism" of these very categories.[89] Even when complemented with other kinds of sources and methods, this approach can result in narratives of endless reaction to colonial institutions and discourses.[90] Katherine McKittrick describes this "analytical habit" as "the tendency to seek out and find marginalized subjects" and then use them to measure scales of "dispossession."[91] In other words, to focus solely on how Maran and Hoyte negotiated the constraints of their particular colonial situations is to cede to a vision of history tied irrevocably to the archives and narratives of empire. It is a vision that reduces life outside the grasp of colonial rule to fragments, *rongés par les termites*, dots in the sky-blue frame of the map.

In the next chapter, I turn my focus toward these fragments and attempt to answer the questions they pose: What did Caribbean administrators themselves think about the ironies—and tragedies—of their positions in African colonies? How did they belittle and transcend the naturalized categories of colonial governments in West and Central Africa? And how did they mobilize new geographies of belonging for their own ends?

FIGURE 3.1. Edwina Violetta Alexis, passport application photograph, April 1917. Public Records and Archives Administration Department, Accra, Ghana, PF 3/3/29.

3

Fragments and Photographs

It has the smell of all colonial buildings, a yellow handwritten papery mustiness which reminds one of khaki breeches, white sea-island cotton shirts, endless reams of paper, carbon duplicates, and ink wells. —DIONNE BRAND, *A Map to the Door of No Return* (2001)

Le Pays Natal

Edwina Violetta Alexis sits in front of a camera in Kumasi. It is April 1917. She is thirty-seven years old, an experienced seamstress. She is waiting for a photograph, waiting for a passport, waiting to travel back home. Her husband is sitting close by with their sixteen-month-old daughter, Ruby. He is three years her senior and one inch her junior. She stares into the lens and quietly imagines her life back in Trinidad. Nearly eight years have passed . . . He had come home bursting with the news—an opportunity with the Gold Coast Agriculture

Department. They had agonized over the decision. In some ways their life in Port of Spain felt constrained—by family, by geography. But the Gold Coast? And with their three sons, all under five? In the end they had come: the transatlantic passage to Southampton, the frenzy of trains and hotels in London, and a long boat ride south from Liverpool along the ports of the West African coastline. They had arrived in Cape Coast in August 1909, settling at Assuantsi. In 1913, after a short trip back to Trinidad, they had moved north to Kumasi.... Nearly eight years have passed, sometimes quickly, mostly incrementally, but now she is sitting in front of a camera, and they are going home.

What else, beyond these itineraries? There are the stark details of her passport application, neatly arranged in a box titled "Description of Wife of Applicant if to Be Included on the Passport."[1] Born Edwina Violetta Bath. Forehead: Small. Eyes: Black. Nose: Prominent. Mouth: Medium size. Chin: Slightly long. Colour of Hair: Black. Complexion: Brown. Face: Long. Any special peculiarities: Walking erect. And there is the photograph, a foggy exposure cropped into a diamond. It speaks only in whispers about her struggles to adapt to life in West Africa, about her skill with a needle and thread, about her loneliness, joys, and worries, about the clothes she is wearing, about the inspiration for her daughter's name, about meals prepared and moments shared.

※

>
> Nightingale Grove,
> Cross Roads P.O.
> St. Andrew,
> Jamaica, B.W.I.
> July 28th 1913.

To the Manager or Superintendent of the Nigerian Railway,
 at Itori Station, Southern Nigeria, West Africa.

> Dear Sir,
>   I shall consider it a favour if you will kindly give me some information regarding Frank Reid, who was an employee on this Railway, at this Station, for some time. He is a Jamaican; colour brown; height about five feet eight inches; disposition quiet and well-mannered. His mother (Mrs. Annie Reid, a Widow) is very anxious about him, as she has not heard from him for some months; he has ever been a most attentive and dutiful son. His last letter to her was written from the above named Station, dated 24/1/13.

Hoping that you can give some information about him, and asking that you will kindly let me have as early a reply as possible.

I remain, etc.,

F.L.Ford (Miss)²

Paris—a rainy morning in late October, 1924. William Beaudu and his wife, Lucie Bouverat, were wandering along the narrow streets near the Gare du Nord, the doctor's words still echoing in Beaudu's head more than half an hour after leaving the clinic: *Délire de persécution. Hallucinations auditives. Surveillance constante.* Bouverat had been in the care of Dr. Edgard Blum for several months. Her health had improved, but she would need continued treatment. Blum had also recommended that Bouverat return to her home in Guadeloupe, where she would benefit from a "familiar climate" and the "moral support" of her family.³ Going back to Dakar, where Beaudu was the vice-president of the Court of Appeal for Afrique Occidentale Française (AOF), was out of the question.

As they turned west and walked across Rue La Fayette, Bouverat implored her husband to find a way back to the Caribbean. Over the past year, Beaudu, who was from Le Carbet, Martinique, had sent three transfer requests to the Ministère des Colonies.⁴ Each time, he had described the fragile condition of Bouverat's health. Each time, he had explained that her recovery depended on a "*retour définitif*" to Guadeloupe, to Bouverat's "*pays natal*," where she would benefit from "childhood memories and her parents." Yet each time, Beaudu's requests were met with bureaucratic indifference, despite his more than two decades in the colonial civil service. But now, with Blum's report, Beaudu thought the result might be different. As they walked toward their hotel near the Place de Clichy, Beaudu pushed the diagnosis aside and began crafting a new letter to the Ministère.

39454.

3rd. September, 1913.

Dear Madam;
    I beg to acknowledge the receipt of your letter of the 28th July last, and I regret to have to inform you, that Mr. Frank Reid, employed as Station

Master at Itori, who was sent to the Lagos Hospital on the 17th March last suffering from cardiac disease, died on the 3rd April.

2. Mr. Reid while on the Nigerian Railways proved himself to be a most efficient officer and his death is greatly regretted.

Yours faithfully,
F. H. Waller
Acting General Manager[5]

They left the Gold Coast in June and made it as far as London, but the war made it impossible to continue on to Trinidad. Edwina Alexis was devastated. They found a small flat near Finsbury Park. Compared with Trinidad, life in London was costly, and with four children their debts quickly accumulated. They received some support through church connections, but by early July, Mark Alexis had to ask the Colonial Office for an extra subsistence allowance.[6] Then in August he sent a petition, complete with a carefully calculated ledger, claiming that the Gold Coast government owed him £115.11.3 in unpaid housing and traveling allowances.[7]

The Colonial Office, five miles away at Whitehall, did not respond. In the meantime, Edwina fell ill. Three months later, Alexis inquired about his petition, pleading with the Colonial Office to "be merciful for the sake of my wife and children." He also requested a transfer back to Trinidad.[8] A week later, Alexis finally had his response: his petition was being "duly considered" and a decision would "be communicated."[9] Alexis wrote back and asked again for a transfer to Trinidad, his "native country."[10] He and Edwina were struggling not only with the financial costs of "support[ing] more than one home," but also with the emotional costs of sustaining multiple networks of relatives and friends, spread thin across the Atlantic. Leave was up at the end of November, however, and with no decision about a transfer forthcoming, they boarded a ship with Ruby and traveled back to the Gold Coast. The three boys stayed behind in London.

No. 39454
Nigerian Railway
Lagos
Dated 3rd. September, 1913.

Sir,

Re Mr. F.L.Reid, West Indian—deceased.

With reference to my letter No. 39454 of the 7th April last, I have the honour to forward a copy of a letter from a Miss J.L.Ford. The officer referred to was Stationmaster at Itori, who died in April last. *It would appear that his death was not reported to his relatives or to the Government of Jamaica.* The information in Miss Reid's letter may be of use to the administrator of the estate.

I have the honour to be,
Sir,
Your obedient servant,
FH Waller
Acting General Manager

The Secretary
Combined Departments
Lagos.[11]

As they continued past a deserted Square d'Anvers, Beaudu thought back to his days as a student. . . . He had graduated from law school in Paris in 1895 and then joined the colonial civil service. Four years later, he began working as a judge in Dakar but had quickly fallen ill with yellow fever. After Beaudu left for France to recuperate, the governor of Sénégal had criticized him, declaring that he was immune to yellow fever because of "his origin" and thus should have stayed in the colony to serve the government.[12] Beaudu eventually recovered and took up an appointment in Cayenne, French Guiana. While back in the Caribbean, he had met Bouverat, and they married in June 1902 . . .

Proceeding along the Boulevard de Clichy, under the shadows of Montmartre, Beaudu thought about their travels together, trying to remember where his wife's troubles had begun. . . . They had lived in Nouvelle-Calédonie without incident from 1907 to 1913. Then, after they had returned to Guadeloupe, a position had come up in Saint-Louis, so the young couple had moved to Sénégal. It was in Saint-Louis, he recalled, that Bouverat had first experienced these "morbid phenomena."[13] After the couple returned to Guadeloupe on leave in January 1916, Bouverat's health had started to improve and so he secured a transfer to Guadeloupe to ensure that his wife "would not relapse."[14] In

Saint-Claude, their situation was relatively stable, and by January 1920 they believed that Bouverat had recovered, so they left Guadeloupe and went back to West Africa.[15] At first Bouverat had remained healthy in Dakar, but before long she again fell ill, believing that she was "the victim of dreadful persecutions at the hands of certain people of [their] *dakarois* community."[16] They left for France in November 1923, and after seeking medical care for nearly a year, Bouverat had finally found some respite at Blum's clinic...

After settling back into their room at the Hotel Clichy on Rue de Bruxelles, Bouverat lay down on the bed while Beaudu began writing his letter to the Ministère des Colonies. Recounting their struggles over the previous decade, he explained that even with "long and costly treatments," doctors in France could only "ameliorate" Bouverat's condition, not heal her. And since she required "constant surveillance," Beaudu continued, he could not take her back to Sénégal, take her to another colony, or leave her alone in France. It was only in Guadeloupe, where they would have the support of her family, that she would be able to recover. "*J'espère ardemment que ma requête trouvera le chemin de votre cœur,*" wrote Beaudu. "*Et je vous remercie d'avance de ce que vous voudrez bien faire... pour me tirer de ma pénible situation.*"[17] After signing the letter, Beaudu carefully slid Blum's report into the envelope. The next morning, he sent it off to the Ministère on Rue Oudinot.

No. 39454
Nigerian Railway
General Manager's Office
Ebute Metta
Dated 7th April 1913.

The Secretary,
    Combined Departments,
        Lagos.

Sir,

Mr. F.L.D. Reid, West Indian.—Deceased.

I regret to have to report the death, in the Lagos hospital on the night of the 3rd instant, of Mr. F. L. D. Reid, a West Indian Clerk Station Master employed in the Traffic Department at Itori.

2. Mr. Reid suffered from cardiac disease on account of which he was placed on sick list on the 17th ultimo.

> I have the honour to be, Sir,
> Your obedient servant,
>
> FH Waller
> Acting General Manager[18]

Back in Kumasi, Mark Alexis continued to send inquiries about a transfer to Trinidad, where his position would be "more suitable and favourable," but there were no vacancies.[19] He also continued to submit petitions about financial matters and other concerns, but his superiors chided him for troubling them with "imaginary grievances."[20] Finally, in September 1921, his leave came up again. He, Edwina, and Ruby returned to London and were reunited with the three other children. Then, at the end of October, the family returned to Trinidad for the first time since 1913. They moved into a new home and found solace among family and friends in Port of Spain.[21] Alexis was still unable to obtain a transfer to Trinidad, however, so in June 1922 he returned to the Gold Coast.[22] This time, Edwina stayed in Trinidad with their children.

The separation wore on the family, while life in West Africa began to take a physical toll on Alexis as he suffered repeated attacks of malaria. He went through a medical exam while on leave in London in August 1925, but the doctor claimed that, based on Alexis's description of the attacks, "the majority of these were imaginary" and that he was "in fair health."[23] Yet the malarial attacks appear not to have been "imaginary." In September 1926, Alexis suffered a cerebral hemorrhage and his right side began to paralyze periodically. The Gold Coast Medical Board diagnosed Alexis with hemiplegia and recommended that he be "invalided out of the service" because he was "unlikely to be capable of rendering further efficient service to the Government."[24] A little more than a month later, Alexis was on a boat heading back to Trinidad. The colonial government had finally accommodated his request for a transfer, but only when he had become expendable. He died in August 1933, at fifty-seven, leaving behind his wife, Edwina, and their four children.

Supreme Court Registry
Lagos, 26th September 1913

The Officiating Secretary
Combined Departments
Lagos

Sir,

With reference to your memo of the 10th instant re. M. P. No. 431/1913, I have the honour to inform you that the Chief Registrar is not administering the estate of the late Mr. F. L. Reid Station Master at Itori.

I have the honour to be,

Sir,

Your Obedient Servant
Chief Registrar[25]

In April 1925, Beaudu secured a temporary position in Martinique, and he and Bouverat returned to the Caribbean. While waiting for a more definitive response about his career, Beaudu again requested a transfer to Guadeloupe, explaining that he and his wife had benefited tremendously from being back in Martinique, his "*petit pays natal*" and that his wife had recovered her "mental equilibrium."[26] When Beaudu finally received a response from the Ministère in April 1926, however, the directive was bewildering: *procureur général* in Réunion. Was it deliberate, he wondered? Or was it just a misunderstanding?

The transfer to Réunion was not entirely random. Back in January 1925, while still in Paris, Beaudu had suggested to the Ministère that if nothing was available in Guadeloupe, he would be willing to go to the Indian Ocean island, where the "climate and lifestyle" would be "similar to that of [Bouverat's] *île natale*."[27] In April 1926, however, when the Ministère notified Beaudu to take up his new position in Réunion, he was shocked, and he sent a desperate letter to the governor-general of Martinique. Réunion would be "a true disaster" for his wife's health, he explained. He had only suggested Réunion to avoid "a forced return to Dakar." He pleaded for an accommodation of some kind, but his efforts were met with silence.[28] Several months later, he and Bouverat were bound for Réunion, where they lived until August 1930. At that point, Beaudu chose to retire for the sake of his wife's "nervous troubles," and they returned to her family and to her "*pays d'origine*."²⁹

One? Or Two?

Many Caribbean administrators became similarly lost in the unforgiving labyrinths of imperial bureaucracies. In each case, the *pays natal* remained a source of emotional orientation, of kinship, of mental and physical renewal. Caribbean administrators realized that they were "not at home in empire," and they longed for places where they did belong.³⁰ In the minds of Edwina Alexis, Lucie Bouverat, and Frank Reid, Trinidad, Guadeloupe, and Jamaica were not colonies or imperial property but places of sustenance. The feeling of being "at home" was a balm for the tolls of colonial life. The *pays natal* was elusive, however—difficult to re-create and sometimes unreachable. These archival fragments are thus a poignant reminder of the regular functioning of pitiless imperial bureaucracies. ("It would appear that his death was not reported to his relatives or to the Government of Jamaica.") They are also a reminder of how the structural residues of these bureaucracies continue to shape our research trajectories.

Scholars have long considered archives as objects requiring analysis in their own right. More than simply repositories of knowledge, archives are sites of exclusion, monuments to authority, technologies of rule.³¹ Reading an archival document is not only about understanding its content, but also about understanding the historical context of its preservation, the form of its collection. This is especially true for investigations in colonial archives, where questions of power and composition are particularly fraught. As Ann Stoler writes, scholars should consider archival research not as "an *extractive* exercise" but as an "ethnographic one."³²

In "ethnographic" reflections on archives, no metaphor is more prevalent than the optical. Lenses, gazes, and frames abound, along with occlusions, obscurities, and myopia.³³ In thinking about the stories of Frank Reid, Edwina and Mark Alexis, and William Beaudu and Lucie Bouverat, this kind of language is irresistible. Africans and Antilleans *appearing* in colonial archives as colonial subjects, *disappearing* as soon as accounts are resolved. Indeed, the final page of Mark Alexis's personnel file is a notice of his death and a one-paragraph explanation about the dispensation of his pension. ("It would appear that his death was not reported.") In the archives of the British and French empires, the lives of such individuals *come into focus* only in relation to the whims of colonial governments. In the *foreground* are petitions, dispatches, passport applications, telegrams, leave allowances, and transatlantic passages—all orbiting around the Colonial Office in London and the Ministère des Colonies in Paris.

The fragments at the beginning of this chapter emerged from this same design, pieced together into coherence using elements from archives in England, France, Ghana, Nigeria, and Trinidad.³⁴ Yet I have also sought to twist this artificial coherence, to interrupt it with personalized narratives that *shift the gaze* and illuminate stories normally *cropped out of the frame*. In addition to the prevailing feelings of alienation and dislocation, other threads link these stories: the clinical gaze of Edwina Alexis's passport application mirrored in Miss F. L. Ford's description of Frank Reid; the "imaginary" illnesses of Mark Alexis, William Beaudu, and Lucie Bouverat; and the family networks, sometimes enduring, sometimes falling apart.

Such fragments, often unremarkable and indistinct, can reveal, in their "apparent muteness ... the remnants of an alternative history rather than the worthless shards left behind."³⁵ Held at the right angle, pieces of broken glass in the sunlight can *diffract* light onto objects in a way that alters our perspectives entirely, unforming the sky-blue frame of the map. Or, at least, that was my experience with a letter from Francis Simmons that I came across in London at the National Archives of the United Kingdom.

An Unknown Ending?

"I might as well mention the ill treatment that the West Indians received out in Nigeria from the head of their department which the head authorities here [in London] know nothing of is quite wrong and is advantage taking upon us while in Nigeria."³⁶ As I read Francis Simmons's letter, I was struck by his story. Simmons was from Princes Town, Trinidad, and in August 1914 he signed a three-year agreement to work as a railway guard in Nigeria. By October 1915, however, he was stranded in London and living at the Harrow Workhouse of the Paddington Board of Guardians. Desperate to get back to Trinidad, Simmons sent a letter to the Crown Agents describing how he had ended up in London.

According to his letter, Simmons fell ill in early April 1915 and missed several days of work at the railway station in Minna, Nigeria. When he sent for the doctor, the doctor refused to attend to him and sent his "dresser" instead, "a native man, that never being to no institute." Simmons sent the man away and asked again for the doctor, but "the doctor never came." Going to the hospital was out of the question—to Simmons the hospital was a place known to "make a sick worst than better." Nevertheless, his condition began to improve when a friend, also from the Caribbean, brought him medicine. A few days

FIGURE 3.2. A postcard of the railway station in Minna, Nigeria, undated. Yale Divinity Library and Atla Digital Library, Missionary Postcard Collection.

later, Simmons reported back to work at the railway station. When he arrived, the stationmaster told him that he would have to "furnish a medical certificate" for the days he had missed. Simmons explained that the doctor had not been willing to see him, much less provide him with a medical certificate. The stationmaster ignored this explanation and sent him home, demanding that he submit a "further statement." By April 23, Simmons had still not produced this "further statement," so the stationmaster suspended him for "insubordination." That same day, Simmons showed up at the railway station to pick up some bananas from Stephen Raymore, a railway guard from Jamaica. When he saw Simmons, the stationmaster informed him that he was suspended and ordered him to leave the property immediately. Simmons again tried to explain himself, but the stationmaster sent for the police, who arrested Simmons for trespassing and held him "among the native prisoners."

Four days later, the British resident minister in Minna released Simmons and told him that he should discuss his issues with the district traffic superintendent, one level up in the bureaucracy from the stationmaster. Following suit, the district traffic superintendent made no effort to help and instead sent Simmons to Nigerian Railway headquarters in Ebute Metta, near Lagos, more than three hundred miles away. There officials also brushed him off. With no one to turn to in Nigeria, Simmons sent a telegram to the colonial secretary of Trinidad asking for help, yet he, too, disregarded Simmons's situation. Then, on May 24, the general manager of the Nigerian Railway terminated Simmons's contract, leaving him stranded. On an annual salary of £72, Simmons could not afford the trip back to Trinidad, and the colonial secretary in Lagos would not cover the cost because Simmons had not fulfilled the terms of his agreement.[37] At this point, a group of West Indian railway workers pooled their money and bought Simmons a ticket back to London.

Simmons arrived in London at the beginning of October 1915, and his situation was precarious. He soon found himself at the Harrow Workhouse, "penniless and without any means of sustenance whatsoever" and "without any relation or friends so many thousand miles away from home." Desperate to return to Trinidad, Simmons appealed to the government as "a British subject" who could "scarcely get a breakfast" and offered to pay back the cost of his passage by working on the ship and by paying out of his subsequent employment.

A few days after receiving Simmons's letter, the Crown Agents passed it along to the Colonial Office. Most of the notes in the thin file on Simmons's case focused on whether Nigeria or Trinidad would have to pay for his "repatriation"— and if they should even consider this option. As one official wrote: "If those who are dismissed are given a free passage to the West Indies, I fear that all those who find Nigeria not such a paradise as they expected will adopt this easy method of getting back to their homes."[38] Of all the comments in the file, not one made reference to the closing lines of the letter regarding the "ill treatment that the West Indians received out in Nigeria." And so, Simmons was stranded in London, hungry and alone in the center of the empire to which he supposedly belonged.

And then, nothing.... There was a draft letter from the Secretary of State for the Colonies to the Crown Agents explaining that the Colonial Office was "not prepared to sanction the grant of a free passage from this country to Trinidad to F. A. Simmons."[39] But the file gave no indication of what happened next. Did the Colonial Office eventually take mercy on Simmons? Did he make it back to Trinidad another way? Did he die alone in London? ("It would appear that his death was not reported.") My ensuing searches resulted only in more dead ends, but the affective ties of some sources are difficult to escape. One day after working at the British Library near Euston Square—chasing other dead ends—I cycled over to the Harrow Workhouse at 313–319 Harrow Road. I thought it might help me to imagine what had happened to Simmons, but instead I found myself looking up at an imposing red brick building that houses the Westminster Register Office. No trace of Simmons. Nor could I find any clues in the Paddington Board of Guardians papers when I visited the London Metropolitan Archives the following week. I shared the story with archive friends and archive strangers, emphasizing the likely tragic ending. ("It would appear...") I occasionally went back to the National Archives to search for Simmons, but I always came up empty, and the strictures of my time in London forced me to move on.

An Extractive Exercise

I continued with my research in West Africa and the Caribbean, but I could not shake Simmons's unknown ending. While in Nigeria I read dozens of files on West Indian railway workers at the archives in Ibadan, including the one on Frank Reid, but found nothing on Simmons. Nor did I come across any mention of him in Trinidad. A year or so later, on a separate research trip to London, I ventured back to the UK National Archives, determined to find out "what had happened." Perhaps, I thought, I had missed something in the registers of correspondence.

The Colonial Office kept copies of all correspondence that came in from the colonies, and, to manage this unwieldy mass, created registers of correspondence organized by colony and by year (e.g., Trinidad 1904 or Gold Coast 1909).[40] Each time a letter came in, a clerk would make note of it in the relevant register by recording the date, sender, and subject, writing a brief description, and assigning a number. The letter itself was then organized chronologically with other correspondence from that colony in a series of bound volumes. Using the registers, Colonial Office staff could more efficiently locate the relevant volume of correspondence on any given issue. This practice changed in 1926, when the Colonial Office began organizing correspondence by subject, assigning descriptive titles to each file. Today, these descriptive titles of Colonial Office correspondence are part of a keyword-searchable online catalogue. For anyone doing research on colonial correspondence before 1926, however, you must follow the same procedure that the Colonial Office staff once did: combing through the registers.

When I first worked at the UK National Archives, I spent many bleary-eyed days reading through the registers for Sierra Leone, the Gold Coast, Nigeria, Barbados, Jamaica, Trinidad, and British Guiana between 1890 and 1926, hoping to come across anything related to West Indians in West Africa. I had found much relevant correspondence, but I also must have missed a lot, since my eyes

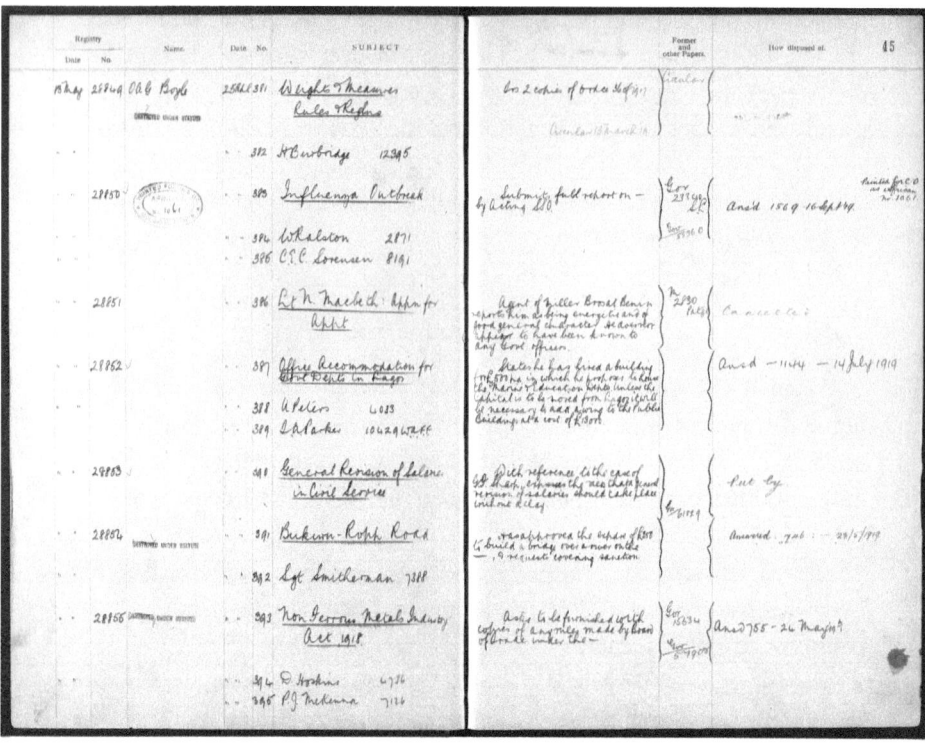

FIGURE 3.3. Double-page layout from the 1919 Nigeria Register of Correspondence. National Archives of the United Kingdom, CO 763/7.

usually glazed over after an hour or so. I thus decided to check the registers again, one last search for Francis Simmons. . . .

. . . Opening the register for Nigeria, 1915, I turned to the pages for October, and there it was. I had missed it. Colonial Office file number 48906. 22 October 1915. F. A. Simmons. Is an inmate of the workhouse. Asks if his passage money to West Indies can be advanced. I quickly requested the volume of Nigeria correspondence covering October 22, 1915 (CO 583/42), then anxiously awaited its retrieval. When it arrived, I stumbled over myself as I thanked the archivist and returned to my desk in the reading room.

It turned out this way: Simmons had sent his long letter to the Crown Agents on October 5, and while the Colonial Office was mulling the question of his "repatriation," he had remained at the Harrow Workhouse. After two weeks of waiting, however, a man named S. J. Langford from the Paddington Board of Guardians wrote directly to the Colonial Office on Simmons's behalf.[41] Langford noted the "slight offence" for which Simmons had been dismissed and explained that he was "destitute" and "desirous of returning to the West Indies." Langford also petitioned the Colonial Office to pay for Simmons to return home. After no response, Langford followed up on November 5. Remarkably, his appeal proved successful, and a few days later the Colonial Office authorized payment for Simmons's passage back to Trinidad.[42] On November 22, seven weeks after arriving in London, Simmons boarded the *Catalina*, headed for Trinidad.[43] Mystery solved.

After wondering about Simmons's fate for more than a year, I was thrilled, to say the least. And yet a hundred questions remained, questions I had not thought of while so narrowly focused on the question of his return to Trinidad. I still had no idea what had happened to him when he disembarked in Port of Spain; nor had I any sense of who he had been before his ill-fated trip to Nigeria. I knew almost nothing about his family and friends, about what he believed in, or even much about his time in Nigeria. The few fragments I had found could be construed as a seamless story only from the vantage point of the Colonial Office. The only mystery I had solved was how the Crown Agents had resolved their accounts. And so I kept thinking about Simmons, not because I was still determined to find out "what had happened"—though I did wonder—but because a yearlong pursuit of his paper trail had challenged my approach to archival research. My fixation on "solving" the Simmons mystery, I realized, was driven not only by affective interest, but also by the form of the Colonial Office archives: their conceit of totality, their sheen of omniscience.

Armed with cameras, tripods, and laptops, researchers (myself included) descend on the UK National Archives from all over the world with this same conceit, drawn by the allure of the metropolitan repository. We request documents ahead of time through the online catalogue, reserve reading tables specially outfitted with camera stands, take thousands of pictures, re-create the colonial logics of the archive on our hard drives and in our cloud storage accounts, revel in the sterile efficiency and uncompromisingly English atmosphere, and then—leave. In a world of limited research funding, this is understandable, but this extractive exercise, and the loss of "experiential friction," as Lara Putnam puts it, is also representative of knowledge production in Western academia.[44] By relying on a method of mass accumulation, *capturing* the archive perpetuates the scholarly cliché of "filling a gap." It is a method that assumes a particular shape of history, *a complete picture* that can be uncovered as long as one reads through the right register, finds the elusive file, and then, stretching out our arms a bit farther...

Reflecting on fragments and the obsession with "archival recovery," Jenny Sharpe suggests that silences "can also be a form of expression, rather than a puzzle of history to be solved."[45] In this light, the traces of people such as Simmons are valuable precisely because of their fragmentary nature. Such stories are often visible only at the blurry edges of the imperial lens, cloudy and distorted compared with the clear pictures at the center, but they are also a reminder that the particular forms of colonial archives were created and are reproduced for particular ends. Whatever narrative coherence these archives peddle, the past was never so seamless. Above all, such fragments challenge us to shift our gaze toward people and networks that transcended the naturalized boundaries of empires.

Pity My Poor State

Thinking in these terms—of fragments and the forms of colonial archives—the most significant moment in the Simmons story might be his arrival in Ebute Metta in May 1915. He had just been released from the Minna prison and had come south to Lagos to plead his case, but when the general manager of the railway terminated his contract, no one in the colonial government was willing to help him, much less listen to him. While he was stranded and isolated, a network emerged: "My friends seeing my poor condition pity my poor state in helping me to secure a passage to London."[46] Who were these friends? Likely they were other railway workers from the Caribbean—more than one hundred had come to Nigeria between 1913 and 1914, and many were based in Ebute Metta, the railway headquarters.[47] Their names do not appear in the Simmons file, but by reading across different archives, the West Indian networks of Lagos come into focus.

For example, one of these friends was almost certainly John Ambleston of Antigua. In December 1913, seven months before Simmons arrived in Nigeria, Ambleston had rallied a group of West Indian railway workers to the defense of Stephen Raymore, a railway guard from Jamaica who later became Simmons's friend at Minna. Raymore had not allowed a European merchant to collect a shipment of packages in Ibadan because he did not present the appropriate paperwork. After an altercation between the two men, police arrested Raymore, and the courts sentenced him to two months in prison. In response, Ambleston submitted a petition to Frederick Lugard, the governor, claiming that key witnesses were missing from the trial. More than a dozen other West Indian railway workers signed the petition, which, Ambleston claimed, voiced the "unanimous sentiment of every one of His Majesty's loyal subjects from the West Indies residing in Nigeria." Lugard did not change Raymore's sentence, but the petition nonetheless reveals an emergent sense of West Indian solidarity. In fact, in

June 1914, Ambleston's petition was republished in *The African Times and Orient Review*, the London-based publication of Marcus Garvey's mentor, Dusé Mohamed Ali.[48]

Another of Simmons's friends was likely Amos Shackleford, a railway worker from Jamaica who also signed Ambleston's petition. Shackleford had first come to Nigeria in 1913 and then returned to Jamaica in 1917 upon completion of his contract.[49] In January 1918, however, he returned to Lagos and began to work as a clerk for S. Thomas & Co., the commercial firm of Saro businessman Peter J. C. Thomas, whom Shackleford had befriended.[50] He eventually left and founded a successful bread-making business, but he and Thomas remained friends and became important advisers and benefactors to many in Lagos.[51] Such networks were especially important in times of ill health and death, as in the case of Donald Kryenhoff of British Guiana.

Like Simmons, Kryenhoff had come to Nigeria on a three-year agreement with the Nigerian Railway in 1914. When he finished his contract, he followed Shackleford over to S. Thomas & Co., where he worked as a shipping agent. Soon thereafter, however, in October 1918, he died of influenza. A number of Africans and West Indians came to the assistance of his family. Peter Thomas made the funeral arrangements, including renting a "motorcar" for Kryenhoff's "West Indian friends" to attend the funeral.[52] Shackleford, meanwhile, submitted an obituary to *The Lagos Standard*, writing that Kryenhoff had "hosts of friends" in Nigeria and that Reverend Thomas Adesina Ogunbiyi had conducted the funeral at the Ebute-Ero Anglican Church.[53] Shackleford also sent word to Kryenhoff's brother-in-law in British Guiana, W. A. Branker, and enclosed a copy of the obituary. ("It would appear that his death was not reported.")

Kryenhoff's wife had died five years earlier, so there were now five children in Georgetown under Branker's care. Kryenhoff had sent back regular remittances to support his children, but with his death, Branker was desperate for the proceeds of the modest estate.[54] Peter Thomas quickly took charge and recruited the help of Joseph Arthur, another railway worker from British Guiana. Arthur was heading back to the Caribbean on leave in April 1919, and he agreed to take Kryenhoff's trunk back to the family.[55] The trunk contained clothing, jewelry, and a shaving kit. The financial part of Kryenhoff's estate remained unresolved, partly because of some missed letters and broken exchanges, but also because Thomas encountered difficulties acquiring Kryenhoff's war bonus from the Nigerian government. Eventually, at the end of December 1920, Thomas settled Kryenhoff's accounts, and the Nigerian government arranged to transfer the £35-15s-1d to Branker.[56] Without the support of Shackleford, Thomas, Arthur, and the rest of the African–West Indian network in Lagos,

Kryenhoff's situation would have ended much differently. His memory would likely have been submerged or even forgotten, and his children would not have received their modest inheritance. ("It would appear that his death was not reported.") Shackleford and Thomas, along with the rest of the network around Kryenhoff, understood the importance of creating social bonds to stave off isolation.[57] It is easy to imagine how a similar network emerged to support Francis Simmons. The arrival of West Indian railway workers in Nigeria was facilitated by the British Empire, but once in West Africa, they created networks that established new forms of solidarity.

Re-creating Home

Feelings of strangerhood and dislocation led Caribbean administrators to rethink their positions in the British and French empires and reimagine their notions of belonging. Crucial to this realization was the experience of migration. Caribbean administrators had grown up in the Caribbean, they had studied in or, at the very least, traveled through Europe, and they had lived and worked in one or more African colonies. By moving between—and writing between—different parts of the British and French empires, they gave form to these empires. They saw far more of the world than their peers, and this mobility allowed them to establish links in a transatlantic imperial community. Simultaneously, however, mobility allowed Caribbean administrators to recognize global patterns of imperial exploitation and racist thinking. Migration thus had the doubled, paradoxical effect of both creating a lived sense of "empire" and rendering the notion of imperial belonging into a glaring fiction. In its place, Caribbean administrators generated new forms of relation that lay outside imperial boundaries. Such insurgent moments, sometimes revealed in times of crisis and death, also emerged in the more mundane exchanges of daily life.

For example:

There was Jules Ninine of Guadeloupe, who organized an informal "*colonie Antillais*" in Cameroon that brought together about a dozen others from Guadeloupe, Martinique, and French Guiana. Among other things, the group served as a relief from "hostility" with a "racial sense" that many of them encountered.[58]

There was Vivian Renwick of Trinidad, who went to Nigeria to work for the Agriculture Department and there met an old friend from Trinidad, John Soloman, who was working on the Nigerian Railway. In 1915, the two spent Christmas together in Ilorin, "chatting and drinking, recalling old friends and other Christmases." The experience made a strong impression on Renwick, who later remembered that "memories of home and friends passed through my mind."[59]

There was Henri Vendôme of Guadeloupe, who in 1914 worked near Kouango, in Oubangui-Chari, with two administrators from French Guiana: Felix Eboué and Juste Poujade. Together they enjoyed whiskey, bridge, and canoe races along the Oubangui River.[60]

There was the "Railway West Indian Employees Recreation Club" in Freetown. Formed in 1917, this group, made up of West Indian railway workers in Sierra Leone, met at the Railway Compound for "reading" and "indoor games." Club members also played cricket, using the grounds of Fourah Bay College. They played against British civil servants, as well as against African clubs, including "Muslim East End."[61]

There was Jean Silvandre from Martinique, who gathered with other *administrateurs Antillais* at the Soudan Club in Bamako in the late 1920s to eat and drink together. They included Maxime Letin, Louis Nottet, Joseph Cleret, and Edouard Labuthie, all from Guadeloupe, and Fernand Forgues and Charles Bayardelle of Martinique.[62] When Silvandre was in Dakar several years later, he became an active member of the "Association des Antillais." He was also the president of the 1936 celebrations in Dakar for the tricentenary of the incorporation of the French Caribbean into the French Empire.[63]

There was George James Christian, the lawyer from Dominica who lived in the Gold Coast and became friends with Percy Roberts of British Guiana. Christian cherished his meals with Roberts and Roberts's wife. "I am looking forward," Christan wrote in January 1925, "to the time when I shall have a chance to come to your end to be indulged by Mrs. Roberts in a good West Indian chop, such as she gave me at Tarquah some time ago."[64]

Amid alienation, racism, and dislocation, Caribbean administrators created new geographical alignments through such exchanges. People from Martinique mixed with people from Guadeloupe and French Guiana, while people from Barbados mixed with people from Jamaica and Trinidad, and so on. As they created such bonds in West and Central Africa, Caribbean administrators also began to rethink their imperial identities. Instead of aligning primarily as "British" and "French," they began to articulate "Caribbean" identities, something that remained uncommon in the stratified colonial societies back home. And when the British and French empires let them down ("It would appear..."), they had their own networks on which to rely. "One sees a discovery actually taking shape," wrote George Lamming about this phenomenon in 1960. "No Barbadian, no Trinidadian, no St. Lucian, no islander from the West Indies sees himself as a West Indian until he encounters another islander in foreign territory."[65]

The lives and networks of Caribbean administrators in Africa appear only as fragments in colonial archives, but when they are assembled in new forms, the center shifts and different perspectives come into focus. Rather than stories of disconnection, such fragments can also yield moments of solidarity and joy, snapshots of how Caribbean people spanned the distances between islands and across the Atlantic. In the chapters that remain, I draw on these fragments to construct narratives that offer different pictures of the past.

A Concert in Kumasi

There was also the fundraising concert in Kumasi in September 1916, organized by John Barbour-James of British Guiana. Among the performers who "enliven[ed] the town" was Edwina Alexis, who sang "Alice, where are Thou."[66]

4

Buried Vocabularies

I am only one-eighth the writer I might have been had I contained all the fragmented languages of Trinidad. —DEREK WALCOTT, "THE ANTILLES: FRAGMENTS OF AN EPIC MEMORY" (1992)

The music of the Fanti language was becoming singable to me, and its vocabulary was moving orderly into my brain. —MAYA ANGELOU, *All God's Children Need Traveling Shoes* (1986)

Not long after leaving the airport in Accra, George Lamming had his first shock: a convoy of obedient young Boy Scouts had arranged themselves to welcome "some dignitary from England."[1] It was 1958, a year after Ghana's independence, but for Lamming the procession recalled the carefully performed rituals of his colonial childhood in Barbados. As the ceremony ended, however, the boys dispersed into a "wild cacophany" of shouts and laughter and play. Lamming could not understand a word of what was happening. "They are speaking Fanti and Ga," a West Indian friend told him. "What often happens is this: when I speak to you in Fanti you will reply in Ga, and although I can't speak Ga and you can't speak Fanti, somewhere in between the meaning is clear." Reflecting on this moment several months later, Lamming identified a fundamental difference between his upbringing in Barbados and the world being fashioned by the young Ghanaian Boy Scouts: "They owed Prospero no debt of vocabulary. English was a way of thinking which they would achieve when the situation required it. But their passions were poured through another rhythm of speed."[2]

When Caribbean administrators arrived in West and Central Africa, agents of Prospero, few had any knowledge of African languages, and they found themselves in the same bewildering position as Lamming. Some from the French Caribbean took African language classes at the École Coloniale in Paris, but those who worked in British colonies had no advance training.[3] In a 1914 letter from Nigeria, for example, a railway worker from Trinidad named Milton Fairley described his frustration with communication: "We had to rely on Domestic Servants who are half savage natives and unable to speak a word of English, hence we could not understand them, nor make ourselves understood."[4] For Fairley, linguistic barriers combined with existing divisions between Africans and West Indians, not unlike the tensions evident in *boun-jouvouko*, the Sango term Central Africans used to describe René Maran.

Elias Buckmire of Grenada found himself in similar circumstances. He arrived in the Gold Coast in May 1909, but after two years at the agricultural station in Kumasi he requested a transfer back to Grenada: "My experience in this country does not encourage the idea of considering the possibility of the renewal of a contract," he wrote.[5] Buckmire's supervisor, W. D. Tudhope, sent the application on to the Gold Coast governor with a letter of support: "It is only natural for Mr. Buckmire to prefer a transfer to the West Indies. . . . He has shown a good knowledge of his work since he took up his appointment and I have always found him keen and interested. Being a black man and requiring an interpreter places him somewhat at a disadvantage however."[6] Anyone without an understanding of African languages in West Africa was certainly "at a disadvantage," but Tudhope coupled linguistic ability with race—"being a black man *and* requiring an interpreter"—thus marking him as doubly disadvantaged.

In other cases, however, Caribbean administrators did learn African languages. Those who did so were often motivated by financial gratuities and prospects of career advancement, but language acquisition was never simply a rote exercise. "Being a black man" and *not* requiring an interpreter in Africa also opened up new social and political networks. For David McNeil-Stewart of

Trinidad, who is the focus of this chapter, learning African languages allowed him to identify buried connections between Africa and the Caribbean. As he learned Fante, Twi, and Ewe, he moved away from Prospero's vocabulary and toward the languages of racial uplift and kinship.

The Language of Empire

The priest and schoolteachers at the Roman Catholic school in Sekondi stared in astonishment. It was October 1910, and David McNeil-Stewart, a sanitary inspector, had entered the school and started "prying behind the school maps and the inkpots on the desks," apparently looking for mosquito larvae.[7] A week later, *The Gold Coast Leader* decried this "idiotic performance," noting that McNeil-Stewart had entered and left the school "without saying a word." The article also labeled him a "West Indian Inspector of Nuisance" and an "*imported* African."[8] Was McNeil-Stewart aware of the reactions around him? If so, what did he make of them? Or was he oblivious, concerned instead with preventing another outbreak of yellow fever in Sekondi?[9] Whatever the case, the newspaper report pondered the "puzzle" of the colonial government hiring a sanitary inspector from Trinidad "whilst natives of better attainments could fill such posts."

Most striking about this incident, perhaps, was McNeil-Stewart's silence. He had come to Sekondi from Trinidad five months earlier, in May 1910, but he seems not to have learned much about the language of social life in his new surroundings. Instead, his outlook remained entrenched in imperial networks. Born in Port of Spain in July 1878, McNeil-Stewart attended the Government Training School in Woodbrook, where he absorbed colonial attitudes about work, race, and the British Empire. He also absorbed the ideas of Anglican missionaries at St. Margaret's Anglican Church in Belmont.[10] Then, in 1909, after eight years as a clerk in the Town Assessor's Office, he began studying tropical sanitation. A year later, on the recommendation of Rubert Boyce, he applied to work as a sanitary inspector in the Gold Coast, and in April 1910 he embarked for Sekondi on a three-year contract. His wife, Octavia, and their two children, Kenneth and Gladys, remained in Trinidad.[11]

Sekondi's natural harbor had made what was once a small fishing village a key site for trade. The British and Dutch had both established forts there in the seventeenth century, and by the late nineteenth century Sekondi had grown into a colonial town. Then, in 1897, the British made Sekondi the terminus of the railway line to Kumasi, and the port soon became the busiest in the Gold Coast. In 1912, two years after McNeil-Stewart's arrival, nearly £3.5 million in imports and exports passed through Sekondi.[12] With this growth came increased concerns about sanitation and disease, and so the colonial government focused on the construction of concrete drains and waterworks, new town layouts and building designs, as well as campaigns to prevent the spread of yellow fever and sleeping sickness.[13]

McNeil-Stewart was directly involved in this work. Over the course of his three years in Sekondi, he seems to have maintained the approach to sanitary work that had caused a commotion at the Roman Catholic school. He also remained unpopular, much like other sanitary inspectors in the Gold Coast, and this animosity continued to spill over into the pages of local newspapers.[14] In March 1913, for example, *The Gold Coast Leader* described McNeil-Stewart as "rude and bumptious and with very little tact and common-sense."[15] A month later, the newspaper's editors derided the "West Indian Sanitary Inspector at Seccondee" as "a malignant type of police officer."[16] The editors claimed they were not opposed to the work of sanitary inspectors but warned that "absolutely nothing [was] being done to teach the people or invite their co-operation," so this work was "of little use." McNeil-Stewart had evidently remained disengaged from those around him, communicating only in the language of empire.

The connections that McNeil-Stewart did make in Sekondi were mostly with other West Indians within the sphere of the colonial government. In March 1913, for example, two anonymous letter-writers, "Jamaica" and "British Guiana," wrote to *The Gold Coast Leader* in defense of McNeil-Stewart's reputation.[17] McNeil-Stewart was also the president of the Sekondi International Club, which included John Barbour-James from the post office, Leonard Muss from customs, Percy Roberts from the prison, and William Simmons from the police—all of whom came from British Guiana. There was also George James Christian, a lawyer from Dominica who had taken part in the 1900 Pan-African Conference in London.[18] The club met regularly, and their social gatherings reveal a small but vital network. In November 1911, for example, the club organized a farewell party for John Maxwell, commissioner of the Western Province, who was returning to England.[19] During this night of "smoking, songs, and recitations," Muss told a story about two miners aboard a ship that "called forth much laughter," while Barbour-James and Christian both sang songs, including "Rocked in the Cradle of the Deep." Later in the evening, McNeil-Stewart presented a formal address in honor of Maxwell, praising him for "rais[ing] the moral tone" of the region and for the "numerous projects set on foot for the betterment of the masses." Such gatherings brought comfort to Caribbean colonial officers who were an ocean away from their families and friends.

In May 1913, at the end of his three-year term in Sekondi, McNeil-Stewart traveled back to Trinidad and reunited with his wife and children. Then, a few months later, he signed a new three-year agreement and returned to the Gold Coast. This time, Octavia accompanied him, while the children, now fifteen and twelve, traveled as far as England, where they continued their schooling. Arriving back in the Gold Coast in November 1913, David and Octavia McNeil-Stewart settled at his new post in Swedru, a small commercial center about fifteen miles north of the coastal city of Winneba.

In Swedru, unlike in Sekondi, McNeil-Stewart and his wife did not have the comfort of a West Indian network, but there was still an echo of the Caribbean there: Swedru was a gateway to the cocoa-growing regions farther north. In Trinidad, cocoa was a major export and along with Tobago, the two islands were among the largest cocoa producers in the world at the turn of the twentieth century.[20] By 1911, however, the cocoa industry in the Gold Coast had become the world leader, exporting more than forty thousand tonnes per year.[21] As trucks rumbled through Swedru, carrying cocoa south to the coast, the sights and smells may have conjured memories in McNeil-Stewart—his father was a cocoa planter on the north coast of Tobago, near Moriah.[22]

(There is a story from Moriah of a healer from West Africa named Gang Gang Sarah who flew to Tobago to care for Africans enslaved on the sugar plantation at Golden Lane. After emancipation, she wanted to return to her homeland. She walked up the hill near Moriah and climbed to the top of a silk cotton tree, but she was no longer able to fly because she had consumed salt, and so she fell to her death.)[23]

It was in Swedru that McNeil-Stewart began studying Fante. This may have been a way of redressing his ignorance about the world around him, but with two children in boarding school in England, there was also a financial incentive. The Gold Coast government awarded £25 to those who passed a lower standard exam and £50 to those who passed a higher standard exam.[24] Whatever the motivation, in December 1915 he passed the lower standard exam, which tested writing, reading, translation, dictation, and conversation.[25] There is no trace of the exam itself in McNeil-Stewart's personnel file, other than the results, so it is difficult to get a sense of how learning Fante may have shaped his daily interactions as a sanitary inspector in Swedru.[26] Yet there are fragments: in early November 1916, *The Gold Coast Leader* again mentioned McNeil-Stewart in its pages, this time only in benign passing: "When will the proposed market shed be built just to protect our poor fish and kenky sellers? Mr. Stewart the Sanitary Inspector at Suedru must see to this."[27] Like cocoa, the mention of "kenky," or *kenkey*, a sour, maize-based dough, may have jolted a connection within McNeil-Stewart—a similar cornmeal dough was known as *conkee* in Trinidad.[28]

BURIED VOCABULARIES 77

Later in November, McNeil-Stewart and his wife left the Gold Coast to see their children in England after three years apart. The family had hoped to continue on to Trinidad, but the threat of German submarines thwarted their plans, and so they remained in London, at a flat on Dennington Park Road in West Hampstead.[29] Then, in March 1917, after they had spent several months together, McNeil-Stewart's leave was up, and he was due to return to the Gold Coast. By this point of the war, however, women and children were not allowed to accompany colonial officers to West Africa, so the family was separated again. Octavia, Kenneth, and Gladys were stranded in London while McNeil-Stewart returned to the Gold Coast alone.

McNeil-Stewart later described the challenges his wife and children encountered in wartime London.[30] Due to the "increased rate of living in England," he explained, they were often unable to buy enough food or coal or warm clothing. During the winter, this left them in "delicate" health, especially his wife, whose "frequent illness" was a result of both "climatic influence" and "nervous breakdowns caused through air raids." McNeil-Stewart also described their difficulties with finding housing due to "exorbitant rents . . . especially when coloured persons were the renters." Finally, he addressed the unique dilemma of "the coloured woman in England," who, "not known in a district for any length of time . . . , had to pay more for [foodstuffs] than the European housewife."

As I read this letter, I tried to imagine the cumulative weight of these years apart, interrupted only by brief moments of reunification. A friend recommended Jean Rhys's *Voyage in the Dark*, a novel about a young woman from the Caribbean in 1930s London, who navigates alienation in a world of "hundreds thousands of white people rushing along" and "dark houses all alike frowning down one after the other all alike all stuck together."[31] I also read Sam Selvon's *The Lonely Londoners*, which centers on Moses Aloetta of Trinidad and other West Indians in 1950s London. In a striking narrative style, Selvon captured the experiences of living in poor housing, working menial jobs, and occasionally finding pleasure and humor amid the racism and bleak weather of the imperial capital. Reading (and inverting) elements from the famous summer passage near the end of Selvon's novel, and mixing in the language from McNeil-Stewart's letter, I imagined a glimpse of Octavia McNeil-Stewart's cold, gray wartime London:

. . . Oh what a time it is when winter come to the city and all them throw on heavy winter coat hiding away from the cold blasts and the coal price going up and not enough warm clothing and rationing and a scarcity of food what a time winter is because everywhere you turn the English people frowning all the tightness and strain in their faces you never think that the grass would ever come green again the trees naked how grim the trees looking and a sort of fog in the distance though right near to you you ain't have no fog but that is only deceiving because if somebody down the other side look up by where you are it would look to them as if it have fog by where you are and this time so the sun in the sky like a forceripe orange and it giving no heat at all and they laboring under very great difficulties obtaining foodstuffs barely sufficient to sustain life during the period of rationing and in every instance nearly had to pay more for them than the European housewife people wouldn't believe you when you tell them the things that happen in the city police notice take cover bugle call all clear back out from the underground and the atmosphere like a sullen twilight hanging over the big city and when is winter a kind of grey nasty color does come to the sky and it stay there and you forget what it like to see blue skies like back home where blue sky so common people don't even look up in the air and you feeling miserable and cold not enough warm clothing or coals and not enough money to keep the family living in anything like comfort all them cold and wet months the population does lie low during the cold months but the unusual demand for houses was so great exorbitant rents were asked for flats especially when West Indians were the renters and they don't want that sort of thing at all they want you to live up to the films and stories they hear about black people living primitive in the jungles of the world oh the things that does happen in this London people wouldn't believe when you tell them they would cork their ears when you talk and say that isn't true police notice take cover bugle call all clear back out from the underground and the frequent illness and their health delicate in that climate and doctor bills and nervous breakdowns and not enough coals and warm clothing all these things happen in the cold wet winter and a sky of grey and no birds whistling and no leaves on the trees and everybody hustling that is life that is London she say when the bitterness of winter get in her she say she would never stay in old Brit'n again as long as she live and sigh a long sigh . . . [32]

Somewhere in Between the Meaning Is Clear

Back in the Gold Coast, McNeil-Stewart arrived alone at his new posting in Kumasi in May 1917. The British had annexed Kumasi in 1901, and the effects of the preceding wars had stripped the Asante capital of its former grandeur—and much of its population. By the time of McNeil-Stewart's arrival, Kumasi was transforming, with new buildings and roads grafted abruptly onto the residues of the old city. Yet the imprint of a new, colonial Kumasi could not escape its past, and it sat awkwardly amid a "ruined but remembered historic urbanism."[33] The railway had arrived from Sekondi in 1903, slicing through the town, and commercial operations had expanded rapidly. Merchants were descending

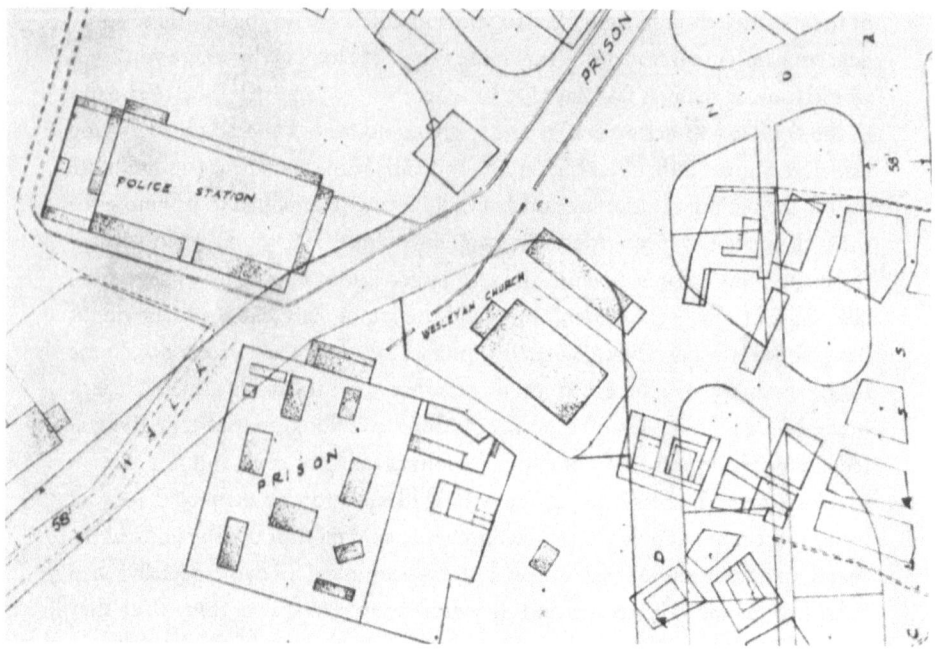

FIGURE 4.1. Police station, prison, and Wesleyan Church, cropped from "Kumasi Town Layout," ca. 1920. Basel Mission Archives, UTC-31.005.01.

on Kumasi from Europe and from around the Gold Coast. The population was also beginning to swell, growing from three thousand people in 1901 to nearly nineteen thousand in 1911. The Sanitary Department was eager to implement its principles of "order" and "improvement," yet sanitary inspectors such as McNeil-Stewart faced many challenges. One young observer remembered the Kumasi of 1920 as an "insanitary town ... with pit wells all about."[34]

For McNeil-Stewart, the imposition of colonial city planning and the rapid growth of makeshift housing around Kumasi would have recalled the urban geography of Port of Spain: railway lines, banks, trading company houses, the courthouse and prison, missionary stations, government schools, the post office, and other administrative buildings—all surrounded by haphazard urban development. Even the street names were similar, carrying the titles and names of British royalty: King, Queen, Duke, Prince, Charlotte. McNeil-Stewart had grown up in Belmont, a settlement just east of Port of Spain, with streets that wound up around the base of the Laventille Hills. Once known as Freetown Valley, the area had been home to former slaves who settled there in the 1840s.

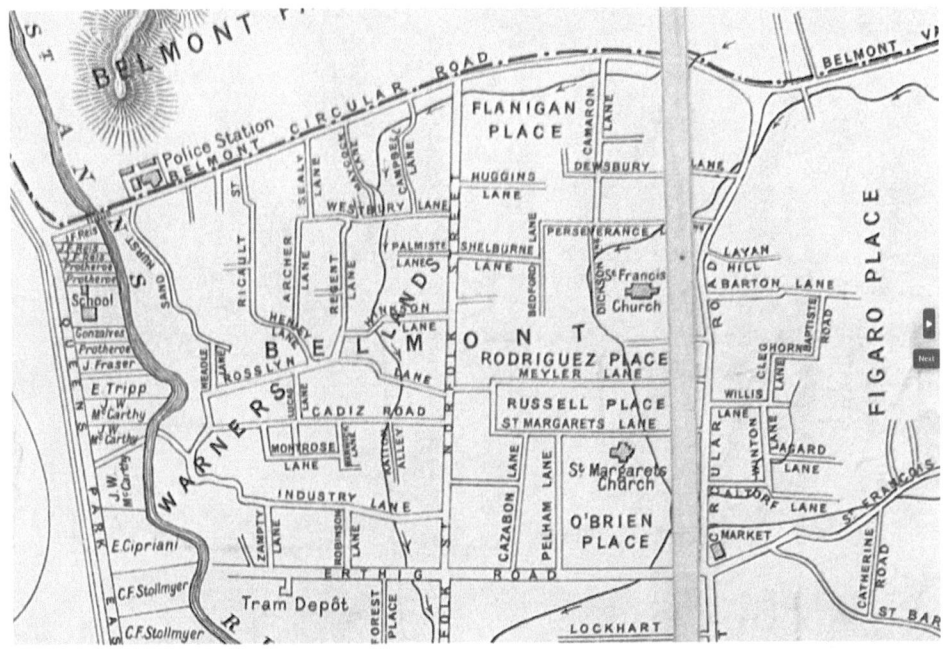

FIGURE 4.2. Belmont, Trinidad, cropped from "Plan of Port of Spain," J. Girod, 1902. National Archives of the United Kingdom, CO 700/Trinidad21.

Those able to find jobs worked as carpenters and masons, mechanics and tailors, domestics, porters, and dock workers. They lived in cramped, poor conditions, laboring in a world transformed by colonial rule, disease outbreaks, and human misery.[35] In Kumasi, the British were leaving similar imprints.

With such connections in mind, McNeil-Stewart returned to his study of Fante, and likely Twi, given his location. Indeed, speaking his coastal Fante in Kumasi would have marked him as even more of an outsider. In July 1917, he took the higher standard Fante exam at the Kumasi courthouse.[36] The examiner, Reverend J. A. Assan, was the "Senior Native Minister" from the Wesleyan mission station. As with the lower standard exam, there were sections on reading, translation, dictation, and conversation. This last section required a "power of understanding natives of different classes and of making [one] self understood by them." It also required examinees to "act as an interpreter between the examiner and a native absolutely ignorant of English." McNeil-Stewart passed the exam, scoring 42 out of 50 for dictation, 74 out of 100 for translation, 80 out of 100 for conversation, and 78 out of 100 for interpretation.

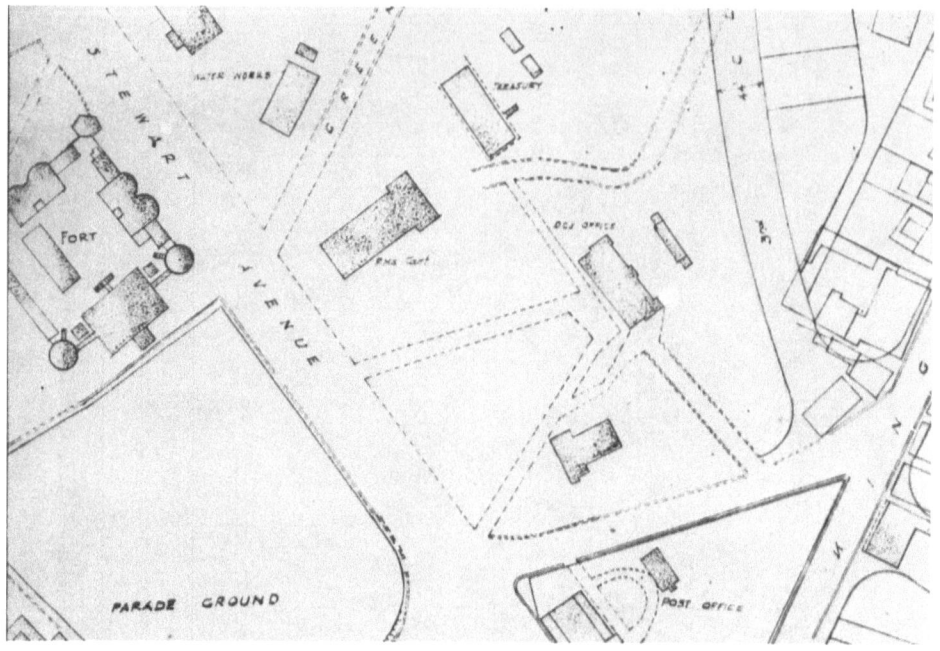

FIGURE 4.3. Fort, courthouse, treasury, waterworks, and post office, cropped from "Kumasi Town Layout," ca. 1920. Basel Mission Archives, UTC-31.005.01.

The content of the exam itself was mostly bland and bureaucratic, focused on daily practicalities and the colonial objectives that guided sanitation work. For example, the text of the dictation section described the following incident:

> Bir a Ahwihwesonmun' baan' amunum ho bian' du tsa dsin. Wāwā kitsa mbrantsen dsindsin; wo de nyimpa yi oabontsi oekohū bebi mbre wotsi. Ahwihwesonmun' bisabisa hon nsem pi, na nkurofun' enyiyi-anu yien,' okyir hon mu duenum kogu efiadsi.

> When the Sanitary Inspector came the disturbances calmed down in the neighborhoods. Wawa held the young men vigorously; they said these people had searched diligently to find out where they live. The Sanitary Inspector asked them many questions, and when the people did not answer them well, he arrested twelve of them and put them in jail.[37]

This situation may have emerged directly from McNeil-Stewart's personal experiences, though many of the details are unclear: What disturbances? Who was Wāwā? Who were "the young men"? The approach of this sanitary inspec-

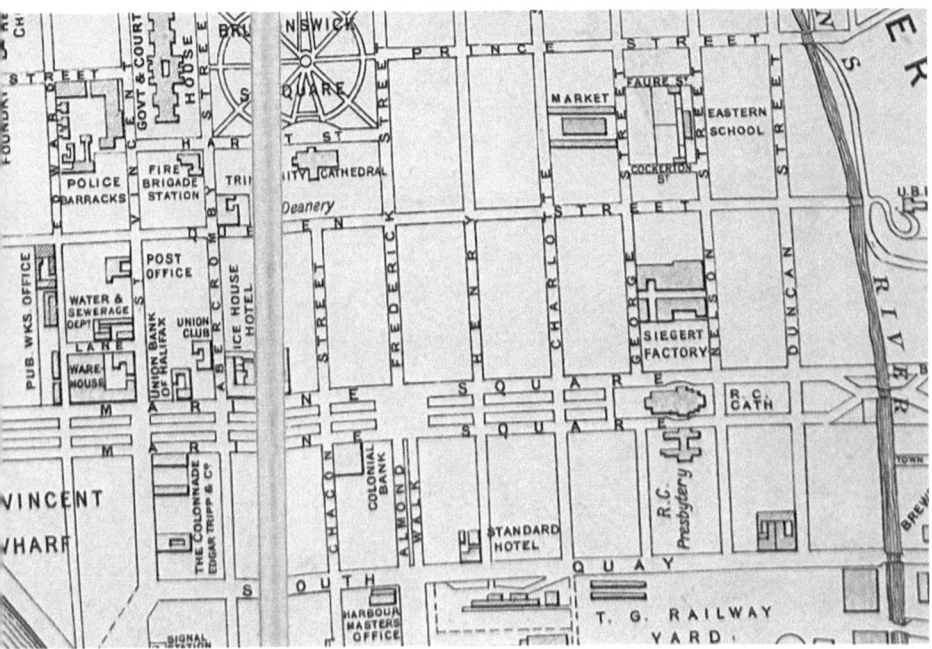

FIGURE 4.4. Downtown Port of Spain, including the post office, police barracks, and courthouse, cropped from "Plan of Port of Spain," J. Girod, 1902. National Archives of the United Kingdom, CO 700/Trinidad21.

tor, arresting those who did not adequately answer his questions, was certainly in keeping with descriptions of McNeil-Stewart. In Sekondi, he had been a "West Indian Inspector of Nuisance" who made no effort to "co-operate" with Africans and acted like "a malignant type of police officer."

Other sections of the exam alluded to the world beyond sanitary work. In the translation section, for example, several of the Fante phrases McNeil-Stewart translated into English reveal local concerns about the war: "Many of the Coomassie people's children go to East Africa"; "The war is for a long time"; "Have you heard that the Germans have destroyed the English ship 'Abosso'?" The British recruited thousands of soldiers from West Africa to fight not only in neighboring Togo, but also in Cameroon and East Africa. Many died, and the effects of losing these "children" for the abstract causes of the war were significant.[38] The *Abosso*, meanwhile, was a steamship torpedoed by a German U-boat in April 1917 on its way from Lagos to Liverpool. McNeil-Stewart had been on a steamship traveling in the opposite direction only a month earlier.

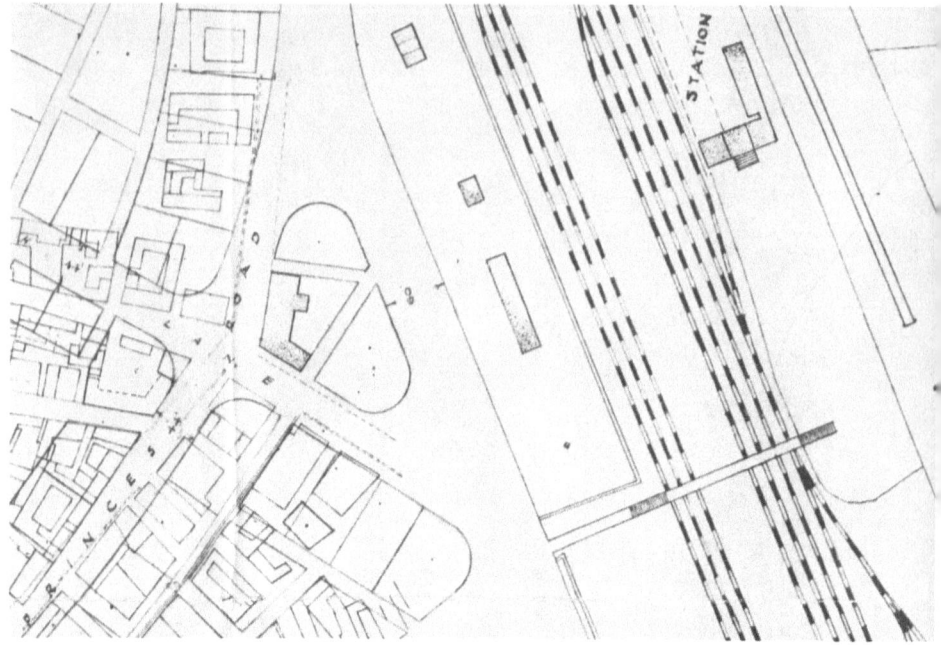

FIGURE 4.5. Princes Road and railway station, cropped from "Kumasi Town Layout," ca. 1920. Basel Mission Archives, UTC-31.005.01.

Another phrase from the translation section reveals how McNeil-Stewart brought the Caribbean with him to the Gold Coast. Referring to a recently arrived governor, the examiner's Fante sentence read:

> Hen enyi dan kwan wo ha; se obaa yedsi botu n'eyim ma oabra mbrosā ton wo hen man yi mu ha.

> We are looking forward to his arrival; when he comes we will bring the issue before him so that he bans the illegal sale of hard liquor here in our country.[39]

McNeil-Stewart translated the sentence as follows:

> We hope his road is here; if he comes we will place before him to forbid the sale of rum in this country.

Why would McNeil-Stewart, who did not drink spirits, translate the Fante word *mbrosā* as "rum"?[40] *Mbrosā*, sometimes written as *mmŏrɔsā* or *mmosā*, comes from two elements: *buro* and *nsa*. *Buro* is used in compound words to designate

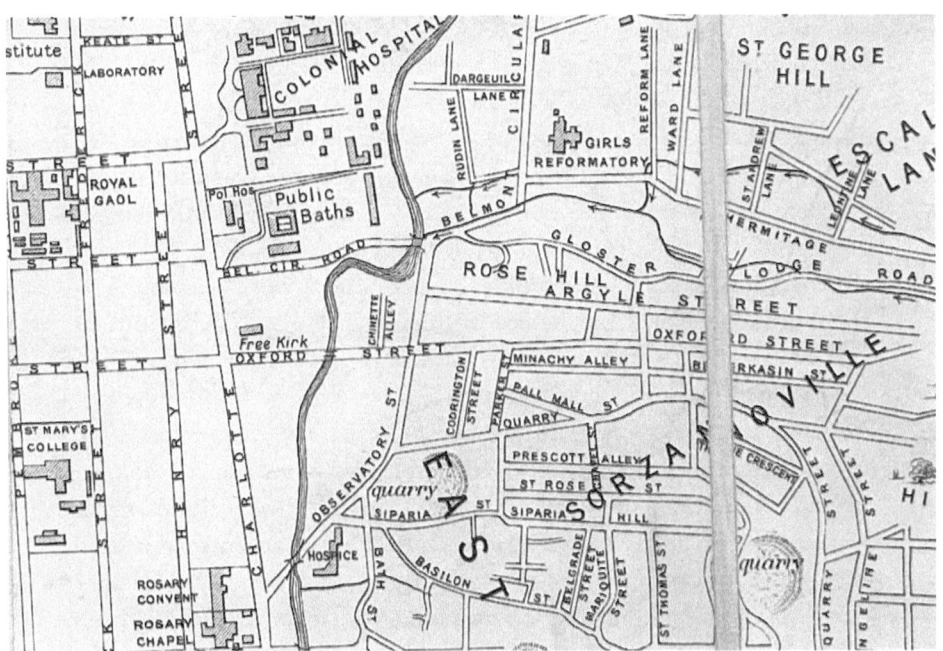

FIGURE 4.6. Colonial Hospital, Royal Gaol, and Charlotte Street, cropped from "Plan of Port of Spain," J. Girod, 1902. National Archives of the United Kingdom, CO 700/Trinidad21.

something of European or foreign origin, such as *aburokyεw*, a European hat, or *oburoni*, a European or other foreigner. *Nsa*, meanwhile, refers to any strong drink or intoxicating liquor, such as palm wine.[41] Put together, *mbrosā* could refer to any imported liquor, such as brandy, scotch, or whiskey. Yet McNeil-Stewart chose to translate *mbrosā* as rum, that most Caribbean of liquors, a word that points to the longer history of imperial networks between Africa and the Caribbean.

First distilled on the sugar plantations of Barbados, rum arrived in West Africa with Europeans in the seventeenth century.[42] Akan-speakers and others gradually incorporated rum, among other liquors, into rituals and rites of passage. Rum was also a key component of the transatlantic slave trade. European slave traders offered rum, along with textiles, weapons, and other goods, in exchange for enslaved people. These trade networks fractured lives and cultures and forcibly dispersed millions of Africans across the Americas, including McNeil-Stewart's ancestors. Within these imperial networks, however, fragments coalesced into new forms. Akan languages such as Twi and Fante, as well

BURIED VOCABULARIES 85

as other African languages, inflected the creoles of the Caribbean, including the creole that McNeil-Stewart grew up speaking in Belmont.[43]

The languages of Trinidad, "accreting and secreting fragments of an old, an epic vocabulary," give voice to this history.[44] When the Spanish arrived in Trinidad in the 1500s, many of the Amerindians living on the island succumbed to slavery and disease. Their vocabularies persisted, but Spanish became the language of power. In the late eighteenth century, however, the demographic and linguistic composition of Trinidad changed dramatically. First, the Spanish government offered concessions to Roman Catholic plantation owners from Martinique, Guadeloupe, and Saint-Domingue, who arrived in Trinidad speaking French and French creoles. Then, in 1797, the British took over the island. French creoles remained dominant until the end of the nineteenth century but gradually mixed with English and English variations.[45] Another major shift occurred in the 1830s. With emancipation, the colonial government contracted thousands of indentured laborers from India to maintain their control over the labor market. These workers brought with them to Trinidad Bhojpuri, Urdu, and Tamil, among other languages.[46] All the while, many in Trinidad were also speaking African languages, a trend that was reinforced when the British brought other indentured laborers to Trinidad from West and Central Africa. Between 1841 and 1861, more than eight thousand Africans arrived in Trinidad, "liberated" from slave ships by the British.[47] By the time of McNeil-Stewart's birth in 1878, the African-born population was smaller, but African languages and cultural practices continued to inform life in Trinidad. The two main groups in Port of Spain were Congo and Yoruba. In the 1870s, East Dry River, just south of Belmont, was known as "Yarriba Village" or "Yarraba Town."[48] In Belmont, meanwhile, a group of Radas from Dahomey founded a vodun healing community in 1868 that remained prominent into the 1950s.[49]

Given McNeil-Stewart's educational trajectory, he likely came from a family with middle-class aspirations, and so, like Vivian Renwick and many others in late nineteenth-century Trinidad, he would have learned to look down on "African" cultural practices. He probably derided their "hog language" while learning "proper" English and singing "Rule Britannia" on Empire Day.[50] Yet when he came to the Gold Coast in 1910 and began to learn Fante, the diverse cultural environment of Port of Spain may have been a source of orientation. Arriving in Kumasi in 1917, and beginning to recognize the similarities of colonial town planning in Africa and the Caribbean, how might he have heard other echoes of Trinidad in the Gold Coast?

... Perhaps, on July 28, 1917, as McNeil-Stewart left his Fante exam at the Kumasi courthouse, he accompanied his examiner, Reverend J. A. Assan, back

FIGURE 4.7. Market square in Kumasi, ca. 1908. Basel Mission Archives, QD-30.044.0083, created by Friedrich Ramseyer.

toward the Wesleyan Church to talk over the results, the sounds of Fante and Twi moving orderly into his brain. Then, parting with Hassan, McNeil-Stewart continued east along the prison road and across the railway towards the crowded Adum market, where food sellers were beginning to wind down for the day. Circulating around the stalls, he encountered women preparing *kenkey*, a maize-based dough similar to *conkee* in Trinidad, while others were pounding cassava into *fufu*, another dough-based mash known by the same name in Trinidad.[51] Heading south now, east of the railway, he passed the Catholic mission and the government school grounds, recalling his time at the Training School in Woodbrook. Looking southeast, he saw the familiar sight of a sugar cane plantation near Fante New Town. Then, crossing back over the railway line, near the store sheds, he overheard recently arrived Fante traders from Sekondi discussing crops of *edwó*, or yams, known as *eddoe* in Trinidad. As he strolled back toward his quarters, McNeil-Stewart thought about his work, remembering a case of leprosy, known in Twi as *kokobey* and in Trinidad as *cocobay*. And, of course, he thought more generally about his position in Kumasi. Ever unpopular, McNeil-Stewart, this West Indian sanitary inspector, was mocked and criticized by the residents of the city, who perhaps labeled him *oburoni*, a foreigner, or even *ɔkɔŋkɔnsání*, a hypocrite or double-tongued traitor, paralleled in Trinidad Creole as *konkonsa*—someone known to be hypocritical or deceptive ...

The language of empire that oriented McNeil-Stewart's education and career had partitioned the histories of Africa and the Caribbean, yet connections endured. They were hidden in plain sight, in the very language he grew up speaking—a "shipwreck of fragments," as Derek Walcott put it.[52] Such connections are conjectural, a leap taken from a word on a colonial language exam. Yet the pages of McNeil-Stewart's exam are a recording of life in 1917 Kumasi, a portal into a collage of words and sounds, names and places. Mixed in with the cadences of Trinidad, these words and sounds combined across the ruptures of Atlantic slavery, encountering one another in fleeting recognition. He is speaking Fante, he is hearing Trinidad Creole, and somewhere in between, perhaps, the meaning is clear.

Linguistic anthropologists are wary of ascribing such connections to linear histories of "origins" and "survivals" between West Africa and the Caribbean.[53] Given the forms and sounds of many of these words, what at first appear to be direct links are often false cognates, coincidences, or loan words filtered through other languages, including other African languages. The compositional terrain of creole languages is murky, to say the least. Moreover, it would be misleading, not to mention essentializing, to suggest that by learning Fante, McNeil-Stewart was knowingly reconnecting a broken link. The fault lines of diaspora remained. What is clear, however, is that there were echoes between late nineteenth-century Trinidad Creole and the languages McNeil-Stewart was learning in the Gold Coast. Rather than ask whether the word *eddoe* in Trinidad Creole *really* came from the Twi word *edwó*, it is perhaps more useful to ask whether such cognates, false or not, resonated with McNeil-Stewart. What were the effects of discovering such correlations? How did they shape his thinking about the British Empire and about the histories that circulated between Africa and the Caribbean?

On August 13, for example, a little more than two weeks after his Fante exam, McNeil-Stewart presided over an "impromptu debate" at the Literary and Recreation Club of Kumasi.[54] The subject of debate, "Whether the coloured races would be benefited after the War," drew arguments for both sides. Some supported the British as "agents of fairplay and justice," but the majority were more pessimistic. One club member, John Arthur, pointed out that "almost all provisions [were] exclusively reserved for the Europeans" and that a "great scheme" was "already afoot" to strip Africans of land rights. McNeil-Stewart, who was the president of the club, sided with the "Noes," alongside many others, including James W. Appiah and Chief Kweku Dua (or Duah), both part of the Asante aristocracy.[55] After seven years in the Gold Coast, and with his family stuck in London, McNeil-Stewart had lost faith in the British Empire. The broader exploitative realities of colonialism in the Caribbean and West Africa were laid bare. Perhaps taking inspiration from these buried vocabularies, McNeil-Stewart began seeking out new forms of belonging.

Poured through Another Rhythm of Speed

At the end of May 1918, after a year in Kumasi, McNeil-Stewart moved to Keta, a coastal town near the border with contemporary Togo. Situated on a narrow strip of land between a lagoon and the sea, Keta was one of several small Anlo settlements that, by the 1680s, had formed a loose military alliance. Over the next two centuries, Keta became an important trading hub, and the Anlo were key players in the slave trade until the 1860s. During this period, Keta periodically came under the control of the Danish, the Akan state of Akwamu, and other invading groups from the west and east. Then, in the late nineteenth century, the British took control of the area, and in 1906 they made Keta into an administrative headquarters, shifting power away from Anloga, the traditional Anlo capital. With its bustling port and lively market drawing traders from across the region, Keta in 1918 was a cosmopolitan colonial town—a center for commerce, Christian missions, and colonial politics.[56]

Arriving in Keta, McNeil-Stewart once again picked up his work as a sanitary inspector, which was no better received than in Sekondi, Swedru, and Kumasi. Here was yet another *yevu* imposing regulations, issuing fines, and bringing people before the courts. Ewe-speakers used *yevu* (plural *yevuwo*), a term usually translated as "cunning dog," to refer to Europeans, as well as Africans who adopted European customs, dress, and language.[57] McNeil-Stewart's Fante and Twi would have been less useful in Keta, though he likely learned some Ewe during his four and a half years there—or at least enough to know when he was being insulted.

In November 1918, with the end of the war, McNeil-Stewart's wife and children were allowed to join him in the Gold Coast. The armistice also meant that the debate from Kumasi on "whether the coloured races would be benefited after the War" was no longer abstract. For McNeil-Stewart, the answer was still "No." In a December 1919 petition, for example, he presented his case for a higher war bonus, pointing out that he had received only one-third of the amount granted to Europeans in the colonial civil service.[58] Six months later, the request was denied. "The Governor does not entertain petition as to the increased War Bonus," wrote his supervisor.[59] Such frustrations, compounding over a decade, led McNeil-Stewart to forge close relationships with several key political figures in Keta, including Togbi Sri II, leader of the Anlo-Ewes, and Samuel Athanasius Pomeyie, Sri II's state secretary. For Sri II and Pomeyie, meanwhile, as well as the other Western-educated African elite of Keta, the arrival of a new sanitary inspector was a welcome opportunity. McNeil-Stewart was a useful ally.

Sri II, born in Taviefe in 1862, attended the Bremen mission school in Keta, where his family was closely linked with the merchant community.[60] As a young man, he worked as a commercial clerk in Sierra Leone and Cameroon, before returning to the Gold Coast. Then, in 1907, he was elected the political and religious leader, or *awoamefia*, of the Anlo.[61] His supporters were Adzovia clan elders who were keen on the "modernization" of the region, and Sri II followed through on this ideal.[62] Upon taking office, he challenged the conventions that had governed his position in the past. He refused to stay in seclusion, rode his bicycle along the littoral, challenged prevailing burial practices, reversed a ban on Western clothing, and welcomed long-resisted Christian churches and schools to Anloga.[63] He also used his connections with the colonial state to expand Anlo power. In 1912, for example, he persuaded the district commissioner to expand the territory of the Anlo state back to its larger, precolonial boundaries.[64] Then, during the war, he offered the British ten thousand soldiers to fight in German Togoland in an effort to reunite Anlo-Ewe people divided by the border.[65] This effort at reunification was ultimately unsuccessful, and after the war the British transferred much of "British Togoland" to the French. Nevertheless, by securing links with the colonial government, Sri II also secured his own power. McNeil-Stewart's relationship with Sri II was mediated by similar dynamics.

> The driver parked at the side of Keta's market and Mr. Adadevo asked me to come and meet his sister, who had a stall on the market's periphery.... When we were introduced, I found that she spoke very scanty English and I expected that she would speak French. The Ewe tribe which occupied Togo and the eastern area of Ghana had been a German colony in the nineteenth century, but after Germany's loss of World War I, the allied victors took away Germany's mandate and gave the area to France.

French became the province's official language in 1920, so I offered to speak French with my host's sister, but her French was only a little better than her English. We smiled at each other and shook hands in exasperation. She spoke rapid Ewe with her brother and niece.... I waved goodbye, anxious to climb into the raised market which was issuing sounds of trade and merriment.[66]

On August 3, 1921, McNeil-Stewart attended a ceremony in Keta in honor of Sri II. Colin Harding, the commissioner for the Gold Coast's Eastern Province, was there to award Sri II the King's Medal for Chiefs, and people from around the region descended on Keta in advance of the occasion.[67] The festivities began in the morning with a procession of students from the three mission schools marching through town. Wearing "bright scarlet and white" uniforms, the students carried banners and were accompanied by a brass band. Eventually, they made their way to the courthouse, where they gathered with the rest of the onlookers. Sri II sat in the center, "wearing a crown of purple and gold, and a brilliant robe of yellow silk." The square was decorated with bunting and flags, and the sound of a cannon called all to attention. Harding made a "spirited address," praising Sri II's loyalty and "sterling worth," and placed a "silver chain around [his] neck." Sri II then gave his own address "in the vernacular," translated into English by Samuel Pomeyie. "We wish once more to assure his Majesty the King-Emperor of our loyalty and obedience to the British Government in all things that are lawful and right," declared Pomeyie. "The British Government, as time and experience show, is the best of all the Governments that at present are existing upon the surface of the globe." Pomeyie also reminded Harding of their desire to reunite with their "kindred people" across the border. At the conclusion of the ceremony, the crowd sang "God Save the King."

Later that day, at a celebratory banquet, McNeil-Stewart gave a toast and remarked on the "complete harmony which had for so long marked the Fia's association with Government and commercial people." There was also music and dancing, which continued until 3 a.m., including two performances by McNeil-Stewart's daughter, Gladys, who sang "The Rosary" and "A Little Love, a Little Kiss" in a "beautiful contralto voice." Leaders such as Sri II used such occasions to signal their ties with the colonial state, and this parade of colonial politics also facilitated McNeil-Stewart's relationships with Sri II and

Pomeyie. Yet their relationships were not circumscribed by the rituals and language of empire.

※

The narrow stairs were bounded by wooden walls, making the entrance dim. I was looking down, making certain of my footfall, when a voice above me drew my attention. I looked up to see an older woman, unusually tall, blotting out the light behind her. She spoke again and in a voice somewhat similar to my own, but I was unable to understand her. I smiled and, using Fanti, said regretfully, "I am sorry, Auntie, but I don't speak Ewe." She put her hands on her wide hips, reared back and let loose into the dim close air around us a tirade of angry words. When she stopped, I offered, in French and in a self-deprecating tone, "I am sorry, Auntie, but I don't speak Ewe." She clapped her hands close enough to my face for me to feel the rush of air, then she raised her voice. My ignorance of the meaning of her words did not prevent me from knowing that I was being denounced in the strongest possible language.[68]

※

A week after the Harding celebration, Sri II sent a letter to the medical officer of Keta and declared that ever since McNeil-Stewart's arrival in 1918, sanitary work in the town had been "carried out with the highest efficiency" and had garnered praise from "every European (Official or non-official) as well as other natives of the Colony passing through."[69] Sri II also described his specific appreciation for McNeil-Stewart:

> His courtesy to the lowest and the most illiterate of my subjects, as well as to the higher and more intelligent ones, his ever willingness to make the ignorant and illiterate people understand sanitary methods which are new to them, instead of unwisely frequently putting them before the Court for things of which they are ignorant, have won for him the love and esteem not only of the people, but also of the Chiefs, the European element (Official and non-official) and likewise mine.

Sri II's praise reflected a change in McNeil-Stewart's approach to sanitary work. Rather than going about his duties "without saying a word," as in Sekondi, he appears to have engaged more meaningfully with the people around him. He was also now willing to explain his role to "the ignorant and illiterate." Instead of arbitrarily arresting the people of Keta and taking them to court like a "malignant type of police officer," he earned their "love and esteem."

While Sri II's letter should be read within the context of colonial politics—it was sent a week before McNeil-Stewart submitted another petition for better compensation—it also hints at the relationships McNeil-Stewart formed with Sri II and his secretary, Samuel Pomeyie. A month earlier, for example, on July 2, 1921, McNeil-Stewart presided over a public meeting in Keta at the Jubilee Memorial Hall.[70] According to one observer, the highlight of the meeting was a "very interesting" speech by Pomeyie in which he called for the creation of an "Anlo Progress Union." This idea, and the name itself, came from the African Progress Union (APU) of London, founded three years earlier by Africans and West Indians in England, including Marcus Garvey's mentor, Dusé Mohamed Ali, and John Barbour-James of British Guiana, McNeil-Stewart's old friend from Sekondi.[71] According to its constitution, the APU sought to "promote the general welfare of Africans and Afro-peoples" and to spread "a knowledge of the history and achievements of Africans and Afro-peoples past and present." The APU was also involved in planning the July 1921 Pan-African Congress in London and proposed an international network of branches, stretching from North America and Europe to the Caribbean and across Africa, including the Gold Coast.[72] Other APU members included John Alcindor of Trinidad, Thomas Hutton-Mills and Joseph Casely Hayford of the Gold Coast, Herbert Bankole-Bright of Sierra Leone, and Amodu Tijani of Nigeria. The Gold Coast press reported extensively on the APU, and Pomeyie must have drawn inspiration from the organization, as well as from McNeil-Stewart and his friendship with Barbour-James.[73] Over the course of a decade in the Gold Coast, McNeil-Stewart had found another rhythm of speed: the language of racial uplift.

※

"Mr. Adadevo, would you please talk to this Auntie. I can't make her understand." The woman fired another salvo, and Mr. Adadevo stepped up and placed himself between me and my assailant. He spoke softly in Ewe. I heard the word "American" while I was watching the woman's face. She shook her head in denial. My protector spoke again, still softly. I heard "American Negro." Still the woman's face showed disbelief. Mr. Adadevo looked at me and said, "Sister, she thinks you are someone else. Do you have your American passport with you?" I hadn't seen my passport in two years, but I remembered having an old California driver's license, which had its identifying photograph. I took the wrinkled, but still slick paper from my wallet and gave it to Mr. Adadevo. He handed the document to the woman who strained to see in the darkness. She turned and walked up the stairs into the light. Mr. Adadevo followed and I followed him. There, the woman, who was over six feet tall, stood peering at the flimsy piece of paper in her dark hand. When she raised her head, I nearly fell back down the steps: she had the wide face and slanted eyes of my grandmother. Her lips were large and beautifully shaped like my grandmother's, and her cheek bones were high like those of my grandmother. The woman solemnly returned the license to Mr. Adadevo who gave it back to me, then the woman reached out and touched my shoulder hesitantly. She softly patted my cheek a few times. Her face had changed. Outrage had given way to melancholia. After a few seconds of studying me, the woman lifted both arms and lacing her fingers together clasped her hands and put them on the top of her head. She rocked a little from side to side and issued a pitiful little moan.[74]

For McNeil-Stewart, Pomeyie, and Sri II, the language of racial uplift in Keta was informed by their connections with the African Methodist Episcopal (AME) Zion Church.[75] Formed in New York City in 1801, the AME Zion Church had spread across the United States and then to the Caribbean. In 1876, the first AME Zion missionaries came to Liberia, and twenty years later, John Bryan Small of Barbados brought the church to Cape Coast.[76] Small had already spent time in the Gold Coast as part of the West Indian regiment in the 1860s, and he knew Fante. In addition to establishing the church in Cape Coast, Small provided opportunities for young men to study at Livingstone College, an AME Zion school in North Carolina where he had studied in the 1880s. One of these young men was James K. Aggrey.

In 1899, AME Zion missionaries also established a church and school in Keta, built on the land of two Anlo elders, Nyaho Tamakloe and Joachim Acolatse.[77] Elites in Keta had long understood the political and economic advantages of sending their children to the Bremen and Catholic mission schools, but they also knew the constraints of colonial racism, and the AME Zion school appeared to offer different possibilities. Nevertheless, the church was slow to make inroads in Keta. For one thing, the AME Zion missionaries struggled to raise funds locally because they had to compete with the better-established missions. They were also often unable to obtain adequate support from headquarters in the United States. With the outbreak of war in 1914, however, the Bremen missionaries were expelled from the Gold Coast, and there was an opportunity.

By this time, Pomeyie was a pastor at the AME Zion church in Keta and the principal of the AME Zion school.[78] Like Aggrey, he had studied at Livingstone College, and he responded to the church's financial challenges by embracing the language of racial uplift. With the Bremen missionaries gone, membership grew, and by 1920, shortly after McNeil-Stewart's arrival in Keta, there were 9,933 members in the church's East Gold Coast Conference.[79] In 1921, Pomeyie suggested the creation of an Anlo Progress Union, and he used this momentum to promote similar initiatives while openly condemning the destructive effects of colonial rule. In March 1922, for example, he gave a speech in Anloga about education with Sri II in attendance. "This is an age of race consciousness," he declared, and without education the "illiterate African ... [will] find himself exploited unaware by 'That Bureaucrat' whose concealed motto is 'Down with the African Native.'"[80] In November 1922, Pomeyie presented similar themes at the AME Zion Church Teacher's Conference in Keta. "Some desipient black people," he stated, "have unnaturally become displeased with their hue and would like to sacrifice all they possess in life to be metamorphosed white." Teachers, he concluded, had the "duty of training the children in the awakened racial consciousness" and to "remain African (Black) in colour."[81]

Pomeyie's language of "racial consciousness," given form by the AME Zion Church, provided a source of respite from the indignities meted out by the "Bureaucrats" of the colonial state. For McNeil-Stewart, the racism in Keta that limited access to education, employment, and trade opportunities was familiar, as it had marked his own experiences in Trinidad, as well as elsewhere in the Gold Coast. The language of racial consciousness thus brought McNeil-Stewart together with Pomeyie, Sri II, and others in Keta, as well as with wider intellectual networks joining West Africa, the Caribbean, and North America.[82]

The woman let her arms fall and stepping up to me, spoke and took my hand, pulling me gently away. Mr. Adadevo said, "She wants you to go with her. We will follow." The girls and the driver had climbed the stairs and we entered the crowded market. I allowed myself to be tugged forward by the big woman who was a little taller than I and twice my size. She stopped at the first stall and addressed a woman who must have been the proprietor. In the spate of words, I heard "American Negro." The woman looked at me disbelieving and came around the corner of her counter to have a better look. She shook her head and, lifting her arms, placed her hands on her head, rocking from side to side.... Their distress was contagious, and my lack of understanding made it especially so. I wanted to apologize, but I didn't know what I would ask pardon for. I turned to Mr. Adadevo and asked if they thought I looked like someone who had died. He answered and his voice was sad, "The first woman thought you were the daughter of a friend. But now you remind them of someone, but not anyone they knew personally."[83]

※

The US-centered language of "racial consciousness," a defining feature of the AME Zion Church, may have united Pomeyie, McNeil-Stewart, and other elites in Keta, but it did not resonate with the majority. As historian Sandra Greene notes, the more prevalent languages of belonging in the region centered on kin groups, lineages, villages, and other political and social communities.[84] Few thought of themselves according to Pomeyie's equated categories of "African (Black)" or as belonging to the same "race" as Pomeyie, let alone McNeil-Stewart. Rather, to many in Keta, Pomeyie and McNeil-Stewart were *yevuwo*.[85] This divergence in ideas about identity and belonging hurt the AME Zion Church in the eastern Gold Coast, and in the 1920s membership dropped significantly—from 9,933 in 1920 to 1,771 in 1931.[86] Funding followed suit. To fight this decline, Greene suggests, church leaders moved from the language of "racial consciousness" to the language of kinship. The key figure in this changing approach was F. K. Fiawoo.

Fiawoo was born in 1891 in Whuti, at the southwestern corner of the Keta Lagoon, and came of age during the rise of the AME Zion Church in the Gold Coast. As with Aggrey and Pomeyie, the church facilitated his schooling in the United States, where he studied from 1925 to 1933. While in the United States, he wrote *Toko Atolia*, now a classic work of Ewe literature, and when he returned to the Gold Coast, he became a pastor in the AME Zion Church. In the 1940s, he also became head of the Zion Secondary School in Anloga. Like his predecessors, however, Fiawoo was not able to raise enough local support for this work. In an attempt to change this, he turned to a story from Atorkor, a town and former slave trade port about a mile from where he grew up.

According to oral traditions, in the 1850s a slave ship stopped at Atorkor to trade with Togbi Ndorkutsu, the leader of Atorkor and a major slave trader. When the crew came to shore, they saw a group of drummers playing and invited them on board their ship to play. The drummers, all men, were joined by some women and children. The captain of the ship offered alcohol to the drummers, and when they became drunk, the crew lifted anchor. The ship then began sailing away from the coast, but the drummers did not notice until it was too late.[87]

Such acts of kidnapping happened elsewhere along the Slave Coast, but Fiawoo used this particular story to bolster his fundraising efforts. Since financial backing for the Zion Secondary School came largely from the United States, Fiawoo began suggesting to Anlos that the school was being supported by "the descendants of their own kidnapped relatives," people who had once been fellow "fishermen and farmers" but had been taken away to North America against their will.[88] This language of (lost) kinship resonated more widely than Pomeyie's language of racial consciousness, especially among those who were not educated at the mission schools. By emphasizing these severed kinship ties, Fiawoo reframed how Anlos conceived of their relationships with the descendants of enslaved people in the United States; funding the school became a way to reconnect with their lost people. Fiawoo's narrative then spread with Zion school graduates across Eweland, and variations of the story are still remembered and retold today.[89]

※

I said, "Mr. Adadevo, you must tell me what's happening." He said, "This is a very sad story and I can't tell it all or tell it well." I waited while he looked around. He began again, "During the slavery period Keta was a good sized village. It was hit very hard by the slave trade. Very hard. In fact, at one point every inhabitant was either killed or taken. The only escapees were children who ran away and hid in the bush. Many of them watched from their hiding places as their parents were beaten and put into chains. They saw the slaves set fire to the village. They saw mothers and fathers take infants by their feet and bash their heads against tree trunks rather than see them sold into slavery. What they saw they remembered and all that they remembered they told over and over. The children were taken in by nearby villagers and grew to maturity. They married and had children and rebuilt Keta. They told the tale to their offspring. These women are the descendants of those orphaned children. They have heard the stories often, and the deeds are still as fresh as if they happened during their lifetimes. And you, Sister, you look so much like them, even the tone of your voice is like theirs. They are sure you are descended from those stolen mothers and fathers. That is why they mourn. Not for you but for their lost people."[90]

McNeil-Stewart left the Gold Coast at the end of 1922 and thus did not have a direct influence on the shift in the 1930s from the language of racial consciousness to the language of kinship. His intellectual trajectory, however, followed a similar transformation. He grew up in the stilted colonial atmosphere of late nineteenth-century Trinidad, where he attended colonial schools and worked for the colonial government. When he arrived in Sekondi in 1910, an agent of the British, he knew the language of empire but was ignorant of other ways of speaking and hearing in West Africa. Learning Fante, however, gave him more direct insights into the world around him, and he began to identify similarities between the destructive geographies of colonialism in Trinidad and the Gold Coast. Learning Fante also allowed him to trace buried linguistic connections between Africa and the Caribbean. Disillusioned with the British Empire, he began to translate Trinidad in West Africa. The language of racial uplift opened possibilities, and he used it to bring together fragments that moved outside the sphere of colonial politics. Yet it was by forging relationships with people such as John Barbour-James, James W. Appiah, Sri II, and Samuel Pomeyie that he learned to speak the language of kinship, joining Port of Spain with Sekondi, Moriah with Swedru, and Belmont with Kumasi and Keta.

When Maya Angelou arrived in Ghana forty years later, the language of Pan-Africanism had spread across the country. This language, linked with a wave of anticolonial movements across the continent—and with the US civil rights movement—allowed Angelou to move through the political networks of Nkrumah's Accra. In other contexts, however, as the passages above reveal, she struggled to communicate. In the Keta market, her French and limited Fante were of little use, and because of her "ignorance" of Ewe, she had to rely on a friend and translator, Mr. Adadevo. She also had to rely on the vocabularies of racial consciousness and kinship: for the woman who confronted her, Angelou was both an "American Negro" and a descendant of the "stolen mothers and fathers" of Keta. Angelou may not have been aware of it, but in Keta these vocabularies were informed by earlier foundations, established by the AME Zion Church and the transatlantic circulations of people like John Bryan Small, Samuel Pomeyie, David McNeil-Stewart, and F. K. Fiawoo. Indeed, the story Angelou was told in the market was informed by Fiawoo's efforts to establish stronger links between the United States and the southeast Gold Coast. Read alongside each other, the experiences of McNeil-Stewart and Angelou in Keta reveal how these kinds of African-diaspora exchanges reconfigured the geographies of belonging between Africa, the Caribbean, and North America across the twentieth century. Their experiences, separated by four decades, were not exact parallels, but as McNeil-Stewart and Angelou navigated moments of alienation and recognition, they drew together similar fragmented vocabularies from across the Atlantic. Somewhere in between, the meaning was clear.

In August 1922, the Gold Coast government decided not to renew McNeil-Stewart's agreement for another three-year term. "Mr. Stewart proved a capable Officer," reads his final certificate of service, "but [he] was neither energetic nor reliable enough to occupy the post he did. Mr. Stewart's engagement was terminated as better and less expensive material now exists in the colony."[91] According to the terms of McNeil-Stewart's agreement, the colonial government would cover the cost of his family's passage back to Trinidad. This journey normally went via England, but in October 1922, just before their departure, McNeil-Stewart requested that they be allowed to travel instead "via Las Palmas" in the Canary Islands.[92] This route, he explained, would be shorter and would thus alleviate the "worry, anxiety, and indisposition caused by the more protracted journey." His wife, Octavia, had "not been enjoying good health for some time," and she would "dread the long and cold journey involved in going via England." (She say she would never stay in old Brit'n again as long as she live.) McNeil-Stewart also pointed out that the Las Palmas route was "sometimes adopted by the Nigerian Government with respect to West Indian Officials in the employment of the Nigerian Civil Service." Perhaps it was just about a shorter, warmer trip, but there was also symbolic power in rejecting London and instead traveling via Las Palmas, a former site of the transatlantic slave trade.

Kenneth

"Sir," wrote Octavia McNeil-Stewart to the colonial secretary in Accra, "I write making a respectful request that you help me to get in touch with my son."[93] It was April 1947, and she had not heard from Kenneth since before the war. Twenty-five years earlier, when she and her husband had left the Gold Coast with their daughter, Gladys, Kenneth had decided to stay in West Africa. Now settled in San Fernando, Trinidad, she was anxiously awaiting an update. After six months passed with no response, she sent another letter to Accra. "I am very anxious to get in touch with Kenneth who is my son," she wrote. "His father David Stewart who is now deceased was at one time a sanitary inspector in the Gold Coast."[94]

As it turned out, a police officer at Asamankese, just northwest of Accra, had been in touch with Kenneth in June 1947, shortly after the arrival of Octavia's initial letter. Kenneth had provided the officer with a mailing address, as well as a brief statement of his whereabouts and activities: he was married and living with his wife on a poultry farm near Oterkpalu; he was the associate editor of *The Gold Coast Observer*, a Cape Coast newspaper; he had property in the capital; and he was earning royalties from the publication of two books of poetry, *If I Had Wings* and *The Gold Coast Answers*. "I am in no difficulties, whatever," he wrote, "financial or otherwise."[95]

By October 1947, however, none of this information had made its way back to Trinidad. Somehow, the colonial secretary's office had failed to send Kenneth's statement to his mother. (It would appear that his death was not reported.) With Octavia's reminder, colonial officials finally sent a copy of the statement back across the Atlantic, and in December 1947, the envelope arrived at 19A Navet Road in San Fernando. "I must take this opportunity to thank you for the kind interest you took in this matter," she responded. "I have written to my son to the address he gave."[96] We can only imagine how Kenneth reacted to this letter, with news from his mother and sister, updates about life in Trinidad, and the shocking report of his father's death. Why he remained in the Gold Coast is another mystery, but the traces left behind suggest that his father had passed on some of his ideas about racial consciousness, kinship, and the enduring connections between Africa and the Caribbean.

When his family left the Gold Coast in 1922, Kenneth, then twenty-four, began working as a writer. In fact, he published his first poem in October 1922, just before his family's departure.[97] It was also around this time that he began to sign his name as Kenneth MacNeill Stewart. This first poem, titled "The Ballad of Africanus," described an idealized "Africa" in glowing rhymes. This was a "land of sunsets and repose," a "land of Eternal Spring." It was a place where, amid "Chieftains," "Kingdoms," "peasants," and "sages old," there was "wild minstrelsy" and "beatitude sublime." More significant than the poem itself, perhaps, was MacNeill Stewart's decision to dedicate the poem to William Essuman Gwira Sekyi, a prominent teacher, lawyer, and writer from Cape Coast, known better as Kobina Sekyi. Following figures such as Joseph Casely

Hayford and Mojola Agbebi, Sekyi was part of a generation of West African intellectuals who denounced the cultural chauvinism of the British, rejected anglicized names and dress, and sought connections with the diaspora.[98] MacNeill Stewart had met Sekyi in London in 1918, when they were both students, and on one occasion, he recalled, Sekyi had presented a poem about "the return of the West Indian and American pilgrims to their long lost alma mater." This poem, MacNeill Stewart wrote, had "exercised a silent but a wonderful influence over me." The second-to-last stanza of "The Ballad of Africanus" makes this influence clear:

> That sun that wakes from sleep again,
> Bereft of tears, bereft of pain,
>   With smiling, budding day,
> To run his fleet impassioned race
> Across the azure seas of space
>   With lily-clouds so gay!

The doubled meanings of "race" in this context, coupled with the "azure seas of space," reflect how MacNeill Stewart drew on the language of "racial consciousness," as well as the wider intellectual currents of Pan-Africanism in the early twentieth century. The stanza also alludes to his own family's trajectory "across the azure seas," or, in Sekyi's terms, their "return" to their "long lost alma mater."

Later in the 1920s, MacNeill Stewart began working as a journalist, and over the next decade he became a prominent, even controversial, figure in the burgeoning newspaper culture of British West Africa.[99] He worked first for *The Gold Coast Pioneer*, then in 1931 became the editor of the *West Africa Times*. This major Accra newspaper, which in 1932 changed its name to the *Times of West Africa*, was established by J. B. Danquah, later one of the United Gold Coast Convention's "Big Six" alongside Kwame Nkrumah. In addition to his editorial duties, MacNeill Stewart developed the highly popular "Ladies Corner" column, written by the pseudonymous "Marjorie Mensah."[100] Around this same time, Nnamdi Azikiwe arrived in Accra, and he edited a rival newspaper, the *African Morning Post*. Azikiwe's political positions garnered much criticism from the Accra elite, including from MacNeill Stewart, whom Azikiwe later described as "an experienced poet" who "donned the garb of a political critic and did not spare me."[101]

In the 1940s, MacNeill Stewart left the city for his farm at Oterkpalu, but he continued writing. He also became a member of the Royal African Society and did some editing for the society's journal, *African Affairs*.[102] He even published several poems in *African Affairs*: "An Idea of Happiness" and "Ode to Stools and Stool Worship," published in 1952 and 1953, were both "mystic" fantasies of village life in West Africa.[103] Even out in Oterkpalu, however, MacNeill Stewart maintained a reputation in Accra. In 1958, one year after Ghana's independence, Moses Danquah edited a special volume titled *Ghana: One Year Old, a First Independence Anniversary*. On the second page, even before the contribution from Nkrumah, was a poem from MacNeill Stewart titled "Ode to Independence."[104] This celebratory poem recounted the injustices of the past, the struggles for freedom, and the importance of living up to the promises of independence. The most distinctive aspect of the poem might be MacNeill Stewart's dissolution of any distinctions between his Caribbean past and that of his fellow Ghanaians. Abandoning the transatlantic imagery of the "azure seas of space," he now folded himself into the language of national kinship. "Remember how *we* suffered," he declared, as he called for the nation to celebrate those who led the fight for the "sacred cause": "*our* noble youth" and "*our* fathers."[105]

Conclusion

Later in 1958, George Lamming arrived in Accra, where he was stunned by the convoy of Ghanaian Boy Scouts and delighted by this "free independent state."[106] While in Ghana, Lamming also traveled north to Kumasi, following the trail of David McNeil-Stewart. When he returned to the coast, he proceeded from Accra to Lomé by car, perhaps through Keta, on the way to Lagos. Lamming's time in West Africa coincided with the arrival of a larger wave of West Indians and African Americans in Ghana, who were traveling to their "long lost alma mater." Among them were Maya Angelou, Julian Mayfield, Malcolm X, Martin Luther King Jr., W. E. B. Du Bois and Shirley Graham Du Bois, Richard Wright, Kamau Brathwaite, Jan Carew, W. Arthur Lewis, and the two famous Trinidadians George Padmore and C. L. R. James.[107] "However present the echoes of slavery," Lamming wrote, "these West Indians have lost the chains which held their ancestors, ankle by ankle, mile after mile, through that night of exile, from the African coast to the Caribbean cradle."[108]

Lamming does not mention Kenneth MacNeill Stewart in his book, but it is possible they met, perhaps at a social gathering of the small West Indian contingent in Accra, which included Cunliffe Hoyte, David McNeil-Stewart's old friend from Trinidad.[109] They might have spoken about writing and poetry, or about the "pleasures" of exile, or about translating between the Caribbean and West Africa. Lamming does, however, mention Neville Dawes, the Jamaican writer, glossed in Lamming's memoir as "N."[110] Dawes, like MacNeill Stewart, came to West Africa because of his father. In fact, Dawes was born in Nigeria, where his father, Levi Dawes, was a teacher from 1908 until 1930.[111] Such connections hardly register in the Pan-Africanist narrative of Nkrumah's Ghana, even as the trajectories of people such as David McNeil-Stewart helped to make this narrative possible. His translations between Trinidad and West Africa were part of a foundation for new languages of kinship and new geographies of belonging.

5

Intimate Geographies

I quickly realized that if I wanted to decode African societies, I would have to converse with the people. But which language should I choose out of so many? —MARYSE CONDÉ, *What Is Africa to Me?* (2017)

"France is not alone!" declared Charles de Gaulle in his famous *appel* on June 18, 1940. "She is not alone! She has a vast Empire behind her." In the wake of the German occupation of France, de Gaulle had retreated to London in search of allies. One of those who responded from this "vast Empire" was Félix Eboué. Born in Cayenne, French Guiana, in 1884, Eboué had worked as a colonial administrator since 1909 and by 1940 was the lieutenant-governor of Chad. Most French colonies aligned with the Vichy government, but Eboué persuaded other leaders in Afrique Équatoriale Française (AEF) to side with the Free French.

In October, de Gaulle travelled to Fort Lamy to meet with Eboué, and early the next month he named Eboué governor-general of AEF.[1] Unsurprisingly, French historians, museums, and governments have commemorated this aspect of Eboué's life with books, plaques, memorials, metro stations, and even enshrinement in the Panthéon in Paris.[2] As the myth goes, here was a descendant of slaves who saved France. Less well known about Eboué, however, is his research on the languages and cultures of Central Africa, which present a different perspective on his life and career.[3]

The remains of Eboué's ethnographic research are held at the Fondation Charles de Gaulle in Paris, a building imbued with Gaullist mythology. Out of power in 1946, de Gaulle returned to his home in Colombey, but he soon began holding weekly meetings at no. 5 Rue de Solférino, which then became the headquarters of his new political party, the Rassemblement du Peuple Français. After his death in 1971, the building was converted into the Institut Charles de Gaulle, and then, in 1992, into the Fondation Charles de Gaulle. The organization has an unambiguous purpose: "To honor the memory of General de Gaulle, to make known, in France and abroad, the example he provided and the lessons he left with his actions and his writings for the defense of the values which are the common heritage of the French people."[4] Entering the Fondation today, one passes through imposing wooden doors into a cavernous hallway ornamented with pillars and looming busts. A winding staircase leads up to de Gaulle's old office, where the desk is presented as if untouched, and the typewriter is carefully staged with other memorabilia, including a model tank and an enormous globe. The library, which also serves as a reading room, is back down on the first floor. Next to the library entrance, a *France libre* flag hangs beside a plaque commemorating each word of the June 18 *appel*. Seated inside the library, one hears the echoed voices of the 1940s and 1950s—Georges Pompidou, Jacques Soustelle, André Malraux, Jacques Foccart.[5] This small room, lined with books and elegantly carved furniture, is laden with the colonial politics of the Algerian War and Françafrique. And it is here, under an enormous painting of the *Général*, that one can read through Eboué's papers.[6]

Organized into a series of twenty-eight cartons, the Fonds Félix Eboué in many ways complements its surroundings. Eboué remained loyal to France until his death in May 1944, and his ethnographic research fits the mold of interwar colonial anthropology, some of which he published in a 1933 book, *Les peuples de l'Oubangui-Chari*.[7] Nevertheless, these fragmentary sources, including drafts of his dictionary and transcriptions of folktales written in Sango and Banda, highlight Eboué's personal relationships and his exchanges with African intellectuals. In other words, this collection offers a counternarrative

FIGURE 5.1. Félix Eboué welcoming Charles de Gaulle to Chad in 1940. Library of Congress, US Office of War Information, Overseas Picture Division, 2017872574.

to the reductive, Gaullist chronicle of Eboué as the savior of Free France and the first Black Frenchman in the Panthéon.

This chapter traces the intimate geographies of Eboué's ethnographic research. How did this work allow Eboué to create networks between the Caribbean, Oubangui-Chari, and Soudan Français (present-day Mali)? And how did these networks shape his intellectual trajectory? In answering these questions, I argue that Eboué's research led him to think differently about his position in the French Empire and about the nature of the empire itself. I also argue that the fictions of Eboué's colonial anthropology, coupled with his transatlantic migrations, made him into a Pan-African symbol, inspiring others to imagine links between Africa and the Caribbean.

A Sleeping Dictionary?

That Eboué ended up in Central Africa at all was somewhat of an accident. In 1901, at sixteen, he left French Guiana on a scholarship to study at the Lycée Montaigne in Bordeaux. There he met René Maran, and they formed a friendship

FIGURE 5.2. Félix Eboué with his classmates at the École Coloniale in Paris, 1908. Eboué is in the front row, second from the left. Raymond Ferjus is in the back row, at the far right. Hoover Institution Library and Archives, Brian Weinstein Papers, Box 18.

reading French poetry and Greek philosophy.[8] He then moved on to the École Coloniale in Paris, where he was known as "Kru-Kru" because of his admiration for the Afrikaner leader Paul Kruger.[9] After graduating in 1908, he was assigned to a position in Madagascar, but one of his peers, Raymond Ferjus, asked to make a trade. Ferjus had been posted to French Congo, and he claimed that he did not want to bring his family there, but he likely also knew that postings to Central Africa were considered demotions.[10] Despite this perception, Eboué agreed to the deal, and in December 1908 he boarded a ship to Brazzaville. After a brief stay there, he continued on to Bangui, a two-week journey up the Congo and Oubangui rivers.

In Bangui, Eboué met Herménégilde Maran, the father of his friend René, who worked for the colonial government in Oubangui-Chari. He also met with the governor, Emile Merwart, who had given him a scholarship to leave French Guiana for Bordeaux eight years earlier and who had been in Bangui since 1906.[11] Merwart assigned Eboué to Bouca, a post about 150 miles north of Bangui. For the next two decades, apart from occasional visits to France and French Guiana while on leave, Eboué remained in Oubangui-Chari.

Arriving in Bouca, Eboué entered a world riven by violence, and like Maran, he was directly involved with the destruction that came with colonial occupation: "recruiting" forced laborers, "pacifying" conflicts, developing agriculture projects, making topographic surveys, and collecting taxes. His approach was often brutal, and in 1914 his district, Ombella-Mondjou, ranked second in the colony for the number of prison sentences given to Africans.[12] Years later, in 1927, he justified this approach in a personal notebook entry on the value of "suffering," writing, "Love, love in itself, leave it to Tolstoy. Man must live and life means blows. But, if we have the iodine to dress the wounds, we agree with our existence which is to live and to fight—all the rest is nonsense. That is all Colonization is—more Nietzsche than Tolstoy. It is necessary to know how to suffer. Only suffering permits organization."[13] A year later, in a letter to Maran, he wrote about the redemptive possibilities of forced labor. Describing the recruitment of workers for the construction of the Congo-Océan Railway, he wrote that he was "sick of it" but also noted what he considered the positive aspects of recruitment: "It is necessary to recognize that an amelioration can be noted in the condition of the workers. As many people may die as before in the work camps, but the survivors who return . . . are in better condition."[14] This positive spin on the brutality of forced labor was hardly exceptional in French colonialist discourse, and for Eboué this attitude was typical.[15]

Alongside this work, Eboué started conducting ethnographic research, a different form of colonial "organization." In fact, as early as 1911 Eboué began collecting word lists in a notebook, with a column of French words and adjacent columns for the equivalent words in Sango, Banda, and Mandjia.[16] Most of the words were basic vocabulary such as *me, you, men, women, children, chicken, eggs, water, eat, drink*, and the words for different body parts. Yet some of the entries, especially the verbs, reveal the alignment of Eboué's word choices with his colonial duties: *Give me that, paper, come quickly, to work, to hit*. That these were some of the first words Eboué was learning—or, at least, choosing to record—reveals how colonial imperatives informed his research and narrowed the scope of language acquisition. Indeed, the word lists themselves appear on the same pages as Eboué's down-to-the-minute schedules of *tournées* (tours), and alongside his calculations of taxes, agricultural production, and rubber collection.

Eboué continued with his linguistic research over the next few years. He also met with Maurice Delafosse while on leave in Paris in November 1912.[17] Then, in 1918, he published a five-language dictionary—French, Sango, Banda, Baya, and Mandjia.[18] In the acknowledgments, he thanked Henri Vendôme, an administrator from Guadeloupe with whom he studied languages in Bouca, and Juste Poujade, an administrator from French Guiana who read the proofs. Eboué also mentioned Narcisse Simonin, with whom he worked in Bozoum.[19] In addition to explaining the grammars and basic structures of the African languages, the dictionary included a glossary of just over one thousand French words and their equivalents in the other languages. He did not elaborate on any of his translations, so it is difficult to make sense of his choices, but even the word-for-word conversions are significant. Read closely, these entries reveal the patterns of his thinking about the effects of colonialism on African cultures and institutions. They also reveal the residues of the relationships he formed in Oubangui-Chari.

CHEF—BIA—MAKŪDJI: For the French word *chef*, meaning leader or chief, Eboué listed two Sango words: *bia* and *makūdji*. *Bia*, or *gbïä*, as it is transcribed in other dictionaries, was borrowed from an Ngbandi word for a centralized leader.[20] The word moved from Ngbandi into the Zande languages spoken by the Nzakara in the eastern parts of Oubangui-Chari in the eighteenth century, when the Bandia, an Ngbandi lineage, invaded Nzakara territory and imposed their political structures.[21] The word then moved into Sango, the trade language along the Oubangui River, and maintained its meaning. In other parts of Oubangui-Chari, however, few groups had centralized leaders prior to the arrival of the French in the late nineteenth century, so there was no use for the word *gbïä*. They instead chose leaders for limited amounts of time and usually only for specific purposes, such as war or hunting.[22] Then, when the French began to impose centralized, territorially defined chiefs, Sango-speakers described them as *makūdji*, a loan word from Lingala.[23]

Eboué's decision to include both *bia* and *makūdji* as the Sango equivalents of *chef* suggests an awareness of the history of Central African leadership institutions. In a draft of a separate Zande dictionary, for instance, he noted that the Zande equivalent for *chef* was *gbia*.[24] Eboué also seems to have understood the problems of political legitimacy created by French-appointed "chiefs," some of whom he befriended. In 1912, for example, he was working at Kouango, northeast of Bangui, and developed close ties with a French-appointed Banziri *chef* named Raymond Sokambi, who had earlier worked with Portuguese merchants.[25] Eboué and Sokambi shared meals and conversations, both aware of the political dynamics at play. Sokambi relied on French support to maintain his power, and Eboué relied on Sokambi to solidify French authority.[26]

Later in his career, the question of chiefs and political legitimacy remained significant to Eboué. For example, in his 1933 ethnography, he stated: "We . . .

dulled the native authority by dividing it and breaking it apart, and we sometimes imposed chiefs on them..., people that local traditions clearly indicated should not have been in these positions."[27] Similarly, when he became governor-general in 1940, he pushed the colonial government to make room for African political institutions—most notably, in his 1941 circular *La nouvelle politique indigène*. "There is a chief designated by custom and this chief should be recognized," he wrote. "If we arbitrarily replace the chief, we divide leadership in two, between official and true leadership."[28]

Eboué's distinction between *bia* and *makūdji* also suggests that learning the languages and histories of Central Africa gave him a clearer understanding of how colonial rule had disrupted African intellectual traditions in Oubangui-Chari. As he wrote to Maran in July 1924:

> I am surprised to note the ravages of the West in these primitive lands. There are no traditions left. The young natives are no longer initiated, and this is terrible, because they are caught "up in the air." With this Latin mania to disrupt everything in order to facilitate assimilation, the natives are wedged between their traditions, which they have forgotten, and our civilization, which is poured to them with an eye-dropper, and which they cannot yet digest.[29]

Eboué's paternalism and his commitment to the "civilizing mission" are evident in this letter, and his assessment that there were "no traditions left" gives too much credit to French influence. Yet in dictionary entries such as *chef*, Eboué subtly acknowledged the history of these "traditions" and the pernicious effects of colonization. Moreover, his characterization of Africans as "wedged between" could have been a self-appraisal. The history of French Guiana was different from that of Oubangui-Chari, but Eboué must have recognized some of these political transformations amid the turmoil of colonial rule.

※

ESCLAVE—MBA—KĀGA: For the French word *esclave*, or slave, Eboué used the Sango word *mba* and the Banda word *kāga*. In these entries, Eboué's inability to accurately describe—or perhaps his inability to hear—tonal differences is evident.[30] With *mba*, for example, he may have been hearing the Sango word *ngbâa*, with a prenasal *ngb* and a descending high-low tone on the vowel. *Ngbâa* means slave, but written as *mba*, without any diacritics or other notation, it is easily confused with the Sango word *mbâ*, with a high tone, which means compatriot or fellow citizen.[31] Eboué does reference tone in the dictionary's introduction, noting that while the importance of "intonation" was "often considerable in *les langues nègres*" it was "impossible to provide this information with only alphabetical signs."[32] The only explanation he gave for his use of diacritics, meanwhile, was that "ā, ē, ī, ō, and ū" referred to "long vowels."[33]

The issues with tonal variation in Eboué's dictionary are even more apparent with his choice of the Banda word *kāga* for *esclave*. In Banda, the word *kanga* with two low tones does mean slave, but *kânga*, with high and low tones, means "attach" or "enclose." In Sango, meanwhile, *kânga* also means "attach" or "enclose."[34] On one hand, Eboué seems to have understood these distinctions because his Sango entries for the French words *amarrer* and *lier* (to tie up, to bind) are both *kāga*. Yet by using the same word—*kāga*—for the Banda translation of *esclave* and the Sango translations of *amarrer* and *lier*, he blurred these distinctions. Was this just a limitation of Eboué's "alphabetical signs" or typesetting options? Perhaps—but even in the handwritten drafts of the dictionary, he used the same word, *kāga*, for each of these translations.

Another possibility is that Eboué did not hear the tonal differences between *kanga* (slave) and *kânga* (to attach or enclose) and was thus drawing an imagined, though erroneous, link between these words. The Sango word *kânga* was likely borrowed from a neighboring Bantu language, and the older Bantu root was **-gàng-*, meaning "to tie up."[35] This root relates to a field of ideas about the physical and metaphorical ties between things and between people, including ideas about healing and social reproduction. For centuries in Central Africa, people were the highest unit of social and economic value, and Africans described the accumulation of people—whether wives, children, pawns, or slaves—in terms of physical and metaphorical ties.[36] Did Eboué learn about the longer history of social organization in Central Africa and suggest a semantic connection between *kāga* (slave) and *kāga* (to attach or enclose)?

Eboué may have been particularly interested in this history because the "ties" of slavery in Central Africa were more flexible than the forms of slavery in the Caribbean that Eboué heard about from his grandmother.[37] In Central Africa, it had once been possible for slaves, especially captives of war, to integrate into their new communities. By the nineteenth century, however, with encroaching slave raids from the north and northeast, the nature of slavery transformed and left little room for mobility.[38] Then, in the early twentieth century, the French imposed new forms of slavery with forced labor camps and prisons. Notably, Eboué translated the French word *prison* into Sango as *da ti kāga* and into Banda as *ada kāga*.[39]

By translating slavery, tying, and prison using *kāga*, Eboué may have believed that he had identified connections between these concepts, and then used his dictionary to hint at the transformations of slavery and social organization in Central Africa. With only Eboué's words, it is impossible to know his reasoning. Yet even if these connections were made because of a misunderstanding of tonal differences, tracing these ideas would have given Eboué insights into the broader history of continuity and change in Central African societies. Despite the layers of confusion and misinterpretation, the process of creating a dictionary necessitated identifying such connections and may have led him to recognize more acutely the effects of colonial rule on ideas about slavery.

POISON—YOLO—OYO: A third group of words demonstrating Eboué's engagement with the social world around him concerns healing. For the French word *poison* (poison) he used the Sango word *yolo* and the Banda word *oyo*. What is significant about these word choices is that Eboué used the very same words—*yolo* and *oyo*—as the equivalents for *fétiche* (fetish or talisman), *médicament* (medicine), and *remède* (remedy). He also used *ho yolo* and *de oyo* for the verb *empoisonner* (to poison).[40] The fact that Eboué used the same words for "medicine" and "poison" suggests that he understood the fluidity of ideas about health. Depending on the dosage, medicines that healed could also become fatal. Scholars of health and healing have analyzed similar dynamics in a range of contexts, though Steven Feierman puts it most succinctly: "Powerful medical substances cannot be used to heal unless they also have the capacity to kill."[41] Eboué evidently understood this therapeutic continuum: *yolo* and *oyo* could refer to objects and substances with the power to cure and destroy. With such an outlook, it seems likely that Eboué also understood the "social basis" of healing, the idea that individual health was inseparable from the broader health of a community.[42]

Eboué may have also recognized the power of healers. For example, in the related entry *guérir* (to heal), Eboué gave the Banda phrase *kubò ka*. *Kubò*, or *kobo*, refers to a disease or illness, while *ka* is a verb that means "to stop" or "to finish." Asking about the word *kobo*, did he also learn that it could refer to spirits that spoke through the mouths of certain women to specify cures for illnesses?[43] For *arc-en-ciel*, meanwhile, or rainbow, Eboué used the Banda word *ebvige*. Did Eboué learn about the connections between *ebviga* and healing?[44] In addition to a rainbow, the word can refer to a quarter-circle of wood marked with lines of black, yellow, and red, planted in the ground near a village to ward off sickness.⁴⁵ As an administrator, Eboué played a role in the incursions of biomedicine, such as mass inoculation campaigns. In his dictionary, however, it seems clear that he understood how such campaigns overlooked the social context of health in Central Africa.

NÈGRE—ZO VUKO: A final example from the dictionary demonstrates Eboué's understanding of the racial and cultural hierarchies of Oubangui-Chari. For the French word *nègre*, Eboué used the Sango term *zo vuko*. *Zo* means human being and *vuko* means the color black. Put together, *zo vuko* translates to "black person." *Zo vuko* is distinct, however, from *vuko zo*, a "person with dark complexion." In Sango, the word order of adjective (*vuko*) and subject (*zo*) changes the texture of a given elocution, and Eboué must have understood such nuances.⁴⁶ This word order is particularly noteworthy with regard to the Sango word *mbunzu*, meaning a European or white person. *Mbunzu* is conspicuously absent from Eboué's dictionary, but other dictionaries explain its variations. *Vuko mbunzu* means a white person with dark complexion, while the inverse, *mbunzu vuko*, refers to "an *évolué*, or African working for the colonial administration, educated in European ways, often used pejoratively with the meaning of 'Black person playing at being European, who slavishly imitates the White.'"⁴⁷

Sango speakers applied the term *mbunzu vuko* to Raymond Sokambi and other *chefs* who spoke French and helped Eboué write his dictionary. Sokambi and Eboué would have discussed the appropriate translations for words such as *nègre*, and during such exchanges they likely also described the nuances of terms such as *mbunzu vuko*, as well as their own experiences with the epithet. Indeed, most Central Africans would have considered Eboué an *mbunzu vuko*, just as some Sango-speakers labeled René Maran a *bounjouvouko*.⁴⁸ The term *mbunzu vuko* may also have been applied to Eboué's children.

From the beginning of his time in Oubangui-Chari, Eboué was imbricated in complex erotic and domestic relations. At his first posting in Bouca, he had a Mandjia "housekeeper," and they had a child, Henri, who was born in 1912, while Eboué was on leave in Cayenne. The specific circumstances of their relationship are unclear, and it is unknown what happened to the woman. Unlike many of his peers, however, Eboué raised the child as his own.⁴⁹ Then, in 1915, while working at Kouango, Eboué married one of Raymond Sokambi's relatives, Bada Marcelline.⁵⁰ According to Banziri custom, he gave her brother a dowry. He also built her a cement house, and in 1919 she gave birth to Eboué's second son, Robert.

Henri and Robert would not have fallen into the category of *métis*, like the children of white *colons* and African women, but they may have been marked with other epithets. For example, for the French word *mensonge* (lie), Eboué used the Banda word *wala*, which means falsity or deceit. Banda-speakers sometimes placed *wala* after the name of a national, ethnic, or racial identity to mark out the boundaries of these identities. Tisserant gives the example of a *Sénégalais wala*, meaning a "fake Senegalese."[51] Were Henri and Robert *Banziri wala*? Or perhaps just *mbunzu vuko* like their father?

Eboué was a French citizen by virtue of his birth in one of the "old colonies" of the Caribbean, and by recognizing his children, he made Henri and Robert French citizens, as well.[52] They were likely marked with other social designations in Central Africa, however, and their status, as well as the status of *métis* children, became important issues to Eboué. As Rachel Jean-Baptiste explains, in the early 1940s, *métis* groups in AEF demanded legal protections that would allow them to make claims on the French state, including the right to the status of citizen. Their demands, however, depended on declaring their superiority over other Africans and thus reinforced racialized binaries. Eboué, by this time governor-general of AEF, considered these claims to *métis* superiority "odd notions of race."[53] Rather than granting special status to *métis*, Eboué sought to expand social and political rights for all Africans, *métis* or not. Greater equality, he believed, would allow "black or *métis* Africans" to "earn the legal status of 'French citizen.'"[54] In making this argument, Eboué was attempting to "decouple race from citizenship," a major challenge to the prevailing imperial system and a precursor to the changes that came after World War II.[55] It is impossible to know, but the experiences of his children with pejorative social designations in Central Africa may have informed his broader thinking about race and citizenship in the French Empire.

As a Caribbean administrator in Central Africa, Eboué was constantly navigating racial hierarchies in his fraught relationships with Africans and Europeans. His inclusion of the Sango term *zo vuko* in the dictionary suggests that he understood—on both a linguistic and a personal level—how colonialism affected ideas about race, difference, and identity. Indeed, despite Eboué's exemplary record, his superiors did not promote him according to his years of service, and he considered his recurring postings to Oubangui-Chari as demotions. "My juniors from the Colonial School are now my seniors," he wrote to Maran in 1925. "Can you imagine anything more disagreeable?"[56] In another letter, Eboué described discrimination in the colonial civil service in plain terms: "The evil acting [governor] of Oubangui-Chari ... heartily dislikes all those of us of color."⁵⁷ This sense of alienation, along with questions about the social positions of his children, may have led Eboué to challenge the racial hypocrisies of the French Empire.

As Eboué collected word lists and wrote his dictionary, he drew on his personal relationships with Raymond Sokambi, Bada Marcelline, and his Mandjia "housekeeper." Who, for example, would have taught him the Mandjia word for *enceinte* (pregnant)? Through these intimate bonds, Eboué learned much about Central African languages and cultures—about leadership institutions, social organization, healing, and discourses of race and difference, even through his sometimes misguided interpretations. For Eboué, the study of African cultures and lifeworlds became consuming and transformative. He accumulated far more material than he could have hoped to publish to advance his career, and what he learned enmeshed him ever more deeply with his friends and family in Central Africa while also helping him identify the similarities of colonial rule in Central Africa and the Caribbean. This does not mean that he was any less committed to the implementation of colonial objectives. Nevertheless, he did begin to think differently about his place in the French Empire and about the nature of the empire itself.

Contes Banda

Eboué continued with his ethnographic work after the publication of his dictionary, but over the next decade his personal relationships pulled him back and forth repeatedly across the Atlantic. Each of these dislocating voyages was marked by moments of connection and separation. Near the end of 1917, when he returned to Cayenne on leave, he brought his son Henri with him, who was mocked for his African background, while his wife, Bada Marcelline, remained in Oubangui-Chari. When he returned to Central Africa in 1918, Henri remained in French Guiana with Eboué's mother. Back in Oubangui-Chari, Eboué transferred to Bambari, where, in May 1919, Bada Marcelline gave birth to Robert. Two years later, in 1921, Eboué returned again to Cayenne, where he reconnected with his son Henri, while his wife and Robert remained in Bambari, supported by Eboué's friend Raymond Sokambi and Sokambi's daughter, Clémentine. In June 1922, still in Cayenne, Eboué married again, this time to Eugénie Tell of Saint-Laurent, French Guiana.⁵⁸ Then, in August 1922, together with Henri, the newly married couple left French Guiana for Paris, where in March 1923 Eugénie Eboué-Tell gave birth to a daughter, Ginette. A few months later, in August 1923, after enrolling Henri in a lycée, Eboué and his wife and new daughter returned to Oubangui-Chari. This time, Eboué

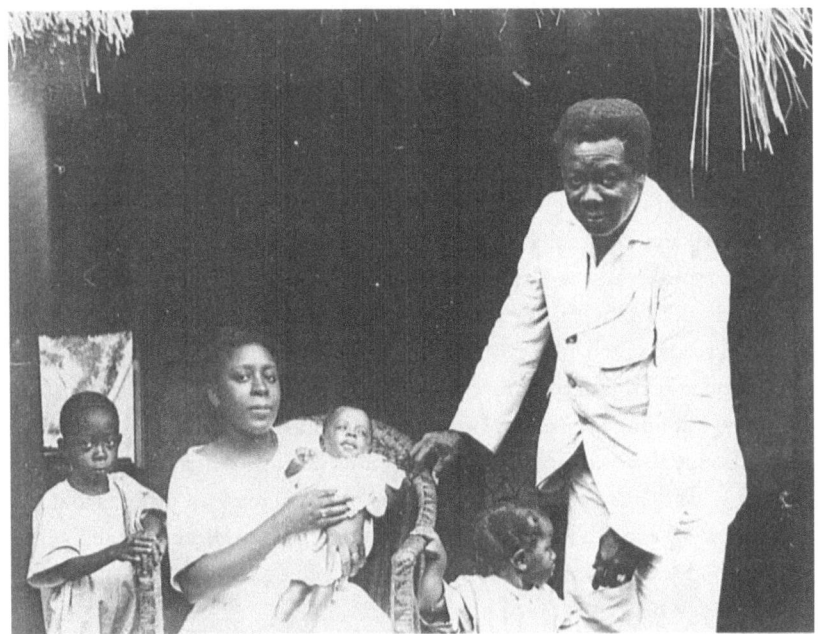

FIGURE 5.3. Félix Eboué with his wife, Eugénie Eboué-Tell, in Bangassou, August 1924. The children are Robert Eboué (left), Charles Eboué (center), and Ginette Eboué (right). Hoover Institution Library and Archives, Brian Weinstein Papers, Box 18.

was posted to Bangassou, and in May 1924 Eboué-Tell gave birth to Charles, a fourth child. Several of Raymond Sokambi's sons joined the Eboués at Bangassou, and they brought Robert with them. Bada Marcelline remained in Bambari, though Eboué continued supporting her financially until her death from leprosy in 1928.[59] After several additional moves between Oubangui-Chari, France, and French Guiana, as well as the death of his mother, Eboué returned to Bambari in September 1928 with his wife and two youngest children, Ginette and Charles, to take up a position as head of the Ouaka district.[60]

For Eboué, this was in some ways a homecoming. He had worked at Bambari from 1918 to 1921, and after settling into new familial arrangements, he was eager to continue with his ethnographic work. In fact, only a month earlier, the lieutenant-governor of Oubangui-Chari had encouraged Eboué to publish more of his research.[61] Equipped with notebooks, pens, and a pamphlet that included a paint-by-numbers questionnaire for colonial ethnography, he set out to collect folktales from around the region.[62] Eugénie played an important role in this work. A gifted pianist, she transposed a number of songs for

Eboué.⁶³ Also key to this project were interpreters, including Paul Doumatchi and Albert Gouandjia.

Eboué had first met Doumatchi in 1918, during his first stint in Bambari. At that time, Eboué had sought out relationships with local leaders, as he had done elsewhere, and one of these leaders was a Banda Linda chief from nearby Ippy who was Doumatchi's father. Eboué urged him to send his son to school in Bambari, and eventually the chief acquiesced. The young Doumatchi thus learned to speak, read, and write in French. Later, he began traveling with colonial officials as an interpreter and clerk. When Eboué returned to Bambari in 1928 and reconnected with Doumatchi, he gave him an official position as an interpreter, first in Bambari and then later in Kouango. The two corresponded regularly, and Eboué addressed Doumatchi in correspondence with the formal *vous*.⁶⁴ Eboué also likely met Albert Gouandjia during his first posting at Bambari.⁶⁵ Gouandjia collaborated with Eboué on small research projects and, on occasion, worked with him as a court interpreter. Gouandjia continued working for the French administration as an interpreter and clerk until his retirement in April 1944.⁶⁶

During their time as Eboué's interpreters, Doumatchi and Gouandjia filled hundreds of pages with stories, word lists, and translations.⁶⁷ These texts reveal a close relationship between Eboué and the two interpreters, though one that remained mediated by a colonial hierarchy. In most cases, the interpreters listened to folktales, transcribed them *mot à mot* into African languages (usually Banda or Sango), and then translated them into French. This material, which Eboué meticulously documented and organized, covers a range of topics: nature, animals, origin stories, and explanatory tales, as well as "trickster" tales centered on the figure of Tere.⁶⁸ Codified into new forms and languages, these texts reveal fascinating intellectual exchanges between the interpreters and Eboué. They also demonstrate how African interpreters used transcription and translation to refract their own ideas and experiences.

One of the *contes Banda* that Gouandjia transcribed and translated for Eboué concerned the relationship between elephants and hippopotamuses. In a notebook titled "Histoire des Animeaux," Gouandjia carefully transcribed the story into Banda on one side of the notebook, and then gave a French translation on the opposing page.⁶⁹ The tale itself explains why elephants lived on land and why hippopotamuses lived in rivers. At one time, the story goes, the animals took turns grazing in the same fields. Where the elephants ate, the vegetation grew back, but where the hippopotamuses ate, it did not. Tired of this pattern, the elephants began plotting to get rid of the hippopotamuses. First, they brought down some trees and laid them by the riverside. Then they

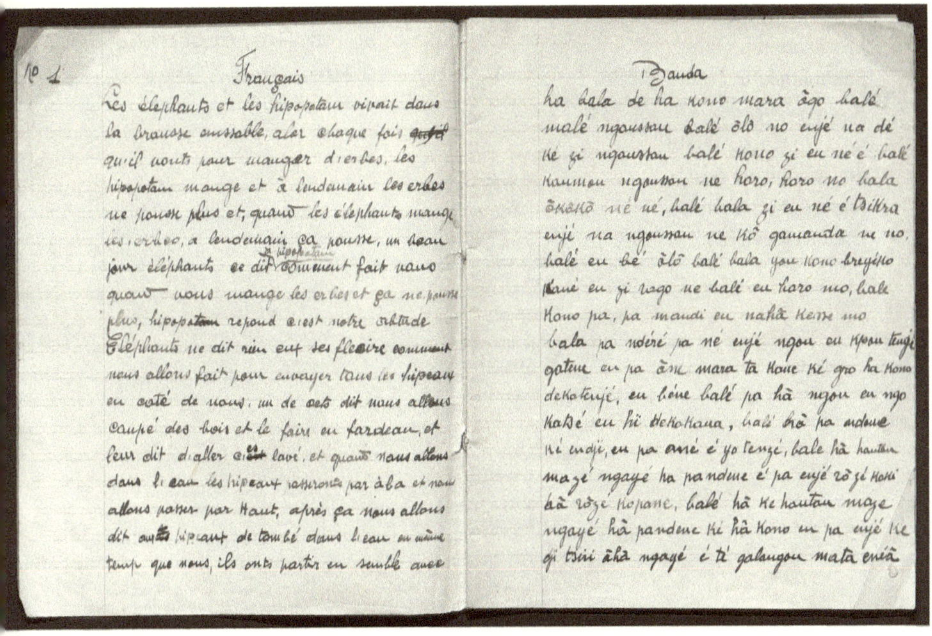

FIGURE 5.4. "Les Éléphants et les Hippopotames," a *conte Banda* transcribed into Banda and translated into French by Albert Gouandjia. Archives Fondation Charles de Gaulle, Fonds Félix et Eugénie Eboué, F22/4, DO1, SO1, 101.

invited the hippopotamuses to bathe in the river. The elephants explained that they would enter upriver, and the hippopotamuses would enter farther downstream. When the time came to go into the river, however, the elephants threw the trees into the river instead of themselves. The hippopotamuses, hearing splashing, believed that the elephants had gone into the river and followed suit. Only after doing so did they realize the trick. Ashamed of their foolishness, the hippopotamuses never left the river again. The elephants, meanwhile, never again had to compete for food on land.

Like all folktales, this story can be read in many ways. For example, one could read the tale as a subtle critique of colonial agriculture regimes. In the 1920s, the initiatives of concessionary companies such as the Compagnie Nouvelle du Kouango Français had severe effects on life in Oubangui-Chari. Combined with onerous taxation, the narrow focus on cotton, coffee, and palm oil drastically limited the scope of agricultural production. Eboué himself was involved with organizing and enforcing cotton production in Oubangui-Chari. Meanwhile, the demands of forced labor and the Congo-Océan Railway made

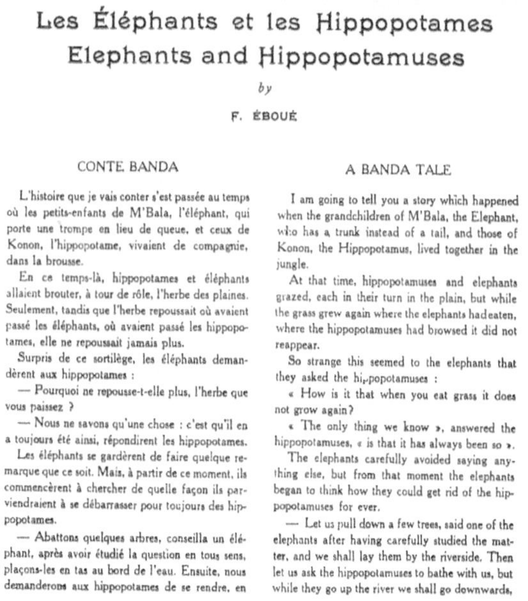

FIGURE 5.5. "Les Éléphants et les Hippopotames," in *La Revue du monde noir*, no. 3 (1932): 35–36. Reproduced from gallica.bnf.fr / Bibliothèque Nationale de France.

Les Éléphants et les Hippopotames

CONTE BANDA

L'histoire que je vais conter s'est passée au temps où les petits-enfants de M'Bala, l'éléphant, qui porte une trompe en lieu de queue, et ceux de Konon, l'hippopotame, vivaient de compagnie, dans la brousse.

En ce temps-là, hippopotames et éléphants allaient brouter, à tour de rôle, l'herbe des plaines. Seulement, tandis que l'herbe repoussait où avaient passé les éléphants, où avaient passé les hippopotames, elle ne repoussait jamais plus.

Surpris de ce sortilège, les éléphants demandèrent aux hippopotames :

— Pourquoi ne repousse-t-elle plus, l'herbe que vous paissez ?

— Nous ne savons qu'une chose : c'est qu'il en a toujours été ainsi, répondirent les hippopotames.

Les éléphants se gardèrent de faire quelque remarque que ce soit. Mais, à partir de ce moment, ils commencèrent à chercher de quelle façon ils parviendraient à se débarrasser pour toujours des hippopotames.

— Abattons quelques arbres, conseilla un éléphant, après avoir étudié la question en tous sens, plaçons-les en tas au bord de l'eau. Ensuite, nous demanderons aux hippopotames de se rendre, en

Elephants and Hippopotamuses

by

F. ÉBOUÉ

A BANDA TALE

I am going to tell you a story which happened when the grandchildren of M'Bala, the Elephant, who has a trunk instead of a tail, and those of Konon, the Hippopotamus, lived together in the jungle.

At that time, hippopotamuses and elephants grazed, each in their turn in the plain, but while the grass grew again where the elephants had eaten, where the hippopotamuses had browsed it did not reappear.

So strange this seemed to the elephants that they asked the hippopotamuses :

« How is it that when you eat grass it does not grow again?

« The only thing we know », answered the hippopotamuses, « is that it has always been so ».

The elephants carefully avoided saying anything else, but from that moment the elephants began to think how they could get rid of the hippopotamuses for ever.

— Let us pull down a few trees, said one of the elephants after having carefully studied the matter, and we shall lay them by the riverside. Then let us ask the hippopotamuses to bathe with us, but while they go up the river we shall go downwards,

---

it impossible to ensure consistent sustenance farming. In fact, in 1930 Eboué expressed concern that farmers should "increase the acreage reserved for food crops."[70] In light of these circumstances, it is possible that Gouandjia was using the tale to criticize the circumscribed state of agriculture in Oubangui-Chari. European concessionary companies, like the hippopotamuses, were a malignant presence. They destroyed existing agricultural systems and made it impossible for Africans, much like the elephants, to feed themselves. The *chicotte*, meanwhile, the whip synonymous with forced labor and colonial punishment, was typically made from hippopotamus hide.

There are dozens of other stories to interpret and analyze in Eboué's archive, but what is particularly significant about this one is that in 1932 he repackaged it and submitted it to the Paris-based journal *La Revue du monde noir*.[71] The *Revue* was founded in Paris in 1930 by Paulette Nardal of Martinique and Léo Sajous of Haiti. While short-lived, with only six editions published between 1930 and 1932, the journal was significant. Its most distinctive feature was its French-English bilingual format. Each page was divided into columns—French on the left, English on the right. Thus, alongside poems by Claude McKay and Langston Hughes one also finds essays by Jean Price-Mars, all in French and English.

Eboué's version of the story in the *Revue* was not markedly different from Gouandjia's version. He formalized the spelling and grammar, added some context, and improvised some dialogue. Yet the framing of the story was completely different. In the notebook, Gouandjia had codified the folktale into Banda and translated it into French on alternating pages. Within the neatly printed lines of the *Revue*, however, there were no descriptions of the decisions Gouandjia and Eboué made about orthography and word boundaries.[72] There was also no mention of Gouandjia.[73] Instead, the folktale appeared in the journal's unique French-English bilingual format. This style mirrored the bilingual layout of Eboué's ethnographic notebooks but omitted the intellectual exchanges between Gouandjia and Eboué, between Banda and French. In fact, the only reference to Banda in the *Revue* was a subtitle, "A Banda Tale," and a short note at the end of the story: "Translated from Banda by Félix Eboué, *Administrateur en Chef des Colonies*." Stripped away from its Central African context and its Central African translator, all that remained was an "African Fable," with only animals as characters.[74]

In his analysis of *La Revue du monde noir*, Brent Hayes Edwards argues that Nardal and Sajous used their French-English bilingual approach to build connections with people who did not speak French—this was "black internationalism as *bilingualism*."[75] Translation, in other words, allowed Africans, Antilleans, and African Americans to establish a sense of unity across linguistic, cultural, and geographic difference. There is no doubt that the *Revue* established connections across the Atlantic and across the boundaries of French and English. Yet Nardal and Sajous's approach precluded the possibility of connections with the millions of Africans and African-descended peoples who did not speak, much less read, French *or* English. This is not to say that Edwards's argument is wrong. If anything, a broader geographical and linguistic scope strengthens his case, and, in fact, he calls for precisely this kind of research.[76] But how was diaspora "practiced" in languages other than French and English? The relationships between Eboué and his interpreters offer one example. By limiting their analysis to mostly French and English sources, however, and to mostly Paris, London, and New York, scholars of diasporic exchanges have elided the ideas and languages of people such as Albert Gouandjia, who also thought deeply about the effects of colonialism and about the possibilities of working across difference.[77]

In the case of this particular *conte Banda*, such elisions began with Eboué himself, but they are also part of a longer, intertwined history of colonialism and knowledge production.[78] Eboué's publications, like the work of other colonial anthropologists, conceal the interpreters and translations that have always accompanied the production of knowledge in colonial contexts.[79] Eboué's archive, however, contains traces of these interactions, making legible the networks that he formed across the divisions of the French Empire. As he collected word lists and folktales, he cultivated close relationships with intellectuals such as Gouandjia and Doumatchi, and his annotations on hundreds of transcriptions reflect genuine engagement. Eboué learned much about their languages and histories, even as he remained steadfast in his commitment to forced labor and cotton production. The ambiguities of Eboué's archive also reflect the ambiguities of his position as a Caribbean administrator in Central Africa. He saw himself as "French," but was frequently marginalized by colonial racism. His lived experience of empire—whether in Cayenne, Paris, or Bambari—challenged his notions of imperial belonging, and these intellectual shifts continued in Soudan Français, where he arrived in 1934, via Martinique.

Géographie Cordiale

In February 1932, the Minister of Colonies assigned Eboué to Martinique after more than twenty years in Oubangui-Chari, so the family moved back across the Atlantic. In Martinique, he worked first as the secretary-general, then, from June 1933, as interim governor. After a change in the French government in February 1934, however, Pierre Laval, the new Minister of Colonies, named Eboué acting governor of Soudan Français. A few months later, Eboué and his family settled into the *quartier administratif* in Koulouba, on a hill overlooking Bamako and the Niger River valley.[80] As governor, Eboué continued his emphasis on distributing colonial power through African leaders. He also focused again on education and agricultural development. Yet his Caribbean background created controversy vis-à-vis the history of slavery in West Africa. Some of Eboué's white subordinates spread stories claiming that "the Muslims had no respect for a descendant of slaves" and that the Touareg "could not bear the sight of Eboué."[81]

In October 1935, a little more than a year after arriving in Koulouba, Eboué began drafting a preface for an *annuaire*, or yearbook, about life in Martinique.[82] He remembered the island fondly, and on a loose piece of typed manuscript he described the "splendors" that "brought glory" to the island's "three centuries of *attachement*—and not *rattachement*" with France. This distinction was important. *Rattachement* refers to the political connection of territories, such as through annexation or occupation, while *attachement* suggests an emotional connection, a sense of mutual affection. In other words, Eboué was describing the relationship between France and Martinique not as an exploitative colonial relationship but, rather, as a relationship informed by equity and warmth. At first glance, this may seem like nothing more than a romanticized and sanitized view of empire. At the end of the preface, however, Eboué proposed a cartography between Africa and the Caribbean that lay outside the reach of the French Empire: "Fort-de-France—Koulouba, a journey already completed; Koulouba—Fort-de-France, a journey in thought, by way of 'intimate geography,' with all of Martinican life in my eyes and in my heart."

The expression I have translated as "intimate geography" was originally *géographie cordiale*, which Eboué took from the title of Georges Duhamel's *Géographie cordiale de l'Europe* (1931).[83] Duhamel based his book on his travels throughout Europe and his efforts to identify the "universal" aspects of European civilization.[84] Eboué, however, shifted Duhamel's focus on Europe to a transatlantic bond between Koulouba and Fort-de-France. Duhamel was looking for unity in Europe, but Eboué, by way of his imagined "journey in thought" back to Martinique, was looking for unity between Koulouba and Fort-de-France, between Africa and the Caribbean. In other words, Eboué was moving outside of imperial time and space, separating Martinique from its colonial relationship with France and joining it with West Africa, leaving Europe outside of this network and off the map.

That very same year, 1935, a young Martinican student named Aimé Césaire began work on a poem that would become *Cahier d'un retour au pays natal*.[85] In the poem, Césaire, in a move similar to Eboué, drew links between Africa and the Caribbean and suggested a new geography beyond Europe. This is not to imply that Eboué's politics were in line with Césaire's. In 1935, Eboué was the acting governor of a French colony, while Césaire was a twenty-two-year-old student living in Paris.[86] Yet in this preface and other writings, there was a noticeable turn for Eboué in the 1930s: a rethinking of imperial geography, coupled with an interest in the connections between Africa and the Caribbean. This shift is particularly clear in Eboué's interactions with Fily Dabo Sissoko, then a young colonial official in Soudan Français.

Sissoko was born in the small village of Horokoto, in the southwestern part of the colony, where his father was *chef de canton*.[87] He studied at the École des Fils de Chefs in Kayes, at the École Normale d'Instituteurs in Saint-Louis, and at the École Normale William Ponty in Gorée. He then became a teacher back in Soudan Français, part of a generation of *"instituteurs-ethnographes"* in Afrique Occidentale Française (AOF).[88] In addition to spreading their own forms of colonial education across West Africa, these intellectuals, like Albert Gouandjia and Paul Doumatchi, played key roles in the production of knowledge: collecting folktales, transcribing oral traditions, and publishing their research.[89]

By the time Eboué arrived in Soudan Français, Sissoko had taken over his father's position as *chef de canton* at Niambia.[90] He had also developed a reputation for challenging French authority. In June 1928, for instance, the lieutenant-governor of Soudan Français wrote to the governor-general of AOF in Dakar and explained that Sissoko was the likely author of a tract that made "venomous" critiques of the government. At the time, Sissoko was working as a teacher in Ségou, and the lieutenant-governor described him as "ambitious and combative" and "driven by a dubious mind." He also mentioned that Sissoko had been the subject of "numerous disciplinary measures."[91]

Eboué and Sissoko met through their roles in colonial government, but they developed a relationship that moved beyond this association. Sissoko was apparently proud of "seeing a black man" in charge of Soudan Français.[92] Both also had a strong appreciation for African history, and they talked extensively about African cultures and ancient African civilizations. Eboué's ethnographic interests from his time in Oubangui-Chari persisted in West Africa, and he encouraged Sissoko to write up more of his own ethnographic research. Their time together ended prematurely when Eboué was named acting governor of Guadeloupe in September 1936, but they stayed in contact, and one can glean traces of their relationship from their correspondence across the Atlantic.[93]

In November 1936, Eboué sent Sissoko a copy of one of his speeches from Guadeloupe, and the following month Sissoko wrote back asking for more information about "this beautiful colony of the Antilles." The "*Géographies* and the Atlas," he explained, were not enough to "sufficiently know" the Caribbean. At the end of the letter, he expressed his gratitude to Eboué. "I am honored to see a *Chef* of your stature taking an interest in little ones like me," he wrote, "and that this *Chef* is a Frenchman and that this Frenchman is *un Noir*!"[94] Sissoko also sent Eboué a copy of an essay that had recently appeared in the *Bulletin de Recherches Soudanaises* titled "La Politesse et les Civilités des Noirs."[95] The journal had recently been established in Bamako with the support of the governor, Matteo Alfassa, and it seems that Eboué wrote an anonymous preface to Sissoko's essay.[96] Much of the text itself was standard colonial ethnography. Sissoko began with the political and social organization of the region, going back to Sundiata in the thirteenth century and to the introduction of Islam. He then described the greetings and other conversational norms that were used in a variety of contexts. At the end of the article, however, Sissoko launched the anti-assimilationist arguments for which he later become known. "The whirlwind of modernism," he declared, was "undermining *la société noire*," along with the impulse to "bring the *Noir* up to the conception of the *Blanc*."[97] He continued by denouncing the "supposedly evolved *Noirs*" who "moved awkwardly" in the attempts to "ape the *Blanc*."[98] Colonization was important, he concluded, but should not be driven by force, which might "obtain immediate submission" but would never reach "the heart of the *Noirs*."[99]

To Eboué, this essay would have provided further support for his own ideas about the necessity of colonial reform, but Sissoko's letter suggests that their relationship also superseded imperial networks. To Sissoko, there may have been distinctions between Antillean, African, and *indigène*, but he, Eboué, and others in Soudan Français were also all *"Noirs."* In March 1937, Sissoko emphasized this racial bond when he sent another publication to Eboué, this time an essay on divination titled "La Géomancie."[100] At the top of the first page, he added a short inscription: "Very respectful wishes and excellent memories (*souvenirs*) from a brother of the race (*frère de race*)." Sissoko thus saw himself as connected to Eboué on two planes of identity: one tied to empire ("Français") and the other tied to race ("Noir"). Their relationship—not to mention their correspondence—was made possible through the networks of the French Empire, but the extraimperial dynamics of their personal bond mirrored their larger ideas about the French Empire and the networks that existed beyond its boundaries.

In August 1938, the Minister of Colonies recalled Eboué from Guadeloupe and sent him back to Central Africa—this time to Chad, where he took over as lieutenant-governor. He and his wife arrived in Fort Lamy (present-day N'Djamena) in January 1939. The following year, in June 1940, de Gaulle delivered his famous speech over the radio. Eboué responded by "rallying" the other colonies of AEF to side with the Free French. Later that year, de Gaulle named him governor-general of AEF, and he and Eugénie moved south to Brazzaville.[101]

Eboué's leadership during this time was unquestionably important, but his experiences with racism did not simply evaporate into a fog of devotion to France and de Gaulle. On one occasion, he went to the Brazzaville railway station to welcome a new administrator from France but was not in uniform. When the young man saw him, he "told Eboué with great authority to pick up his bags." Eboué politely took the luggage, but when this new administrator formally met the governor-general later that day, he was "shocked and frightened to learn that the 'porter' was his *chef*."[102] Eboué continued to put his faith in France and the empire, but in light of such experiences, he also continued to draw on his imagined *géographie cordiale* between Africa and the Caribbean. For example, on July 21, 1943, Eboué gave a speech in Brazzaville in honor of Victor Schoelcher, France's Wilberforce.[103] Near the end of the speech, he offered a "cordial salute to the children of Madinina and Karukera." This salute, he continued, mixing imperial and pre-Columbian geographies, was made on behalf of "all the people of *Afrique Équatoriale Française*."

Despite his transatlantic migrations and the upheaval of war, Eboué maintained his relationship with Sissoko. In December 1943, for instance, Sissoko sent him a draft of an essay about the "cultural evolution of colonial peoples."[104] Sissoko had been working on the essay since at least 1937, when he submitted an early version of the essay to a conference held in Paris on this subject.[105]

The essay also expanded on ideas from his 1936 article that denounced those who advocated for assimilation. "We are *Nègres et Français*," he declared. "But the fact of being *français* does not annihilate... the primordial fact of being *Nègre*."[106] The "assimilated," he continued, "or the one who thinks they are, is a wreck [*épave*]."[107] His main conclusion, as in 1936, was that "the *Blanc* should try all appropriate means to evolve [*faire évoluer*] the *Noir* according to their stage of evolution."[108] This argument about evolutionary "stages" was in some ways representative of French colonial writers such as Maurice Delafosse and Georges Hardy, yet even as his language reinforced notions of hierarchy, Sissoko affirmed a "cultural equivalence" between civilizations.[109] Moreover, unlike Delafosse and Hardy, he declared pride in being "*Nègre*."

Sissoko sent the essay to Eboué in December 1943. This was only a few weeks before the Brazzaville conference, where French officials gathered to discuss the future of the empire, and Eboué relied on Sissoko's essay to make his own anti-assimilation arguments at the conference.[110] Also significant was the handwritten message that Sissoko had added at the top of the first page: "To M. Félix Eboué, Governor General of the Colonies, respectful wishes from a brother who has never lost hope in the Race."[111]

The two never met again, but one can trace Eboué's influence on Sissoko in some of his other work. *La savane rouge*, for example, which Sissoko wrote between 1936 and 1960, resembles some of Eboué's thinking about ethnography and geography.[112] In part 1, "Les cheminements du destin," Sissoko describes his journeys between 1911 and 1918 from his home in Horokoto to school in Saint-Louis and Dakar, then back to Horokoto via Conakry and Bamako. Along this itinerary, he delves into the histories of each place he passes through, noting Bandiagara as the city where Tidiani Tall, the nephew of El Hadj Omar, defeated Massina in 1864, and describing Sundiata's defeat of Soumaoro Kanté near Kirina.[113] The book was published in January 1962, six months before Sissoko's arrest for opposing the policies of Mali's first president, Modibo Keïta. He was sentenced to the Kidal prison, where he died in 1964.

When Eboué was sitting at the conference table in Brazzaville in January 1944, his mind, like the minds of the other men around the table, was focused on how to organize the empire after the war. Yet Eboué's friendship with Sissoko, laden with a racial bond, suggests that Eboué may have also imagined alternatives to the geography of the (Free) French Empire. His thoughts may have turned to his childhood in the Caribbean and to the intimate networks of family and friends he had developed in Oubangui-Chari and Soudan Français. Eboué's interest in African cultures and languages transcended colonial imperatives, and his research notes and personal relationships gesture to a recognition of the perspectives, beliefs, and political institutions of Africans. In the end, Eboué's politics remained grounded in the paternalistic language of colonial reform, grounded in the structure of the French Empire.[114] Yet his example—of building transatlantic connections and engaging seriously with African intellectuals—was a significant precedent. These "intimate geographies," tied to his ethnographic research, laid a foundation for creating future links between Africa and the Caribbean.[115]

Eboué as Symbol

After the *ralliement* of 1940, Eboué became an important symbol in the French Empire, but his ethnographic research had already made him somewhat of a Pan-African symbol in the African–Antillean–African American networks of interwar Paris. For example, when he made a second contribution to the *Revue du monde noir* in 1932, Paulette Nardal, one of the editors, noted that Eboué had "for long years . . . studied the Ethnology of certain African peoples" and praised him as a "distinguished precursor" for students hoping to "avail themselves of the riches which the black race and the African continent offer to them."[116] Eboué became acquainted with the Nardal sisters and with Léo Sajous, the other main force behind the *Revue*, through his friend René Maran. Years later, an anonymous *souvenir* in the French press recalled one of their evenings together:

> I see him again, on rue Bonaparte, in the studio of his dear friend, René Maran, the famous black writer. It was in '32. The African wall-hangings, blue from the night and striated with muted red, the small statues made of ebony and the walls with shelves full of books make an appropriate setting for his conversation: he tells us about Oubangui, Chad, as a scholar, as a colonial, as a man passionately attached to the social progress of black humanity, as a realist too. There is also Dr. Léo Sajous, the Director of *La Revue du Monde Noir* . . . It was that evening that we sensed the crucial role that Félix Eboué could be called to play one day as part of the black race and as part of the Empire.[117]

This description of Eboué as a "scholar" surrounded by bookshelves, "African wall-hangings," and "small statues made of ebony" suggests the power of his ethnographic work, even with its misinterpretations and the omissions of his interpreters. In a Paris overtaken by *l'art nègre*, Eboué's tales of Central Africa gave him an aura of authenticity and considerable standing, even among groups with whose politics he did not align.[118] Eboué's knowledge of Central African languages and cultures made a significant impression, especially for those who had not been to Africa. In October 1931, for example, Sajous declared that he wanted to take *"un petit tour"* to Africa—to Liberia, Sierra Leone, Cameroon, Ethiopia, and Belgian Congo—and then open a store in Paris where he would sell "black products." He noted that in this way he could "continue the *Exposition nègre* in its own way."[119] The Colonial Exposition took place in Paris from May to November 1931, and Eboué had participated in the event.

Maran also introduced Eboué to Alain Locke during one of Locke's visits to Paris, and Locke was captivated by Eboué's research. Eboué, who owned a copy of Locke's *The New Negro*, later sent Locke some knives from Oubangui-Chari for an art exhibition in Harlem.[120] In his return letter, Locke thanked Eboué and noted his preference for "old objects that don't show European influence," such as the knives, because they could be used to "show our people the ancient power of our race."[121] Through Locke, Eboué's reputation spread beyond France and to the United States. In 1939, for example, when the French Minister of Colonies transferred Eboué from Guadeloupe to Chad, Mercer Cook, a professor at Howard University and a friend of Maran's, wrote an article in *Opportunity* lamenting the loss of Guadeloupe's "first negro governor."[122]

After 1940, African American organizations and newspapers began following Eboué more closely. In 1941, for instance, the National Association for the Advancement of Colored People (NAACP) sent Eboué a letter declaring that "thirteen million American Negroes have been stirred by the steadfast resistance of French Equatorial Africa. . . . We applaud your courage." The letter also stated: "American Negroes have a great concern with and interest in Africa. . . . [W]e join with you and the other citizens of French Equatorial Africa in the struggle."[123] Two years later, Walter White, the secretary-general of the NAACP, even began inquiring about making a film based on Eboué's life.[124] In April 1944, Eboué responded to the NAACP and declared his "sympathy and solidarity . . . to the brave people of the United States of America who fight courageously for the liberty of the world and betterment of the human condition."[125] Eboué saw Americans as allies in the war against Germany, but the NAACP regarded Eboué as someone who represented the possibility for connections between Africans and African-descended peoples around the world.

Eboué's influence also spread to British Guiana. In 1942, a lawyer in Georgetown named Mohammad Omar sent him a letter of effusive praise:

> I am an Afrikan unadulterated, a Muslim, and a British subject. . . . Every Demararian is proud of your achievements, as colonial secretary of Martinique, and as Governor of Guadeloupe, and finally as Governor of Lake Chad Territory. . . . Your instrumental stand in AFRIKA at Lake Chad,

FIGURE 5.6. A stamp commemorating the life and career of Félix Eboué, 1945. Reproduced from www.wikitimbres.fr.

against the Vichy traitors to France, will live forever, let me assure your Excellency, that every Afrikan adores you for this. My fervent hope is to get to AFRIKA as soon as possible, and your Excellency, I should be proud to have the honour of serving under you.[126]

Eboué's role in the *ralliement* of Free France undoubtedly influenced the letter, yet Omar's association of Eboué with "AFRIKA" reveals the Pan-African symbol that he had become. Thirty years earlier, Omar had been affiliated with Dusé Mohammed Ali and *The African Times and Orient Review* in London, and he evidently saw Eboué as a representation of new connections between Africa and the Caribbean.[127]

George Padmore also sensed Eboué's symbolic power, and he attempted to use it to support his own political ends. In 1944, for instance, while based in London, Padmore wrote an article for *The Chicago Defender* claiming that

Eboué had won the "first round in the fight for self-government in Africa."[128] In other articles, Padmore praised the "native forces recruited by Governor General Félix Eboué" and claimed that "the first troops to battle their way to Hitler's 'Eagles' Nest' amidst the steep Alpine crags near Berchtesgaden were the African 'Black devils,' troops of the late African General Félix Eboué."[129] Such perceptions of Eboué—whether in France, the United States, British Guiana, or England—were informed more by the idea of Eboué than by his actual pronouncements and actions. In April 1944, just a month before Eboué's death, Walter White of the NAACP interviewed him in Cairo and asked if he ever thought of the "eventual abolition of the colonial system..., which would mean complete independence and freedom for the natives of Africa." Eboué replied: "We are Frenchmen and we are loyal to France."[130]

Some years after Eboué's death, no less a figure than Frantz Fanon offered his own praise of Eboué. In a February 1955 essay, "Antillais et Africains," Fanon explained that Eboué, "though an Antillais, had spoken to the Africans at the Brazzaville conference, calling them 'my dear brothers.' And this brotherhood was not evangelical, it was based on color. The Africans adopted Eboué. He was theirs. The other Antillais could come, but their pretensions to superiority [*prétentions de toubabs*] were known."[131] On one hand, this was an odd thing for Fanon to write, especially in light of Eboué's call for a "native bourgeoisie," an idea that Fanon later condemned as hollow and artificial.[132] Yet in claiming that Eboué placed himself on equal footing with "the Africans," Fanon, like many others, revealed his power as a symbol for Africa-Caribbean links.[133]

Conclusion

In her 2012 memoir, *La vie sans fards*, the Guadeloupean writer Maryse Condé described her own intimate geographies between the Caribbean and Africa.[134] In the 1960s, she moved between Côte d'Ivoire, Guinée, Ghana, and Sénégal, meeting revolutionaries and writers such as Sékou Touré, Amilcar Cabral, Wole Soyinka, and Ousmane Sembène. This was also a time of upheaval in her personal and family relationships. When she left Guinée for Ghana in 1963, she was also leaving her husband, Mamadou Condé, and assuming sole responsibility for her four children. She credits her survival during this time to the generosity of close friends and several strangers. Yet, like other Antilleans in Africa, Condé often struggled to find her place.

In the 1960s, teachers, doctors, lawyers, and others from Haiti, Guadeloupe, Martinique, and French Guiana came to former French colonies in West Africa, not unlike the West Indians and African Americans who came to Kwame

Nkrumah's Ghana. In her memoir, Condé reflects on the tensions of these African-Antillean relationships. "Throughout the African continent, a huge gap separated [Antilleans] from Africans," she writes. "Weren't they former slaves, the Africans would say in contempt, failing to distinguish between domestic slavery and the Atlantic slave trade."[135] To Antilleans, meanwhile, with their attitudes of superiority, Condé suggests that "Africa was a mysterious and incomprehensible landscape which, in the end, frightened them."[136]

For Condé, who found herself "attracted to and intrigued by" Africa, such divisions also entered her own family. The father of three of her children was Guinean, but that only seemed to make things more complicated. "Your mother's a *toubabesse*," mocked the children at her son's school in Conakry.[137] In the end, after nearly a decade across four different countries, Condé did not find her place, and she returned to France. She did, however, find a place for her memories of living in West Africa, and in the closing lines of her memoir, she explains how these memories informed the creation of her acclaimed novels:

> L'Afrique enfin domptée se métamorphoserait et se coulerait, soumise, dans les replis de mon imaginaire. Elle ne serait plus que la matière de nombreuses fictions.[138]

> Africa, finally subdued, would transform itself and slip, domesticated, into the folds of my imagination and be nothing more than the subject of numerous narratives.[139]

Like Condé, Eboué's writing about Africa created fictions, imposing form and fragmentation on African cultures, languages, and histories. He did not write any novels, as far as I can tell, but his dictionary and collections of folktales were also works of imagination that "subdued," "transformed," and "domesticated." Eboué's archive, however, reveals that his "*nombreuses fictions*" were possible only because of extensive personal networks. His ethnographic research necessitated relationships with his unnamed "housekeeper," Bada Marcelline, Raymond Sokambi, Albert Gouandjia, Paul Doumatchi, and Fily Dabo Sissoko. They not only taught him languages and shared stories and experiences but also brought him emotional and material comfort. These intimate geographies shaped Eboué's intellectual trajectory, leading him across the fault lines of the Atlantic and toward new ideas about the future of the French Empire. After his death, meanwhile, Eboué himself became the subject of fiction and fantasy. Despite his politics, he came to represent the possibility of building connections between Africa and the Caribbean, even connections that lay outside imperial boundaries.[140]

In some ways, Eboué's engagement with African languages was exceptional. When Eslanda Goode Robeson traveled to Central Africa in 1946, she met several people who had worked with Eboué, and they explained that he could not only speak several Central African languages but could also communicate using a talking drum.[141] Even basic language acquisition, however, allowed Caribbean administrators to interact more directly with Africans and, sometimes, break through the fog of colonial stereotypes. In doing so, Caribbean administrators learned about African cultures and histories and sometimes forged close connections. These exchanges rarely led to the creation of political organizations, journals, or anticolonial manifestoes. Moreover, Caribbean administrators who learned African languages often used this knowledge to be more effective colonial officers. This was certainly the case with Eboué. Nevertheless, language acquisition engendered connection, and exchanges with African intellectuals created openings for thinking differently about the geography of empire. In the next chapter, I consider how colonial education—and Caribbean teachers—created similar openings between Barbados, British Guiana, Jamaica, the Gold Coast, and Nigeria.

6

Old Talk

"The headmaster occupied a rather unusual position in the social structure of a West Indian territory," wrote C. L. R. James in a 1959 draft of "Notes on the Life of George Padmore."[1] Headmasters, he added, were "the real centres of intellectual life, in the towns as well as in the country," and a "channel of communication between the local community and the leaders of a highly artificial society." James, who grew up in early twentieth-century Trinidad, was the son of a headmaster, as was his childhood friend, George Padmore.[2] As James suggests, headmasters and teachers in this period played crucial social roles. They were not just instructors, but also civic leaders, historians, and career advisers—intermediaries between their communities and colonial governments.[3] In the late nineteenth century, when West Indian teachers began working in the government schools of the Gold Coast and Nigeria, they continued to play this dual role.

The British established government schools in West Africa in the late nineteenth century, alongside existing missionary schools. In addition to an underlying emphasis on Christianity and imperial loyalty, the main imperatives of these schools were basic arithmetic, reading and writing, the history and geography of Europe, and technical skills. For boys, there was often additional focus on agricultural work, manufacturing, blacksmithing, and carpentry. For girls, there was extra attention on domestic training, such as sewing and household work. Above all, the British designed curriculums to support the economic and administrative needs of colonies, hoping to train bookkeepers and low-level clerks.[4] Yet these schools never operated solely as straightforward stepping stones into the civil service. There were always discrepancies between colonial policies and the "unanticipated results" of colonial education, and these discrepancies allowed West Indian teachers to make "unanticipated" contributions.[5] As in the Caribbean, West Indian teachers in West Africa were intermediaries, channels of communication in highly artificial societies.

This chapter narrates the intertwined memories of three West Indian teachers who worked in the Gold Coast and Nigeria: Edith Goring of Barbados, Joseph Britton of British Guiana, and Lebert Josiah Veitch of Jamaica. Like other Caribbean administrators, West Indian teachers came to Africa with a sense of superiority. They were educated in colonial schools and taught within a colonial education system, and they brought this training with them. Like others from the Caribbean, however, they had to reckon with complex forms of racism and alienation in Africa. As teachers, they responded to these circumstances in unique ways. In their classrooms, they recognized the falsity of stereotypes about African intellectual inferiority, and they cultivated feelings of racial pride among their students. They also pushed against the parameters of colonial education, "following the rules, yet creating new forms at the same time."[6] In doing so, I argue, they brought together disconnected histories and geographies and created durable, transatlantic networks.

The structure of this chapter adopts the same spirit. It follows the general rules of a historical narrative but also creates new forms. Rather than retracing the stories of these three teachers chronologically and adopting the voices of the colonial documents from which their stories unfold, I have assembled a series of layered, interconnected recollections, taking speculative cues from objects, sounds, events, conversations, and metaphors to move across time, space, and memory. This depends on some conjectural leaps, but these are leaps grounded by letters, newspapers, memoirs, and other sources. I use this structure in part to draw attention to the scattered archival forms of these histories—including archives in Ghana, Nigeria, the United Kingdom, and Jamaica—but also to center the inner worlds of Goring, Britton, and Veitch and to imagine how they may have remembered key moments from their own lives. In other words, the argument is enacted in the prose itself. The chapter brings together fragmented memories to create connections unconstrained by imperial categories and epistemologies. These anachronic shapes reveal otherwise invisible resonances, subtle harmonies that reflect the efforts of West Indian teachers to span the distances in between.

November 21, 1938

Rain, rain, rain... A morning laden with cloud soon passed into noon at number 60 Ivanhoe Drive in Harrow. It was Edith Barbour-James's fifty-ninth birthday. When she was a child, her mother might have consoled her by saying that her birthday had brought showers of blessing.[7] Barbour-James was preparing for a trip home to Barbados, where she had not been for eight years, and that time she had traveled alone. This time her husband, John, would accompany her. The preparation for these journeys was always complicated—tickets, trains, trunks, lodgings, clothing—and there was still so much to do before their departure from Southampton.[8] More than two decades of teaching in Barbados and then the Gold Coast had made organization a necessity, but there was more than careful planning wrapped up in these transatlantic voyages—the goodbyes, the anticipation of home. Moving slowly from room to room, she thought of the letters she had received from Barbados last year about the trial of Clement Payne, the trade-union leader, and about the rebellion in Bridgetown, with stories of stones and bottles and turned-over cars and smashed store fronts on Broad Street. The tension and violence had spread to the country, too, even to St. George's, her home parish, ending only after three days and at least fourteen dead. This year there had been similar unrest in Jamaica.[9] Outside the window, the clouds were thick under the gray sky. She checked her lists again, and as she relayed instructions, she thought back to another departure, in September 1906, when she had first left Barbados for the Gold Coast...

She was twenty-seven years old and had been teaching for eight years, but her life, she remembered, was constrained by the stifling atmosphere of Little England. She was teaching at St. George's Girls School, where she had developed a reputation as a "good disciplinarian," a head teacher who provided her school with the right "tone."[10] But then came an opportunity to teach in West Africa. It was only later that she learned more about the circumstances surrounding her appointment to the Government Girls' School in Cape Coast. The Gold Coast governor, Herbert Bryan, had "preferred to ask for the appointment of a European Mistress," but he had also noted that, because there was no "European nursing sister... attached to the Hospital" in Cape Coast, a

"European Mistress" would have to live "without a companion of her own sex," a situation that would be "lonely and prejudicial to good work."[11]

The memory was amusing now. Apparently, loneliness did not afflict West Indian women, or at the very least, was not "prejudicial" to their work. She had learned much of this background from her counterpart at the Government Boys' School in Cape Coast, Joseph Britton, who had come to the Gold Coast from British Guiana in 1885. Before her arrival, Britton told her, the Girls' school had been in a "deplorable state of inefficiency."[12] Yet things had turned around. Bringing with her the ideals of the British colonial education system, she had helped the school recover its form. It had even met the standards of Lady Elizabeth Clifford, the governor's wife . . .

Glancing up at a bookshelf in the hallway, Edith saw Clifford's book, *Our Days on the Gold Coast*. She had not looked at it in years but was now reminded of Clifford's visit to the Cape Coast Girls' School in 1916, and she opened the book to find the relevant pages: "I recall the brightness and smartness of the little Girl Guides whom I had the honour of inspecting at Cape Coast Castle; the intelligent faces, upright bearing, and excellent work of the girls of the Government School, under their most efficient, energetic, and business-like West Indian headmistress."[13] At the time, Edith remembered, she had been in awe of this distinguished visitor. But the act of "inspecting" the young Girl Guides at the Cape Coast Castle . . .

Rereading that word now, in that context, cast the meeting in a different light, linking Clifford with the castle's original purpose. The artificial ceremony of Clifford's visit, she recalled, had followed the same colonial choreography of the annual Empire Day celebrations in Cape Coast, the same rituals she had grown accustomed to as a child in Barbados. In Cape Coast, everyone gathered for Empire Day in Victoria Park, next to the Cape Coast Castle.[14] There were always flags waving sternly overhead and students standing in precise lines, sometimes delivering recitations. The girls from the Government School would be arranged neatly by height, wearing white dresses and singing in harmony:

When Britain first, at heaven's command
Arose from out the azure main
Arose, arose from out the azure main
This was the charter, the charter of the land
And guardian angels sang this strain:

Rule, Britannia! Britannia, rule the waves
Britons never, never, never shall be slaves!

FIGURE 6.1. Empire Day celebration in Cape Coast, May 24, 1912. Reproduced with permission of Special Collections at the School of Oriental and African Studies. MMS/17/07/06/03/14/001.

Then there were the speeches, the cheers for the king, and the short parade. Joseph Britton had always been at these celebrations, as well, with his students from the Government Boys' School.... She had learned much from Britton about teaching, but the more important lessons concerned the politics of Cape Coast society. The networks Britton had built in this old Fante town, with Africans and other West Indians, had grounded her, and his departure in 1912 had left a hole. In fact, it was on Empire Day in 1912, she remembered, that Joseph Casely Hayford had publicly announced Britton's plan to retire after twenty-seven years in the Gold Coast. In an impassioned address, Casely Hayford had expressed his "appreciation, and that of the native inhabitants," for Britton's "services to the Colony."[15] Word had already spread around town, however, through his former students, and testimonials were pouring into local newspapers.

She remembered one writer in *The Gold Coast Leader* who called for a grand celebration so that the "genial old gentleman" would not leave "without a signal mark of appreciation by all classes of the population."[16] One of Britton's former students, H. O. Kuofie, called for the creation of a "Committee of gentlemen" to plan a retirement party and celebrate Britton's "noble work," which, Kuofie noted, had "borne good fruit in the many sons of the Gold Coast."[17] A number of these "sons," Edith thought, were now prominent figures of Gold Coast society. There was E. J. P. Brown, for instance, who was a lawyer, historian, and politician.[18] Another was Vidal Buckle. He had become a lawyer, as well, and was the father of Desmond Buckle, whom she knew from their interactions in the League of Coloured Peoples in London. And Frederick Nanka-Bruce. He had been a student of Britton's in Accra and was one of the first African doctors in the Gold Coast. He had been active in the National Congress of British West Africa alongside Casely Hayford.

The retirement party itself had taken place on July 30, 1912. Edith had helped to plan the event—decorating the Government Boys' School and preparing refreshments.[19] Among the distinguished guests she knew were Adelaide Casely Hayford, George Amissah, Eva Amissah, Dr. Richard Akinwande Savage, Reverend Egyir-Asaam, J. P. H. Brown, Josiah Spio-Garbrah, Peter Awoonor Renner, Reverend Samuel Attoh-Ahuma, and Joseph William de Graft Johnson.[20] The evening featured a number of speeches, and all praised Britton for his tireless work ethic and steadfast commitment to education. The tribute that came back to her most clearly, however, was from Samuel Isaac Wilberforce, one of Britton's former students, who said, "Your noble work has been evinced by the specimens of boys produced who are scattered all over the West Coast holding prominent positions of trust and responsibility. These numerous pupils of yours bear a lasting testimony of your good services rendered to our Country and Race which will never be effaced from the annals of the history of the Gold Coast Colony."[21]

Following these remarks, Edith recalled, Wilberforce and four other former students—Josiah Spio-Garbrah, Thomas Aikins, Daniel Sackey, and J. A. Aggrey—presented Britton with a gold watch and chain, as well as photographs of "Old Government School boys" who had moved to Kumasi, Calabar, Accra, Zungeru, and elsewhere. It was clear to her that Britton was deeply moved by these tributes and had struggled to find adequate words of gratitude at the end of the evening: "I feel happy to know that my labours have not been in vain," he had said in a slow, measured tone. "I have endeavoured by precept and example . . . to show you the right course in life." The closing words of his address had brought on long applause: "The secret of the success which everybody tells me has attended my work is the love I have for it, for the good of you all, and for the uplifting of the race." A few days later, on the morning of August 3, 1912, Edith had gathered with a crowd on the Cape Coast beach and watched Britton's steamer slowly disappear over the horizon, leaving West Africa for the last time . . . [22]

August 3, 1912

... On board the steamer, Britton turned and looked back at Cape Coast. Drifting away, he imagined himself again at the retirement party, grateful for his former students and his friends, Edith Goring in particular. After six years working alongside each other, he would miss her dearly. He thought, too, of Samuel Wilberforce's address and remembered when Wilberforce had first entered the school in Cape Coast. He had stumbled over the name, taken aback. Born in 1853 in Berbice, British Guiana, he knew Wilberforce as a name that stood in for the abolition of slavery. It was also a name, he had learned, that the British used to smooth over their role in the slave trade. "These numerous pupils of yours," Wilberforce had declared, "bear a lasting testimony of your good services rendered to our Country and Race which will never be effaced." In that moment, he thought, Wilberforce had moved beyond the legacy of his namesake, gesturing, with the language of racial uplift, to connections outside the empire and to the shared legacies of the slave trade in Africa and the Caribbean. Britton had not always thought in such terms, but the lines of racial division, so much a part of his upbringing in British Guiana, had also dominated life in West Africa. What had sustained him in Cape Coast for so many years was a sturdy community of friends, many of whom had attended the celebration a few days earlier.

Looking again at the outlines of Cape Coast from the ship, Britton thought back to September 1885, when he had first arrived on this beach, without any kind of network.... The sense of European superiority in the colonial government had been immediately apparent. His initial appointment in 1885 was as a schoolmaster in Cape Coast, but after only a few months the governor had dismissed him for "insubordination." It was only thanks to the Anglican Bishop of Sierra Leone, Ernest Ingham, that the governor offered him another post in the Colonial Secretary's Office in Accra.[23] Then, with Ingham's continued support, he had resumed teaching in February 1889 as headmaster of the Government School in Accra. It was there that he taught Frederick Nanka-Bruce. The governor had taken pains to make it clear that if a "trained European" was appointed to the school, he would have to step down to "2nd Master."[24] Four years later, in 1893, he returned to the government school at Cape Coast, but such judgments on his status continued, sometimes only insinuated, or whispered in government correspondence.[25] His salary had slowly increased, but the salary of the "European Principle Teacher" in Cape Coast, Walter J. Pitt, always remained higher.[26] Walter Pitt. The name reminded him of a different celebration, only a year earlier, during which his "Race" had been all but "effaced."

. . . It was June 22, 1911, the coronation service in honor of King George V in Cape Coast, and the town was humming with anticipation. Both Britton and George Amissah, lay readers in the Anglican Church, had been busy preparing for the upcoming ceremony at Christ Church. He had presided over the previous coronation service in Cape Coast in 1902, so he returned to his notes, updating them with small changes. At the last minute, however, the colonial government had replaced him and Amissah with two English officials, Pitt and J. L. Atterbury. One writer in *The Gold Coast Leader*, Britton remembered, had expressed "profound regret" at the "exclusion" of Britton and Amissah, two "Black functionaries," from the service.[27] The writer also noted the "striking coincidence" that this exclusion had occurred at the same time that the British had banned "representative Black Soldiers at the Coronation of King George V" in London.[28] There was nothing to be done, but he and Amissah had taken some solace in the printed words of solidarity. "One may make allowances for the colour line in everyday life," the writer noted, "but when it finds its way into the Church it warps one's religious ardour and makes one undecided as to the whiteman's sincerity in his own religion."[29] This had been one of many moments of recognition. In the eyes of the colonial government, West Indians and Africans were not British, no matter their education or devotion. Instead, he and Amissah were "Black functionaries," linked together by the "colour line" that had followed him from Berbice to Cape Coast. They had nonetheless attended the coronation ceremony and loyally sang "God Save the King," but such moments weakened imperial bonds. . . . Gazing back once more toward Cape Coast, his thoughts turned away from the 1911 coronation and ahead to British Guiana, his destination. This long journey had begun there more than twenty-seven years earlier, and he read, once again, the brief notice from *The Daily Chronicle* that he had kept with him for all these years: "Mr. Britton's object in visiting the land of his forefathers is not generally known; but in any case we wish him a successful and prosperous journey."[30]

July 5, 1946

The funeral took place at East Queen Street Baptist Church in Kingston.[31] As Lebert Josiah Veitch listened to the eulogy, delivered by Reverend R. O. C. King, he reflected on the trajectory of his younger brother's life. Dr. Felix Gordon Veitch had been a prominent Baptist minister and physician. He had also been a politician. In 1929, he won a seat on Jamaica's Legislative Council, representing Hanover for Marcus Garvey's People's Political Party.[32] Then, in 1944, he ran as a candidate with Alexander Bustamante's Jamaica Labour Party, taking a seat for Hanover Western and becoming the first speaker of Jamaica's House of Representatives. And in January 1945, he had been honored with the Order of the British Empire for "public services in Jamaica." All that, thought Veitch, cut tragically short at age fifty-nine. Sitting in the familiar environment of this storied church, he looked around at some of the other mourners. There were many family members, of course, including his two other brothers, Josiah and Sidney. Bustamante was there as well, sitting among a coterie of the political class. He was one of the other pallbearers. Turning, Veitch also saw Johnnie Mills, one of his first students at the school in Sturge Town.[33] He remembered that difficult parting—leaving Sturge Town for the Wesley Church School in Kingston and then, soon after, in 1904, leaving Jamaica for Nigeria, where he spent much of the next thirty years.

After the service, the funeral procession wound its way north toward St. Andrew Parish Church for the interment. Driving up Duke Street, and then past the racecourse toward Half Way Tree, they passed the grounds of Mico College, and he suddenly lost sight of the Kingston he knew. The earthquake in 1907 had left its mark. When he had first come to the city as a student to attend Mico and train as a teacher, the venerable institution had been down on Hanover Street. Now Mico was here, north of the city, and Mills, his former student from Sturge Town, was the principal. Wandering back through the intervening years, he thought again about those nervous weeks before embarking for Nigeria in December 1904—unsure of the future, and leaving behind a younger brother and sister who were dependent on him.[34] The city he saw now from the funeral procession was hardly recognizable compared with the one he knew in those days.... "Permit me most respectfully to approach you, humbly thanking you for the great privilege you have bestowed upon us," he had written to the secretary of state for the colonies. "We proceed to Nigeria to assist in the development of that distant portion of His Gracious Majesty's Empire."[35] In May 1904, the director of education in Nigeria had requested two schoolmasters from Jamaica, and the superintending inspector of schools chose Veitch and Hylton Wright Lynch.[36] They each signed three-year agreements at the end of November and on December 8 had departed Jamaica for Nigeria, via England.[37]

His first school in Nigeria was the Government High School in Bonny, in the southeast. He had arrived there in January 1905, and in addition to general subjects, he taught woodworking, agriculture, and typewriting. He was also responsible for running the Church Missionary Society's "Book Depot," which promoted literacy and Christianity.[38] He had also been eager to establish connections outside the school. Early on he had forged a friendship with Dandeson Coates Crowther, the archdeacon of the Niger Delta Pastorate, an African-run missionary group. Veitch and Crowther had similar experiences with colonial racism, and they were also both outsiders in the Niger Delta—Crowther was the son of Samuel Ajayi Crowther, the best known of the "returnees" from Sierra Leone. For Veitch, this friendship had been especially important after the earthquake in Kingston in January 1907.... When he moved on to Ibadan several years later, Veitch made similar connections with members of the African Church.[39] At their anniversary celebration in 1914, he gave a short address about education that was met with a warm ovation, but it was his attire, he recalled, that had provoked the most acclaim. Two years after the event, someone had submitted an "appreciation" of him to *The Nigerian Pioneer* and referred specifically to his clothing from that evening.[40] As the writer recalled, rather than the "conventional evening dress with the inevitable high collar and cuffs," he had appeared wearing the "highly valued Yoruba principal dress of Etù gown of the purest texture." The author of this "appreciation" also claimed that Veitch had inspired him to "go back entirely to the use of our national or tribal dress." In the early 1920s, Veitch had heard about the growth of Garveyism in Ibadan, and he now wondered whether his presence there, a West Indian from Garvey's Jamaica, had left a foundation for that interest.[41]

August 3, 1912

As the ship turned away from the shoreline, Britton's memories of life in Cape Coast continued to float through his mind. Ever loyal to the empire, he never made public comments about racism, but in his roles as a teacher and church official he found subtle ways to promote a world beyond such barriers, and these efforts endeared him to the Fante society of Cape Coast. He remembered in particular the column that Reverend Samuel Attoh-Ahuma had written in March 1904: "Mr. Joseph A. Britton, the only beautiful exception among the host of our brethren from elsewhere..., has proved himself honest in the belief that what is sauce for the Gold Coast African is sauce alike for any other African."[42] Many West Indians, Britton knew, carried their own air of superiority in the Gold Coast, and Reverend Attoh-Ahuma, once the principal of the African Methodist Episcopal (AME) Zion Church in Cape Coast, had always been attentive to the tensions of such relationships.[43] Yet he had also been attentive to the possibilities of creating connections between the Gold Coast, the United States, and the Caribbean. Britton had learned much from Attoh-Ahuma and had tried to incorporate these kinds of connections into his teaching and into the Bible studies he led for many years at Christ Church...

With the Cape Coast Castle now moving out of view, Britton thought of one Bible study in particular, from November 1904, on "gather up the fragments."[44] He pulled out his well-thumbed pocket Bible and turned to John, Chapter 6. After feeding the crowd of five thousand with only five loaves and two fish, Jesus had instructed his disciples to "gather up the fragments." This passage was typically associated with lessons in frugality, but that was not the only subject of discussion that Sunday afternoon. As he prepared for the Bible study, he had thought about a translation of "fragments," or κλάσμα, as "remnants," a word that resonated with the writings of Old Testament prophets.[45] Both Jeremiah and Isaiah had prophesied about a "gathered remnant," and he turned to those pages again. From Jeremiah 23:3: "Saith the Lord . . . 'I will gather the remnant of my flock out of all countries whither I have driven them, and will bring them again to their folds; and they shall be fruitful and increase.'" And from Jeremiah 31:7: "For thus saith the Lord . . . 'Behold, I will bring them from the north country, and gather them from the ends of the earth.'" And from Isaiah 11:11: "The Lord shall set his hand again the second time to recover the remnant of his people, which shall be left, from Assyria, and from Egypt, and from Pathros, and from Cush, and from Elam, and from Shinar, and from Hamath, and from the islands of the sea."

Rereading these passages—God gathering "remnants" from the "ends of the earth" and from "the islands of the sea"—he saw again the links with ideas about "providential design."[46] In the late nineteenth century, he remembered, there had been more and more talk of the providential design of the transatlantic slave trade—the idea that God had ordained the trade so that enslaved Africans and their descendants could learn under a "superior" race and then "redeem" Africa with Christianity. His old supporter, Bishop Ingham, had often talked about this idea, as had Edward Blyden and many of the West Indians who came to West Africa.[47] Born only nineteen years after abolition, Britton was keenly aware of how slavery and its legacies had shaped his upbringing in British Guiana. Cape Coast, meanwhile, where he had lived and worked for more than two decades, had been a major slave-trading port in West Africa, and he was often reminded of this history. The Cape Coast Castle had maintained its prominent place in town—directly across the street from Christ Church, where he led his Bible studies. In many ways, Cape Coast was a site of fracture. Yet as he prepared his Bible study in November 1904, he had also thought about this history, about his work, and about his students. Cape Coast, he thought, was also a place where fragments and remnants could be gathered together again and made whole . . .

FIGURE 6.2. Christ Church in Cape Coast, view from the Cape Coast Castle, with the Wesleyan Church in the background at far right, 1901. National Archives of the United Kingdom, CO 1069/34/22.

The ship was now finding its way out to open water. As Cape Coast faded into the distance, he found a copy of his remarks from the retirement party. Rereading them, he placed himself back among his friends and former students at the Cape Coast Government Boys' School and caught himself as he quietly repeated his closing words: "Although I will be many miles away from you, my heart will always be here where I have received nothing but kindness."[48]

November 21, 1938

Even after Britton's retirement party, Edith remembered, his name and influence had lived on in Cape Coast, and as she walked downstairs, she prompted her husband, John, about his countryman. Right away, he mentioned the "Brittonite Club" that had formed shortly after Britton's departure from Cape Coast. Josiah Spio-Garbrah, John reminded her, along with several other former Britton students, had established the club in honor of their teacher only a month after his departure.⁴⁹ Spio-Garbrah had been Britton's student in the 1890s and was named his successor as principal teacher at the Cape Coast Boys' School.⁵⁰ The club's stated goal, she now remembered, was to "preserve the name of their dear old master from extinction."⁵¹ By 1918, the club had mostly faded out, but Spio-Garbrah had ensured that Britton's legacy persisted.⁵² Less than a year after Britton's departure, she recalled, Spio-Garbrah and his wife had a son and named him Britton.⁵³ In fact, as she thought of it now, Spio-Garbrah's life trajectory had also reflected the continued influence of his former teacher. In 1923, he became the first African inspector of schools in the Gold Coast, a position that Britton himself never reached.⁵⁴ And in the mid-1920s, Spio-Garbrah was involved in the creation of Achimota College in Accra alongside James Kwegyir Aggrey, an institution Britton would certainly have supported . . .⁵⁵

Breaking off from these memories, Edith confirmed with John the location of their Southampton lodgings, where they would stay the night before boarding the *Colombie* on the twenty-fifth.⁵⁶ For John, this discussion about accommodations, mixed with memories of Britton's departure from the Gold Coast, had conjured the memory of his own final departure from West Africa in May 1917. That had been shortly after Caroline's death, when he had retired to London to take care of their children.⁵⁷ When he had first taken up his position in the Gold Coast in 1902, Caroline and their five children had come only as far as London, where he visited them when on leave. He and Caroline had had three more children in London, though by 1919 five of their eight children had died. Amid these tragedies, there had also been one final indignity in the Gold Coast, a far cry from Britton's grand send-off . . .

In May 1917, John had arrived in Sekondi, bound for London, but when he boarded his ship, no accommodations were available, so he returned to shore. While he waited for the next boat, he took a room in the Government Rest House. What followed, he only learned about years later, when John Maxwell, then the commissioner for the Gold Coast's Western Province, had retired back to England. After settling in at the Rest House the manager, Charles Watt, had consulted Maxwell about this "irregularity."⁵⁸ Maxwell, who had known Barbour-James for many years, informed Watt that Barbour-James could stay at the Rest House until his departure.⁵⁹ The next day, however, a medical officer in Sekondi named Malcolm Hay alerted Watt that there was a "native" in the Rest House. "The Rest House," Hay pointed out, was "reserved for Europeans" and was "situated in the Segregation Area."⁶⁰ Watt immediately wrote back to Hay and explained that this particular "native," John Barbour-James, was a government official from British Guiana and that "the matter" had already been settled with Maxwell.⁶¹ Hay, unconvinced by this solution, then wrote to Maxwell himself to find out whether the commissioner had indeed "sanction[ed]" Barbour-James's stay at the Rest House.[62] Hay also expressed general concern with the segregation policy in the Gold Coast: "I can hardly believe that the Government go to such enormous expense in acquiring land for a European Segregation area and then deliberately house people of the Negro Race thereon." Further revealing his essentialized racial thinking, Hay had declared: "It appears that I was wrong in supposing Mr. James was a 'native' and I now find he was born in the West Indies but I think you will agree that I may be excused in having judged him a West African entirely on naked eye appearances." Hay had initially objected to Barbour-James's presence in the Rest House on the grounds that he was a "native," but when Hay found out that Barbour-James was a colonial official from the Caribbean, he had recalibrated his reasoning and made his objection on the grounds that Barbour-James was "of the Negro Race." As John understood it, the underlying issue was thus not *where* he was from but, rather, racial difference—the fact that to the "naked eye" he was not white. For Hay and others, he had learned, his presence in the Rest House was a violation not only of segregation policy, but of colonial ideas about race, difference, hierarchy, and place.[63]

... As Edith listened to John retell this story, she reflected, once again, on how the rigid lines of racial thinking superseded categories based on geography or nation such as "European," "British," "West Indian," or "African." A person of African descent from the Caribbean could aspire to "Europeanness," but could never be a "European."

July 8, 1946

A few days after his brother's funeral, Veitch was traveling back from Kingston to his home in Hanover, but Dandeson Crowther and his other friends in Nigeria remained on his mind. The journey took him through St. Ann, his home parish, and through Saint Ann's Bay, where Marcus Garvey had grown up. One of his friends in Nigeria, Amos Shackleford, a fellow Jamaican, had been keen on Garvey's ideas, and he remembered his debt to the Garveyite networks in Nigeria and England. ... In August 1918, the colonial government transferred Veitch from Bonny to King's College in Lagos. Four months later, after recovering from an awful bout of influenza, he arrived in the capital, where the governor informed him that he would have to find his own living quarters.[64] This was a surprise, because until that point, his living quarters had always been provided.[65] While looking for a place to live, he stayed with several other West Indians, including Amos Shackleford and John Ambleston of Antigua.[66] Both had come to Nigeria to work for the railway, though Shackleford had since joined S. Thomas & Co., a Lagos shipping company run by the Saro businessman Peter J. C. Thomas.⁶⁷ Veitch also spent a night at the home of Ernest Ikoli, his former student from the Bonny Government School.

Within a week, he found a room in Ebute Metta, near the railway headquarters, at £10 per month. When he inquired about a housing allowance to cover the cost of his rent, however, the governor informed him that he had "no right to free quarters or an allowance in lieu thereof" and that free quarters were "meant for European officers and should not have been given to him" in the first place.⁶⁸ The issue of his housing allowance was eventually resolved when, in July 1919, Dusé Mohamed Ali sent a letter of support on Veitch's behalf to the Colonial Office. Ali, the London-based editor of *The African Times and Orient Review* and Garvey's former mentor, claimed that Veitch deserved free quarters even if they were meant only for "Europeans." "It is true that Mr. Veitch is a coloured man," he wrote, "but it appears from his communication that his engagement was on European lines rather than native lines, because he is not a native of Nigeria, but a West Indian."⁶⁹ Two months later, the colonial government relented and granted Veitch his housing allowance.⁷⁰ This network came together again in September 1920 when Shackleford, Ambleston, and Ikoli co-founded the Lagos branch of Garvey's Universal Negro Improvement Association (UNIA).⁷¹ Shackleford was president; Ambleston was treasurer; and Ikoli was secretary. Peter Thomas had likely played a role, as well, Veitch thought, given the connections to his business and the fact that he attended the 1921 Pan-African Congress in London.⁷² Veitch never had an official position in the Lagos UNIA branch, but he remained entrenched in—and grateful to—the city's African-West Indian networks.⁷³

November 21, 1938

As she finished packing, Edith saw her wedding dress near the back of the closet, hanging next to the carefully sewn veil she wore on that special day. She had retired from her position as headmistress of the Cape Coast Government Girls' School in May 1920, and then followed John's path to London. A few months later, in October 1920, they married at St. Dunstan's Anglican Church in Acton. The wedding itself reflected the connections they had established and continued to sustain between the Caribbean, West Africa, and London. Among the attendees were Herbert Macaulay and Amodu Tijani of Lagos, who, she remembered, had come to London to appeal a ruling about land in Lagos with the Privy Council.⁷⁴ The ceremony was covered in the Gold Coast

FIGURE 6.3. John Barbour-James and Edith Goring on their wedding day, at St. Dunstan's Anglican Church in Acton, West London, October 19, 1920. Still from "Wedding of Colour," British Pathé. Reproduced with permission.

press, and there was even a small film crew.[75] After the wedding, she and John settled into the family home at 84 Goldsmith Avenue in Acton, nicknamed "Kaieteur" for the waterfall in British Guiana.

The house became a locus of African and West Indian politics in London. John had already been involved with the African Progress Union (APU), she remembered, and through him she met some of the key figures in the organization: John Richard Archer of Liverpool, the first Black mayor in England; John Alcindor, a doctor from Trinidad; and Kwamina Tandoh, a businessman from the Gold Coast.[76] At the inaugural dinner in December 1918, John had made a speech, sung a song, and presented a toast.[77] After settling in London, Edith had joined the APU alongside her husband, and over the next several years the organization brought together people from Africa, the Caribbean, and the United States. Among those who attended meetings and informal gatherings were W. E. B. Du Bois, Dusé Mohammed Ali, Joseph and Adelaide Casely Hayford, Robert Broadhurst, Herbert Bankole-Bright, and Solomon Plaatje.

The group also sent a delegation to the 1921 Pan-African Congress in London. John had served as treasurer and vice-president of the APU, and when Alcindor died in 1924, he also acted as chair.[78] Joseph Britton, their old friend from Cape Coast, was occasionally involved as well.[79] Through the 1920s, she and John continued to promote African and Caribbean arts and culture events around the city.[80] They also inaugurated an annual "Africa Day" celebration in Acton with speeches from figures such as H. Hudson Phillips of Grenada and J. C. de Graft Johnson of the Gold Coast. "Africa Day" festivities also included music by Alyce Fraser of British Guiana, among others.[81] More recently, John had been giving public lectures on "African and Afro-West Indian subjects," with his daughter Amy joining him and performing solos.[82] As they had learned in the Gold Coast, the strongest politics emerged from networks that brought together Africa and the Caribbean.

July 8, 1946

Passing near Runaway Bay now, Veitch turned from the Caribbean Sea and looked up in the direction of Sturge Town, his first school, where he had taught Johnnie Mills. He thought, too, of his first school in Nigeria, at Bonny, and about Ernest Ikoli, and about his other former students in Nigeria. . . . After moving to Lagos, Ikoli had inserted himself in Nigerian politics as a journalist. In one article from 1920, he had argued that the colonial government should incorporate more Africans into its upper levels and had praised the work of "black men" who had "nurtured" the Education Department, mentioning Veitch and several others.[83] Ikoli had also become a key member of the Nigerian Youth Movement, along with another one of Veitch's former students from King's College in Lagos, Hezekiah Oladipo Davies. . . . The road along the north coast was a familiar one, but travel was slow, and Veitch's thoughts turned to his family in England. After retiring in August 1930, he had lived for five years in the southeastern part of that country, in the town of Deal, with his wife and three children: Dorothy, Herbert, and Patricia, then twenty, seventeen, and thirteen. His move to England had coincided with the emergence of the League of Coloured Peoples (LCP), a group founded in London in 1931 by Harold Moody, a doctor from Jamaica.[84] The League was committed to promoting the "welfare of Coloured Peoples" and to "improv[ing] relations between the Races."[85]

Veitch became an LCP member and connected with several other West Indians who had worked in West Africa, including John Barbour-James and his wife, Edith, who, as he learned, had also been a teacher. Through the LCP, he also met a younger generation of African and Caribbean students, including Stella and Stephen Thomas, the children of his Lagos friend, Peter J. C. Thomas, and a fellow Jamaican, Una Marson. Hezekiah Oladipo Davies, his former student from Lagos, came to London in 1934 and joined the LCP, as well as the West African Students' Union (WASU).[86] There was also Johnstone Kenyatta of Kenya and Desmond Buckle of the Gold Coast.[87] These African-West Indian networks in the United Kingdom came to a peak, Veitch remembered, during the Italy-Ethiopia crisis of 1935...

The threat of Italian invasion had sparked protests across West Africa, the Caribbean, and Europe. In London, his former student H. O. Davies was involved as a correspondent for *The Nigerian Daily Times*.[88] *The Nigerian Daily Telegraph*, meanwhile, edited by Ernest Ikoli and Dusé Mohammed Ali, called for a public demonstration in Lagos in July 1935.[89] Several months later, Veitch had read, two thousand people attended a public meeting in Lagos to discuss the invasion of Ethiopia, and Ikoli had presided over the gathering.[90] When Davies returned to Nigeria in 1938, he joined Ikoli in reviving the Nigerian Youth Movement. Ikoli was vice-president and Davies was secretary.[91] Veitch still occasionally saw their names in print when there was news from Nigeria...

It was sixteen years now since he had left West Africa, but those connections had endured, and he thought of Nigeria often. When he had returned to Jamaica and settled in Hanover, in the hills southwest of Lucea, near Jericho, he had nicknamed his home "Bonnyville" after the site of his first school in Nigeria. He never thought that he was responsible for the politics and careers of his former students, but he had always found ways to contribute more to their classes than explaining the geography of the British Isles and the history of England since the Norman Conquest.[92]

November 22, 1938

Edith woke up the next day still thinking about where these networks had taken her and John since 1920—since 1906, for that matter. The APU had splintered by the late 1920s, and for the previous seven years their political work had centered on Dr. Harold Moody's organization, the League of Coloured Peoples.[93] She was a member of the LCP executive committee from April 1934 until April 1937, while John served as vice-president from January 1935 until the end of 1937. John's daughter Amy was a member of the LCP, too. She also remembered meeting Lebert Josiah Veitch through the LCP. Originally from Jamaica, Veitch had taught for twenty-five years in Nigeria, and after retiring in 1930 he had spent several years in Deal, Kent, where he lived with his English wife. He had been involved with the LCP until leaving for Jamaica in October 1935, and she wondered what had become of him.... Putting on her glasses and walking downstairs, Edith thought of other connections she and John had made through the organization, especially with young Africans and West Indians who had come to London. They included Una Marson of Jamaica, Johnstone Kenyatta of Kenya, Desmond Buckle of the Gold Coast, H. O. Davies and Stella Thomas of Nigeria, and W. Arthur Lewis of St. Lucia. These interactions occurred in London, but in many cases, she reflected, they emerged from pre-existing networks in West Africa. Stella Thomas was the daughter of Peter J. C. Thomas of Lagos, an old friend of L. J. Veitch. H. O. Davies had been one of Veitch's students at King's College Lagos. Desmond Buckle was the son of Vidal Buckle, one of Joseph Britton's former students.[94] And Arthur Lewis's older brother, George Stanley Lewis, had lived in the Gold Coast since 1929, where he was a close friend of George James Christian, the lawyer from Dominica. John knew Christian from his time in Sekondi, and Christian was also part of the LCP, even serving on the executive committee in 1938.[95]

Another notable member of the LCP, Edith recalled, was C. L. R. James of Trinidad, who joined in 1933 when he arrived in London. He had been a member of the executive committee in 1934, and the LCP newsletter, *The Keys*, occasionally featured his writing.[96] He had also attended several of the annual LCP conferences, on some occasions making speeches.[97] In 1936, *The Keys* published a review of his play "Toussaint L'Ouverture," starring Paul Robeson.[98] And only a month ago, he had published a new history of Haiti titled *The Black Jacobins: Toussaint Louverture and the San Domingo Revolution*.[99]

James's comrade George Padmore was not a member of the organization, but the League nonetheless promoted his public lectures and published a review of his 1936 book, *How Britain Rules Africa*.[100] There were sometimes tensions here, too, however. The approach of her generation had generally remained within the structure of the British Empire—standing in lines, wearing white dresses, and singing "God Save the King." Yet these networks of people from Trinidad and the Gold Coast; from Jamaica and Nigeria; and from Barbados, the United States, and South Africa had begun to undermine the allure of those lines, and costumes, and refrains. She wondered how these young students and writers would reckon with that old imperial structure that had shaped their world...

But for now it was time to go—first to the station, then on to Southampton, and then, finally, to Barbados.

July 9, 1946

Arriving home at Bonnyville, Veitch sat and looked out over the hills, down toward the Caribbean Sea. He missed his brother; he had missed so much of his life away in Nigeria. He thought, too, of his own family—of his wife and children and now grandchildren, all living in England. It had been a little more than a decade since he had made his return to Jamaica. He had missed his daughter Patricia's wedding in Deal in September 1939. Her husband, Henri Franklin, had flown for the Royal Air Force. And his older daughter Dorothy, meanwhile, had moved to London and worked at Whitehall during the war...

Fifteen years had passed since that "Nigerian reunion dinner" at the South Camp Road Hotel in Kingston.[101] Amos Shackleford had been there, along with Gwendolyn James, who sang a song to mark the occasion. Two months later, Shackleford and James had married and gone back to Nigeria together. By that point, Shackleford had become the "Bread King" of Lagos and a close friend of Herbert Macaulay, Dandeson Crowther's nephew.[102] Veitch remembered Shackleford speaking about Nigeria then as his "home" and "country."[103] Levi Dawes, another teacher, had been there too, with his son Winston. Dawes had followed Veitch's path, from Sturge Town to Nigeria, then retired to Jamaica in 1930. James Clarke had missed the dinner because he was still teaching in Nigeria, but when he returned in 1932 he began giving public lectures about life in West Africa. Dawes had given similar lectures, as had Veitch himself, but Clarke was the most prolific speaker.[104] Clarke gave lectures at the St. Andrew's Kirk Literary and Debating Society at Cochrane Hall in Kingston, at a meeting of the Kingston Teachers' Association, and to the Literary Society of the famous East Queen Street Baptist Church in Kingston.[105] In all of these lectures, Veitch reflected, he and other West Indian teachers brought "Africa" to the Caribbean—through photographs, cloth, brass work, agricultural knowledge, and stories of education, religion and progress. These objects and stories presented a significantly different narrative of Africa and Africans from those to which many in the Caribbean were accustomed. And the lectures were popular. To Veitch, this suggested there was great interest in Jamaica for learning more about the links between Africa and the Caribbean, just as there was in West Africa.... From Bonnyville, those connections sometimes seemed far away, caught in the past, but in his memories, his old friends in Nigeria were always close at hand. That "distant portion of His Gracious Majesty's Empire" was not so distant after all... [106]

Afro-Atlantic Dialogue

In an important 1999 article, "The English Professors of Brazil," J. Lorand Matory argued that scholars of the African diaspora should view Africa not as an ancestral homeland separated from the diaspora by time and space but, rather, as a coeval and engaged catalyst in the movement of people, goods, and ideas around the world.[107] Matory demonstrated that the ideas and writings of a group of Afro-Brazilians who traveled between Brazil and Nigeria at the turn of the twentieth century resulted in major cultural transformations on both sides of the Atlantic. In Lagos, Afro-Brazilians interacted with "Westernized" Africans and played a central role in creating a "Yorùbá tradition." They also helped to transmit these ideas back to Brazil, where they propagated this new "tradition," which included "purely African" religions such as Candomblé. Such exchanges, Matory argued, were part of an "Afro-Atlantic dialogue."

Edith Goring, Joseph Britton, and Lebert Josiah Veitch, "English Teachers of the West Indies," created their own forms of Afro-Atlantic dialogue. The colonial archives that hold their stories partition and conceal these connections by reproducing the divisions of the British Empire, yet by centering their inner worlds in a new form, their dialogues across time and space come into view. Goring, Britton, and Veitch all learned from their experiences in West Africa, especially from their interactions with students and friends. They worked persistently against the threat of fragmentation, and they created new networks of belonging across the Atlantic. The British Empire made this "dialogue" possible, but the efforts and examples of Goring, Britton, and Veitch established a foundation for later diasporic exchanges that transcended imperial boundaries.

1968

By the late 1960s, Joseph Britton was remembered in Ghana not for his role as a teacher but, rather, for forming the country's first football club. According to Stephen Borquaye, in his 1968 biography of the legendary Accra Hearts of Oak Sporting Club, football arrived in Ghana with "a Jamaican educationist, a Mr. Briton, who was headmaster of the Government Boys School at Cape Coast."[108] Britton, Borquaye explained, was an "all-round sportsman" who taught his students to play cricket and lawn tennis and then in 1903 "introduced" football.[109] Interest in the game quickly moved beyond the school grounds, so Britton also established a local football club, Excelsior. This name—the Latin word for "ever upward" or "still higher"—could not have been more appropriate. Uplift, whether through schooling or sports, was central to Britton's educational approach. His initiative proved successful, and the popularity of football spread along the coast.[110]

Perhaps the most significant aspect of this account was Borquaye's slippage in describing Britton as "a Jamaican." Borquaye wrote his book in the wake of Kwame Nkrumah's Pan-Africanist boycott of the 1966 World Cup, and the popular symbolism of Marcus Garvey and Jamaica did not disappear with the 1966 military coup.[111] Indeed, Ghana's national football team, the Black Stars, had the same name as Garvey's shipping line. In many newly independent African countries, the football team was a symbol of national unity. In the case of Ghana, however, the football team was also a symbol of Pan-African unity, and memories of Joseph Britton, the teacher from the Caribbean, were braided into this powerful narrative.

7

Poetry and Peripheries

It was June 1957, and Henri Jean-Louis was in Paris. He was eighty-two years old, worn down by a life of travel between the Caribbean, West and Central Africa, and Europe. Yet as he squinted through his cataracts and scrawled another poem, his vision of decolonization came into focus once again:

> Je retourne en Afrique, en mon noir territoire
> Graver sur son vieux sol une page d'Histoire:
> Je vais la réveiller d'un long sommeil du soir
> En réanimant son âme au feu d'un encensoir.

> I am returning to Africa, to my black territory
> To mark on its old ground a page of History:
> I will awaken her from a long night of sleep
> By reviving her soul at the fire of a censer.[1]

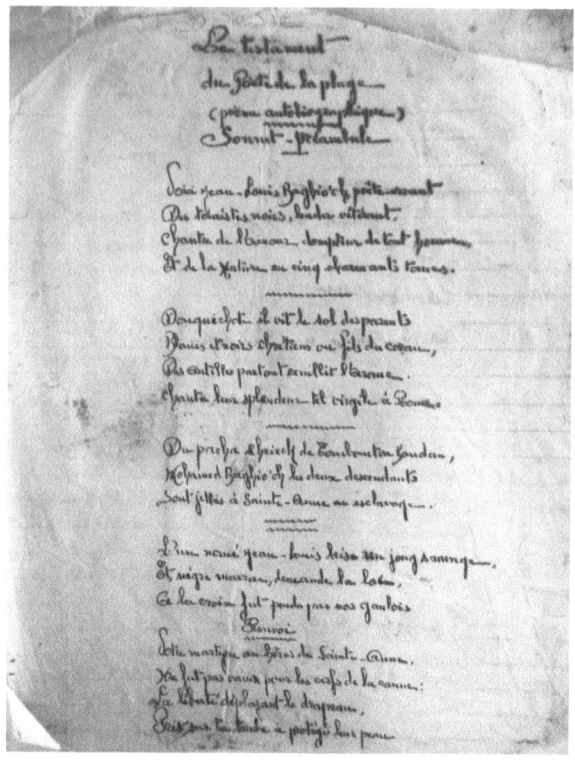

FIGURE 7.1. Manuscript of "Le testament du Poète de la plage," a poem by Henri Jean-Louis from 1946. ATM, FJL, Box 1, Folder 33. Reproduced with permission of Wyck Jean-Louis.

Nearly sixty years later, when I first read this poem in Martinique, I wondered where it fit into the life of a former colonial judge from Guadeloupe. Jean-Louis had worked as a magistrate in Brazzaville for two years, before resigning in 1926. He remained in Central Africa, however, working as a lawyer and defending African interests against the colonial government.

> La Confédération Africo-Musulmane
> D'Arabes et de Noirs de mon génie émane
> Pour donner à la race un unique Drapeau
> Guidant leur Liberté sans distinction de peau.

> The Africo-Muslim Confederation
> Of Arabs and Blacks from my spirit emanates
> To provide for the race a single Flag
> Guiding their Liberty without the distinction of skin.

In 1931, he settled in Paris, where his wife and four children lived, but continued to travel to West and Central Africa. Then, in 1933, he returned to the Caribbean, but he never lost sight of his connections with Africa:

Or, je viens le denier, moi, Mohammed Baghio'oh,
Unifier notre Afrique en un République.

Yet, I come last, myself, Mohammed Baghio'oh
To unify our Africa into a Republic.

June 1957 in Paris. This was the midst of the Algerian War and three months after Ghana's independence. On one level, Jean-Louis's poem had a clear Pan-Africanist message, denouncing colonialism and calling for a unified "African Republic." Yet the poem's meanings seemed more ambiguous. Why the invocations of a French revolutionary "Liberté" and a Catholic *encensoir* awakening a continent? What flag? Surely not the tricolore. Who was Mohammed Baghio'oh? And why did Jean-Louis insist on expressing his politics through poetry?

This chapter responds to these questions by following Henri Jean-Louis's journeys around the Atlantic world and analyzing his ideas about decolonization. The structure of the chapter follows my pursuit of Jean-Louis, as well as my puzzlement, as I tried to make sense of his meandering intellectual trajectories and the bewildering sources he left behind. Gradually I began to understand how poetry allowed Jean-Louis to escape social and political constraints and to carve a political trajectory that was otherwise inaccessible. Similarly, by following Jean-Louis's example, and his fragmentary archive, I saw opportunities to escape the constraints of a plodding historical narrative. In the first half of the chapter, I describe my search for Jean-Louis across a series of archives, before moving, in the second half, to the remarkable Fonds Jean-Louis.

Requêtes

My first encounter with Jean-Louis was in 2013. I was sitting at a table on the fourth floor of Memorial Library in Madison, Wisconsin, reading Véronique Hélénon's *French Caribbeans in Africa*.[2] Jean Symphorien Henri Jean-Louis, Hélénon wrote, was born on December 5, 1874, in Sainte-Anne, Guadeloupe. Also known as "Baghio'o," he had worked as a colonial judge in Brazzaville, resigned in 1926, and then remained in Central Africa. After resigning, Hélénon continued, he became the "judicial counselor" for Richard Duala Manga Bell of Cameroon. In 1929, he helped write two petitions for Manga Bell and sent them to the League of Nations. The petitions asked for the removal of France's mandate in Cameroon. Jean-Louis also apparently spent time in Paris, joining "various associations that defended blacks in France and the colonies." I found a few more references to Jean-Louis in books by Philippe Dewitte and Oruno Lara and quickly added his name to my "do more research" list.[3]

Some months later, I followed Hélénon's footnotes to the Archives Nationales d'Outre-Mer in Aix-en-Provence, France, and worked my way through his personnel file: EE/ii/1427. There was no shortage of dreary administrative detail. Jean-Louis studied literature and law in Paris and in 1918 registered as a lawyer in Guadeloupe. In 1921, he was appointed prosecutor in Martinique; then in 1923 he went to Brazzaville, where he worked as a judge. In May 1925, while Jean-Louis was on leave in France, the Minister of Colonies transferred him to a position in Madagascar, but Jean-Louis refused to go, choosing instead to resign from the colonial civil service. The EE/ii/1427 file also contained some hints about Jean-Louis's role in the "various associations that defended blacks in France and the colonies." In September 1931, for instance, Auguste Dirat, the interim governor-general of Afrique Occidentale Française (AOF), wrote to his counterpart in Brazzaville asking for information on Jean-Louis.[4] Dirat explained that a month earlier, Jean-Louis had come to Dakar and "made contact with people suspected of having extremist opinions." He also claimed that Jean-Louis was a member of the Ligue de Défense de la Race Nègre (LDRN) in Paris; that he was linked with "Léo Sajoux" and "Tiemoko Garan Kouyaté"; and that he had come to Dakar to promote a publication called "*La Revue du monde noir.*" Sajous and Kouyaté, I knew, were key members of interwar *Paris Noir*, and the *Revue* was a landmark bilingual publication.[5]

With these clues from Jean-Louis's personnel file, I moved to the SLOTFOM files—Service de Liaison avec des Originaires des Territoires de la France Outre-Mer. Between 1916 and 1954, intelligence agents from SLOTFOM monitored colonial subjects in France. They infiltrated organizations such as the LDRN, co-opted informants, and wrote detailed monthly reports. For scholars of interwar France, the SLOTFOM files are well-trodden terrain, and I uncovered a number of details about Jean-Louis's time in Paris in these and other files in Aix.

While still on leave in Paris in 1925, for example, Jean-Louis joined the Comité de Défense de la Race Nègre (CDRN) and was made honorary president.[6] Founded in April 1925, the CDRN was led by Joseph Gothon-Lunion, a militant communist lawyer from Guadeloupe, and Lamine Senghor, a Marxist war veteran from Sénégal. Another key member was Tiemoko Garan Kouyaté of Ségou, Soudan Français. In January 1926, Jean-Louis returned to Central Africa and started working as a lawyer in Brazzaville, Pointe Noire, and Port-Gentil.[7] The colonial government in Brazzaville was not enthusiastic about his continued presence in Central Africa, however, and in November 1926 the governor-general of AEF wrote to the Minister of Colonies describing Jean-Louis as an "Antillais de couleur" and a "notorious communist."[8] Over the next few years, I learned, Jean-Louis divided his time between Brazzaville, Douala, Dakar, and Paris, slowly building up a network.

Many of the Africans and Antilleans in interwar Paris seemed to revere Jean-Louis. They valued his personal experiences of working and traveling in West and Central Africa, as well as his condemnations of French colonial abuses. When I later traveled to Paris, I found a remarkable description of Jean-Louis in the microfilmed files of the Internationale Communiste at the Archives Départementales de la Seine-Saint-Denis. In a report from October 1925, Joseph Gothon-Lunion praised Jean-Louis in strong terms:

> *Un noir de valeur.* . . . In a short amount of time he has acquired considerable influence. . . . On many occasions his interventions have curbed the arbitrary rule of the government [in AEF]. . . . This valiant comrade refused to take up his new post [in Madagascar]. "As a *nègre*, I must defend *les nègres*," he said. . . . He confided to me that he does not need more than two years to rouse all of Equatorial Africa against French imperialism. The crimes, he declared, are daily realities. Accustomed to suffering, the unfortunate natives have become indifferent to pain. They are buried in an extreme fatalism.[9]

By January 1927, however, disputes over communism and assimilation threatened to break up the CDRN. There was also a personal rivalry between Lamine Senghor and Gothon-Lunion, as well as a division between Africans and Antilleans. Most Africans wanted Senghor to remain head of the organization, while most Antilleans wanted new leadership. At the end of January, Senghor expelled Gothon-Lunion from the CDRN.[10] The next month, at a particularly tense meeting, the members of the CDRN voted "unanimously" for René Maran to take over as president. Maran refused, remarking that they were "stupid to make divisions between themselves, and would be better served by defending their race than getting into disagreements about communism."[11] In the end, Senghor's group, supported by Kouyaté, left the CDRN and formed the LDRN.[12]

After this split, Jean-Louis attended several LDRN meetings. At a gathering in November 1929, for example, he informed the others that "Africa has its own civilization, its traditions and customs, just like any other region." According to a police informant in attendance, Jean-Louis "undoubtedly knew more than all the others about what was happening in the colonies and about the harmful effects of colonization."[13] This was likely the case, as Jean-Louis, by this time, had spent time in French colonies in the Caribbean, Central Africa, and West Africa. Others at the meeting called for Jean-Louis to put together "some pamphlets about his travels and memories of his years in the colonies." Another report on the meeting noted that Jean-Louis then outlined his plans to publish several articles and volumes that would "discuss above all the injustices."[14] Yet Jean-Louis, for his part, was hesitant about the political alignment of the LDRN. In October 1930, he noted that the organization was "essentially communist."[15]

The following year, Jean-Louis helped to cofound the journal *La Revue du monde noir*, along with Paulette Nardal of Martinique, Léo Sajous of Haiti, and several others. Jean-Louis also contributed an article to the inaugural issue: "Introduction to a Study on Creole Art and Literature."[16] It was in August 1931 that he traveled to Dakar on behalf of the *Revue* to promote the journal and sell subscriptions and, apparently, to make "contact with people suspected of having extremist opinions."[17] These included Magatte Bâ, manager of the *Périscope Africain*, a Dakar newspaper, and Arthur Beccaria, leader of the Dakar branch of the LDRN.[18] In the SLOTFOM files, I learned that the Minister of Colonies notified Auguste Dirat, the interim governor-general of AOF, about the trip and described Jean-Louis as "a disreputable individual" who belonged to the French socialist party, the Section Française de l'Internationale Ouvrière (SFIO). The Minister also wrote that Jean-Louis's ideas were "hostile to our influence in Africa."[19]

In another series of files in Aix, I found more details about Jean-Louis's involvement with Richard Manga Bell of Douala. Jean-Louis had first met Manga Bell in 1923, when his ship to Brazzaville was stopped in Cameroon. In 1929, however, he became Manga Bell's lawyer.[20] Over the next two years, Jean-Louis helped Manga Bell submit two petitions to the League of Nations in Geneva. These petitions, which were among other petitions written by the Douala chiefs, demanded the return of land that Germany had expropriated and that France had taken over after the war. The petitions also asked the League of Nations to remove France from its "mandate" in Cameroon. In a letter to a group of Douala leaders, Jean-Louis explained that he would promote their cause by raising their concerns in the French press and with the Ligue des Droits de l'Homme. He also assured them that he would send pamphlets to each French deputy and use his connections with several Antillean politicians in Paris: Alcide Delmont, one of the deputies for Martinique, and Henry Lémery, the senator for Martinique.[21] The campaign was ultimately unsuccessful, but Jean-Louis's work on behalf of Manga Bell and the Douala chiefs further illustrated his ability to create networks between Africans and Antilleans. His commitment to combating colonial injustices also demonstrated his eagerness to defend Africans against European governments, regardless of national or even imperial boundaries.

As I gathered together these and other materials in Aix, Jean-Louis's story emerged as a powerful example of the kind of networks I was tracing between Africa and the Caribbean. Yet as I put in my *requêtes* for carton after carton of SLOTFOM files, I seemed to be falling into the same trap that had distorted my view of Francis Simmons. The fragments I had uncovered about Jean-Louis were the residues of a surveillance agency. I could read between the lines, and I could read against and along the grain, but my obsession with "archival recovery" was still reproducing a geography centered at the Ministère des Colonies, a geography that Jean-Louis himself seemed to transcend. As he told Kouyaté in February 1934: "The affairs of the blacks in France no longer interest me. I would prefer to work with the Africans and work seriously on Cameroon."[22] The bonds that Jean-Louis had created in Africa—whether in Brazzaville, Douala, or Dakar—evidently inspired a stronger commitment than the circles of interwar Paris. Yet I was unsure about how to follow Jean-Louis beyond the constraints of a colonial archive. Then came a surprise from the Caribbean.

A few months earlier, I had written to the Bibliothèque Nationale in Paris, hoping to find other traces of Jean-Louis. Yveline Baratta of the Bibliothèque put me in touch with Charles W. Scheel, a professor of American and Caribbean literature at the Université des Antilles in Martinique. Scheel had a special interest in Jean-Louis's son, Victor Jean-Louis, who had published several novels under the same pen name as his father, Jean-Louis Baghio'o, and whom Scheel had befriended in Italy in 1982.[23] After a few exchanges, Scheel told me about the *valise*. In May 2013, he had been at the Jean-Louis family apartment in Paris, searching for materials about Henri Jean-Louis. At one point, he and Victor's daughter, Dr. Wyck Jean-Louis, decided to try their luck in the basement storage unit. There, in a far corner, under old skiing equipment, they found a suitcase packed with pamphlets, typescripts, and hundreds of handwritten pages—all from the pen of Henri Jean-Louis. The Jean-Louis heirs entrusted this collection to the care of Dominique Taffin, then the head of the Archives Territoriales de Martinique.[24] I planned a trip. "Tin-trunk" archives do not always live up to their promise, but with Jean-Louis's suitcase, the abundance of intriguing material was overwhelming.[25] There was one complication though—almost all of his writing was rhyming poetry.

Fonds Jean-Louis

Jean-Louis was a prolific writer and poet. Most of his poems were only one or two pages long, and most followed straightforward ABAB rhyming patterns. From 1933, when he returned to Guadeloupe, until his death in 1958, he usually wrote thirty to forty poems per year, and sometimes many more. In 1957, for instance, he wrote more than one hundred poems, despite being nearly blind from cataracts. Between 1911 and 1950, he had produced several short collections of essays and poetry, but most of his work had never been published. These seemingly simplistic writings revealed a fascinating intellectual trajectory—from suggesting the creation of a French Union in the 1930s to calling for the creation of a "Republic of Africa" in the 1950s. Jean-Louis also used his poetry to write about assimilation, slavery, and Pan-Africanism.

As I read through Jean-Louis's writing, I was frequently struck by his creative breadth and capacious political visions. The African-Antillean networks that he had joined in Africa and Europe had laid the groundwork for the rest of his political life, sowing the seeds for his ideas about geography and decolonization. Moreover, since Jean-Louis usually noted the date and place of writing, the collection allowed me to track his physical trajectory alongside his intellectual detours.[26] The Fonds Jean-Louis thus provided illuminating details of how he began to envision alternatives to the geography of empire.

All of this, constrained in a suitcase—the metaphor was irresistible. Jean-Louis's mobility was inseparable from his intellectual trajectory, and the suitcase, bursting with poems, was a perfect symbol for the real and imagined networks that he created with his travels between the Caribbean, Africa, and Europe. Yet the suitcase also became a container. In a basement storage unit, the suitcase immobilized Jean-Louis's thinking and partitioned his networks, not unlike the cartons of SLOTFOM files and the dull administrative tenor of his personnel file, EE/ii/1427.

Opening the suitcase, however, raised difficult issues of narrative and fragmentation. When I arrived at the archives in Martinique, I found the poems organized into three cartons, mostly by date. Reading through the poems, I struggled to imagine an appropriate form for these fragmentary sources. The obvious temptation was a biographical mode, tracking Jean-Louis chronologically across the poems and adding context from his life. I went through the collection systematically—reading, taking notes, taking photographs. Yet each poem, each fragment, pushed away from this system and toward a chronology of its own making. The poems defied the kind of representation I was imposing and challenged the linear conventions of History.

In *Poetics of Relation*, Édouard Glissant describes how French imperialism projected outward not just political and economic power, but also cultural and linguistic dominance, "with the aim of providing legitimacy."[27] Yet "beneath" these projections of domination, he suggests, poetic thought carved its own "trajectories." First, "from the Center to the peripheries," then "from the peripheries to the Center," and finally a third stage, that "curved" and "abolished" the earlier trajectories entirely. In this stage, Glissant writes, "The poet's word leads from periphery to periphery.... [T]hat is, it makes every periphery into a center; furthermore, it abolishes the very notion of center and periphery."[28] Reading these lines, it is easy to see Glissant's thinking illuminated in the life and poetry of Henri Jean-Louis: studying law in Paris, working as a colonial judge in Brazzaville, and then, over twenty-five years, creating a poetic oeuvre between Africa and the Caribbean that utterly rejected the "vectorization of this world into metropolises and colonies."[29]

One way to begin is to return to Paris, in June 1957:

> Sous un pont de la Seine on aperçoit un nègre
> aux chaussures bleus, aveugle, un ancien magistrat.
>
> Under a bridge by the Seine, one sees a *nègre*
> with blue shoes, blind, a former magistrate.[30]

Perhaps you can see him there, an old man under a bridge, looking out through old eyes, across that old river. How many times had he walked along the Seine— as a student, as a lawyer, as a father and husband, as a political activist? Now he sits, with blue shoes, scribbling in a brown-covered Bloc steno notebook. On the first page, he has written "Lettres africaines: Coup d'oeil d'un nègre sur Paris et le monde." And on several other pages are plans for other books, never to be completed: "Une Enquête sur le Monde Arabe" and "Une Enquête sur l'Afrique Noire."

Another way to begin is in Central Africa, in October 1924. Another notebook, this one mostly illegible:

> J'ai oublié de dire qu'hier soir en G—j'ai fait la connaissance d'un sieur Le—... parler de Marcus Garvey.
>
> I forgot to say that yesterday evening in G—I met a M. Le—... talking of Marcus Garvey.[31]

Garvey's influence is apparent in Jean-Louis's other writing from this period, especially the idea of creating a "Black Empire" in Africa. In February 1925, a few months after this conversation about Garvey, Jean-Louis drafted a short exposition on "The Political Organization of Africa," written on the back of AEF court documents. He explained that Africans were "reduced to the state of serfs" and outlined his ideas for a new *"politique indigène."*[32] He began with a straightforward question: "How can you organize a liberated Africa (*Afrique délivré*)?" His proposed solution was a return to the political structures that were in place "before the conquest." Among these, according to Jean-Louis, were "the King of Gabon, the King of BaKongo, the King of the Batekes, the Sultan of Oubangui, the Sultan of Chad, the Sultan of Cameroun, and the King of Katanga." Above these kings would be an "Emperor, the leader of the Congo Empire." This "Emperor of Congo" would also be the leader of a "confederation" called the "United States of Africa," made up of the Congo Empire and the three "independent states" of Ethiopia, Egypt, and Liberia. With such a political system in place, Jean-Louis argued, the population of Central Africa would "double in 30 years" and the "African Republic" would become "the world's top power." In his "epilogue," Jean-Louis declared himself to be "a supporter of Colonization" but warned that France had a responsibility to "develop the natural riches of its colonies," "maintain peace among the turbulent populations," and "cultivate their primitive civilization." "The Union of France and the black Race," Jean-Louis continued, could be "legitimate and durable" but had to start from "justice and humanity." In closing, he stated: "I do not despair the spirit of justice or the philanthropic feelings of the French people. Yet it is time . . . for the government to show these in AEF."

Or we could begin near the end, in April 1958, after Jean-Louis had traveled back to Guadeloupe after his last trip to Paris in 1957. Living then at his sister's home in Sainte-Anne, four months before his death, Jean-Louis reflected on his origins:

> Je suis un caraïbe et descends des Incas
> Qui formaient au Mexique un fameux syndicat
> Mes aïeux ont conquis l'Archipel des Antilles;
> Ma famille nommait le Cacique des Isles.

> Or, un jour de Malheur le Démon débarqua
> Sur notre beau rivage, et ce seul fait marqua
> La fin de notre Empire...
>
> I am a Carib descended from the Incas
> Who formed in Mexico a renowned federation
> My ancestors conquered the Archipelago of the Antilles;
> My family named the Cacique of the Islands.
>
> Yet, one Tragic day the Devil landed
> On our beautiful shore, and this marked
> The end of our Empire...[33]

This starting point, this "Tragic Day," also marked Jean-Louis's criticisms of imperialism. In 1935, for instance, he was living in Martinique. This was a significant year on the island, punctuated by lavish celebrations of the three hundred years since the arrival of Pierre Bélain d'Esnambuc. Jean-Louis must have seen the statue of Esnambuc erected in the center of Fort-de-France that year, and in a poem titled "Assimilation," he was quick to emphasize the destructive effects of French colonialism in the Caribbean:

> Ministres de la France, écoutez les chorales
> Qui chantent nos malheurs, nos hontes, nos revers
> Le bon peuple Antillais, lançant sa plainte orale
> Vous dit: « Faites cesser un régime pervers. »
>
> Ministers of France, listen to the choirs
> That sing our woes, our disgraces, our setbacks
> The good Antillean people, letting out their complaints
> Say to you: "End this perverse regime."[34]

As with his notebook from Central Africa, however, Jean-Louis's criticisms of empire remained bracketed by a France-centered political system. His words still led from the peripheries to the Center. In the final two stanzas, he rhymed "assimilation" into the French "nation," rather than demanding independence:

> Trois siècles sont passés depuis que, chère France,
> Nous te crions en vain nos peines, nos souffrances,
> Pour que nos îles soient filles de la Nation.
>
> Nous voulons vivre au sein de la Mère-Patrie:
> Avec piété, ferveur, et même idolâtrie
> Français, nous demandons notre ASSIMILATION!

> Three centuries have passed since, dear France,
> We have been crying out in vain with our struggles, our sufferings,
> So that our islands could be daughters of the Nation.
>
> We want to live in the heart of the Mother-Country:
> With devotion, fervor, and even idolatry
> Frenchmen, we demand our ASSIMILATION!

Jean-Louis was not blindly promoting assimilation into France, however, with no understanding of what had happened during the preceding three centuries. For him, this was assimilation into France on an equal basis, something that would make "all French people sons of the same mother" and put an end to the "perverse regime" of colonial rule.[35] In some ways, this was a precursor to Aimé Césaire's and Léopold Senghor's efforts to achieve non-national sovereignty after World War II.[36]

In 1936, Jean-Louis further developed his ideas about assimilation in an extended poem/open letter to Léon Blum, then the prime minister of France, head of the SFIO, and a supporter of the Ligue des Droits de l'Homme.[37] In the letter, Jean-Louis posed a critical question: "Given the financial situation of the Metropole, is she truly capable of attending to the economic and social development of her colonial subjects?" Jean-Louis evidently understood the direction in which France and its empire were headed, and he answered his own question rather plainly: "Doubt is permitted."[38] His proposed solution was for France to transform its empire into an allied confederation by making its colonies into "Dominions," much like Canada, New Zealand, and Australia in relation to Britain. Jean-Louis argued that this would create a "genuine society of free people, people conscious of their rights as well as their obligations" instead of a "vague and powerless *société des nations* at the heart of which the strong devour the weak." He also claimed that such a reorganization would help prevent war in Europe. His criticism of the League of Nations, meanwhile, was likely a reference to the petitions he had written on behalf of Manga Bell from Douala.

A war poem, from August 1944, "La Victoire de la France," presented a reimagined version of the Allied victory.[39] Jean-Louis described African soldiers marching north from Chad across the Sahara Desert to Tunisia, defeating Rommel, and then continuing across Europe to liberate France, before finally arriving in Paris and marching through the Arc de Triomphe. Throughout,

Jean-Louis emphasized the role of the "valiant soldiers of Chad" in "saving France from the teeth of the sharks." He highlighted the crucial role of African soldiers in preserving the prewar geography of Europe, and he called for France to recognize their efforts. Jean-Louis thus still understood "liberation" within the contours of France, but he also saw the need for correctives to those contours. Near the end of the war, the French removed West African troops from the front for political reasons, and it was likely no coincidence that Jean-Louis wrote this poem on August 26, 1944. This was one day after the German surrender and the same day of the victory march along the Champs-Élysées in Paris that explicitly excluded African soldiers.[40] Jean-Louis dedicated the poem to "the memory of Governor General Félix Eboué," who had died three months earlier in Cairo, and at the end of the poem he declared that Eboué deserved a place in the Panthéon in Paris. Five years later, in 1949, this prophecy came true.

Jean-Louis's ideas about "assimilation" into France, about the "legitimate and durable" links between France and its colonies, did not survive World War II. In October 1947, he wrote an inversion of his poem on assimilation titled, appropriately, "Contre l'Assimilation":

> Nul Antillais ne veut d'une Assimilation
> Qui le prive du droit d'avoir sa République
> Et lui-même gérer ses affaires publiques
>
> Notre avenir est dans la Confédération
> Des Isles d'Amérique, ou l'union Caraïbe
> Dont la Commune mer de ses flots nous imbibe.
>
> No Antillean wants an Assimilation
> That deprives them of the right to have their own Republic
> And to control their own public affairs
>
> Our future is in Confederation
> Of the Islands of the Americas, or the Caribbean union
> Whose Common sea of waves saturates us.[41]

Jean-Louis was looking for new political formations to replace the link between the Antilles and France, and he advocated for a "*union Caraïbe.*" His geography of decolonization was thus tied into the idea of Caribbean unity, not atomized independence. He drew on the geographical structure of empires, but he adjusted their political and social inequalities. This idea was not unlike the short-lived West Indian Federation of the late 1950s and early 1960s. Indeed, Jean-Louis's thinking about a Caribbean Confederation likely traced back to his time in Trinidad between 1937 and 1939.

It was in Trinidad that Jean-Louis nearly met Marcus Garvey, during the latter's brief stay on the island. In Trinidad, Jean-Louis was offering lessons in French and Latin at 39 Ana Street, in Woodbrook, and he published a short pamphlet in English, *Visions of Africa*.[42] Apart from one letter to Jean-Louis from Garvey, there is no trace of their interactions, but Garvey's ideas, already important to Jean-Louis, took on further significance.[43] Jean-Louis's arrival in Trinidad also coincided with Tubal Uriah Butler's famous strike on the oilfields in June and July 1937.[44] This strike left a mark on Jean-Louis, and he wrote about Butler in a long draft letter to Garvey from 1937, describing Butler's "devotion" to the people and exclaiming that his name would "pass on into prosperity."[45] At the end of the letter, Jean-Louis added a quick poem in English:

> God save our Saviour,
> Long live our Saviour!
> God save Garvey!
> Send him victorious,
> Happy and glorious,
> Long to reign over us
> God save Garvey![46]

Jean-Louis's subversion of the British national anthem into a pro-Garvey hymn was a sign of things to come—drawing on the forms of empire but changing the content. In another Trinidad poem, "Epitre aux Peuples Européens: La Vie ou la Mort," Jean-Louis was more direct in his condemnations of empire. In presenting the "facts of colonization," he explained:

> Christophe Colomb ensanglante le monde
> Transformant l'Amérique en un charnier immonde.
>
> Christopher Columbus bloodied the world
> Transforming the Americas into a vile mass grave.[47]

He also gave a stark warning to the "civilized" people of Europe:

> Vos femmes, vos enfants, tout ne sera que flammes
> Si vous ne décidez ce que le cœur réclame:

> Transformer des sujets en frères citoyens,
> Leurs pays en Etats avec murs mitoyens
> Oui, chaque colonie en simple République. . . .
>
> Peuples Européens, vous mourrez dès demain
> Dans la flamme et le feu qu'allumeront vos mains.
>
> Your women, your children, all will be in flames
> If you do not follow what the heart demands:
> Transform subjects into brother citizens
> Their lands into States with common walls
> Yes, every colony into a single Republic. . . .
>
> Europeans, you will die starting as soon as tomorrow
> In the flame and the fire that you will light with your own hands.[48]

Jean-Louis's violent imagery, combined with his reconceptualization of the French Empire into a "single Republic," made for a powerful geographical argument, one that struck at the core of the imperial worldview. Yet it was after World War II, drawing on his time in Trinidad, that he became clearer in his call for Caribbean confederation.

In "Speech à Truman," from March 1947, he demanded independence for the colonies of the Caribbean. He even used Garvey's call of "Africa for the Africans" but adapted it to the Caribbean:

> Les Antilles aux Antillais, c'est leur destin
> Naturel, nous a dit Schoelcher le philanthrope
> L'Indépendance en tout mettra fin au festin
> Sanglant et ruineux des gerfauts de l'Europe.
>
> The Antilles for the Antilleans, it is their natural
> Destiny, Schoelcher the philanthropist told us
> Total independence will put an end to the
> Bloody and ruinous feast of the falcons of Europe.[49]

In an August 1949 poem, "Union Nationale des Isles d'Amérique," Garveyism continued to imbue his ideas about a Caribbean confederation:

> Je rime à l'amour de ma race, au réveil
> Des peuples de couleur trop longtemps au sommeil.
>
> I rhyme to the love of my race, to the awakening
> Of the people of color who have been dormant too long.[50]

This proposed "Union Nationale" even bore the same initials as Garvey's Universal Negro Improvement Association.⁵¹

Jean-Louis's calls for a *union Caraïbe* were a striking precedent to the efforts of West Indian politicians in the 1950s, though he also moved beyond imperial boundaries to include the entire archipelago.⁵² Moreover, this idea was not just grounded in Garveyism or the slogan of "Les Antilles aux Antillais." Jean-Louis also drew on the history of slavery and revolution in the Caribbean. He suggested, for example, that the capital of this *union Caraïbe* be named "Delgrès-ville," the "*belle capitale*" where the "tree of federalism would flourish."⁵³ Louis Delgrès had been the leader of the fight against reenslavement in Guadeloupe at the beginning of the nineteenth century, and Jean-Louis drew direct links between Delgrès's efforts and the struggle against colonialism in the twentieth century. He also claimed a personal link to the legacy of Delgrès. In a number of poems from the mid-1940s, he noted that his great-uncle "Jean-Louis dit Baghio'o" had fought to defend the abolition of slavery in 1794 in Sainte-Anne, Guadeloupe, and was hanged by the French.⁵⁴ Jean-Louis claimed that the mission handed down to him by his ancestor was to "save liberty from the hands of the White Masters and from the feet of the Black Lackeys."⁵⁵

During this same immediate postwar period, Aimé Césaire had pushed for and achieved "departmentalization" for Martinique, Guadeloupe, Guyane, and Réunion.⁵⁶ Curiously, there is no mention of Césaire in any of Jean-Louis's writings. For Jean-Louis, an intellectual who moved between Guadeloupe and Martinique in the 1940s, Césaire would have been unavoidable, so it is possible that Jean-Louis's calls for independence, his rejection of assimilation, and his condemnation of "Black Lackeys" were aimed at Césaire and his political allies.

Back to Brazzaville. In February 1925, Jean-Louis signed a draft essay about political organization in Africa as "Mohamed Baghio'o," but then crossed it out and signed instead as "Jean d'Afrique."⁵⁷ The latter pseudonym did not reappear, but in the 1940s, when he began writing about his connections with West Africa, he did return to "Mohamed Baghio'o." In July 1948, for example, while in Sainte-Anne, Guadeloupe, he wrote a "*poème autobiographique*" that outlined his lineage from Timbuktu:

Du pacha cheikh de Tombouctou Soudan,
Mohamed Baghio'oh les deux descendants,
Sont jetés à Sainte-Anne en esclavage.

L'un nommé Jean-Louis brise un joug sauvage
Et, nègre marron, demande la loi,
A la croix fut pendu par nos gaulois.

From the Pasha Cheikh of Timbuktu Soudan,
Mohammed Baghio'oh the two descendants
Were thrown to Sainte-Anne in slavery.

The one named Jean-Louis broke his cruel yoke
And, as a *nègre marron*, demanded the law
From the cross he was hanged by our *gaulois*.[58]

With this claim of "Mohamed Baghio'oh" as an ancestor, Jean-Louis was likely referring to Mohammed Baghayogho, a prominent scholar in late sixteenth-century Timbuktu.[59] Born circa 1523 near Djenné, Mohammed Baghayogho went to Mecca in the early 1580s and was in Timbuktu by 1583, where he became Imam of the Sidi Yahya mosque. It is possible that Jean-Louis read about Mohammed Baghayogho when he was studying literature at the Sorbonne between 1901 and 1905. Indeed, Octave Houdas's French translation of the *Tarikh es-Soudan* was published in Paris in 1900.[60] At the very least, Jean-Louis likely took his spelling of "Baghio'oh" from Houdas, who used "Baghyo'o." There is no reference in this or other works to Mohammed Baghayogho's descendants being enslaved, however. In the aftermath of the Moroccan invasion of Timbuktu in 1591, many of the city's scholars were taken back to Morocco, including Mohammed Baghayogho's better-known student, Ahmad Baba. Yet Mohammed was spared, perhaps because of his family's link with a Moroccan saint, and he died in Timbuktu in 1594. Nevertheless, by linking the story of "Mohamed Baghio'oh" with the story of his great-uncle Jean-Louis dit Baghio'oh of Sainte-Anne, who fought against slavery in Guadeloupe, Jean-Louis connected the histories of West Africa and the Caribbean.

In other poems from this period, Jean-Louis described himself not only as the descendant but also the reincarnation of Mohamed Baghio'o. For example, in a March 1950 poem, "De la Métempsycose," Jean-Louis claimed that "by the laws of metempsychosis" he was "St. John, Socrates; and after Jean de la Croix, / And Mohamed Baghio, then Voltaire."[61] Jean-Louis also made connections between his ancestor and his political concerns. In an October 1950 poem called "Humanité," he explained that the "Antillean Republic" would one day sing "its own Marseillaise," composed by "the Guadeloupean, Mohamed Baguioh, the legitimate heir of the *cheick des Tidganias*."[62] Jean-Louis thus saw himself as a new Mohammed Baghio'o, the Muslim scholar from Timbuktu, and as the descendant of "Jean-Louis Baghio'oh," who fought against reenslavement in Guadeloupe. The possibilities of these imagined transatlantic connections were neutralized by departmentalization in the French Caribbean, but Jean-Louis evidently found inspiration in bringing this history into the present.

Jean-Louis's geography of decolonization was informed by journeys across time and space, but he also continued to ground these wide-ranging visions in concrete realities. For instance, in an uncharacteristically long poem from July 1954 (sixty stanzas), Jean-Louis described colonialism as a "sickness" and demanded independence in French Indochina. This was just two months after the French defeat at Dien Bien Phu. Jean-Louis also foreshadowed the next stage in his own thinking by calling for unity in Africa:

> Que l'Afrique du Nord, librement unifié
> A notre Afrique Noire, en Bloc soit edifié
> Les Arabes, les Noirs, ont même Religion
> Ils vont se métisser dans leur propre région.
>
> That North Africa, freely unified
> To our Black Africa, built into a Bloc
> The Arabs, the Blacks, have the same Religion
> They will mix in their own region.[63]

This call for Vietnamese independence, alongside an expression of Pan-African unity, was framed through the structure of a Soviet "Bloc" and in some ways prefigured the alignments of the Bandung Conference of April 1955. Yet this possibility of unity was also articulated with a quintessentially Antillean verb: *métisser*.

By 1956, Jean-Louis was back in Paris. One day, walking slowly along the Boulevard Saint-Michel, he met a young student from Sénégal, Cheikh Hamidou Kane:

> It was as if this voice were waking him. In front of Samba Diallo an old
> Negro was standing. In spite of his advanced age, which had not bent his

body, he must have stood at the same height as the young man. He was wearing old clothes, and the collar of his shirt was of doubtful cleanliness. A black beret cut across his thatch of white hair, and its edges had thus the semblance of being buried in a skull-cap. He was carrying a white cane, and Samba Diallo fixed his attention on his eyes, to see if he was blind. No, the man was not blind, though the whole central surface of his left eye was covered by a white film. His right eye showed no abnormality, though it presented the stigmata of fatigue. As he smiled, his mouth disclosed old yellow teeth, far apart and out of line.[64]

Fictionalized as "Pierre-Louis" in Kane's 1961 book, *L'Aventure ambiguë*, the Jean-Louis character asks Kane's narrator, Samba Diallo, about "taking a table somewhere."[65] Over a drink, Pierre-Louis describes his great-grandfather, Mohammed Kati, the "author of the *Tarikh El Fettâch*," who was enslaved and named "Pierre-Louis Kati," but then stopped using the name Kati "so as not to dishonor it."[66] He also explains that he worked as a magistrate in Africa but then went to the "other side of the bar" and "defended my compatriots from Gabon and Cameroon." Over the course of a remarkable conversation, Pierre-Louis also condemned the racist thinking at the heart of colonialism:

> People have wanted us to believe ... that the Germans were racists—fundamentally, more than the other white nations of the West. That is false. Hitler, yes, and his Nazis, as well as all the world's Fascists, without doubt; but otherwise the Germans are no more racist than the civil or military settlers of all nationalities. Remember Kitchener at Khartoum, the French armies in the conquest of Algeria, Cortez in Mexico, and so on.[67]

Algeria was certainly on Jean-Louis's mind. In June 1957, he wrote three related poems: "La Guerre Franco-Algérienne," "L'Indépendance de l'Algérie," and "Note sur la Constitution de l'Algérie." He also kept a newspaper clipping next to these poems from René Martin about the Algerian War. Near the end of the article, Jean-Louis starred and emphasized several sections on the need to reform the "structure of the French Union." The *loi-cadre*, passed in 1956, Jean-Louis underlined, had been like "shooting French soldiers in the back" and played into the "game" of the Front de Libération Nationale.[68]

Jean-Louis's conversation with Kane also allowed him to relive his days as a lawyer, when he was defending Africans against colonial injustices, and he put this theme directly into his poetry. In "L'Avocat de l'Afrique," for example, written in another of his brown-covered Bloc steno notebooks, Jean-Louis reprised this role but now defended Africans against Europeans and Americans:

Je suis le Défenseur du pauvre et du petit
Contre un Colonialisme à très gros appétit
C'est pourquoi je retourne en mon pays, l'Afrique
Le protège contre l'Europe et l'Amérique.

I am the Defender of the poor and the weak
Against a Colonialism with a great appetite
That is why I will be returning to my land, Africa
To protect it against Europe and America.⁶⁹

By the mid-1950s, Jean-Louis's poetry focused increasingly on African independence. This focus, however, remained tied to his connections with his ancestor, Mohamed Baghio'oh of Timbuktu. Jean-Louis claimed that Baghio'oh had tried to unify "Arab and Black Africa" and now pledged to fulfill the efforts of his ancestor. In his August 1956 poem "La Confédération Arabo-Africaine," he stated: "With my soul and my spirit, I will govern Africa . . . under the name of Sultan of the Black United States."⁷⁰ Describing his return to Africa, Jean-Louis compared himself to Lenin returning to Russia in 1917 to lead the Bolshevik Revolution.⁷¹ He appointed himself "Sultan Mohammed Baghio'o."⁷² He reiterated his "dream of forming an Empire in Africa."⁷³ And he claimed that "the Arab and the Black . . . with three hundred million hearts" would "form the 3rd Empire of the World."⁷⁴ Jean-Louis's continued adherence to a Garveyesque "Black Empire" in Africa was never more explicit. He credited Garvey for "posing the question" and declared that he would lead a new "Confédération Africo-Musulman" under a "black, green, and red flag."⁷⁵ He also called for all the "children" of Africa to return to the continent and unify with Arabs into a "Republic" against the European "sharks."⁷⁶

Jean-Louis's radical and capacious thinking about leading an African Republic or Black Empire was surpassed only by his other grand idea: an international socialist confederation. In June 1957, he wrote a poem titled "Excursion d'un poète et juriste nègre en URSS." This poem was self-referential but also represented a link to Joseph Gothon-Lunion, a fellow Guadeloupean lawyer who had traveled to Moscow and whom Jean-Louis had met in Paris in the 1920s. In the poem, Jean-Louis claimed that a "Union Républicaine, Humaine, et Socialiste" of China, Russia, Africa, and India offered an alternative to the war-mongering of France and England, citing the examples of the French war in Algeria and the

British at Suez.⁷⁷ Similarly, in a July 1957 poem titled "The Union of Socialist Nations," Jean-Louis declared that such a confederation would stand up against the "capitalist bloc, the oppressors of workers and Liberty," and would bring "peace and fraternity" to the world.⁷⁸ It seems likely that the 1955 Bandung Conference and Ghana's independence in 1957 influenced Jean-Louis's idea of a nonaligned "confederation," and he held on to this dream until his death.

By the end of 1957, Jean-Louis had returned to Guadeloupe and was living with his sister, Laurence Jean-Louis, at her home in Sainte-Anne. One of Jean-Louis's last poems was "La Revanche de Carthage sur Rome," written on July 21, 1958. In "La Revanche," Jean-Louis expressed his admiration for Hannibal's defeat of the Roman army at the Battle of Cannae and again called for the formation of an "African Empire." He also advocated for the creation of a "Grand Empire Uni Socialiste Oriental" of India, China, Africa, and Russia:

Le G. E. U. S. O. gouvernera le monde
Et maintiendra la paix dans ces Etats immondes
En proie des préjugés de race et de nation
Qu'ils appellent, hélas! la Civilisation!

La Civilisation de Haine et de Misère
De seigneurs et de serfs, de science et de guerre
Où toutes les nations en armes soit debout
Pour piller le voisin et la mort est au bout.

The G. E. U. S. O. will govern the world
And will maintain peace in the vile Countries
By preying on the prejudices of race and nation
That they call, alas! Civilization!

The Civilization of Hatred and Misery
Of lords and serfs, of science and war
Where all the nations are at arms and ready
To pillage their neighbor and death is at the end.⁷⁹

For Jean-Louis, the imperial legacies of European empires had spread only the civilization of "Hatred and Misery" and "of science and war." The "G. E. U. S. O.," by contrast, would promote "peace" in a divided world and would "prey" on the

FIGURE 7.2. Henri Jean-Louis Baghio'o (1874–1958), ca. 1945. Archives Privées Jean-Louis. Reproduced with permission of Wyck Jean-Louis.

prejudices of "race and nation." Jean-Louis thus maintained his faith in large political structures, such as empires and confederations, but wanted to base them on humanity and socialism, not racism, nationalism, exploitation, slavery, and violence. A little more than a month later, Jean-Louis died at the hospital in Saint-Claude, not far from Matouba, where Louis Delgrès had made his final stand.

Conclusion

Jean-Louis's geographical reconceptualizations of the world were as radical and imaginative as those of any anticolonial thinker. As he traveled, his views on empire evolved continuously, from denouncing the treatment of Africans in Brazzaville to calling for independence in Africa and the Antilles; from promoting a Caribbean federation to suggesting the creation of an African Republic and an international socialist confederation. His migrations and his interactions with people from around the world, both within and beyond imperial boundaries, led him to envision an alternative geography of decolonization, one inflected, but not circumscribed, by empire. None of Jean-Louis's plans came to fruition, and few of his poems were ever published. Instead, his ideas remained enfolded in a suitcase. Yet the power of his imagination, and the networks he left behind, are a striking symbol in themselves. Perhaps a metaphor of constrained cosmopolitanism is the right one for Jean-Louis, after all. Constrained by an empire, and eventually by a suitcase in a basement storage unit, he nonetheless envisioned another world. This, I think, goes some way toward explaining why he abandoned his earlier political expositions for a poetics of the periphery.

Another of Glissant's ideas that surfaces in Jean-Louis's story is *errance*, or errantry. The "thinking of errantry," Glissant explains, "silently emerges from the destructuring of compact national entities that yesterday were still triumphant and, at the same time, from difficult, uncertain births of new forms of identity."[80] This is precisely the kind of "thinking" that developed not just in Jean-Louis, but also among many other Caribbean administrators in Africa. As René Maran and Cunliffe Hoyte reckoned with the contradictions of colonial categories, they began to see more clearly the logics and boundaries of "French" and "British" identities. Meanwhile, who better understood the "destructuring of compact national entities" than Francis Simmons, stranded in the "center" of the empire to which he supposedly belonged? And what about Edwina and Mark Alexis, William Beaudu and Lucie Bouverat, Miss F. L. Ford, and the family of Frank Reid? The indifference of colonial bureaucracies overwhelmed and sometimes fragmented their lives.

Yet alongside these categories and bureaucracies, out of these fragmentations, "new forms of identity" emerged. These connections, however "uncertain," sometimes coalesced into foundations. One thinks here of Edwina Alexis singing or of David McNeil-Stewart and his moments of recognition between Kumasi and Belmont, between Fante and Trinidad Creole, "poured through another rhythm of speed." One thinks, too, of Félix Eboué learning languages in Central Africa, remembering his own ties to the Caribbean, and developing a *géographie cordiale*. And one recalls Edith Goring, Joseph Britton, and Lebert Josiah Veitch, their long sojourns as teachers in the Gold Coast and Nigeria and their subtle influences on their students to connect colonial exploitation and racism across the Atlantic.

Few Caribbean administrators took as radical a stance as Henri Jean-Louis. In fact, most remained loyal to the French and British empires, at least in their official pronouncements. Yet even those who held fast to their imperial identities could not avoid the alienation of doubled marginalization. As Caribbean administrators moved between the Caribbean, Africa, and Europe, they also saw through the myth of imperial belonging. They became aware of the global implications of imperialism far more quickly than people who remained in the Caribbean or who traveled only between the Caribbean and Europe. In African colonies, Caribbean administrators not only encountered racism; they also witnessed the destructive effects of colonial ideologies on African cultures and institutions. Caribbean administrators were part of the colonial establishment, but they understood that the British and French implicated them in the same underlying racial thinking. Out of migration and rigid imperial categories came "new forms of identity."

Caribbean administrators rarely formed associations or leagues or *comités*. They rarely published journals or manifestoes or issued grand declarations. For them, "Africa" was not just a symbol, and "Africans" were more than abstractions. They knew personally the difficulties of uniting vastly diverse groups of people under a singularized identity and were much less eager to make such claims. Nevertheless, they formed connections with Africans in daily exchanges—as colleagues, teachers, and students; by eating food and drinking together; through marriage; by learning languages; and by learning about African cultures and histories. These exchanges, however mundane, were the basis of important intellectual work. Such connections, forged across the fault lines of the Atlantic, created a foundation from which others could imagine new political and geographical connections.

Epilogue

There were also the *fonctionnaires* working in Africa. Through them one saw a land of savages, of barbarians, of natives. —FRANTZ FANON, "ANTILLAIS ET AFRICAINS" (1955)

In 1955, after graduating from Cambridge University, Kamau Brathwaite headed to the Gold Coast as an education officer. "I ended up in a village in Ghana," he later wrote. "Slowly, slowly, ever so slowly; obscurely, slowly but surely, during the eight years that I lived there, I was coming to an awareness and understanding of community, of cultural wholeness.... I came to connect my history with theirs, the bridge of my mind now linking Atlantic and ancestor, homeland and heartland."[1] For Brathwaite, his time in West Africa was a turning point. The connections he formed were an inspiration, and they remained so when he returned to the Caribbean in 1962.[2] The Ghana that Brathwaite encountered in the late 1950s, however, was very different from the Gold

Coast where Joseph Britton had taught between 1885 and 1912, or where David McNeil-Stewart had worked as a sanitary inspector between 1910 and 1922. Brathwaite may have "slowly" come to a sense of "cultural wholeness" in West Africa, but few from Britton's generation made such realignments.

At the turn of the twentieth century, when Caribbean administrators arrived in West and Central Africa, they brought with them the ideas and attitudes of their colonial upbringings. They tended to look down on Africans, and they took comfort in their attachments to the British and French empires. As they reckoned with assimilation, racism, and dislocation, however, they questioned their notions of imperial belonging and forged links with Africans through language, cross-cultural exchange, and nascent ideas about racial solidarity. They also began turning away (slowly, slowly) from London- and Paris-centered geographies. To be sure, the networks of Caribbean administrators were dependent on imperial channels, but their migrations across the deaf sea nonetheless created foundations from which new geographies could be imagined—including the possibility of Brathwaite living and working in Ghana.

Was Brathwaite aware of this history? It seems likely. One of his friends in Ghana was Neville Dawes, a writer from Jamaica whose father, Levi Dawes, had worked as a teacher in Nigeria from 1908 until 1930. There was also Kenneth MacNeill Stewart, the son of David McNeil-Stewart, who had remained in the Gold Coast after his family returned to the Caribbean in 1922.[3] And Cunliffe Hoyte, who retired in 1939, stayed in Ghana until his death in Adabraka in 1966.[4] For others who came to Ghana on the eve of independence, attracted by the rise of Kwame Nkrumah, these earlier networks were important precedents.

Frantz Fanon also knew this history, and while he was critical of the stereotyped "Africa" brought to the Caribbean by Antillean *fonctionnaires*, he drew on their example, as did others of his generation. In addition to Maryse Condé, there was Paul Niger and Guy Tirolien of Guadeloupe, who both worked for the French in Soudan Français. And, of course, Fanon himself first went to Algeria not as a revolutionary, but as a doctor at a colonial hospital.

In the archives of the British and French empires, the histories of these networks and possibilities between the Caribbean and Africa are fragmented—crumbs, dots, islands, cheap paper shredded upon the water. The same imperial fault lines have informed our research trajectories. By focusing on London and Paris, and by adhering to particular categories, sources, and methods, scholars have rendered invisible African diasporic exchanges that took place in other parts of the world and in other languages. To challenge this fragmentation, I have tried to follow the paths that Caribbean administrators followed themselves. I have also tried to follow the poetics of Brathwaite and Aimé Césaire in an effort to cast these fragments together in new forms.

On the sleeve of the original 1968 edition of *Rights of Passage*, Brathwaite included a short reflection on a dust storm in St. Lucia:

> i suddenly realized that what i was witnessing—that milky haze, that sense of dryness—was something i had seen and felt before in ghana. it was the seasonal dust-cloud, drifting out of the great ocean of sahara— the harmattan. by an obscure miracle of connection, this arab's nomad wind, cracker of fante wood a thousand miles away, did not die on the sea-shore of west africa, its continental limit; it drifted on, reaching the new world archipelago to create our drought, imposing an african season on the caribbean sea.[5]

The histories of Caribbean administrators in Africa often appear in a similar haze. Their migrations, networks, and ideas drift, obscurely, in and out of view, even as their trajectories across the Atlantic created new geographies of belonging and made legible the lines of an unformed map.

Notes

INTRODUCTION

1. For eyewitness accounts of the earthquake, see "The 1907 Earthquake," in Paton and Smith, *The Jamaica Reader*, 199–202; Caine, *The Cruise of the Port Kingston*; and Treves, *The Cradle of the Deep*. See also Smith, "A Tale of Two Tragedies."

2. "News Telegrams," *Lagos Standard*, January 23, 1907, 6.

3. On the Niger Delta Pastorate and the growth of independent churches in late nineteenth-century Nigeria, see Ajayi, *Christian Missions in Nigeria, 1841–1891*; Hanciles, "Dandeson Coates Crowther and the Niger Delta Pastorate"; and Tasie, *Christian Missionary Enterprise in the Niger Delta, 1864–1918*.

4. In 1807, British ships began patrolling the West African coast to "liberate" Africans aboard slave ships, and about 75,000 "liberated Africans" ended up in Sierra Leone. Some of those who were originally from Nigeria later returned. The best known of these Saro returnees was Samuel Ajayi Crowther. For a recent history of "liberated Africans" in West Africa, see Anderson, *Abolition in Sierra Leone*.

5. Lebert Josiah Veitch, letter to the editor, *Lagos Standard*, June 5, 1907, 6–7.

6. "Current Items," *Daily Gleaner*, June 29, 1907, 2.

7. Their arrivals were part of a longer history of migration from the Caribbean to Africa. In the late eighteenth century, for example, the British deported maroons from Jamaica to Sierra Leone via Nova Scotia. Others came in subsequent decades as missionaries, soldiers, and civil servants or seeking to escape the constraints of the postemancipation Caribbean. On these migrations, see Banton, *More Auspicious Shores*; Blyden, *West Indians in West Africa, 1808–1880*; Dyde, *The Empty Sleeve*; Nicol, "West Indians in West Africa"; and Wariboko, *Ruined by "Race."*

8. Traces, as Paul Wenzel Geissler and Guillaume Lachenal suggest, "always point to the absence of their cause" and are "always remains of something alive." Geissler and Lachenal, "Brief Instructions for Archaeologists of African Futures," 16.

9. Brathwaite, "Islands," in *The Arrivants*, 204–5.

10. See, e.g., Stovall, *Paris Noir*; Edwards, *The Practice of Diaspora*; Wilder, *The French Imperial Nation-State*; Stephens, *Black Empire*; Boittin, *Colonial Metropolis*; Makalani, *In the Cause of Freedom*; Matera, *Black London*; and Goebel, *Anti-imperial Metropolis*.

11. This tendency also characterizes many of the ships launched by the call to study colony and metropole in a "single analytic field." Stoler and Cooper, "Between Metropole and Colony," 4. On the "staging" of African history in the twentieth century, see Hanretta, *Islam and Social Change in French West Africa*. For a similar critique, see Mann, "Locating Colonial Histories."

12. Feierman, "Colonizers, Scholars, and the Creation of Invisible Histories," 206. The larger argument in this section draws from Feierman's essay.

13. Recent works on "back to Africa" migrations from the United States tend to be similarly grounded in the imperial grasp of US historiography, often overlooking the methods and languages employed by historians of Africa. Two important exceptions are Lindsay, *Atlantic Bonds*, and Vinson, *The Americans are Coming!*

14. An important model in this regard from the postindependence period is Bedasse, *Jah Kingdom*.

15. The two main historiographical reference points for this topic are Blyden, *West Indians in West Africa*, and Hélénon, *French Caribbeans in Africa*.

16. The British Security Service, for example, kept personal files on figures such as C. L. R. James, Jomo Kenyatta, Kwame Nkrumah, and Nnamdi Azikiwe. NAUK, KV2—The Security Service: Personal Files. In France, meanwhile, the Service de Liaison avec des Originaires des Territoires de la France Outre-Mer monitored colonial subjects in France and wrote monthly reports on "les milieux indigènes," including "la colonie noire." ANOM, SLOTFOM III.

17. See Trouillot, *Silencing the Past*, esp. chap. 3. Keguro Macharia similarly suggests that "encounters" between Africans and Afro-Caribbeans in the twentieth century "generate[d] forms of being together unimagined and unimaginable within white-supremacist frames." Macharia, "On Being Area-Studied," 185.

18. I was also following Brent Hayes Edwards's suggestion to trace diasporic connections outside of colonial metropoles. Edwards, *The Practice of Diaspora*, 9. On this point, see also Putnam, *Radical Moves*; and Putnam, "Circum-Atlantic Print Circuits and Internationalism from the Peripheries in the Interwar Era."

19. Lisa Lowe describes a "practice of reading across archives" to disrupt the "discretely bounded objects, methods, and temporal frameworks canonized by national history." Lowe, *The Intimacies of Four Continents*, 6. Jean Allman reckons with similar issues in the writing of postcolonial African history. Allman, "Phantoms of the Archive."

20. On the power of the "colonial library," see Mudimbe, *The Invention of Africa*. Here I am also following the arguments of Chakrabarty, *Provincializing Europe*; Lowe, *The Intimacies of Four Continents*; Mignolo, *Local Histories, Global Designs*; as well as Ranajit Guha's *Subaltern Studies* collections.

21. Guha, "The Prose of Counter-Insurgency."

22. "Discipline," as Katherine McKittrick writes, "is empire." McKittrick, *Dear Science and Other Stories*, 36.

23. Brathwaite, "Islands," 204.

24. Ferdinand, *A Decolonial Ecology*.

25. Wynter, "Novel and History, Plot and Plantation." See also Scott, "The Re-enchantment of Humanism."

26. Glissant, *Caribbean Discourse*, 66.

27. Glissant, *Poetics of Relation*, 33–34.

28. Lamming, *The Pleasures of Exile*, 16.

29. Maximin also suggests that the geography of the Caribbean "evades (*déjoue*) representations of space, its scales and boundaries." Maximin, *Les fruits du cyclone*, 89, 100, 107–8. Similar declarations about the underlying connections of the Caribbean islands mark the work of many other scholars, poets, novelists, and artists, including Derek Walcott, Alejo Carpentier, and Antonio Benítez-Rojo.

30. Césaire, *Cahier d'un retour au pays natal* (1983), 54–55. The translation is from Eshleman and Smith, *Aimé Césaire*, 75.

31. Césaire, *Cahier d'un retour au pays natal* (1983), 55. The translation is from Edwards, "Aimé Césaire and the Syntax of Influence," 11. My analysis of this passage also draws from Edwards's article.

32. Eshleman and Smith, *Aimé Césaire*, 74–75. In their 2017 translation of Césaire's "Séisme," Eshleman and A. James Arnold also translate "*informe*" as "unformed." Arnold and Eshleman, *The Complete Poetry of Aimé Césaire*, 532–33.

33. For background on *Documents*, see Hollier, "La valeur d'usage de l'impossible."

34. Leiris, "De Bataille l'impossible à l'impossible *Documents*," 689.

35. Bataille, "Informe," 382.

36. Bataille, *Encyclopaedia Acephalica*, s.v. "Formless," 51–52. This volume includes the complete collection of the "Dictionnaire." On Bataille and *informe*, see also Bois and Krauss, *Formless*.

37. Alastair Brotchie, "Introduction," in Bataille, *Encyclopaedia Acephalica*, 23.

38. Frobenius, "Dessins rupestres du sud de la Rhodésie." On Césaire, Bataille, and the colonial context of interwar France, see Edwards, "The Ethnics of Surrealism."

39. Césaire, "Cahier d'un retour au pays natal." On the different versions of the *Cahier*, see Arnold, *The Original 1939 Notebook of a Return to the Native Land*; and Gil, "Bridging the Middle Passage." My thanks to Alex Gil for sharing the different versions of the poem.

40. Césaire, *Cahier d'un retour au pays natal* (New York, 1947); and Césaire, *Cahier d'un retour au pays natal* (Paris, 1947).

41. Césaire, *Cahier d'un retour au pays natal* (Paris, 1956). Césaire inserted this section just before the strophe about geography quoted in one of the epigraphs for this book. As far as I can tell, this was the first time Césaire had used *informe* in his poetry. The word also appears in the poem "Séisme," published in *Les Lettres Nouvelles* in 1959.

42. The 1956 edition of the *Cahier* was published in June 1956, and four months later, Césaire made his decisive departure from the French Communist Party. "The anticolonialism of French communists still bears the marks of the colonialism it is fighting," he wrote in his famous letter of resignation. Near the end of the letter, he also denounced the "petrified forms" that "obstruct[ed]" the path forward. Césaire, "Letter to Maurice Thorez," 150, 152.

43. Wilder, *Freedom Time*.

44. Brathwaite, "Caliban's Garden," 4. This essay was originally part of Brathwaite's 1990 lecture series, "Conversations with Caliban," at the University of Kent.

45. See, e.g., Brathwaite, "The African Presence in Caribbean Literature"; Brathwaite, *The Arrivants*; Brathwaite, *The Development of Creole Society in Jamaica, 1770–1820*; Brathwaite, *History of the Voice*; and Brathwaite, *Middle Passages*.

46. Brathwaite, *Contradictory Omens*, 64.

47. Brathwaite, "Caribbean Man in Space and Time," 1. This essay was reprinted in 2021 in *Small Axe*, along with an introductory essay by Kelly Baker Josephs, "Caribbean Studies in Digital Space and Time." My analysis in this section draws on Josephs's essay and from Putnam, "To Study the Fragments/Whole."

48. Brathwaite, "Caribbean Man in Space and Time," 3–4.

49. Brathwaite, "Caribbean Man in Space and Time," 11.

50. Josephs, "Caribbean Studies in Digital Space and Time," 106–7.

51. Brathwaite, "Islands," 204–5.

52. Nancy Rose Hunt suggests that historians might use form to "create shapes, suggest meanings and tones, confront enigmas, enable surprise, and even please the senses." Hunt, "History as Form, with Simmel in Tow," 128, 144.

53. Hunt, "History as Form, with Simmel in Tow," 137.

54. In my use of sources, I follow the example of McKittrick, who, drawing on Glissant, writes that "subaltern spatial practices . . . are written into and expressed through the poetics of landscape . . . through theoretical, fictional, poetic, musical, or dramatic texts." McKittrick, *Demonic Grounds*, xxiii.

55. On "orchestrated fragments," I take inspiration from Edwards, "The Taste of the Archive."

56. Walcott, *Omeros*, 135.

57. Walcott, *Omeros*, 137.

58. Walcott, *Omeros*, 138–39. Earlier, in Book Two, Afolabe appears as a slave building a fort in St. Lucia. He is described as "Achille's ancestor," and "the small Admiral" renames him Achilles—not Achille. Walcott, *Omeros*, 82–83. On this point and other acts of naming in *Omeros*, see McKinsey, "Missing Sounds and Mutable Meanings."

59. Walcott, *Omeros*, 150.

60. McKittrick, *Demonic Grounds*, xvii.

61. Glissant, *Caribbean Discourse*, 66–67. On transversals and Atlantic history, see Kazanjian, *The Brink of Freedom*, 5–10.

CHAPTER 1. FROM THE CARIBBEAN TO AFRICA

1. NAUK, CO 111/529, Barbour-James Colonial Service Application, November 5, 1901.

2. This description of Barbour-James's childhood in Epsom comes from his application form and from Jan Carew's 1958 novel, *The Wild Coast*, about life in Tarlogie, a village on the Corentyne coast close to Epsom.

3. NAUK, CO 111/529, Barbour-James to Governor of British Guiana, November 23, 1901.

4. NAUK, CO 111/529, Governor of British Guiana to Secretary of State for the Colonies, December 4, 1901.

5. NAUK, CO 111/529, Colonial Office Minutes, February 5, 1902.

6. NAUK, CO 111/531, Barbour-James, President of the Victoria Institute Villagers Association, to Government Secretary, March 14, 1902. On imperial culture and the Boer War in the British Caribbean, see Smith, *Strolling in the Ruins*, esp. chap. 1.

7. NAUK, CO 111/531, Governor of British Guiana to Secretary of State for the Colonies, March 21, 1902.

8. NAUK, CO 96/363, Colonial Office Correspondence, April 1902.

9. John Barbour-James arrived in the Gold Coast in July 1902. In 1904, Caroline Barbour-James and the children settled in London, where John visited them while on leave until his retirement in 1917. Green, *Black Edwardians*, 70–78; and NAUK, CO 100/52, Gold Coast Blue Book 1902.

10. As Faith Smith writes about this "quiet period" in Caribbean history, "The diasporic and the imperial, far from being mutually exclusive spheres, are better understood relationally, as not only thwarting and displacing but also shaping or enlivening each other." Smith, *Strolling in the Ruins*, 10.

11. "Islands ruled by sugar cane" is from Kamau Brathwaite, "Calypso," in Brathwaite, *The Arrivants*, 48. For overviews of the nineteenth-century Caribbean, see Ibarra and Laurence, *General History of the Caribbean*; Knight, *The Caribbean*; Knight and Palmer, *The Modern Caribbean*; Larcher, *L'autre citoyen*; and Palmié and Scarano, *The Caribbean*.

12. Scarano, "Labor and Society in the Nineteenth Century," 59.

13. In some contexts, conditions actually worsened with emancipation. For example, enslaved women in Jamaica who gave birth to six or more children were exempt from field labor, but during the "apprenticeship" years (1834–38), the government removed this exemption. Heuman, "Peasants, Immigrants, and Workers," 350.

14. Beckles, *A History of Barbados*, 158. For a study of these dynamics in Antigua, see Lightfoot, *Troubling Freedom*.

15. Brereton, "Society and Culture in the Caribbean," 103.

16. At least 238,000 laborers from India came to British Guiana, 145,000 to Trinidad, 39,000 to Guadeloupe, 21,500 to Jamaica, 6,748 to Martinique, 2,570 to Grenada, 1,820 to St. Vincent, and 1,550 to St. Lucia. Heuman, "Peasants, Immigrants, and Workers," 356–58; and Knight, *The Caribbean*, 132.

17. Between 1853 and 1879, almost nineteen thousand Chinese indentured laborers came to the Caribbean. Most ended up in British Guiana, but five hundred also arrived in Guadeloupe, while in 1859 alone, another five hundred arrived in Martinique. And between 1841 and 1865, roughly thirty-six thousand African indentured laborers, mostly "liberated Africans" whom the British brought to Sierra Leone and Saint Helena, arrived in the British and French Caribbean. Heuman, "Peasants, Immigrants, and Workers," 356–58; Knight, *The Caribbean*, 132; and Schuler, *Alas, Alas, Kongo*.

18. For an account of Indian indentured labor in the Caribbean, see Kale, *Fragments of Empire*.

19. On these uprisings, see Holt, *The Problem of Freedom*; Heuman, *"The Killing Time"*; Nicolas, *L'insurrection du sud à la Martinique*; Adélaïde-Merlande, *Les origines du mouvement ouvrier en Martinique*; Beckles, *Great House Rules*; Fallope, *Esclaves et citoyens*; and Teelucksingh, *Labour and the Decolonization Struggle in Trinidad and Tobago*.

20. Flores-Villalobos, *The Silver Women*; Giovannetti-Torres, *Black British Migrants in Cuba*; Maddox, *A Home Away from Home*; and Putnam, *The Company They Kept*.

21. Knight, *The Caribbean*, 133.

22. Brereton, *Race Relations in Colonial Trinidad, 1870–1900*, 69.

23. Brereton, "Society and Culture in the Caribbean," 107–8.

24. Palmer, *Inward Yearnings*, 13.

25. Knight, *The Caribbean*, 211.

26. Warner, *Critical Perspectives on Léon-Gontran Damas*, 18.

27. James, *Beyond a Boundary*, 29–30.

28. Glissant, *Caribbean Discourse*, 7; and James, "Black Experience in Twentieth-Century Britain," 377–79.

29. Hall, "Negotiating Caribbean Identities," 8.

30. Rodney, *A History of the Guyanese Working People, 1881–1905*, 115, quoted in Knight, *The Caribbean*, 218. On education and class divisions in the French Caribbean, see Hélénon, *French Caribbeans in Africa*, 23–30.

31. The French Ministry of Colonies generally sent Caribbean administrators to Africa but also sent them to Asia, especially before World War I. Hélénon, *French Caribbeans in Africa*, 38–40, 95; and Weinstein, *Eboué*, 22. I have not found evidence of the British sending West Indians to British colonies outside of Africa and the Caribbean, although this appears to have been a possibility. When Hubert Nurse, the father of Malcolm Nurse/George Padmore of Trinidad, applied for a position in West Africa in February 1912, he noted on his application form, "West Coast of Africa or N. or S. Nigeria. East Indies not desired." NAUK, CO 295/473, Hubert Nurse Application Form, February 15, 1912.

32. Louis, *Conversation avec Aimé Césaire*, 22.

33. Renwick, "Forty Years On . . . ," 192–94. The title of this section is from Walcott, *Omeros*, 137.

34. NAUK, CO 295/492, Renwick Application for Promotion; Renwick, "Forty Years On . . . ," 202.

35. On images of Africa in the Americas, see Appiah, *In My Father's House*; Curtin, *The Image of Africa*; Mayer, *Artificial Africas*; Pieterse, *White on Black*; and Sidbury, *Becoming African in America*.

36. Palmer, *Inward Yearnings*, 10.

37. Glissant, *Caribbean Discourse*, 6.

38. "The coloured people," continued James, are "not savages" and their "whole outlook is that of Western civilization modified and adapted to their particular circumstances." James, *The Life of Captain Cipriani*, 49–50. My thanks to Minkah Makalani for bringing this reference to my attention.

39. Renwick, "Forty Years On . . . ," 194.

40. On African indentured labor in the British Caribbean, see Schuler, *Alas, Alas, Kongo*. For the French Caribbean, Hélénon notes that between 1857 and 1862, the French brought 15,000 African indentured laborers to Guadeloupe, 10,500 to Martinique, and 1,828 to French Guiana. See also Mam Lam Fouck, *La Guyane au temps de l'esclavage*, 223. According to Brereton, in 1891 there were 2,055 Africans living in Trinidad, approximately 1 percent of the total population. Brereton, *Race Relations in Colonial Trinidad, 1870–1900*, 153. Renwick was born in Port of Spain on June 17, 1892. NAUK, CO 295/492, Renwick Application for Promotion.

41. A rich literature has detailed the re-creation of African cultures in the Americas in the nineteenth century. See, e.g., Falola and Childs, *The Yoruba Diaspora in the Atlantic World*; Gomez, *Exchanging Our Country Marks*; Matory, *Black Atlantic Religion*; and Warner-Lewis, *Central Africa in the Caribbean*.

42. Brereton, *Race Relations in Colonial Trinidad, 1870–1900*, 134. On "ethnic" markers and the transatlantic slave trade, see Sweet, "Mistaken Identities?"

43. Stewart, *Three Eyes for the Journey*; and Warner-Lewis, *Central Africa in the Caribbean*.

44. Ebroin, *Quimbois, magie noire et sorcellerie aux Antilles*; and Paton, *The Cultural Politics of Obeah*.

45. Brereton, "Society and Culture in the Caribbean," 106. See also Sweet, "The Evolution of Ritual in the African Diaspora."

46. *Trinidad Chronicle*, January 16, 1872, quoted in Brereton, *Race Relations in Colonial Trinidad, 1870–1900*, 154. For more on the Radas of Belmont, see Carr, "A Rada Community in Trinidad"; and Senah, "Rada."

47. Blanche, "6000 'engagés volontaires' en Afrique et en Guadeloupe, 1858–1861"; and Hélénon, *French Caribbeans in Africa*, 65–66. One of these groups had still preserved Kikongo traditions such as recipes, folktales, and songs into the 1990s.

48. Colonial laws such as the 1898 Obeah Act in Jamaica typically condemned "African" practices and rituals. The middle classes looked down on Africans, and journalists regularly caricatured and mocked obeah practitioners. Paton, *The Cultural Politics of Obeah*.

49. Weinstein interview with Yves Gratien, December 2, 1967, quoted in Weinstein, *Eboué*, 10.

50. Renauld, *Félix Eboué et Eugénie Tell*, 31.

51. Rouse-Jones and Appiah, "Interview with Dr. Ralph Hoyte."

52. The Hoyte family was related to the family of George Padmore/Malcolm Nurse. Padmore's grandfather, Alphonso Nurse, settled in Belmont after relocating to Trinidad from Barbados and British Guiana. UWISC, GPC, Box 1, Folder 2, "Mr. Alphonso Nurse," *Port of Spain Gazette*, 1929.

53. Baghio'o, *Le colibri blanc*, 24. This novelized memoir, compiled and written by Jean-Louis's son, Victor Jean-Louis, was based on Henri Jean-Louis's earlier drafts. Jean-Louis was likely referring to Mohammed Baghayogho, who was a prominent scholar in Timbuktu in the sixteenth century. For more on this link, see chapter 7 in this volume.

54. Baghio'o, *Le colibri blanc*, 13–14.

55. Baghio'o, *Le colibri blanc*, 14, 23, 40.

56. As in other parts of West Africa, British opposition to Aro slave trading was deeply hypocritical. British slave trading in the eighteenth century had reoriented the economic patterns of the Niger Delta around slavery, while British merchants in the twentieth century continued to buy palm products produced by slave labor. Afigbo, "The Calabar Mission and the Aro Expedition of 1901–1902"; and Falola, *Colonialism and Violence in Nigeria*.

57. Some Caribbean people also fought in these military conquests. On West Indian soldiers in Africa, see Dyde, *The Empty Sleeve*; and Ellis, *The History of the First West India Regiment*. The French military also recruited soldiers from the Caribbean to participate in colonial campaigns, though the practice was less common. Hélénon, *French Caribbeans in Africa*, 3–4. See also Lara, *Le commandant Mortenol*.

58. There is a substantial literature on Africans who worked for European colonial governments. See, e.g., Brunschwig, *Noirs et blancs dans l'Afrique noire française*; Hunt, *A Colonial Lexicon*; Lawrance et al., *Intermediaries, Interpreters, and Clerks*; Moyd, *Violent Intermediaries*; Ochonu, *Colonialism by Proxy*; and Otim, *Acholi Intellectuals*. Colonial governments also sometimes transported Africans from one colony to another, such as the laptots from West Africa who worked for the French in Central Africa. Whitehouse, *Migrants and Strangers in an African City*.

59. NAUK, CO 96/573, Colonial Office file on a gratuity for Mark Alexis of Trinidad.

60. NAUK, CO 96/521, Note on West Indian Railway Staff in the Gold Coast, September 23, 1912. British officials became so preoccupied with this question that the secretary of state for the colonies launched an enquiry into "the extent to which . . . West Indian subordinates of African extraction . . . [were] liable to suffer from tropical diseases as compared with Europeans." Several months later, Dr. C. B. Hunter, the senior medical officer in Accra, conducted a "statistical comparison between the health of European and that of West Indian Officials during the years 1903 to 1912" and indicated that "West Indians of African extraction do not enjoy better health in the Gold Coast than European Officials." PRAAD, ADM 1/1/206, Secretary of State for the Colonies to Governor of the Gold Coast, May 20, 1913; NAUK, CO 96/538, Acting Governor of the Gold Coast to Secretary of State for the Colonies, November 20, 1913; and NAUK, CO 96/538, Dr. C. B. Hunter to Principal Medical Officer, November 18, 1913.

61. Hélénon, *French Caribbeans in Africa*, 84.

62. On providential design and the transatlantic slave trade, see Drake, *The Redemption of Africa and Black Religion*; Jenkins, *Black Zion*; Sidbury, *Becoming African in America*; Smith, *Conjuring Culture*; and Vinson, *The Americans Are Coming!*, esp. chap. 1.

63. On these initiatives, see Clegg, *The Price of Liberty*; and Sanneh, *Abolitionists Abroad*.

64. NAUK, CO 267/413, Governor of Sierra Leone to Secretary of State for the Colonies, December 7, 1894.

65. "Bishop Ingham's Mission to the West Indies," *Lagos Weekly Record*, November 2, 1895, 4–5.

66. Janzen, "Tensions on the Railway."

67. François Manchuelle called Roger's novel *Kélédor* "one of the best examples in a Francophone text of . . . the theory of 'providential design.'" Manchuelle, "The 'Regeneration of Africa,'" 583.

68. Hélénon, *French Caribbeans in Africa*, 94–95.

69. Hélénon, *French Caribbeans in Africa*, 108–9.

70. In the United States, three of the main proponents of providential design and emigration to Africa were Alexander Crummell, Martin Delany, and Henry McNeal Turner. Adeleke, *UnAfrican Americans*; and Moses, *Alexander Crummell*.

71. Blyden, "The Call of Providence to Descendants of Africa in America," 27. The phrase "Go up and possess the land" comes from Numbers 13 and Deuteronomy 1.

72. On Blyden's intellectual transformations, see Odamtten, *Edward W. Blyden's Intellectual Transformations*. On Blyden's influence on Caribbean administrators, see Janzen, "Tensions on the Railway."

CHAPTER 2. MIDDLE PASSAGES

Epigraphs: PRAAD, ADM 1/1/211, Harcourt to Governor of the Gold Coast, January 20, 1914; NAUK, CO 583/72, Bland to Central Secretary Lagos, December 30, 1918; and ANOM, AFFPOL/592, "Exposé de Monsieur le Gouverneur de Coppet."

1. Maran to Bocquet, February 1, 1910, quoted in Bocquet, "Préface," 15.

2. French maritime law ruled Maran's official birthplace as Fort-de-France, Martinique. Ikonné, *Links and Bridges*, 258.

3. Maran to Gahisto, January 23, 1912, in Fonkoua, *Correspondance Maran-Gahisto*, 118. Apart from "Mardi," this letter appears undated. Elsewhere, however, Gahisto introduces the letter as having arrived ten days after a letter from January 10, 1912. Gahisto, "La genèse de Batouala," 105–6.

4. Maran's father, Herménégilde Maran, was still in Bangui when his son arrived, but he left for France in November 1910 and died shortly thereafter. Maran later described his joy in reconnecting with his father, writing, "Six months of daily work revealed to us our real feelings and our flaws. We began to love each other even more for not having known each other before. . . . We also cried a lot, both of us, for a long time, before the departure of the boat that would separate us forever." Maran to Paul Culine, November 29, 1910, quoted in Gahisto, "La genèse de Batouala," 100.

5. ANOM, FP/8APOM/4, Report sent by Maran to Chef de la Circonscription, December 22, 1910; and ANOM, FP/8APOM/4, Report sent by Chef de la Circonscription to Lieutenant-Governor, December 22, 1910.

6. ANOM, FP/8APOM/4, Chef de la Circonscription to Lieutenant-Governor of Oubangui-Chari, December 22, 1910.

7. On the inconsistent classifications of West Indian and African civil servants in the Gold Coast, see Ray, *Crossing the Color Line*, chap. 2.

8. For more detailed overviews of French colonialism in Central Africa, see Birmingham and Martin, *History of Central Africa*; Cordell, *Dar al-Kuti and the Last Years of the Trans-Saharan Slave Trade*; Giles-Vernick, *Cutting the Vines of the Past*; Ceriana Mayneri, *Sorcellerie et prophétisme en Centrafrique*; and Nzabakomada-Yakoma, *L'Afrique Centrale insurgée*.

9. Coquery-Vidrovitch, *Le Congo au temps des grandes compagnies concessionaires, 1898–1930*.

10. Ralph Austen and Rita Headrick note that during labor recruitment in Oubangui Chari, "villagers unable to flee were tied together and brought naked to the forests to tap rubber vines." Austen and Headrick, "Equatorial Africa under Colonial Rule," 35.

11. On *regroupement*, see Giles-Vernick, "Na lege ti guiriri (On the Road of History)."

12. UCAD, FRM, MS 24, 9–11, Maran to Paul Culine, September 16, 1910.

13. Maran to Gahisto, June 19, 1911, in Fonkoua, *Correspondance Maran-Gahisto*, 108.

14. Maran to Gahisto, October 11, 1912, in Fonkoua, *Correspondance Maran-Gahisto*, 152, 150.

15. Maran to Bocquet, August 1913, quoted in Bocquet, "Préface," 53.

16. Maran to Gahisto, April 10, 1914, in Fonkoua, *Correspondance Maran-Gahisto*, 202.

17. Bocquet, "Préface," 53; and Dennis, "The René Maran Story," 77.

18. Maran to Gahisto, December 18, 1914, in Fonkoua, *Correspondance Maran-Gahisto*, 228.

19. Maran to Gahisto, June 19, 1911, in Fonkoua, *Correspondance Maran-Gahisto*, 11.

20. Tuffrau, "Hommage," 256.

21. NATT, CSO 7505/1909, Engagement of Sanitary Inspectors.

22. Rodger claimed that the proper training took too long, so he asked that the Colonial Office "obtain . . . Sanitary Inspectors from the West Indies." NATT, CSO 7505/1909, Governor of the Gold Coast to Secretary of State for the Colonies, October 11, 1909.

23. PRAAD, PF 3/32/473, Cunliffe Hoyte Personnel File.

24. For overviews of this history, see Austin, *Labour, Land, and Capital in Ghana*; Getz, *Slavery and Reform in West Africa*; Law, *From Slave Trade to "Legitimate" Commerce*; McCaskie, *Asante Identities*; and Perbi, *A History of Indigenous Slavery in Ghana*. More generally, see Lovejoy, *Transformations in Slavery*.

25. On these African-West Indian tensions, see Janzen, "Tensions on the Railway."

26. "Railway," letter to the editor, *Gold Coast Leader*, July 27, 1907, 4.

27. The phrase was made most famous by Marcus Garvey in the 1910s and 1920s through the Universal Negro Improvement Association. Adi and Sherwood, *Pan-African History*, viii; Asante and Mazama, eds., *Encyclopedia of Black Studies*, 131; and Shepperson, "Notes on Negro American Influences on the Emergence of African Nationalism," 301.

28. PRAAD, PF 3/32/473, Hoyte to Medical Officer of Health, Accra, March 10, 1915.

29. For a recent study of sanitation work in the Gold Coast, see Amoako-Gyampah, "Sanitation and Public Hygiene in the Gold Coast (Ghana) from the Late 19th Century to 1950."

30. NAUK, CO 98/20, Gold Coast Medical and Sanitary Report 1911, 64.

31. NAUK, CO 100/61, Gold Coast Blue Book 1911.

32. PRAAD, PF 3/32/473, Petition from Hoyte to the Medical Officer of Health, Accra, March 10, 1915; PRAAD, PF 3/32/473, Petition from Hoyte to Governor of the Gold Coast, July 26, 1915.

33. Accompanying Hoyte's July petition were ten pages of handwritten "self-explanatory" tables detailing his lack of upward mobility and static salary grade, as well as a comprehensive list of the thirty documents and letters to which he referred in the petition.

34. James, "Black Experience in Twentieth-Century Britain," 377–79.

35. ANOM, FP/8APOM/4, Fonds Fraisse, "Documents sur René Maran," Maran to Lieutenant-Governor of Moyen-Congo, June 25, 1915. The month on this letter page is missing due to termites. Maran's personnel file, ANOM, AEF/GGAEF/C//74/Maran, shows that his leave in 1915 began on June 24. The space where the month appears on this page is too short to be juillet, septembre, octobre, novembre, or décembre, so it is either "juin" or "août." From the traces on the edges, it appears to be "juin."

36. On the architecture and legacies of the Hotels ABC, see Sacks, "Lived Remainders."

37. *Fonctionnaires de couleur* also carried echoes of *gens de couleur*, an important category in the history of the French Caribbean.

38. PRAAD, PF 3/32/473, Principal Medical Officer to Colonial Secretary, October 29, 1914.

39. PRAAD, PF 3/32/473, Basel Mission to Secretary for Native Affairs, January 7, 1915.

40. PRAAD, PF 3/32/473, Basel Mission to Acting Chief Commissioner of Ashanti, January 31, 1916.

41. I have retained Hoyte's version of the text, even though many of his orthographic usages are no longer current. For example, Hoyte uses *e* instead of *ɛ*, *o* for *ɔ*, *dśi* for *ji*, *nśo̱* for *ŋshɔ*, and so on. Nevertheless, they reveal how he heard and transcribed the dictation portion of the exam. They are also reflective of the texts he used to study for the exam.

42. My thanks to Seth Nii Moi Allotey and Hermann von Hesse for their help with translation from Ga to English.

43. On Ga history and the growth of Accra, see Parker, *Making the Town*, esp. chap. 1. See also Odotei, "The Ga and Their Neighbors, 1600–1742."

44. Zimmermann, *A Grammatical Sketch and Vocabulary of the Akra- or Gã-Language*, 1:183.

45. Reindorf, *History of the Gold Coast and Asante*, 10.

46. Reindorf, *History of the Gold Coast and Asante*, 10, 84, 95. "Lɛtebɔi," also known as Nii Boi Tono, was both a political and a spiritual leader.

47. Hoyte also likely used Zimmermann's book in preparation for his exams. In October 1914, when he was studying for his lower standard examination, he asked his supervisor for "a list of books recommended for study." PRAAD, PF 3/32/473, Hoyte to Medical Officer of Health, Accra, October 23, 1914.

48. Both *nyomo* and *nyon* come from the Ga verb *nyo* (to fall, to sink, or to go down). Parker, *Making the Town*, 90; and Zimmermann, *A Grammatical Sketch and Vocabulary of the Akra- or Gã-Language*, 2:242.

49. A 2010 study from Osu showed that *nyon* was one of several "abusive words used to describe slave descendants." Yankholmes et al., "Awusai Atso," 59. *Tsulo* is a Ga word, while *odonko* and *awowa* were borrowed from Twi.

50. On the changing meanings of land and property in nineteenth- and twentieth-century Accra, see Sackeyfio, "The Politics of Land and Urban Space in Colonial Accra."

51. PRAAD, PF 3/32/473, Notes between David Alexander, Senior Sanitary Officer, and Principal Medical Officer in March and August 1915.

52. "Accra," *Gold Coast Leader*, October 14, 1916, 3.

53. On Jamot in Central Africa, see Bado, *Eugène Jamot, 1879–1937*; and Lachenal, *The Doctor Who Would Be King*.

54. Doungouyolo gave a declaration of these events to Jean Bonneveau, the head of the district, in Bangui on June 9, 1918. ANOM, AEF/GGAEF/C//74/Maran, Bonneveau to Lieutenant-Governor of Oubangui-Chari, June 10, 1918.

55. ANOM, AEF/GGAEF/C//74/Maran, Testimony of Oroumbia to Jean Bonneveau in Fort-Crampel, July 20, 1918.

56. The other details about these incidents come from the testimony of Mayo, Onandago, Yamengue, Yabanza, Oroumbia, Gripendé, Dalenguere, Gaouranga, Dori, Bissinzali, Yarissi, Badingouanzé, Coupé, Idja, Mendina, Gouvinda, Tingui, Yapende, and Niama. They gave their testimony to Jean Bonneveau and Michel Sodji, an interpreter from Dahomey, in Fort-Crampel between July 20 and July 29, 1918. ANOM, AEF/GGAEF/C//74/Maran.

57. ANOM, AEF/GGAEF/C//74/Maran, Extract of the Minutes of the Tribunal de 1ère Instance de Bangui, Oubangui-Chari, AEF, June 26, 1919.

58. ANOM, AEF/GGAEF/C//74/Maran, Maran to Rapporteur de la Commission d'enquête, August 6, 1919.

59. For another account of the "affaire Mongo," see Rubiales, "Désillusion et frustration."

60. Maran to Gahisto, May 18, 1918, in Fonkoua, *Correspondance Maran-Gahisto*, 419.

61. "Lettre inédite de René Maran à André Fraisse."

62. Maran, "René Maran s'explique . . ." *Le Libertaire*, 1959, 2, quoted in Dennis, "The René Maran Story," 82.

63. "Lettre inédite de René Maran à André Fraisse," 11.

64. ANOM, AEF/GGAEF/C//74/Maran, Maran to Governor of Oubangui-Chari, June 6, 1918.

65. "A Black man I am, a 'boy' they want me to become." ANOM, EE/ii/6175/35, Maran Personnel File, Maran to Governor of Oubangui-Chari, June 9, 1918.

66. ANOM, AEF/GGAEF/C//74/Maran, Maran to Governor-General of AEF, June 3, 1918.

67. This was likely Maran's spelling of *mbunzu*, meaning "a European."

68. Maran had some familiarity with Central African languages. In one of his notebooks he carefully transcribed the meanings of hundreds of village names and basic vocabularies. UCAD, FRM, MS 31.

69. ANOM, AEF/GGAEF/C//74/Maran, Maran to Governor-General of AEF, June 3, 1918.

70. Maran, *Batouala*, 11. Maran also declared, "The natives were broken down by incessant toil for which they were not paid, and were even robbed of the time to sow their own crops. They saw disease come and take up its abode with them, and saw famine stalk their land, saw their numbers grow less and less." Maran, *Batouala*, 15–16. On *Batouala* and the ambiguities of its subtitle, see Edwards, *The Practice of Diaspora*, chap. 2. On the creation of Maran's preface, see Scheel, "René Maran."

71. Fabre, "René Maran, the New Negro and Négritude"; Onana, *René Maran*; Rubiales, "Notes sur la réception du Goncourt 1921 en France"; and Steemers, "Appropriation of a Controversial Novel."

72. ANOM, AEF/GGAEF/C//74/Maran, Maran to Chef de la Circonscription, March 3, 1923. In a letter to Gahisto later that month, Maran made similar comments. He wrote, "If the good reputation of France was not at stake, I would have been executed long ago, and in an awful manner, by the Ministry of Colonies, and by the *fonctionnaires* of Oubangui-Chari." Maran to Gahisto, March 19, 1923, in Fonkoua, *Correspondance Maran-Gahisto*, 669.

73. Eboué to Maran, November 20, 1922, quoted in Weinstein, *Eboué*, 81; ANOM, AEF/GGAEF/C//74/Maran, René-Boisneuf to Minister of Colonies, January 14, 1923; and Dennis, "The René Maran Story," 157.

74. PRAAD, PF 3/32/473, Hoyte to Medical Officer of Health, Kumasi, August 21, 1916; PRAAD, PF 3/32/473, Hoyte to Governor of the Gold Coast, August 21, 1916; and PRAAD, PF 3/32/473, Hoyte to Colonial Secretary of the Gold Coast, August 21, 1916.

75. PRAAD, PF 3/32/473, Letters and minutes from Colonial Secretary to Principal Medical Officer to be communicated to C. M. G. Hoyte, September 5, September 12, 1916.

76. PRAAD, ADM 1/1/239, Hoyte to Under Secretary of the State for the Colonies, September 26, 1917.

77. Hoyte also alluded to the 1916 Easter Rising in Ireland—specifically, to the executions of three Irish journalists and activists on April 26, 1916: Frances Sheehy Skeffington, Patrick James McIntyre, and Thomas Dickson. The executions were unwarranted, so in Dublin on June 7, 1916, the British court-martialed Captain Bowen-Colthurst, who had ordered the executions. The court found him guilty of murdering the three men but also found him to be insane, and he spent the remainder of his life in Canada. Hoyte made direct reference to the report, "Royal Commission on the Arrest and Subsequent Treatment of Mr. Francis Sheehy Skeffington, Mr. Thomas Dickson, and Mr. Patrick James McIntyre," and stated that he was aware of "the recent manifestations on the part of this Empire in righting wrong and removing abuses."

78. According to Hoyte's calculations, he had "saved to the Treasury a sum exceeding £250." PRAAD, ADM 1/1/239, Hoyte to Under Secretary of the State for the Colonies, September 26, 1917.

79. Hoyte was referring to Gold Coast General Order 52(1) and General Order 76 and West African Pensions Law no. 748, para. 1.

80. PRAAD, ADM 1/1/239, Secretary of the State for the Colonies to Governor of the Gold Coast, October 5, 1917; and PRAAD, PF 3/32/473, Governor of the Gold Coast to Secretary of State for the Colonies, March 20, 1918.

81. PRAAD, PF 3/32/473, Hoyte Petition to Governor of the Gold Coast, July 26, 1915. Hoyte was quoting from Macaulay's essay "Machiavelli," which appeared in Macaulay, *English Essays*, 398. Macaulay's father, Zachary Macaulay, was an abolitionist as well as governor of Sierra Leone from 1794 to 1799. Interestingly, there was another Thomas Babington Macaulay in early nineteenth-century Sierra Leone, who was the son of "liberated Africans" enslaved in Nigeria. He married Abigail Crowther, daughter of Samuel Ajayi Crowther, and their son was Herbert Macaulay.

82. PRAAD, PF 3/32/473, Petition from Hoyte to Governor of the Gold Coast, July 26, 1915.

83. Rouse-Jones and Appiah, "Interview with Dr. Ralph Hoyte." When he retired, his pension paperwork listed him as a "Non-European Officer." PRAAD, PF 3/32/473, "West African Pensions Form."

84. See, e.g., Conklin, *A Mission to Civilize*; and Cooper and Stoler, *Tensions of Empire*.

85. On the history of colonial studies, see Cooper, *Colonialism in Question*. For an earlier overview in the context of African historiography, see Cooper, "Conflict and Connection."

86. Brown, *"We Were All Slaves"*; Allman and Tashjian, *"I Will Not Eat Stone"*; and Cooper, *Decolonization and African Society*.

87. Cooper, *Colonialism in Question*, 203.

88. Schoenbrun, "Conjuring the Modern in Africa," 1403.

89. Feierman, "Colonizers, Scholars, and the Creation of Invisible Histories"; and Hanretta, *Islam and Social Change in French West Africa*, 4–11.

90. In 2005, Gary Wilder suggested that this scholarship, preoccupied with an "analytic of failure," was producing "important but by now unsurprising conclusions." Wilder, *The French Imperial Nation-State*, 78–79.

91. McKittrick, *Dear Science and Other Stories*, 48–49; and McKittrick, *Demonic Grounds*, 14.

CHAPTER 3. FRAGMENTS AND PHOTOGRAPHS

1. PRAAD, PF 3/3/29, Mark Alexis Personnel File, Passport Application. For an exquisite analysis of photography, West Indian women, and imperial archives, see Flores-Villalobos, "'Freak Letters.'" My analysis in this chapter is also informed by Campt, *Listening to Images*.

2. NAI, N 431/1913, F. L. Ford to Manager of Nigerian Railway, July 28, 1913.

3. ANOM, EE/ii/2294/5, William Beaudu Personnel File, Report of Docteur Edgard Blum, October 22, 1924.

4. ANOM, EE/ii/2294/5, Beaudu to Minister of Colonies, November 27, 1923; ANOM, EE/ii/2294/5, Beaudu to Director, July 14, 1924; and ANOM, EE/ii/2294/5, Beaudu to Minister of Colonies, October 8, 1924.

5. NAI, N 431/1913, Waller to F. L. Ford, September 3, 1913.

6. NAUK, CO 96/586, Alexis to Under Secretary of State for the Colonies, July 9, 1917.

7. PRAAD, PF 3/3/29, Alexis to Under Secretary of State for the Colonies, August 9, 1917.

8. NAUK, CO 96/586, Alexis to Under Secretary of State for the Colonies, November 8, 1917.

9. PRAAD, ADM 1/1/240, Gilbert Grindle, Assistant Under Secretary of State for the Colonies, to Alexis, November 14, 1917.

10. NAUK, CO 96/586, Alexis to Under Secretary of State for the Colonies, November 15, 1917.

11. NAI, N 431/1913, Waller to Colonial Secretary, September 3, 1913, emphasis added.

12. ANOM, EE/ii/2294/5, Notes of the Governor of Sénégal, November 11, 1900. See also Hélénon, *French Caribbeans in Africa*, 79–84.

13. ANOM, EE/ii/2294/5, Beaudu to Minister of Colonies, October 25, 1924.

14. ANOM, EE/ii/2294/5, Beaudu to Director, January 31, 1916.

15. ANOM, EE/ii/2294/5, Beaudu to Minister of Colonies, October 25, 1924.

16. ANOM, EE/ii/2294/5, Beaudu to Minister of Colonies, October 8, 1924.

17. ANOM, EE/ii/2294/5, Beaudu to Minister of Colonies, October 25, 1924. "I ardently hope that my request will find the way to your heart. . . . And I thank you in advance for whatever you can do . . . to get me out of my painful situation."

18. NAI, N 431/1913, Waller to Colonial Secretary, April 7, 1913.

19. PRAAD, PF 3/3/29, Alexis to Governor of the Gold Coast, February 20, 1918. In August 1918, the governor of Trinidad informed the Colonial Office that there were no vacancies in the Trinidad Agriculture Department. Alexis also made transfer requests in February and September 1921. NAUK, CO 295/517, Governor of Trinidad to Secretary of State for the Colonies, August 9, 1918; PRAAD, PF 3/3/29, Governor of the Gold Coast to Secretary of State for the Colonies, February 21, 1921; and PRAAD, PF 3/3/29, W. D. Tudhope to Colonial Secretary of the Gold Coast, September 8, 1921.

20. PRAAD, PF 3/3/29, Gold Coast Director of Agriculture to Colonial Secretary of the Gold Coast, April 24, 1920.

21. NAUK, CO 295/539, Alexis to Secretary of State for the Colonies, December 5, 1921.

22. PRAAD, PF 3/3/29, Alexis African Service Sheet.

23. PRAAD, PF 3/3/29, W. T. Prout to Under Secretary of State for the Colonies, August 7, 1925.

24. PRAAD, PF 3/3/29, Proceedings of Medical Board Examination of Mark Alexis, October 29, 1926.

25. NAI, N 431/1913, Chief Registrar to Colonial Secretary, September 26, 1913.

26. ANOM, EE/ii/2294/5, Beaudu to Director, September 3, 1925.

27. ANOM, EE/ii/2294/5, Beaudu to Minister of Colonies, January 25, 1925.

28. ANOM, EE/ii/2294/5, Beaudu to Governor-General of Martinique, April 3, 1926.

29. ANOM, EE/ii/2294/5, Beaudu to Minister of Colonies, August 22, 1930.

30. Guha, "Not at Home in Empire." There was more to this feeling than the "anxiety" that Ranajit Guha describes among British administrators in India, however, because

Caribbean administrators longed not for the metropole but rather for a home outside of empire.

31. See, e.g., Chakrabarty, *Provincializing Europe*; Hamilton et al., *Refiguring the Archive*; Stoler, *Along the Archival Grain*; and Trouillot, *Silencing the Past*.

32. Stoler, *Along the Archival Grain*, 47.

33. An early and influential text in this regard was Pratt, *Imperial Eyes*.

34. Listing these countries, it is hard not to think of Lara Putnam's insights about transnational historical research. "You should not have to use archives in five countries to get a job," she writes. "And if you do use archives in five countries, as readers we must presume that you did not get to know all five especially well." Putnam, "The Transnational and the Text-Searchable," 401.

35. Edwards, "The Taste of the Archive," 948.

36. NAUK, CO 583/40, Simmons to Crown Agents, October 5, 1915.

37. According to Simmons's agreement, he was entitled to a free passage back to Trinidad only "on the satisfactory completion" of his three-year agreement. The colonial government in Nigeria appears to have ignored section 8 of this agreement, however, which states, "In the event of the person engaged being incapacitated by accident or by ill-health from carrying out the terms of this agreement, the Government may terminate the same and in such case shall provide the person engaged with a free second class passage back to [Trinidad]." NAUK, CO 583/22, "West Indian Railway Employees," June 1914; and NAUK, CO 741/1, "List of Appointments, Increments, Reductions, and Leave Granted during September 1914."

38. NAUK, CO 583/40, Note by Colonial Office official in file on Simmons, October 13, 1915.

39. NAUK, CO 583/40, Draft letter in file on Simmons, October 16, 1915.

40. On the Colonial Office holdings at the UK National Archives, see Banton, *Administering the Empire, 1801–1968*.

41. NAUK, CO 583/42, S. J. Langford, Acting Clerk to the Guardians, to Secretary of State for the Colonies, October 22, 1915.

42. This decision was hardly one of compassion, however. As the Secretary of State for the Colonies noted, if they did not send Simmons back to his "native Colony," he would be "for some time at least a charge of public funds." NAUK, CO 583/42, Draft letter from Secretary of State for the Colonies to Governor of Nigeria, November 8, 1915.

43. NAUK, FamilySearch Genealogy Service, List of Outgoing Passengers, *Catalina*, November 22, 1915.

44. Putnam adds that "when historians research far from home but don't stay around long enough to be inconvenienced, insulted, or instructed, the quality of their analysis suffers." Putnam, "The Transnational and the Text-Searchable," 394, 396.

45. Sharpe, *Immaterial Archives*, 56.

46. NAUK, CO 583/40, Simmons to Crown Agents, October 5, 1915.

47. Many of the railway workers who arrived in 1914 were recruited by F. H. Waller during his tour of Barbados, Trinidad, and British Guiana in June and July 1914. Janzen, "Tensions on the Railway." Waller was the same general manager of the Nigerian railway who reported the death of Frank Reid.

48. "Nigerian Justice," *African Times and Orient Review*, June 30, 1914, 353–56.

49. NAUK, CO 137/699, Governor of Jamaica to Secretary of State for the Colonies, October 15, 1913. On Shackleford, see Okonkwo, "Amos Stanley Wynter Shackleford"; Okonkwo, "The Garvey Movement in British West Africa"; and Okonkwo, "A Jamaican Export to Nigeria!"

50. *Saro* is a Yoruba term for the descendants of "liberated Africans" who returned to Nigeria from Sierra Leone in the nineteenth century. On Shackleford's friendship with Thomas, see chapter 6 in this volume.

51. Shackleford was not the first West Indian to establish himself in Lagos. One earlier example is Robert Campbell, born in Jamaica in 1829, who arrived in Lagos in 1862 and ran a newspaper. On Campbell, see Blackett, "Return to the Motherland."

52. NAI, N 939/1920, "Kryenhoff Statement of Account."

53. Amos Shackleford, letter to the editor, *Lagos Standard*, November 13, 1918, 7.

54. NAI, N 939/1920, W. A. Branker to Colonial Secretary of British Guiana, January 19, 1920.

55. Arthur later found himself in similar difficult circumstances. He retired from the railway in 1938 after twenty-five years of service but remained in Nigeria. By 1950, he had fallen on hard times. In a letter to the Nigerian government, he described himself as "a West Indian recruited in 1914 to work for Nigerian Railway." He also noted that King George V had decorated him for conscientious Empire Service, but that since World War II he was reduced to "beggary." The administration did not offer Arthur any support. Arthur to Chief Secretary of Government, April 14, 1950, Nigerian Railway Corporation Headquarters, Ebute Metta, Nigeria, SL 696; Lindsay, *Working with Gender*, 67, 75 n. 59; and Lisa Lindsay, personal communication with the author, April 28, 2015.

56. The details of this story are from NAI, N 939/1920.

57. In October 1914, Kryenhoff himself had come to the support of a West Indian railway worker. Theophilus Augustus King of British Guiana died of heart disease en route to Nigeria to work as a signaler on the railway. He was "buried at sea" near Madeira on October 30. Kryenhoff, who was on the same boat, ensured that King's belongings were "sealed and weighed" properly and returned to King's "legal heirs" in Demerara. On this case, see NAI, N 4248/1914.

58. FCDG, FFE, F22/20, Folder 1, Jules Ninine to Félix Eboué, November 20, 1940.

59. Renwick, "Forty Years On . . . ," 216.

60. Weinstein, *Eboué*, 48.

61. Members of the cricket teams included Leslie A. Barnett, Horatio Llewellyn Lake, Leonard Willoughby Blackmann, and H. Smart, among others. "R.W.I.E Recreation Club," *Sierra Leone Weekly News*, March 16, 1918, 5; "Athletics," *Sierra Leone Weekly News*, December 28, 1918, 2; and "Civil Service Cricket Tournament—1919," *Colonial and Provincial Reporter*, February 1, 1919, 6.

62. ANOM, ANS, 17G/243, "Incident du Soudan Club de Bamako."

63. From 1946 until 1955, Silvandre was deputy for Soudan Français in the Assemblée Nationale: "Jean Silvandre, 1896–1960," Assemblée Nationale website, accessed January 22, 2022, http://www2.assemblee-nationale.fr/sycomore/fiche/(num_dept)/6839.

64. UWISC, GJC, Box 3, Folder 72, George Christian to Percy Roberts, January 26, 1925.

65. Lamming, *The Pleasures of Exile*, 214.

66. "Coomassie," *Gold Coast Nation*, October 12, 1916, 1507; and "Coomassie," *Gold Coast Leader*, November 4, 1916, 2.

CHAPTER 4. BURIED VOCABULARIES

1. Lamming, *The Pleasures of Exile*, 161. On Boy Scouts in Ghana and its competitor, the Young Pioneers, see Ahlman, *Living with Nkrumahism*, chap. 3.
2. Lamming, *The Pleasures of Exile*, 162.
3. Hélénon, *French Caribbeans in Africa*, 41.
4. NATT, CSO 7452/1912–1926, Milton Fairley to Colonial Secretary of Trinidad, February 8, 1914.
5. NAUK, CO 96/511, Elias Buckmire to W. D. Tudhope, Director of Agriculture, September 30, 1911.
6. NAUK, CO 96/511, Tudhope to Colonial Secretary of the Gold Coast, November 7, 1911.
7. "Seccondee," *Gold Coast Leader*, November 5, 1910, 4.
8. "Seccondee," *Gold Coast Leader*, November 5, 1910, 4, emphasis in original.
9. In April 1910, there was an outbreak of yellow fever in Sekondi that resulted in at least twelve deaths. NAUK, CO 1071/155, Gold Coast Colonial Report 1912, 43–44.
10. When he applied to work in the Gold Coast, McNeil-Stewart listed Reverend Herbert Melville of St. Margaret's in Belmont as a reference. NATT, CSO 7505/1909, McNeil-Stewart Application for Colonial Employment.
11. NATT, CSO 7505/1909, Engagement of Sanitary Inspectors. The Colonial Office offered to pay for McNeil-Stewart's wife to travel to West Africa but was unwilling to pay for the two children. PRAAD, PF 3/32/922/923, McNeil-Stewart Personnel File, McNeil-Stewart to Under Secretary of State for the Colonies, April 8, 1913.
12. The colonial report for 1912 lists £3,475,832 in total trade at the Sekondi port. For comparison, the total value of trade that moved through the Accra port in 1912 was £2,320,094. NAUK, CO 1071/155, Gold Coast Colonial Report 1912, 13.
13. On sanitation measures and town planning in Sekondi and other urban centers in the Gold Coast, see Amoako-Gyampah, "Town Planning, Housing, and the Politics of Sanitation and Public Health in the Gold Coast (Colonial Ghana), c. 1880–1950."
14. In 1912, for example, there were 5,590 convictions in the Gold Coast for "offences against sanitary laws and regulations." NAUK, CO 1071/155, Gold Coast Colonial Report 1912, 30.
15. "Editorial Notes," *Gold Coast Leader*, March 22, 1913, 3–4.
16. "Editorial Notes," *Gold Coast Leader*, April 19, 1913, 3–4. McNeil-Stewart was the only West Indian sanitary inspector in Sekondi, though this same phrase seems to have been used in reference to Cunliffe Hoyte in 1911. See chapter 2 in this volume.
17. The latter was likely John Barbour-James, who worked at the post office in Sekondi. The editors of *The Gold Coast Leader* refused to publish these letters, however, declaring them "presumptuous and impertinent." "Editorial Notes," *Gold Coast Leader*, April 19, 1913, 3–4. British Guiana's letter, which praised McNeil-Stewart's work, was later published in *The Gold Coast Nation*, May 8, 1913, 294.
18. On Christian's remarkable story, see Rouse-Jones and Appiah, *Returned Exile*.
19. "Seccondee," *Gold Coast Leader*, December 9, 1911, 3.

20. Bekele, "The History of Cocoa Production in Trinidad and Tobago."

21. Austin, "Vent for Surplus or Productivity Breakthrough?"; and Dickson, *A Historical Geography of Ghana*.

22. NATT, CSO 7505/1909, McNeil-Stewart Application for Colonial Employment. On roads and transportation through Swedru and other parts of the Gold Coast during this period, see Wrangham, "An African Road Revolution."

23. Rita Pemberton, "Ancestors Weep: Lessons from the Silk Cotton Tree," *Trinidad and Tobago Newsday*, December 10, 2020, https://newsday.co.tt/2020/12/10/ancestors-weep-lessons-from-silk-cotton-tree; Joseph, "History and Public Memory in Tobago," 261–65; and Brand, *A Map to the Door of No Return*, 43–44. In Brand's retelling of the story, Gang Gang Sarah does return to Africa.

24. McNeil-Stewart's annual salary was £180, while the annual cost of keeping both children in school in England was £84. PRAAD, ADM 1/1/178, Secretary of State for the Colonies to Governor of the Gold Coast, August 6, 1909; and PRAAD, PF 3/32/922/923, McNeil-Stewart to Under Secretary of State for the Colonies, April 8, 1913.

25. PRAAD, PF 3/32/922/923, General Instructions for Language Exam.

26. McNeil-Stewart scored 15 out of 20 for reading, 14 out of 20 for translation, 7 out of 10 for writing, and 36 out of 40 for conversation. PRAAD, PF 3/32/922/923, Acting Provincial Commissioner to Colonial Secretary, Accra, July 4, 1916.

27. "Agona-Nsaba," *Gold Coast Leader*, November 4, 1916, 3.

28. Lise Winer suggests that *conkee* in Trinidad Creole, sometimes called *paime*, may come from the Fante word *kenkey*. Winer, *Dictionary of the English/Creole of Trinidad and Tobago on Historical Principles*, 241.

29. PRAAD, PF 3/32/922/923, McNeil-Stewart to Governor Guggisberg, December 1919; and PRAAD, PF 3/32/922/923, McNeil-Stewart Agreement, February 5, 1917.

30. PRAAD, PF 3/32/922/923, McNeil-Stewart to F. G. Guggisberg, December 1919.

31. Rhys, *Voyage in the Dark*, 17.

32. This passage combines elements from Sam Selvon's *The Lonely Londoners* with language from McNeil-Stewart's 1919 letter describing his family's hardships in wartime London. Selvon, *The Lonely Londoners*, 101–10; and PRAAD, PF 3/32/922/923, McNeil-Stewart to F. G. Guggisberg, December 1919. On air raids in London during World War I, see Grayzel, *At Home and Under Fire*, chap. 3.

33. McCaskie, *Asante Identities*, 144.

34. Kwabena Bonsu, ASSC, 9.66, quoted in McCaskie, *Asante Identities*, 145–46. The statistics and descriptions of Kumasi in this section are from McCaskie, *Asante Identities*, chap. 4; McCaskie, "'Water Wars' in Kumasi, Ghana"; and Yeboah, "Phoenix Rise."

35. On life in late nineteenth-century Port of Spain, see Brereton, *Race Relations in Colonial Trinidad, 1870–1900*, chap. 6; and Warner-Lewis, *Trinidad Yoruba*, chap. 2.

36. PRAAD, PF 3/32/922/923, Report on the Examination of Mr. David McNeil Stewart, July 28, 1917.

37. I have reproduced the Fante text as it appears on the exam. My thanks to Efua Osam for her help with the translation from Fante to English.

38. For an overview of recent scholarship on World War I in Africa, see Samson, "Unravelling the Past." On West Africans in East Africa during the war, see Killingray and Matthews, "Beasts of Burden."

39. I have reproduced the Fante text as it appears on the exam. My thanks again to Efua Osam for her help with the translation from Fante to English.

40. During his initial medical exam in Trinidad in 1909, McNeil-Stewart claimed that he did not drink spirits, though did drink an "occasional glass of beer." NATT, CSO 7505/1909, Medical Examination of Officers in Cases of Transfer.

41. Christaller, *A Dictionary of the Asante and Fante Language*, 40–41, 54, 320, 371, 417. In Twi, rum is also known as *aworonte* while *apo so nsa* refers to an "overseas drink." Akyeampong, *Drink, Power, and Cultural Change*, 15, 27.

42. On the history of rum and alcohol in Ghana, see Akyeampong, *Drink, Power, and Cultural Change*; Akyeampong and Ntewusu, "Rum, Gin, and Maize"; and Dumett, "The Social Impact of the European Liquor Trade on the Akan of Ghana (Gold Coast and Asante), 1875–1910."

43. There is an abundance of scholarship about African influences on Caribbean creoles. See, e.g., Alleyne, *Comparative Afro-American*; Allsopp, *Dictionary of Caribbean English Usage*; Ferreira, "Caribbean Languages and Caribbean Linguistics"; Holm, *Pidgins and Creoles*; Warner-Lewis, *Central Africa in the Caribbean*; and Warner-Lewis, *Trinidad Yoruba*.

44. Walcott, "The Antilles," 70.

45. On English, French, and Creole in 1860s Trinidad, see Thomas, *The Theory and Practice of Creole Grammar*.

46. Mahabir, *The Still Cry*.

47. Brereton, *Race Relations in Colonial Trinidad, 1870–1900*, 134. By 1891, there were about two thousand African-born people in Trinidad.

48. *The Chronicle*, October 17, 1871, March 30, 1877, quoted in Warner-Lewis, *Trinidad Yoruba*, 41. See also Warner-Lewis, *Central Africa in the Caribbean*.

49. Carr, "A Rada Community in Trinidad"; and Senah, "Rada."

50. Warner-Lewis, *Guinea's Other Suns*, 30.

51. References in this section come from Allsopp, *Dictionary of Caribbean English Usage*; Christaller, *A Dictionary of the Asante and Fante Language*; and Winer, *Dictionary of the English/Creole of Trinidad and Tobago on Historical Principles*.

52. Walcott, "The Antilles," 70.

53. On the early outlines of such debates, see Alleyne, *Comparative Afro-American*; Allsopp, *Dictionary of Caribbean English Usage*; and Aub-Buscher, "African Survivals in the Lexicon of Trinidad French-Based Creole."

54. "Coomassie," *Gold Coast Leader*, September 15, 1917, 2.

55. James W. Appiah, misprinted in this article as "J. M. Appiah," was the father of Joe Appiah, a leading nationalist politician and Nkrumah's onetime ally, as well as the grandfather of Kwame Anthony Appiah. James Appiah also worked with McNeil-Stewart on the Kumasi Red Cross Committee, where McNeil-Stewart was president and Appiah was secretary. "Coomassie," *Gold Coast Leader*, September 29, 1917, 3.

56. On early twentieth-century Keta, see Akyeampong, *Between the Sea and the Lagoon*; Greene, *Gender, Ethnicity, and Social Change in the Upper Slave Coast*; and Greene, *Sacred Sites and the Colonial Encounter*.

57. Greene, *West African Narratives of Slavery*, 204–5.

58. PRAAD, PF 3/32/922/923, McNeil-Stewart to F. G. Guggisberg, December 1919.

59. PRAAD, PF 3/32/922/923, Senior Sanitary Officer to McNeil-Stewart, May 20, 1920.

60. On Togbi Sri II, see Akyeampong, *Between the Sea and the Lagoon*, chaps. 2–3; Agboada, "The Reign and Times of Togbi Sri II of Anlo, 1906–1956"; Greene, *Sacred Sites and the Colonial Encounter*, esp. chaps. 2–3; and Mamattah, *The Ewes of West Africa*, 204–10.

61. On this contentious election, sometimes dated to 1906, see Akyeampong, *Between the Sea and the Lagoon*, 112–13. The Anlo elders who helped install Sri II were keen to use their connections with the colonial government for their own ends, including smuggling across the border into German Togoland. Greene, *Sacred Sites and the Colonial Encounter*, 43.

62. For example, when Anloga burned in 1911, Sri II and his political advisers attempted to plan a "modern" town that aligned with the aims of the British government. Greene, *Sacred Sites and the Colonial Encounter*, 76.

63. On the implications of these religious changes in southeastern Ghana, see Greene, *Sacred Sites and the Colonial Encounter*; and Venkatachalam, *Slavery, Memory, and Religion in Southeastern Ghana, c. 1850–Present*.

64. Akyeampong, *Between the Sea and the Lagoon*, 113.

65. Sri II and other Anlo leaders were also eager to alleviate the harsh taxes and forced labor regulations endured by Anlo-Ewe people in German Togoland. Notably, while Sri II offered soldiers to fight in Togo, he refused to send soldiers to East Africa. Akyeampong, *Between the Sea and the Lagoon*, 191–92; and Greene, *Gender, Ethnicity, and Social Change in the Upper Slave Coast*, 142.

66. Angelou, *All God's Children Need Traveling Shoes*, 201–2. This memoir describes Angelou's time in Ghana between 1962 and 1965. Excerpts from *All God's Children Need Traveling Shoes* by Maya Angelou, copyright © 1986 by Caged Bird Legacy LLC. Used by permission of Random House, an imprint and division of Penguin Random House LLC. All rights reserved. Reproduced with permission of the Licensor through PLSclear.

67. My description of this event comes from "Notable Events at Quittah," *Gold Coast Leader*, October 15, 1921, 7–8; and "Quittah," *Gold Coast Leader*, October 1, 1921, 3. Harding had begun his career in southern Africa working for the colonial police in what was then northwestern Rhodesia. On Harding, see Vickery, *Black and White in Southern Zambia*. See also Harding's autobiography, *In Remotest Barotseland*.

68. Angelou, *All God's Children Need Traveling Shoes*, 202.

69. PRAAD, PF 3/32/922/923, Togbi Sri II to Medical Officer of Keta, August 11, 1921.

70. "Quittah," *Gold Coast Leader*, August 6–13, 1921, 8. McNeil-Stewart was also the president of the Literary and Social Club, and he occasionally hosted parties at his bungalow. "Quittah," *Gold Coast Leader*, April 23, 1921, 3.

71. "The African Progress Union," *Gold Coast Leader*, August 20, 1920, 5–6; and "African Progress Union Dinner," *Gold Coast Leader*, March 26, 1921, 4–5.

72. Weston Library, Oxford University, H2/70, *Constitution of the African Progress Union* (London: Furnival Press, 1918).

73. On March 26, 1921, *The Gold Coast Leader* featured a full-page write-up on the African Progress Union meeting of February 18, 1921. The article described speeches by John Barbour-James, Joseph Casely Hayford, Herbert Bankole-Bright, and Thomas Hutton-Mills, among others. "African Progress Union Dinner," *Gold Coast Leader*, March 26, 1921, 4–5, reprinted from *West Africa*, February 26, 1921.

74. Angelou, *All God's Children Need Traveling Shoes*, 203–4.

75. On Pomeyie (1889–1938), see Mamattah, *The Ewes of West Africa*, 439–40.

76. On the AME Zion Church in West Africa, see Greene, *West African Narratives of Slavery*, chap. 8; and Yates, "The History of the African Methodist Episcopal Zion Church in West Africa, Liberia, Gold Coast (Ghana) and Nigeria, 1900–1939."

77. In 1907, these two men were part of the group that ensured the selection of Sri II as *awoamefia*. Greene, *Sacred Sites and the Colonial Encounter*, 43–44.

78. "Quittah," *Gold Coast Leader*, July 4, 1914, 6.

79. This number included students. Yates, "History of the African Methodist Episcopal Zion Church in West Africa, Liberia, Gold Coast (Ghana) and Nigeria, 1900–1939," 148.

80. "Quittah," *Gold Coast Leader*, April 22, 1922, 8.

81. Samuel Athanasius Pomeyie, "The Ideal Teacher, and Racial Consciousness," *Gold Coast Independent*, November 11, 1922, 523.

82. For example, in July 1922, McNeil-Stewart gave an address on sanitation at an AME Zion Church conference. *Missionary Seer*, vol. 22, no. 9, September 1922, 8.

83. Angelou, *All God's Children Need Traveling Shoes*, 204–5.

84. Greene, *West African Narratives of Slavery*, 198.

85. According to Greene, this term was used to describe Europeans as well as Africans "who were seen as having adopted aspects of European culture." Greene, *West African Narratives of Slavery*, 204–5.

86. Greene, *West African Narratives of Slavery*, 205.

87. This version of the "Atorkor Incident" comes from Bailey, *African Voices of the Atlantic Slave Trade*, 33–34; and Greene, *West African Narratives of Slavery*, 187–88. Both of their accounts are based on oral histories collected in Atorkor and elsewhere in the region, including from Ndorkutsu's great-grandson.

88. Greene, *West African Narratives of Slavery*, 210.

89. In her analysis of this "reconfigured" story, Greene explains that while conducting research in Anloga in 1978, several men stopped her in the market square and "insisted" that she was "a descendant of people from Atorkor." Greene, *West African Narratives of Slavery*, 212.

90. Angelou, *All God's Children Need Traveling Shoes*, 206. For a powerful reflection on these passages from Angelou's memoir, see Mukoma wa Ngugi, "Blackness, Africans, and African Americans."

91. PRAAD, PF 3/32/922/923, Certificate of Service.

92. PRAAD, PF 3/32/922/923, McNeil-Stewart to Medical Officer at Keta, October 6, 1922.

93. PRAAD, CSO.2–12–1212, Octavia McNeil-Stewart to Colonial Secretary's Office, Accra, April 28, 1947.

94. PRAAD, CSO.2–12–1212, Octavia McNeil-Stewart to Colonial Secretary's Office, Accra, October 6, 1947.

95. PRAAD, CSO.2–12–1212, Kenneth MacNeill Stewart to Sergeant-in-Charge, Asamankese, June 26, 1947.

96. PRAAD, CSO.2–12–1212, Octavia McNeil-Stewart to Colonial Secretary's Office, Accra, December 6, 1947.

97. Kenneth MacNeill Stewart, "The Ballad of Africanus," *Gold Coast Leader*, October 21, 1922, 3.

98. See, e.g., Sekyi's satirical play from 1915, *The Blinkards*. Sekyi was also a member of the National Congress of British West Africa and the Aborigines' Rights Protection Society. For analysis of this generation of intellectuals, see Esedebe, *Pan-Africanism*; Langley, *Pan-Africanism and Nationalism in West Africa, 1900–1945*; and Zachernuk, *Colonial Subjects*.

99. On newspapers and print culture in West Africa, see Peterson et al., *African Print Cultures*.

100. MacNeill Stewart attempted to publish some of these columns in London, and in a 1934 legal case he claimed that he was the sole author of all the Marjorie Mensah columns and thus owned the copyright. The court, however, found that many of the columns had been written by Mabel Dove, who married J. B. Danquah in 1933, and by Ruby Quartey-Papafio. On MacNeill Stewart and this case in particular, see Newell, *The Power to Name*, 164–66; and Prais, "Imperial Travelers," chaps. 4, 6.

101. Azikiwe, *My Odyssey*, 259. Also quoted in Prais, "Imperial Travelers," 255.

102. "Quarterly Notes," *African Affairs* 51, no. 205 (October 1952): 305. The editor of *African Affairs* at this time was Henry Swanzy. Since 1946, Swanzy had also run the British Broadcasting Corporation's famous *Caribbean Voices* program, taking over from Una Marson. Jarrett-Macauley, *The Life of Una Marson, 1905–65*.

103. Kenneth MacNeill Stewart, "An Idea of Happiness," *African Affairs* 51, no. 203 (April 1952): 155–56; and Kenneth MacNeill Stewart, "Ode to Stools and Stool Worship," *African Affairs* 52, no. 208 (July 1953): 185–87.

104. MacNeill Stewart, "Ode to Independence," 2.

105. MacNeill Stewart, "Ode to Independence," 2, emphasis added.

106. Lamming, *The Pleasures of Exile*, 163.

107. The most comprehensive book on this topic is Gaines, *American Africans in Ghana*. See also Okuda, "Caribbean and African Exchanges."

108. Lamming, *The Pleasures of Exile*, 155.

109. Alongside Hoyte there was also George Stanley Lewis of St. Lucia, the brother of W. Arthur Lewis, who came to the Gold Coast in 1929. When he died in Ghana in December 1999, the funeral program listed Hoyte alongside Lewis and several others as the West Indian "Pioneers" who "settled in the Gold Coast." UWISC, GJC, Box 1, Folder 19, "Burial and Thanksgiving Service for the Life of George Stanley Lewis."

110. Lamming, *The Pleasures of Exile*, 155.

111. Neville Dawes was born in Warri, Nigeria. Baugh, "Neville Dawes, 1926–1984"; and Dawes and Dawes, *Fugue and Other Writings*. Kwame Dawes, the son of Neville Dawes, is a prolific author, poet, and playwright and the George Holmes Distinguished Professor of English at the University of Nebraska-Lincoln.

CHAPTER 5. INTIMATE GEOGRAPHIES

1. On the intertwined memories of Eboué and de Gaulle in Central Africa, see Bernault, *Démocraties ambiguës en Afrique Centrale*, 137–47. Of the many books on Eboué, the most comprehensive remains Weinstein, *Eboué*. For a more recent biography, see Capdepuy, *Félix Eboué*.

2. Eboué died in Cairo in May 1944, but in 1949 the French government relocated his remains to the Panthéon, alongside the remains of Victor Schoelcher.

3. Janzen, "Linga's Dream?"

4. "Historique de la Fondation," Charles de Gaulle Foundation website, accessed February 19, 2023, https://www.charles-de-gaulle.org/la-fondation/historique.

5. On de Gaulle's meetings at no. 5 Rue de Solférino between 1946 and 1958, see Jackson, *De Gaulle*, esp. pt. 3.

6. Eboué's son-in-law, Pierre Fontaine, donated the collection to the Fondation in 1999. FCDG, FFE, F22, "Inventaire détaillé."

7. Eboué, *Les peuples de l'Oubangui-Chari*. On the links between colonialism and anthropology, see Asad, *Anthropology and the Colonial Encounter*; Pels and Salemink, *Colonial Subjects*; and Said, *Orientalism*. On colonial anthropology in France, see Conklin, *In the Museum of Man*; Sibeud, *Une science impériale pour l'Afrique?*; and Wilder, "Colonial Ethnology and Political Rationality in French West Africa."

8. Weinstein, *Eboué*, 17–21.

9. Kruger, who died in July 1904, was revered by many in France and was welcomed to the country in 1900 when he came to ask for support in the fight against the British. Eboué apparently hung a poster of Kruger in his room and grew a beard like Kruger's. Maran, *Félix Eboué*, 12–14.

10. Florence Bernault writes that those who were assigned to AEF considered it "at best an inglorious stage at the beginning of a career, at worst a repressive measure (*sanction*)." Bernault, *Démocraties ambiguës en Afrique Centrale*, 45. Phyllis Martin similarly notes that Brazzaville was considered "the impoverished capital of an imperial backwater" and that "Central Africa ranked at the bottom of French colonial priorities." Martin, *Leisure and Society in Colonial Brazzaville*, 8, 12.

11. Kalck, *Central African Republic*, 55.

12. "Rapport d'Ensemble sur la situation générale de l'Oubangui-Chari en 1914," 48, quoted in Weinstein, *Eboué*, 44.

13. Eboué notebook entry, December 1927, quoted in Weinstein, *Eboué*, 56.

14. Eboué to Maran, March 21, 1928, quoted in Weinstein, *Eboué*, 116. Between 1925 and 1932, approximately 42,000 men were taken from Oubangui-Chari. Sautter, "Notes sur la construction du chemin de fer Congo-Océan (1921–1934)," 258–59, quoted in Weinstein, *Eboué*, 100. For a recent overview of the construction of the Congo-Océan Railway, see Daughton, *In the Forest of No Joy*.

15. Conklin, *A Mission to Civilize*, esp. chap. 7.

16. FCDG, FFE, F22/1, Eboué Notebook, 1911.

17. On Delafosse and colonial anthropology in France, see Amselle and Sibeud, *Maurice Delafosse*.

18. Eboué, *Langues sango, banda, baya, mandjia*.

19. Eboué and Narcisse Simonin later coauthored "Les Bayas de l'Ouham Pende."

20. In this section I have relied on the insights of Marcel Diki-Kidiri, as well as a number of dictionaries: Bouquiaux et al., *Dictionnaire sango-français*; Calloc'h, *Vocabulaire français-sango et sango-français, langue commerciale de l'Oubangui-Chari, précédé d'un abrégé grammatical*; Giraud, *Vocabulaire des dialectes sango, bakongo et a'zandé*; Taber, *A*

Dictionary of Sango; Tisserant, *Dictionnaire Banda-Français*; and Tisserant, *Sango, langue véhiculaire de l'Oubangui-Chari*.

21. When the Bandia conquered the western parts of Nzakara territory, they imposed their hierarchical, centralized political system but adopted Nzakara language and culture in daily life. Traces of Ngbandi words, however, such as *gbïä*, endured in Nzakara political organization. On Bandia history, see de Dampierre, *Un ancien royaume bandia du Haut-Oubangui*.

22. De Dampierre, *Un ancien royaume bandia du Haut-Oubangui*, 14.

23. The word is also spelled *mokonji* or *mokönzi*. Pierre Kalck, who was a colonial administrator in Oubangui-Chari, suggested that "the idea of a chief whose competence was restricted to a given geographical area was so alien to traditional Central African conceptions that the people invented a new term, of foreign origin, to refer to these official chiefs." Kalck, *Central African Republic*, 28. Didier Gondola similarly explains that in late nineteenth-century Congo, Bobangi traders began using the term *mokonzi* for the leaders of new, larger villages or settlements. Gondola also claims that *mokonzi* derived from the Bobangi word *konza*, a term that "conjures up images of wealth and prosperity." Gondola, *Tropical Cowboys*, 27. See also Harms, *River of Wealth, River of Sorrow*, 143.

24. FCDG, FFE, F22/5, Folder 2, "Notes sur la Grammaire et le Vocabulaire de la langue Zande."

25. Weinstein, *Eboué*, 45, 166.

26. On Eboué's relationship with Sokambi and other leaders, and their suppression of rebellions, see Weinstein, "Eboué and the Chiefs."

27. Eboué, *Les peuples de l'Oubangui-Chari*, 67.

28. Eboué, *La nouvelle politique indigène pour l'Afrique Équatoriale Française*, 15. Elsewhere in the document, Eboué claimed that chiefs were part of a "true native bourgeoisie" and that they should be considered "members of a natural aristocracy," not "employee[s] of the state." Eboué believed that this aristocracy, this elite class of "*notables évolués*," would help to run AEF. Eboué, *La nouvelle politique indigène pour l'Afrique Équatoriale Française*, 18–19, 25–27. Bernault explains that the *évolués* did not end up becoming the intermediary class that Eboué envisioned, in large part because the French made it incredibly difficult to achieve this status. Bernault, *Démocraties ambiguës en Afrique Centrale*, 89–92, 332–33.

29. Eboué to Maran, July 24, 1924, quoted in Maran, *Félix Eboué*, 80.

30. This was also the case with *makūdji*, normally written *mokönzi*. Instead of noting the prenasalized consonant, *nz*, Eboué seems instead to have nasalized the *ū*, which does not reflect the phonology of Sango.

31. Bouquiaux et al., *Dictionnaire sango-français*, 223.

32. Eboué, *Langues sango, banda, baya, mandjia*, 6.

33. Eboué, *Langues sango, banda, baya, mandjia*, 6.

34. Bouquiaux et al., *Dictionnaire sango-français*, 144.

35. Yvonne Bastin et al., "Bantu Lexical Reconstructions 3," Royal Museum for Central Africa, Tervuren, Belgium, no. 1331, https://www.africamuseum.be/en/research/discover/human_sciences/culture_society/blr; and Vansina, *Paths in the Rainforests*, 298. For analysis of *-gàng-* in an Atlantic context, see de Luna, "Sounding the African Atlantic";

and Rey, "Kongolese Catholic Influences on Haitian Popular Catholicism." It is also possible that the Sango word *kânga* came from the Bantu root **-kúng*, "to gather."

36. Guyer and Belinga, "Wealth in People as Wealth in Knowledge"; Kopytoff and Miers, *Slavery in Africa*; and Vansina, *Paths in the Rainforests*.

37. On Eboué's childhood, see Weinstein, *Eboué*, chap. 1.

38. Cordell, *Dar al-Kuti and the Last Years of the Trans-Saharan Slave Trade*. See also Ceriana Mayneri, *Sorcellerie et prophétisme en Centrafrique*, 25–32.

39. Eboué may have been oblivious to the tonal differences of *kanga* and *kânga*, but he was familiar with colonial prisons. In 1920, two years after the publication of the dictionary, the governor-general of AEF specifically disparaged Eboué for what he considered unwarranted use of the *Code de l'Indigénat*, the code of laws used to put Africans in prison without trials for a maximum sentence of fifteen days. Weinstein, *Eboué*, 64. On the history of confinement in Africa, see Bernault, *Enfermement, prison, et châtiments en Afrique du 19e siècle à nos jours*.

40. Subsequent dictionaries provide similar translations. See Bouquiaux et al., *Dictionnaire sango-français*; Taber, *A Dictionary of Sango*; and Tisserant, *Dictionnaire Banda-Français*.

41. Feierman, *Peasant Intellectuals*, 11.

42. On the "social basis" of health and healing in Africa, the classic texts are Feierman, "Struggles for Control"; Feierman and Janzen, *The Social Basis of Health and Healing in Africa*; Janzen, *Lemba, 1650–1930*; and Janzen, *The Quest for Therapy*.

43. Tisserant, *Dictionnaire Banda-Français*, 204.

44. Other dictionaries use *evinga* or *avinga*. Diki-Kidiri proposes *axînga*, using the *x* to represent the labiodental flap in Banda. Marcel Diki-Kidiri, personal communication with the author, March 13, 2024.

45. Tisserant, *Dictionnaire Banda-Français*, 41–42.

46. In Sango, qualifying adjectives such as *vukö* normally appear before the noun they refer to, while quantifying adjectives usually appear after the noun. When qualifying adjectives are positioned after a noun, however, it produces a special meaning. Marcel Diki-Kidiri, personal communication with the author, March 13, 2024.

47. Bouquiaux et al., *Dictionnaire sango-français*, 233, 352, 396; and Taber, *A Dictionary of Sango*, 123.

48. On Maran and this term, see chapter 2 in this volume. A more recent dictionary suggests that Sango speakers use *mbunzu vuko* to refer to all Antilleans. Chaduteau, *Sango, langue nationale de Centrafrique*, 145.

49. As Rachel Jean-Baptiste notes, most *colons* who had children with African women "did not acknowledge paternity, provide financial resources, or maintain contact." Jean-Baptiste, *Multiracial Identities in Colonial French Africa*, 7. On the "sexual economy" of Central Africa, see also Jean-Baptiste, *Conjugal Rights*.

50. Weinstein, *Eboué*, 48.

51. Tisserant, *Dictionnaire Banda-Français*, 470–71. On *métis* children in Central Africa, see Jean-Baptiste, *Multiracial Identities in Colonial French Africa*. On *métis* children in West Africa, see Jones, *The Métis of Senegal*; Saada, *Les enfants de la colonie*; and White, *Children of the French Empire*.

52. On the history of citizenship in the French Caribbean, see Dubois, *A Colony of Citizens*; and Larcher, *L'autre citoyen*.

53. ANOM, AEF/GGAEF/5D44, Note regarding the ordinance project creating the Charity Protecting Métis of the Empire, General Directorate of Administrative and Political Affairs, April 11, 1941, quoted in Jean-Baptiste, *Multiracial Identities in Colonial French Africa*, 149.

54. Jean-Baptiste, *Multiracial Identities in Colonial French Africa*, 155.

55. Jean-Baptiste, *Multiracial Identities in Colonial French Africa*, 193. On citizenship in the French Empire after World War II, see Cooper, *Citizenship between Empire and Nation*.

56. Eboué to Maran, November 9, 1925, quoted in Weinstein, *Eboué*, 93.

57. Eboué to E. L. Boutin, August 30, 1928, quoted in Weinstein, *Eboué*, 110.

58. On the remarkable political career of Eugénie Eboué-Tell, see Joseph-Gabriel, *Reimagining Liberation*, esp. chap. 3.

59. Weinstein interview with Pierre Sondjio, brother of Bada Marcelline, June 30, 1968, quoted in Weinstein, *Eboué*, 115.

60. Henri and Robert Eboué remained in France, in boarding schools.

61. Weinstein, *Eboué*, 117.

62. FCDG, FFE, F22/4, Folder 2. The pamphlet was prepared by Joseph Halkin, a professor at the Université de Liège and author of *Les Ababua (Congo Belge)* (Brussels: A. de Wit, 1911). Among the different categories in the questionnaire were social organization, religion, family life, intellectual life, and language. Eboué's copy is heavily annotated.

63. When Eugénie Eboué-Tell first came to Oubangui-Chari in 1923, she brought a piano with her, hauled upriver in a large canoe. Weinstein, *Eboué*, 86.

64. Weinstein interview with Paul Doumatchi, Ippy, July 19, 1968. Weinstein, *Eboué*, 118–19. See also the *Journal Officiel de l'Afrique Equatoriale Française*, October 1, 1930, 835, and March 15, 1931, 217.

65. ANOM, AEF/GGAEF/D/4(3)/40, "Rapport Trimestriel, circonscription de la Ouaka, June 30, 1930."

66. *Journal Officiel de l'Afrique Equatoriale Française*, March 1, 1944, 198.

67. This collection is located in FCDG, FFE, F22/4, Folder 1.

68. The "folktale character" Tere changes "depending on the ethnic group" and is alternatively known as Ètèrè, Tòrò, Tòlò, and Tùnlè, among others. In different contexts, he is "a spirit of the earth, a civilizing hero, a cunning and deceitful character, a clever man caught in his own traps or a fool." Bouquiaux et al., *Dictionnaire sango-français*, 338. See also Ceriana Mayneri, *Sorcellerie et prophétisme en Centrafrique*, 80–88.

69. FCDG, FFE, F22/4, Folder 1. Gouandjia titled the notebook "Histoire des Animeaux," instead of "Animaux."

70. ANOM, AEF/GGAEF/D/4(3)/40, "Rapport Trimestriel, circonscription de la Ouaka, June 30, 1930."

71. Félix Eboué, "Les Eléphants et les Hippopotames," *La Revue du monde noir* no. 3 (1932): 35–36.

72. There was no standardized written Banda in 1930, so Gouandjia had to create orthographic conventions intuitively. That Gouandjia's work is possible to decode and understand more than ninety years later makes the text a remarkable achievement in its own right. On Banda languages, see Cloarec-Heiss, *Dynamique et équilibre d'une syntaxe*.

73. Garane, "The Invisibility of the African Interpreter."

74. In the table of contents for issue 3 of *La Revue du monde noir*, the story is described as an "African Fable."

75. Edwards, *The Practice of Diaspora*, 120.

76. Edwards suggests that scholars consider diasporic "conjunctures" beyond Paris—in Havana, Fort-de-France, Cotonou, Dakar, and elsewhere. Indeed, his powerful arguments about translation need not be limited to exchanges in cities or other imperial hubs. Edwards, *The Practice of Diaspora*, 9.

77. Another of Eboué's interpreters, Michel Goumba, was the father of Abel Goumba, who worked alongside Barthélemy Boganda in the 1940s and 1950s. Abel Goumba was also Boganda's student in Grimari. See Goumba, *Les mémoires et les réflexions politiques du résistant anti-colonial, démocrate et militant panafricaniste*.

78. As V. Y. Mudimbe famously articulated, Western scholars have often distorted "Africa" by expressing "African modalities in non-African languages" and by using the "anthropological and philosophical categories" of Western scholarship. Mudimbe, *The Invention of Africa*, 186.

79. Niranjana, *Siting Translation*, 2. On translation, invisibility, and colonialism, see also Cheyfitz, *The Poetics of Imperialism*; Robinson, *Translation and Empire*; and Venuti, *The Translator's Invisibility*.

80. Weinstein, *Eboué*, 156. Henri remained in France, while Robert and Charles traveled only as far as Dakar, where they enrolled at a lycée. Ginette accompanied her parents to Soudan Français.

81. Weinstein interview with Governor-General R. Bargues, March 26, 1968. Weinstein, *Eboué*, 163–64.

82. FCDG, FFE, F22/4, Folder 5, Draft preface for the *Annuaire de la vie martiniquaise*. The volume was published the following year in Martinique: Sylvestre and Lotaut, *Annuaire de la vie martiniquaise, 1936*. Eboué's preface in the published version was largely unchanged from this draft.

83. Duhamel, *Géographie cordiale de l'Europe*. It is possible that René Maran recommended Duhamel's book to Eboué. Maran later wrote reviews of Duhamel's 1948 book, *Le bestiaire et l'herbier*, and his 1949 work, *La pesée des âmes*. UCAD, FRM, Res. 5182.

84. "I go from town to town," Duhamel wrote, "from border to border, from people to people, sometimes joyful, sometimes disappointed, sometimes singing in the secret of my heart the funeral march of Europe, sometimes celebrating Europe's recovery and glory." Duhamel, *Géographie cordiale de l'Europe*, 21.

85. Césaire began writing the poem in summer 1935 while on a vacation in Croatia with a school friend, Petar Guberina. Césaire saw an island that reminded him of Martinique and was inspired when Guberina told him that the island was known as "Martin" or "Martinska." In Césaire's words, "After buying a *cahier d'écolier*, I started to write *Cahier d'un retour au pays natal*." Césaire, *Nègre je suis, nègre je resterai*, 26.

86. There are some connections between Eboué and Césaire. In 1933, Eboué had signed off on Césaire's scholarship from Martinique to continue studying in France. FCDG, FFE, F22/7, Folder 5, "Boursiers de la Martinique dans la Metropole, pendant l'année scolaire 1933–1934." Moreover, Eboué's son Henri was a friend of Césaire and other Antillean students in 1930s Paris. Weinstein, *Eboué*, 148–49. And, one of the contributors to the

Annuaire was Eugène Revert, who had been Césaire's teacher at the Lycée Schoelcher in Fort-de-France. Césaire credited Revert with moving beyond the curriculum and teaching about the natural marvels of Martinique. Louis, *Conversation avec Aimé Césaire*, 23–27.

87. For accounts of Sissoko's life and literary career, see Ministère de la Culture du Mali, *Tradition et modernité dans l'oeuvre littéraire de Fily Dabo Sissoko*; and Sidibe, *Fily Dabo Sissoko, un grand sage africain*.

88. Labrune-Badiane and Smith, *Les hussards noirs de la colonie*, 26. On this generation, see also Jézéquel, "Collecting Customary Law."

89. Labrune-Badiane and Smith, *Les hussards noirs de la colonie*, 11–12. When Eboué arrived in Soudan Français in 1934, Sissoko had already published an analysis about "l'enfant Bambara." Sissoko, "Enquête sur l'enfant noir de l'AOF."

90. Labrune-Badiane and Smith, *Les hussards noirs de la colonie*, 365.

91. ANOM, ANS, 17G/58, Lieutenant-Governor of Soudan Français to Governor-General of AOF, June 16, 1928.

92. Weinstein, *Eboué*, 163.

93. Weinstein, *Eboué*, 174. While in Soudan Français, Eboué was also in contact with Maximilien Quénum of Dahomey, and in 1936 he reviewed a draft of Quénum's *Au pays des Fons*, later published in 1938. Quénum sent Eboué a letter of gratitude, describing Eboué as a "guide" and a teacher" and noting that Eboué's name was "well-known in Dahomey." FCDG, FFE, F22/4, Folder 1, Quénum to Eboué, April 4, 1936.

94. FCDG, FFE, F22/3, Folder 8, Sissoko to Eboué, December 23, 1936. Sissoko was fifteen years younger than Eboué, and so he may have approached Eboué as a *koroké* (elder brother) and as a possible patron. My thanks to Greg Mann for bringing this possibility to my attention.

95. FCDG, FFE, F22/6, Folder 2, Sissoko, "La Politesse et les civilités des Noirs."

96. Labrune-Badiane and Smith, *Les hussards noirs de la colonie*, 304–5. In his letter to Eboué, Sissoko wrote, "I understood from the beginning that the Editor's note [*N.D.L.R*] which serves as an introduction and preface to my work, was from your pen. For this I thank you very sincerely, with all my heart." FCDG, FFE, F22/3, Folder 8, Sissoko to Eboué, December 23, 1936.

97. Sissoko, "La politesse et les civilités des Noirs," 12.

98. Sissoko, "La politesse et les civilités des Noirs," 12.

99. Sissoko, "La politesse et les civilités des Noirs," 14.

100. FCDG, FFE, F22/6, Folder 2, Sissoko, "La géomancie." The inscription was made by Sissoko at Horokoto on March 8, 1937.

101. Charles left for Cairo from Fort Lamy to attend a French Jesuit school. The other three children were in France.

102. MSRC, EGR, Box 13, Eslanda Goode Robeson, "Félix Eboué: The End of an Era," *New World Review* (October 1952): 47–48; and MSRC, EGR, Box 17, Diary no. 1, 1946, "African Trip," 57 (back). Weinstein, who recounts a similar version of this story, also notes that arguments between French administrators and African clerks in Brazzaville sometimes resulted in the senior administrators saying, "If you don't like my decision, you can go see *your* governor general, le gros singe, to complain." Weinstein, *Eboué*, 262.

103. FCDG, FFE, F22/18, Folder 3, "Message aux Antillais," July 21, 1943.

104. FCDG, FFE, F22/19, Folder 3, Fily Dabo Sissoko, "Vue d'ensemble de l'évolution culturelles des peuples coloniaux."
105. The conference was held in Paris in September 1937. Sissoko submitted a paper, "Les Noirs et la culture," but was not invited to appear in person. Labrune-Badiane and Smith, *Les hussards noirs de la colonie*, 454–55.
106. FCDG, FFE, F22/19, Folder 3, Sissoko, "Vue d'ensemble de l'évolution," 5.
107. FCDG, FFE, F22/19, Folder 3, Sissoko, "Vue d'ensemble de l'évolution," 19.
108. FCDG, FFE, F22/19, Folder 3, Sissoko, "Vue d'ensemble de l'évolution," 21.
109. Labrune-Badiane and Smith, *Les Hussards noirs de la colonie*, 459–60. On the ideas of Delafosse, Hardy, and other colonial reformers, see Wilder, *The French Imperial Nation-State*.
110. Labrune-Badiane and Smith, *Les hussards noirs de la colonie*, 507.
111. FCDG, FFE, F22/19, Folder 3, Sissoko, "Vue d'ensemble de l'évolution," 1.
112. Sissoko, *La savane rouge*. My thanks to Greg Mann for suggesting this connection. Sissoko does not mention Eboué in *La savane rouge*, but he does appear briefly in the context of the *ralliement* in *Une page est tournée*, a collection of Sissoko's essays published in 1959. Sissoko, *Une page est tournée*, 33, 37.
113. Sissoko, *La savane rouge*, 37, 35. On geography and the "voyage" in Sissoko's work, see Diallo, "La fonction initiatique du voyage dans l'oeuvre littéraire de Fily Dabo Sissoko."
114. In fact, Eboué's ethnographic research seems to have entrenched in him a commitment to an "enlightened" colonialism. In *La nouvelle politique indigène*, from 1941, he wrote, echoing Sissoko, "We will strive to develop [the native's] sense of dignity, responsibility, [and] moral progress ... but we will do so within the framework of his own natural institutions." Eboué, *La nouvelle politique indigène pour l'Afrique Équatoriale Française*, 12.
115. Eugénie Eboué Tell was among those who built on her husband's legacy. She also articulated her own vision of transatlantic connections. Elected to the French Senate from Guadeloupe in 1946, she demanded more support for African war veterans. "I ask the government and the entire assembly to consider that it is high time that we give satisfaction to the brothers of our race, to my brothers at the very least, in short, to our brothers." Eugénie Eboué-Tell, "Débats parlementaires, assemblée nationale," October 5, 1946, 4714, quoted in Joseph-Gabriel, *Reimagining Liberation*, 95.
116. Paulette Nardal, "Awakening of Race Consciousness," *La Revue du monde noir* no. 6 (1932): 30; and Félix Eboué, "La Musique et le Langage des Banda," *La Revue du monde noir*, no. 6 (1932): 32–34.
117. FCDG, FFE, F22/23, Folder 1, "Un épisode oublié de la vie du Gouverneur Général Félix Eboué," newspaper unknown, date unknown. The author, "A.," may have been Andrée Nardal, one of Paulette Nardal's sisters and a contributor to the *Revue*.
118. Eboué described the articles of *Légitime Défense*, a journal created by Martinican students, as "abominable," and he disapproved of Maran's involvement in groups such as the Comité de Défense de la Race Nègre. Weinstein, *Eboué*, 140, 106–7. On *Légitime Défense* and *Négritude*, see Edwards, *The Practice of Diaspora*, 187–98.
119. ANOM, SLOTFOM II/21, "Rapport de Joe," October 8, 1931.
120. Weinstein, *Eboué*, 107.

121. Locke to Eboué, July 30, 1928, quoted in Dennis, "The René Maran Story," 189. Also quoted in Weinstein, *Eboué*, 108.

122. Mercer Cook, "Guadeloupe Loses Its First Negro Governor," *Opportunity* 17, no. 4 (April 1939), 112.

123. LOC, NAACPR, pt. 2, General Office File, 1940–56, Box 2: A3, Félix Eboué, 1941–44, NAACP to Félix Eboué, December 17, 1941.

124. LOC, NAACPR, pt. 2, General Office File, 1940–56, Box 2: A3, Félix Eboué, 1941–44, Walter White to Lowell Mellet, Bureau of Motion Pictures, Office of War Information, February 25, 1943.

125. LOC, NAACPR, pt. 2, General Office File, 1940–56, Box 2: A3, Félix Eboué, 1941–44, Eboué to Walter White, April 8, 1944.

126. FCDG, FFE, F22/3, Folder 8, Mohammad R. Omar to Félix Eboué, January 14, 1942. Omar was also known as B. Basil Marshall.

127. *African Times and Orient Review*, August 1913, 77–78.

128. George Padmore, "Eboué Wins First Round in Fight for Self-Government in Africa," *Chicago Defender*, March 4, 1944, 4.

129. George Padmore, "Race Troops Help Crack Mareth Line: Eboué Men Rip Nazis in Flank Attack," *Chicago Defender*, April 3, 1943, 1; and George Padmore, "Negro Troops Take Hitler's Alps Hideout," *Chicago Defender*, May 12, 1945, 1.

130. White, *A Rising Wind*, 121. Also quoted in Weinstein, *Eboué*, 309–10.

131. Fanon, "Antillais et Africains," 267. Weinstein cites part of this passage in the introduction to his biography of Eboué. Fanon also praised Eboué in *Black Skin, White Masks* while lambasting René Maran. After labeling Maran a "black abandonment neurotic," Fanon declared, "When we read such passages we cannot help thinking of Félix Eboué, unquestionably a Negro, who saw his duty quite differently in the same circumstances." Fanon, *Black Skin, White Masks*, 71, 79.

132. For Fanon's condemnation of the "native bourgeoisie," see *The Wretched of the Earth*.

133. For example, Walter Rodney, perhaps intentionally, labeled Félix Eboué an "African." Rodney, *How Europe Underdeveloped Africa*, 267. Aimé Césaire also praised Eboué. In December 1945, he pointed out that "all French overseas Territories" had elected representatives to the French Chamber of Deputies, and that this "represent[ed] the first application of the program of reforms outlined by M. Eboué, late Governor General of French Equatorial Africa, and adopted at the Brazzaville Conference." Thyra Edwards, "Two French Deputies Chide U.S.," *Chicago Defender*, December 29, 1945, 11.

134. Condé, *La vie sans fards*. In 2017, the book was translated into English by Condé's husband, Richard Philcox, as *What Is Africa to Me? Fragments of a True-to-Life Autobiography*.

135. Condé, *What Is Africa to Me?*, 35. Sékou Touré also used this language when he met Condé. "So you are from Guadeloupe," he said to her. "You're one of the little sisters that Africa once lost and now found again." Condé writes that she did not then have the "nerve" to replace the word *lost* with *sold*. Condé, *What Is Africa to Me?*, 71.

136. Condé, *What Is Africa to Me?*, 35.

137. Condé, *What Is Africa to Me?*, 89. *Toubab* refers to a white person or foreigner in Guinée, Sénégal, and several other West African countries.

138. Condé, *La vie sans fards*, 334.

139. Condé, *What Is Africa to Me?*, 290. The French word *fiction*, which Philcox translates as *narrative*, could also be translated as *fiction* or *fantasy*, or even *dream*.

140. Here I am following Justin Izzo, who argues that "ethnographic fictions" sought not only to make sense of "imperial formations" but also to "imagine connections across and outside them." Izzo, *Experiments with Empire*, 8.

141. MSRC, EGR, Box 17, Diary no. 1, 1946, "African Trip," 55. My thanks to Lorelle Semley for bringing this reference to my attention. For more on Robeson in Central Africa, see Joseph-Gabriel, *Reimagining Liberation*, esp. chap. 6.

CHAPTER 6. OLD TALK

1. UWISC, CLRJ, Box 18, Folder 345, C. L. R. James, manuscript of "Notes on the Life of George Padmore." A published version of "Notes" appeared in eleven installments, from October 1959 to January 1960, in *The Nation*, the newspaper of Trinidad's People's National Movement. James was the newspaper's editor.

2. At the time, Padmore was known as Malcolm Nurse. Grantley Adams's father was also a headmaster. James, "Notes on the Life of George Padmore." On James's childhood in Trinidad, see his autobiography, *Beyond a Boundary*.

3. More recent scholars of the Caribbean have echoed James's emphasis on the importance of headmasters and teachers. Franklin Knight, for example, writes that teachers have long acted as intellectuals, lay preachers, and even "quasi-legal arbiters" and remain "a potent force in the politics of the English-speaking Caribbean." Knight, *The Caribbean*, 218.

4. On the history of education in Ghana and Nigeria, see Ferrell, "Fighting for the Future"; Foster, *Education and Social Change in Ghana*; Graham, *The History of Education in Ghana*; Omolewa, "Educating the 'Native'"; Steiner-Khamsi and Quist, "The Politics of Educational Borrowing"; and White, "Talk about School."

5. Foster, *Education and Social Change in Ghana*, 103–4.

6. Feierman, *Peasant Intellectuals*, 13.

7. Some of the descriptive language in this sentence and elsewhere in the chapter comes from George Lamming's 1970 novel, *In the Castle of My Skin*. The novel begins with a description of a flood on the protagonist's ninth birthday; chapter 3 describes Empire Day at a school in Barbados; and chapter 9 describes the 1937 rebellion in Bridgetown.

8. NAUK, FamilySearch Genealogy Service, List of Passengers, *Colombie*, November 25, 1938.

9. On the 1937 labor rebellion in Barbados, see Beckles, *Great House Rules*, esp. chap. 5. On the 1938 labor rebellion in Jamaica, see Holt, *The Problem of Freedom*.

10. In 1904, 85 percent of her students had passed through the Standards; 89 percent passed through the following year. NAUK, CO 28/266/22, Inspector of Schools for Barbados to the Governor of Barbados, August 16, 1906.

11. NAUK, CO 96/443, Acting Governor of the Gold Coast to the Secretary of State for the Colonies, June 11, 1906.

12. NAUK, CO 96/443, Acting Governor of the Gold Coast to the Secretary of State for the Colonies, June 11, 1906. This letter quotes from Britton's description of the school.

13. Clifford, *Our Days on the Gold Coast, in Ashanti, in the Northern Territories, and in the British Sphere of Occupation in Togoland*, 209–10. Lady Clifford was the wife of Gold Coast Governor Hugh Clifford.

14. My descriptions of this event are from "Empire Day Celebrations," *Gold Coast Leader*, June 1, 1912, 2.

15. "Empire Day Celebrations," *Gold Coast Leader*, June 1, 1912, 2.

16. "General News," *Gold Coast Leader*, April 20, 1912, 2.

17. H. O. Kuofie, letter to the editor, *Gold Coast Leader*, June 1, 1912, 7. Since leaving Cape Coast, Kuofie had taken up a position in Aboh, Nigeria, working for the Forestry Department.

18. "A Farewell Gathering," *Gold Coast Leader*, April 25, 1908, 2. Brown also became a member of the Legislative Council and wrote a history of the Gold Coast. Brown, *A Gold Coast and Asianti Reader*. In his acknowledgments, Brown thanked Josiah Spio-Garbrah, another former Britton student, and James E. Kwegyir Aggrey. On these and other members of the early twentieth-century Gold Coast elite, see Doortmont, *The Pen-Pictures of Modern Africans and African Celebrities by Charles Francis Hutchison*.

19. My descriptions of this celebration come from "Grand Conversazione—A Unique Send-off. Mr. Jos. A. Britton Honoured," *Gold Coast Nation*, August 1, 1912, 110; "The Retirement of Mr. J. A. Britton," *Gold Coast Leader*, August 3, 1912, 2; and "The Retirement of Mr. Britton," *Gold Coast Leader*, August 3, 1912, 4.

20. This was likely Joseph William de Graft-Johnson Sr. (1860–1928), a close associate of Joseph Casely Hayford and a cofounder of the Gold Coast Aborigines' Rights Protection Society. It may have been his son, also Joseph William de Graft-Johnson (b. 1893), who became headmaster of the Cape Coast Wesleyan School in 1921 and later wrote *Towards Nationhood in West Africa*. Reverend Egyir-Asaam and J. P. H. Brown were both involved in founding and managing *The Gold Coast Leader*.

21. The transcript of Wilberforce's speech is from "Grand Conversazione."

22. "General News," *Gold Coast Leader*, August 3, 1912, 2.

23. On Ingham, see chapter 1 in this volume.

24. "Mr. Britton understands that if at any time a trained European is appointed to be Headmaster of the School, he will take up the position of 2nd Master." NAUK, CO 96/200, Governor of the Gold Coast to Secretary of State for the Colonies, March 29, 1889; and NAUK, CO 100/35–43, Gold Coast Blue Books, 1885–93.

25. In February 1902, for example, the governor explained to the Colonial Office that there was no need to hire a new "European headmaster" at Cape Coast because the school was already being "efficiently conducted by the native Principal teacher Mr. J. A. Britton." NAUK, CO 96/395, Governor of the Gold Coast to Secretary of State for the Colonies, February 22, 1902.

26. Britton's annual salary increased from £60 in 1886 to £200 in 1912, but the salary of the "European Principal Teacher," Walter J. Pitt, was £315. NAUK, CO 96/531, J. A. Britton Pensions Form, enclosure in letter from Governor of the Gold Coast to Secretary of State for the Colonies, May 26, 1913; and NAUK, CO 100/62, Gold Coast Blue Book 1912.

27. "Coronation Day," *Gold Coast Leader*, July 1, 1911, 3–5.

28. The British apparently imposed this ban because white women in England had "lavished so much attention on black soldiers" at the coronation of Edward VII, George V's father, in 1902. Boyle and Bunie, *Paul Robeson*, 248.

29. "Coronation Day," *Gold Coast Leader*, July 1, 1911, 3.

30. "Berbice Items," *Daily Chronicle* (Demerara), May 22, 1885, 3.

31. My description of this funeral comes from "Many Pay Last Tribute to Rev. F. Gordon Veitch," *Daily Gleaner*, July 6, 1946, 12.

32. Garvey had also personally supported Veitch's election campaign in Hanover. "Speech by Marcus Garvey," in Hill, *The Marcus Garvey and Universal Negro Improvement Association Papers*, vol. VII, 333, 340 n. 13.

33. In his later memoir, Mills described Veitch as "original in the extreme" and claimed that Veitch was "most winning in his ways and humour.... [T]he villagers loved him; the children feared and loved him. All were very sorry when he left for Wesley Church School in Kingston." Mills, *J. J. Mills*, 22–23.

34. In a letter he wrote before leaving Jamaica, Veitch asked for a salary advance because his brother and sister were "dependent" on him, a matter that was giving him "a little anxiety." NAUK, CO 137/642, Veitch to Superintending Inspector of Schools, November 15, 1904.

35. NAUK, CO 137/642, Veitch to Secretary of State for the Colonies, December 8, 1904.

36. NAUK, CO 520/24, Archibald Douglas to Colonial Secretary of Southern Nigeria, May 16, 1904.

37. NAUK, CO 137/642, Governor of Jamaica to Secretary of State for the Colonies, December 8, 1904.

38. NAUK, CO 592/3, 1906 Annual Report on the Education Department of Southern Nigeria; and NAI, NC 70/1919, "Conditions of Appointment of West Indians." Methodist, Presbyterian, and Anglican missionaries all ran "book depots" in Nigeria. Apart from books, the book depots sold paper, writing implements, and so on. In rural areas, the depots were connected to larger central book depots. These networks facilitated the dispersion of books and other materials to regions removed from urban centers. My thanks to Caitlin Tyler-Richards for this explanation.

39. In 1901, Jacob Kehinde Coker founded the "African Church Organization" in Lagos after a split with the Anglican Church Missionary Society. Anderson, *African Reformation*, 60–64.

40. "Mr. L. J. Veitch, West Indian Headmaster of the Bale School, Ibadan: An Appreciation," *Nigerian Pioneer*, August 4, 1916, 7.

41. On Garveyism in Ibadan in the early 1920s, see Watson, "Literacy as a Style of Life"; and Williams, "Garveyism, Akinpelu Obisesan and His Contemporaries." I have not found evidence of a connection between Akinpelu Obisesan and Veitch.

42. Attoo, "Scrutineer," *Gold Coast Leader*, March 26, 1904, 3. "Attoo," a frequent contributor to *The Gold Coast Leader*, was likely a pseudonym for Reverend Samuel Richard Brew Attoh-Ahuma. He was also Britton's friend and gave a speech at Britton's retirement party in July 1912. Newell, *The Power to Name*, 30.

43. Like James K. Aggrey and Samuel Pomeyie, Attoh-Ahuma studied at Livingstone College in the United States. Doortmont, *The Pen-Pictures of Modern Africans and African Celebrities by Charles Francis Hutchison*, 110–11.

44. "The members of the Reading Club attended Service in a body on last Sunday afternoon at the Christ Church, when Mr. Britton gave them a splendid address on 'Gather up the fragments.'" "General News," *Gold Coast Leader*, November 26, 1904, 2.

45. Britton served as an interim preacher on numerous occasions, as well as an organist, and his extensive church activities were regularly reported in Gold Coast newspapers. "Bishop Hamlyn," *Gold Coast Leader*, December 6, 1913, 5; "General News," *Gold Coast Leader*, June 6, 1903, 1; "Among the Churches," *Gold Coast Leader*, September 27, 1902, 4; and "Dedication of the New Organ at Christ Church," *Gold Coast Leader*, April 6, 1912, 2.

46. In fact, the South African Garveyite J. C. Humble used the passage from Jeremiah 23 for similar purposes in 1925. Vinson, *The Americans Are Coming!*, 91.

47. On Ingham and providential design, see chapter 1 in this volume.

48. "The Retirement of Mr. J. A. Britton."

49. "General News," *Gold Coast Leader*, August 31, 1912, 2.

50. "General News," *Gold Coast Leader*, January 11, 1913, 2; and NAUK, CO 100/62, Gold Coast Blue Book, 1912.

51. "The Britton Club," letter to the editor, *Gold Coast Leader*, January 18, 1913, 5. In the letter, the club's secretary, James Marmah, praised "the character, the spirit, the vigor, the nobleness, the sincerity, and the faith" of Britton's work, and explained that members were committed to Britton's "methods, principles in life, manners of teaching, and philosophizing."

52. In September 1917, a club member wrote to *The Gold Coast Leader* regretting that there had been no recent meetings. "Has the Brittonite Club Proved a Failure?" *Gold Coast Leader*, September 1, 1917, 7. The last mention of the club in the Gold Coast press was in January 1918. A correspondent from Lomé declared, "From Cape Coast we hear of a Brittonite club in honour and memory of Mr. Britton, a West Indian, who did so much in uplifting many Fanti youths who are well-to-do today." "Lome," *Gold Coast Leader*, January 12, 1918, 7–8.

53. Britton Spio-Garbrah later followed the example of his father and his namesake, becoming a teacher at Achimota College. Then, in the late 1940s, he studied at the University College of North Wales, where he became a close friend of Ivor Wilks and "patiently initiated Ivor into the intricacies of Gold Coast politics." According to Wilks, after they received their degrees in 1951, Spio-Garbrah "was returning home to the Gold Coast, and I was moving to Oxford to do postgraduate work. Sadly and solemnly, we shook hands. 'You must come to my country one day,' he said. 'I will,' I replied, but we both knew how very unlikely that was!" Two years later, in September 1953, Wilks arrived in Accra to teach at the University College of the Gold Coast, and the two men renewed their friendship. By this point, Britton Spio-Garbrah was an avid supporter of Kwame Nkrumah and the Convention People's Party, and in the 1960s he was a foreign diplomat for the Nkrumah government. On the life of Britton Spio-Garbrah, see "Britton Spio-Garbrah, May 1913—Nov[ember] 1988: Educator, Administrator, Ambassador," *West Africa*, vols. 3974–75, November 22–28, 1993, 2119. On Wilks and Spio-Garbrah, see Hunwick and Lawler, *The Cloth of Many Colored Silks*, 8.

54. NAUK, CO 100/73, Gold Coast Blue Book 1923–24.

55. Aggrey was a teacher at the Wesleyan Centenary Memorial School in Cape Coast during Britton's time at Cape Coast Government School. I have not found any traces of a

connection between them, but they must have interacted at annual exams or other events that brought Cape Coast schools together.

56. NAUK, FamilySearch Genealogy Service, List of Passengers, *Colombie*, November 25, 1938.

57. Caroline Barbour-James died on March 12, 1917, and John arrived back in London in June 1917. On John Barbour-James and his family, see Green, "Barbour-James, John Alexander"; Green, *Black Edwardians*, esp. 70–78; and Green, "John Alexander Barbour-James (1867–1954)."

58. PRAAD, PF 3/36/354, Barbour-James Personnel File, Charles Watt to Malcolm Bell Hay, May 15, 1917. Watt described the situation and his actions in his letter to Hay.

59. PRAAD, PF 3/36/354, telegram from John Maxwell to Watt, May 14, 1917, quoted in letter from Watt to Hay, May 15, 1917.

60. PRAAD, PF 3/36/354, Hay to Watt, May 15, 1917.

61. PRAAD, PF 3/36/354, Watt to Hay, May 15, 1917.

62. PRAAD, PF 3/36/354, Hay to Maxwell, May 18, 1917.

63. Maxwell later forwarded the case to the colonial secretary in Accra and asked whether Barbour-James, a "coloured native of the West Indies," or "any other officer in a similar position," was "entitled to accommodation in the Segregation Areas." The colonial secretary approved of Maxwell's approach and stated that, for future cases, "the occasional stay of a West Indian in a rest house would not add materially to the danger of Europeans becoming infected with disease since, owing to the necessity of allowing native servants to live in the compounds of bungalows in Segregation Areas, the total segregation of Europeans is never possible." PRAAD, PF 3/36/354, Maxwell to Colonial Secretary, July 11, 1917; and PRAAD, PF 3/36/354, Colonial Secretary to Maxwell, August 23, 1917.

64. NAUK, CO 583/75. My descriptions of this incident are from a letter Veitch wrote to the acting governor general of Nigeria, February 13, 1919.

65. Before coming to Nigeria, the British administration had assured Veitch that it would always provide him with "furnished quarters with the necessary furniture." NAUK, CO 583/75, Veitch to Acting Governor General of Nigeria, February 13, 1919.

66. "The people with whom I lodged during this time are all West Indians and strangers like myself." NAUK, CO 583/75, Veitch to Acting Governor General of Nigeria, February 13, 1919; and NAUK, CO 583/83, Veitch to the Secretary of State for the Colonies, July 5, 1919. In the same correspondence, Veitch named Shackleford, Ambleston, and Ikoli.

67. Okonkwo, "A Jamaican Export to Nigeria!," 51–52. Ambleston and Shackleford had also come together to support the railway guard Stephen Raymore in June 1914. See chapter 3 in this volume.

68. NAUK, CO 583/75, Veitch to Acting Governor General of Nigeria, February 13, 1919; and NAUK, CO 583/75, Colonial Office official "D. C. C.," June 26, 1919.

69. NAUK, CO 583/75, Dusé Mohamed Ali to Colonel Aubrey Herbert, July 18, 1919. Ali had corresponded with Herbert during World War I while attempting to arrange for Black war correspondents. In intraoffice correspondence, Herbert and other colonial officials had derided Ali as "that nigger editor." Duffield, "Dusé Mohamed Ali and the Development of Pan-Africanism, 1866–1945," 315–17.

70. NAUK, CO 583/78, Secretary of State for the Colonies to the Governor of Nigeria, September 23, 1919; and NAUK, CO 583/78, Governor of Nigeria to Secretary of State for the Colonies, October 31, 1919.

71. "Universal Negro Improvement Association and African Communities' League: Lagos Branch," *Lagos Weekly Record*, September 25, 1920, 7. See also Hill, *The Marcus Garvey and Universal Negro Improvement Association Papers*, vol. X, 709–11. On Garveyism in West Africa, see Okonkwo, "The Garvey Movement in British West Africa."

72. Asante, *Pan-African Protest*, 120. Asante writes that Thomas made a "significant contribution" to the Pan-African Congress.

73. Two years later, for example, Veitch attended a party in Lagos organized by Peter Thomas, and Ikoli was among the other guests. "List of Invitees in Connection with the 'At Home' Given by Mr. and Mrs. Peter Thomas," *Nigerian Pioneer*, December 29, 1922, 8a. The article listed both Veitch and Ikoli among the "Africans," alongside Ladipo Oluwole and W. G. Nicol, one of Veitch's colleagues at King's College.

74. Macaulay and Amodu Tijani were in London to challenge land appropriation by the colonial government in Apapa, Lagos. Courts in Lagos had ruled against them, but their appeal to the Judicial Committee of the Privy Council was successful, and they received £22,500 in compensation for the land. On this history, see Ibhawoh, *Imperial Justice*, chap. 5.

75. "Wedding of Colour," *Gold Coast Leader*, November 13, 1920, 7. For film footage of the wedding that shows Barbour-James, Goring, Macaulay, and Tijani, see "Wedding of Colour," British Pathé, accessed December 17, 2023, https://www.britishpathe.com/asset/48477.

76. On the African Progress Union, see chapter 4 in this volume.

77. "The African Progress Union: Inaugural Meeting and Dinner, Great Eastern Hotel, London, December 18, 1918," *West Africa*, vol. II, nos. 102–6, January 11–February 8, 1919.

78. Reports on the APU's annual meetings from 1918 to 1924 are located in the weekly newspaper *West Africa*. See vol. II, nos. 102–6, January 11, 1919–February 8, 1919, vol. V, no. 245, October 8, 1921, vol. VI, no. 309, December 30, 1922, vol. VII, no. 354, November 10, 1923, and vol. VIII, no. 369, February 23, 1924.

79. "African Progress Union," *West Africa*, vol. VI, no. 309, December 30, 1922, 1617.

80. "A Coaster's London Log," *West Africa*, vol. XIII, no. 664, October 19, 1929, 1405.

81. Press coverage for "Africa Day" appeared in *West Africa*, vol. XIII, no. 625, January 19, 1929, 24, vol. XV, no. 733, February 14, 1931, 152, and vol. XVIII, no. 911, July 14, 1934, 772.

82. "Mr. J. A. Barbour-James as Lecturer," *West Africa*, vol. XIX, no. 942, February 16, 1935, 171.

83. Ernest Ikoli, "The Regrading of the African Staff of the Nigerian Civil Service," *Lagos Weekly Record*, August 14, 1920, 7.

84. On the League of Coloured Peoples and its membership, see Macdonald, *The Keys*.

85. *The Keys*, vol. I, no. 1, July 1933.

86. Davies also became the president of WASU.

87. In London, Kenyatta went by his Christian baptismal name. In 1953, at the request of Kwame Nkrumah, H. O. Davies traveled to Kenya to defend Kenyatta and the other members of the "Kapenguria Six." Terretta, "Anticolonial Lawyering, Postwar Human Rights, and Decolonization across Imperial Boundaries in Africa."

88. Matera, *Black London*, 72. For the best analysis of these protests in West Africa, see Asante, *Pan-African Protest*.

89. Ali had moved to Lagos in 1921 and established a new publication, *The Comet*. Asante, *Pan-African Protest*, 120–22.

90. The meeting took place in Lagos on September 20, 1935. Ikoli, along with Eric Olawolu Moore, condemned Italy's invasion of Ethiopia and praised British Foreign Secretary Samuel Hoare's recent speech at the League of Nations. On September 11, 1935, Hoare had pledged British support for "collective resistance to all acts of unprovoked aggression." Many took this as British support for Ethiopia, so when Britain did nothing to prevent the invasion several weeks later, there were further protests across West Africa, fomented by the Italian defeat of Addis Ababa in May 1936. Documents on British Foreign Policy, 2d series, XIV, app. 4, "Sir S. Hoare's Speech at the League Assembly September 11, 1935," 789, quoted in Mallet, *Mussolini in Ethiopia, 1919–1935*, 215.

91. Arifalo, "The Rise and Decline of the Nigerian Youth Movement, 1934–1941."

92. Years later, in his memoir, H. O. Davies wrote fondly of "Mr. L. J. Veitch, a vivacious West Indian, who taught History and Geography" at King's College Lagos. Davies, *Memoirs*, 28.

93. Background information on the LCP and its membership comes from Macdonald, *The Keys*.

94. Desmond Buckle later joined the Communist Party of Great Britain. Adi, "Forgotten Comrade?"

95. *The Keys*, vol. V, no. 4, April–June 1938. Christian carefully preserved his LCP membership card. UWISC, GJC, Box 2, Folder 43. Christian also made donations to WASU. UWISC, GJC, Box 8, Folder 195, Ladipo Solanke to Christian, December 9, 1936.

96. C. L. R. James, "The West Indies Cricket Team, 1933," *The Keys*, vol. I, no. 1, July 1933, 11–13; C. L. R. James, "West Indies Self-Government," *The Keys*, vol. I, no. 4, April–June 1934, 72, 84; and C. L. R. James, "Abyssinia and the Imperialists," *The Keys*, vol. III, no. 3, January–March 1936, 32, 39–40.

97. At the 1933 conference, James gave a speech titled "The West Indian" and explained "how the black man in the West Indies had been shorn of all African civilization and had been engulfed by Western civilization. This meant that there was no spirit of nationalism, which gave force to democratic movements in other countries." "Conference Report," *The Keys*, vol. I, no. 1, July 1933, 5. At the annual conference in April 1936, James discussed "Economic Organisation in the Tropics." *The Keys*, vol. III, no. 4, April–June 1936, 48.

98. "Toussaint L'Ouverture," *The Keys*, vol. III, no. 4, April–June 1936, 68–69.

99. *The Black Jacobins* was published in London by Secker and Warburg in October 1938. *The Keys* published a review of *The Black Jacobins* in December 1938. "Black Jacobins," *The Keys*, vol. VI, no. 2, October–December 1938, 12–13. On the "making" of *The Black Jacobins*, see Douglas, *Making The Black Jacobins*.

100. In 1937, the newsletter promoted one of Padmore's upcoming lectures, "The Negro in the Modern World." "Forthcoming Events," *The Keys*, vol. V, no. 1, July–September 1937, 22. See also "The British in Africa" (review of George Padmore's *How Britain Rules Africa*), *The Keys*, vol. IV, no. 1, July–September 1936, 10–11. In 1939, *The Keys* also printed an excerpt from an essay by Eric Williams, "The Abolition of the Slave System in Britain." *The Keys*, vol. VII, no. 1, July–September 1939, 11–13.

101. "Nigerian Reunion Dinner in Jamaica," *Daily Gleaner*, November 21, 1931, 12.

102. Okonkwo, "A Jamaican Export to Nigeria!"

103. In July 1931, before traveling back to Jamaica from Nigeria, Shackleford wrote to Macaulay, "I take away to the West Indies with me the very highest esteem for the Community in which I lived and worked and am looking forward with some anticipation to the day when I shall come back home. . . . Wishing you a long life pregnant with further useful work for our great country." UISC, HMP, Box 91, File 3, Shackleford to Macaulay, July 12, 1931.

104. In September 1916, while on leave in Sturge Town, Dawes gave an address to the local branch of the Jamaican Agriculture Society. "The Process of Agriculture," *Daily Gleaner*, September 19, 1916, 16. When he retired, he gave "Lecture on Africa" at the Mount Nebo Baptist Church in St. Catherine. "Latest News of the Religious Denominations," *Daily Gleaner*, February 19, 1932, 21. And in 1937, Dawes gave the lecture "Nigeria" to the Jamaica Union of Teachers Conference, which demonstrated his "wealth of knowledge on the mannerisms, crafts and attainments of Africans." Accompanying the report was a photograph of Dawes holding "an intricately hand-carved ebony stool, the product of African handcraft." "Lecture on Africa," *Daily Gleaner*, January 14, 1937, 27. As for Veitch, in December 1927, when he returned to Jamaica on leave with his wife and children, he gave a lecture on Nigeria. A writer for *The Daily Gleaner* noted that Veitch's "delights [were] not so much to tell of the dark side of life there but to tell of wonderful progress of the people." "Mr. L. J. Veitch Returned after Long Stay in Nigeria," *Daily Gleaner*, January 11, 1928, 19.

105. "Current Items," *Daily Gleaner*, October 31, 1932, 2; "Lecture on Africa," *Daily Gleaner*, November 4, 1932, 15; "Teachers of City Given Address by Mr. J. A. Clarke," *Daily Gleaner*, March 4, 1933, 16; and "East Queen Street Baptist Church Literary Society," *Daily Gleaner*, September 29, 1933, 19.

106. NAUK, CO 137/642, Veitch to Secretary of State for the Colonies, December 8, 1904. In May 1949, Dorothy Bruce, Veitch's eldest daughter, visited her father in Jamaica, bringing her son Christopher. "Current Items," *Daily Gleaner*, May 11, 1949, 2. Three years later, in September 1952, Veitch died at Bonnyville at eighty. NAUK, FamilySearch Genealogy Service, Veitch Death Certificate, September 23, 1952.

107. Matory, "The English Professors of Brazil." Matory elaborates on this argument in *Black Atlantic Religion*.

108. Borquaye, *The Saga of Accra Hearts of Oak Sporting Club*, 27.

109. In fact, football was introduced to the Gold Coast in the 1880s by British settlers and colonial civil servants. Darby, "'Let Us Rally around the Flag,'" 225–26. On the broader diffusion of football across Africa, see Alegi, *African Soccerscapes*.

110. The Accra Hearts of Oak Sporting Club was founded in Accra in 1910.

111. Darby, "'Let Us Rally around the Flag.'"

CHAPTER 7. POETRY AND PERIPHERIES

1. ATM, FJL, Box 2, Folder 54, "Espérance," June 4, 1957.

2. Hélénon, *French Caribbeans in Africa*, 103.

3. Dewitte, *Les mouvements nègres en France, 1919–1939*, 130, 257, 259; Lara, *La naissance du panafricanisme*, 5, 7, 313.

4. ANOM, EE/ii/1427, Jean-Louis Personnel File, Governor-General of AOF to Governor-General of AEF, September 8, 1931.

5. On *Paris Noir* in the interwar years, see Boittin, *Colonial Metropolis*; Edwards, *The Practice of Diaspora*; Goebel, *Anti-imperial Metropolis*; Stovall, *Paris Noir*; and Wilder, *The French Imperial Nation-State*.

6. ANOM, AEF/GGAEF, 5D/65, "Note sur la propagande révolutionnaire intéressant les pays d'outre-mer," April 1925. On the CDRN, see also correspondance in the archives of the Ligue des Droits de l'Homme at the Bibliothèque de Documentation Internationale Contemporaine in Nanterre, F Delta Res 798/65.

7. ANOM, EE/ii/1427, Jean-Louis Personnel File.

8. ANOM, SLOTFOM IX/2, Governor-General of AEF to Minister of Colonies, November 20, 1926.

9. ADSSD, Archives Microfilmées de l'Internationale Communiste, 3 MI 6/110, Joseph Gothon-Lunion, "Rapport sur la question coloniale," October 25, 1925.

10. ANOM, AEF/GGAEF/5D/70, "Note sur la propagande révolutionnaire intéressant les pays d'outre-mer," January 31, 1927, February 28, 1927, and March 31, 1927. On this schism, see also Boittin, *Colonial Metropolis*, 89–95; and Dewitte, *Les mouvements nègres en France, 1919–1939*, 150–53.

11. ANOM, AEF/GGAEF, 5D/70, "Note sur la propagande révolutionnaire intéressant les pays d'outre-mer," March 1927.

12. ANOM, AEF/GGAEF, 5D/70, "Note sur la propagande révolutionnaire intéressant les pays d'outre-mer," April 1927.

13. ANOM, AEF/GGAEF, 5D/68, "Rapport de Paul," November 3, 1929.

14. ANOM, AEF/GGAEF, 5D/68, "Rapport de Joe," November 3, 1929.

15. ANOM, SLOTFOM II/21, "Rapport de Joe," October 11–16, 1930.

16. Jean Louis, "Introduction to a Study on Creole Art and Literature," *La Revue du monde noir*, no. 1 (1931): 8–11.

17. ANOM, EE/ii/1427, Jean-Louis Personnel File, Governor-General of AOF to Governor-General of AEF, September 8, 1931.

18. ANOM, ANS, 21G/44 (Police et Sûreté), Governor-General of AOF to Minister of Colonies, August 29, 1931, 44. On Beccaria, see Keller, *Colonial Suspects*, chap. 5.

19. ANOM, SLOTFOM V/28, Minister of Colonies to Governor-General of AOF, September 17, 1931.

20. Jean-Louis, *Visions of Africa*, 8–9.

21. ANOM, TGO//31, Jean-Louis to Chiefs of Douala, December 1, 1929; ANOM, TGO//31, Commissaire de la République in Cameroon to Minister of Colonies, March 17, 1930; ANOM, TGO//31, Commissaire de la République in Cameroon to Minister of Colonies, May 22, 1930; and ANOM, TGO//31, Minister of Colonies to Commissaire de la République in Cameroon, June 23, 1930.

22. ANOM, SLOTFOM II/3, "Rapport de Moise," February 3, 1934.

23. See, e.g., Scheel, "Jean-Louis Baghio'o père et fils"; and Scheel, *Victor Jean-Louis Baghio'o par lui-meme*.

24. With the documents in Martinique, Scheel organized the entire collection and created a chronological inventory of more than seven hundred entries. This detailed inventory provided a much clearer picture of Jean-Louis's biography, and I remain indebted

to Scheel for this work. For his short biography of Jean-Louis, see Charles W. Scheel, "Henri Jean-Louis Baghio'o," *Île en île*, June 4, 2016, http://ile-en-ile.org/baghio_henri_jean-louis.

25. On "tin-trunk" archives in African historiography, see Barber, *Africa's Hidden Histories*.

26. This, too, was possible only because of Scheel's careful organization of the collection.

27. Glissant, *Poetics of Relation*, 28.

28. Glissant, *Poetics of Relation*, 28–29.

29. Glissant, *Poetics of Relation*, 32.

30. ATM, FJL, Box 2, Folder 55, "Sous un pont de la Seine," June 1957.

31. ATM, FJL, Box 1, Folder 2, Jean-Louis Notebook, October 1924.

32. ATM, FJL, Box 1, Folder 3, Jean-Louis Notebook, February 1925.

33. ATM, FJL, Box 2, Folder 58, "Paroles d'un Caraïbe," Sainte Anne, Guadeloupe, April 14, 1958.

34. ATM, FJL, Box 1, Folder 10, "Assimilation," Fort-de-France, 1935.

35. ATM, FJL, Box 1, Folder 10, "Notre Assimilation," 1935.

36. Cooper, *Citizenship between Empire and Nation*; and Wilder, *Freedom Time*.

37. ATM, FJL, Box 1, Folder 17, "Le monde et les Colonies: Lettre ouverte à Monsieur Léon Blum," 1936.

38. This is the core argument of Frederick Cooper's work on the end of the French empire in the 1950s and early 1960s. Cooper, *Citizenship between Empire and Nation*; and Cooper, *Decolonization and African Society*.

39. ATM, FJL, Box 1, Folder 29, "La victoire de la France," August 26, 1944.

40. For more on this *blanchissement*, or "whitening," see Mann, *Native Sons*, 19–20.

41. ATM, FJL, Box 3, Folder B, "Contre l'Assimilation," October 18, 1947.

42. Jean-Louis, *Visions of Africa*.

43. Scheel, "Jean-Louis Baghio'o père et fils," 70.

44. On the 1937 strike and riots, see Thomas, *The Trinidad Labour Riots of 1937*.

45. ATM, FJL, Box 1, Folder 20, "Discours à Marcus Garvey," Trinidad, 1937.

46. ATM, FJL, Box 1, Folder 20, "Discours à Marcus Garvey," Trinidad, 1937.

47. ATM, FJL, Box 1, Folder 23, "Epitre aux Peuples Européens: La Vie ou la mort," September 1938.

48. ATM, FJL, Box 1, Folder 23, "Epitre aux Peuples Européens: La Vie ou la mort," September 1938.

49. ATM, FJL, Box 1, Folder 34, "Speech à Truman," March 17, 1947. Jean-Louis also used "*Les Antilles aux Antillais*" in ATM, FJL, Box 1, Folder 34, "Evangile de Baghio'oh," July 5, 1947.

50. ATM, FJL, Box 1, Folder 41, "U. N. I. A. - Union Nationale des Isles d'Amérique," August 6, 1949.

51. Scheel, "Jean-Louis Baghio'o père et fils," 70.

52. For example, in January 1949's appropriately titled "L'Union Antillaise," Jean-Louis took an imagined journey from Trinidad to St. Kitts and described it as "*notre archipel*." ATM, FJL, Box 1, Folder 41, "L'Union Antillaise," January 18, 1949.

53. ATM, FJL, Box 1, Folder 39, "Delgrès-ville, capitale des Antilles," May 16, 1948.

54. ATM, FJL, Box 1, Folder 29, "Soleil d'Octobre," October 1, 1944; ATM, FJL, Box 1, Folder 37, "Le testament du Poète de la plage," n.d., likely 1946; ATM, FJL, Box 1, Folder 34, "Tu reverras notre île," January 16, 1947; and ATM, FJL, Box 1, Folder 39, "Delgrès-ville, capitale des Antilles," May 16, 1948.

55. ATM, FJL, Box 1, Folder 29, "Soleil d'Octobre," October 1, 1944.

56. On Césaire's "untimely" call for departmentalization, see Wilder, "Untimely Vision."

57. ATM, FJL, Box 1, Folder 3, Jean-Louis Notebook, February 1925.

58. ATM, FJL, Box 1, Folder 37, "Le testament du Poète de la Plage," July 14, 1948. The poem was written on Bastille Day, a celebration of the French Revolution, so Jean-Louis's reference to "*nos gaulois*" is particularly poignant. Jean-Louis also seems to have written an earlier version of this poem, likely in 1946. ATM, FJL, Box 1, Folder 33, "Le testament du Poète de la Plage," n.d.

59. On Mohammed Baghayogho, also spelled Baghayughu, see Gomez, *African Dominion*; Hunwick, "A Contribution to the Study of Islamic Teaching Traditions in West Africa"; and Massing, "Baghayogho." My thanks to Greg Mann for pointing out this connection.

60. al-Sa'di, *Tarikh es-Soudan*.

61. ATM, FJL, Box 2, Folder 47, "De la Métempsycose," March 29, 1950.

62. ATM, FJL, Box 3, Folder 1, "Humanité," October 1950. In fact, Jean-Louis had already written a national anthem for his proposed Caribbean federation, titled "L'Antillaise."

63. ATM, FJL, Box 2, Folder 45, "Les Héros de la Paix," July 29, 1954.

64. Kane, *Ambiguous Adventure*, 129. Kane's book was first published in French in 1961, but I am quoting from the English translation.

65. Kane, *Ambiguous Adventure*, 130.

66. Kane, *Ambiguous Adventure*, 130. As with his change to Jean-Louis's name, it appears that Kane used "Mohamed Kati" as a replacement for "Mohammed Baghio'o." At the time in France, based on the work of Maurice Delafosse and Octave Houdas, it was believed that the *Tarikh al-fattash* was written by a sixteenth-century scholar named Mahmud Kati. Mauro Nobili and Mohamed Shahid Mathee, however, suggest that the Delafosse and Houdas version of the *Tarikh al-fattash* "conflates two different chronicles." The first, they argue, was written by Ibn-al-Mukhtar in the seventeenth century, and the second in the 1820s by a Fulani scholar. Nobili and Mathee, "Towards a New Study of the So-called *Tārīkh al-Fattāsh*," 39–40.

67. Kane, *Ambiguous Adventure*, 132–33.

68. René Martin, "Le sens d'un crise," newspaper and date unknown, likely June 1957.

69. ATM, FJL, Box 2, Folder 58, "L'Avocat de l'Afrique," November 1956.

70. ATM, FJL, Box 2, Folder 48, "La Confédération Arabo-Africaine," August 6, 1956.

71. ATM, FJL, Box 2, Folder 54, "Espérance," June 4, 1957.

72. ATM, FJL, Box 2, Folder 56, "Le Drapeau de le C.A.M," March 7, 1958.

73. ATM, FJL, Box 2, Folder 55, "L'Afrique aux Africains," October 5, 1957.

74. ATM, FJL, Box 2, Folder 55, "Seconde lettre au President Pinay," October 15, 1957.

75. ATM, FJL, Box 2, Folder 55, "Seconde lettre au President Pinay," October 15, 1957; and ATM, FJL, Box 2, Folder 56, "Le Drapeau de la C.A.M," March 7, 1958.

76. ATM, FJL, Box 2, Folder 58, "L'Afrique aux Africains: Hymne National de la République de l'Afrique Noire," May 15, 1958.

77. ATM, FJL, Box 2, Folder 54, "Excursion d'un poète et juriste nègre en URSS," June 9, 1957.

78. ATM, FJL, Box 2, Folder 51, "L'Union des Nations Socialistes," July 2, 1957.

79. ATM, FJL, Box 2, Folder 58, "La Revanche de Carthage sur Rome," July 21, 1958.

80. Glissant, *Poetics of Relation*, 18.

EPILOGUE

1. Brathwaite, "Timehri," 38.

2. This is especially apparent in his famous trilogy, *The Arrivants*, which combined three earlier collections of poetry: *Rights of Passage* (1967), *Masks* (1968), and *Islands* (1969).

3. On Kenneth MacNeill Stewart, see chapter 4 in this volume.

4. Rouse-Jones and Appiah, "Interview with Dr. Ralph Hoyte."

5. Brathwaite reproduced this passage at the beginning of his 1974 essay, "The African Presence in Caribbean Literature," 73. My thanks to Brent Hayes Edwards for bringing this passage to my attention.

Bibliography

ARCHIVES AND LIBRARIES

Alma Jordan Library, Special Collections, University of the West Indies, St. Augustine (UWISC), St. Augustine, Trinidad
C. L. R. James Collection (CLRJ)
George James Christian Papers (GJC)
George Padmore Collection (GPC)
Oral and Pictorial Records Programme
Archives Départementales de la Seine-Saint-Denis (ADSSD), Paris, France
Archives Microfilmées de l'Internationale Communiste
Archives Fondation Charles de Gaulle (FCDG), Paris, France
Fonds Félix et Eugénié Eboué (FFE)
Archives Nationales d'Outre-Mer (ANOM), Aix-en-Provence, France
Affaires Politiques (AFFPOL)
Fonds AOF, Microfilmées des Archives Nationales du Sénégal (ANS)
Fonds Privé (FP)
Gouvernement Général de l'AEF (AEF/GGAEF)
Personnel Files (EE/ii)
Série géographique Togo-Cameroun (TGO)
Service de Liaison avec les Originaires des Territoires Français d'Outre-Mer (SLOTFOM)
Archives Territoriales de Martinique (ATM), Fort-de-France, Martinique
Fonds Henri Jean-Louis (FJL)
Bibliothèque Centrale, Université Cheikh Anta Diop (UCAD), Dakar, Sénégal
Fonds René Maran (FRM)

Bibliothèque Nationale de France, Paris, France
British Library, London, England
Center for Research Libraries
    African Newspapers Database
Kenneth Dike Library, University of Ibadan, Special Collections (UISC), Ibadan, Nigeria
    Herbert Macaulay Papers (HMP)
Library of Congress (LOC), Washington, DC, USA
    National Association for the Advancement of Colored People Records (NAACPR)
Moorland-Spingarn Research Center, Howard University (MSRC), Washington, DC, USA
    Eslanda Goode Robeson Papers (EGR)
National Archives of Nigeria, Ibadan Branch (NAI), Ibadan, Nigeria
    Central Secretary's Office (CSO)
        Annual Files, 1913–1921, N series (N)
        Annual Files, 1913–1921, NC series (NC)
National Archives of Trinidad and Tobago (NATT), Port of Spain, Trinidad
    Colonial Secretary's Office (CSO)
    Trinidad Yearbooks
National Archives of the United Kingdom (NAUK), London, England
    Colonial Office Files (CO)
        Annual Reports, Blue Books, Official Correspondence
    FamilySearch Genealogy Service
Public Records and Archives Administration Department (PRAAD), Accra, Ghana
    Colonial Secretary's Office (CSO)
    Official Correspondence (ADM)
    Personnel Files (PF)
Weston Library, Oxford University, London, England
    Papers of the Anti-Slavery Society
    Papers of Arthur Creech Jones

NEWSPAPERS AND PERIODICALS

African Times and Orient Review
Chicago Defender
Colonial and Provincial Reporter
Daily Gleaner

Daily Chronicle (Demerara)
Gold Coast Independent
Gold Coast Leader
Gold Coast Nation
Journal Officiel de l'Afrique Equatoriale Française
The Keys
Lagos Standard
Lagos Weekly Record
Missionary Seer
The Nation (Trinidad)
Nigerian Pioneer
Opportunity
Port of Spain Gazette
La Revue du monde noir
Sierra Leone Weekly News
Trinidad Chronicle
West Africa

PUBLISHED PRIMARY AND SECONDARY SOURCES

Adélaïde-Merlande, Jacques. *Les origines du mouvement ouvrier en Martinique: 1870–1900*. Paris: Karthala, 2000.

Adeleke, Tunde. *UnAfrican Americans: Nineteenth-Century Black Nationalists and the Civilizing Mission*. Lexington: University Press of Kentucky, 2014.

Adi, Hakim. "Forgotten Comrade? Desmond Buckle: An African Communist in Britain." *Science and Society* 70, no. 1 (January 2006): 22–45.

Adi, Hakim, and Marika Sherwood. *Pan-African History: Political Figures from Africa and the Diaspora since 1787*. London: Routledge, 2003.

Afigbo, A. E. "The Calabar Mission and the Aro Expedition of 1901–1902." *Journal of Religion in Africa* 5, no. 2 (1973): 94–106.

Agboada, Napoleon K. "The Reign and Times of Togbi Sri II of Anlo, 1906–1956." BA thesis, University of Ghana, 1984.

Ahlman, Jeffrey. *Living with Nkrumahism: Nation, State, and Pan-Africanism in Ghana*. Athens: Ohio University Press, 2017.

Ajayi, J. F. Ade. *Christian Missions in Nigeria, 1841–1891: The Making of a New Élite*. London: Longmans, 1965.

Akyeampong, Emmanuel K. *Between the Sea and the Lagoon: An Eco-social History of the Anlo of Southeastern Ghana c. 1850 to Recent Times*. Athens: Ohio University Press, 2001.

Akyeampong, Emmanuel K. *Drink, Power, and Cultural Change: A Social History of Alcohol in Ghana, c. 1800 to Recent Times*. Portsmouth, NH: Heinemann, 1996.

Akyeampong, Emmanuel K., and Samuel E. Ntewusu. "Rum, Gin, and Maize: Deities and Ritual Change in the Gold Coast during the Atlantic Era (16th Century to 1850)." *Afriques* 5 (2014): 1–20.

Alegi, Peter. *African Soccerscapes: How a Continent Changed the World's Game*. Athens: Ohio University Press, 2010.

Alleyne, Mervyn C. *Comparative Afro-American: An Historical-Comparative Study of English-based Afro-American Dialects of the New World*. Ann Arbor, MI: Karoma, 1980.

Allman, Jean. "Phantoms of the Archive: Kwame Nkrumah, a Nazi Pilot Named Hanna, and the Contingencies of Postcolonial History-Writing." *American Historical Review* 118, no. 1 (2013): 104–29.

Allman, Jean, and Victoria Tashjian. *"I Will Not Eat Stone": A Women's History of Colonial Asante*. Portsmouth, NH: Heinemann, 2000.

Allsopp, Richard. *Dictionary of Caribbean English Usage*. Oxford: Oxford University Press, 1996.

al-Sa'di, Abdul-Rahman. *Tarikh es-Soudan*. Edited and translated by Octave Houdas. Paris: Ernest Leroux, 1900.

Amoako-Gyampah, Akwasi Kwarteng. "Sanitation and Public Hygiene in the Gold Coast (Ghana) from the Late 19th Century to 1950." PhD diss., University of Johannesburg, 2019.

Amoako-Gyampah, Akwasi Kwarteng. "Town Planning, Housing, and the Politics of Sanitation and Public Health in the Gold Coast (Colonial Ghana), c. 1880–1950." *Journal of the History of Medicine and Allied Sciences* 80, no. 1 (2025): 42–66.

Amselle, Jean-Loup, and Emmanuelle Sibeud, eds. *Maurice Delafosse: Entre orientalisme et ethnographie, l'itinéraire d'un africaniste (1870–1926)*. Paris: Maisonneuve and Larose, 1998.

Anderson, Allan. *African Reformation: African Initiated Christianity in the Twentieth Century*. Trenton, NJ: Africa World Press, 2001.

Anderson, Richard Peter. *Abolition in Sierra Leone: Re-building Lives and Identities in Nineteenth-Century West Africa*. Cambridge: Cambridge University Press, 2020.

Angelou, Maya. *All God's Children Need Traveling Shoes*. New York: Random House, 1986.

Appiah, Kwame Anthony. *In My Father's House: Africa in the Philosophy of Culture*. Oxford: Oxford University Press, 1993.

Arifalo, S. O. "The Rise and Decline of the Nigerian Youth Movement, 1934–1941." *African Review* 13, no. 1 (1986): 59–76.

Arnold, A. James. *The Original 1939 Notebook of a Return to the Native Land: Bilingual Edition*. Middletown, CT: Wesleyan University Press, 2013.

Arnold, A. James, and Clayton Eshleman, trans. *The Complete Poetry of Aimé Césaire: Bilingual Edition*. Middletown, CT: Wesleyan University Press, 2017.

Asad, Talal, ed. *Anthropology and the Colonial Encounter*. New York: Humanities Press, 1973.

Asante, Molefi Kete, and Ama Mazama, eds. *Encyclopedia of Black Studies*. London: Sage, 2005.

Asante, S. K. B. *Pan-African Protest: West Africa and the Italo-Ethiopian Crisis, 1934–1941*. London: Longman Group, 1977.

Aub-Buscher, Gertrud. "African Survivals in the Lexicon of Trinidad French-Based Creole." *Society for Caribbean Linguistics* 23 (April 1989): 1–18.
Austen, Ralph A., and Rita Headrick. "Equatorial Africa under Colonial Rule." In *History of Central Africa*, vol. 2, edited by David Birmingham and Phyllis Martin, 27–94. London: Longman Group, 1983.
Austin, Gareth. *Labour, Land, and Capital in Ghana: From Slavery to Free Labour in Asante, 1807–1956*. Rochester, NY: University of Rochester Press, 2005.
Austin, Gareth. "Vent for Surplus or Productivity Breakthrough? The Ghanaian Cocoa Take-off, c. 1890–1936." *Economic History Review* 67, no. 4 (2014): 1035–64.
Azikiwe, Nnamdi. *My Odyssey: An Autobiography*. New York: Praeger, 1970.
Bado, Jean-Paul. *Eugène Jamot, 1879–1937: Le médecin de la maladie du sommeil ou trypanosomiase*. Paris: Karthala, 2011.
Baghio'o, Jean-Louis. *Le colibri blanc: Mémoires à deux voix*. Paris: Éditions Caribéennes, 1980.
Bailey, Anne C. *African Voices of the Atlantic Slave Trade: Beyond the Silence and the Shame*. Boston: Beacon Press, 2005.
Banton, Caree A. *More Auspicious Shores: Barbadian Migration to Liberia, Blackness, and the Making of an African Republic*. Cambridge: Cambridge University Press, 2019.
Banton, Mandy. *Administering the Empire, 1801–1968: A Guide to the Records of the Colonial Office*. London: University of London Press, 2008.
Barber, Karin, ed. *Africa's Hidden Histories: Everyday Literacy and the Making of the Self*. Bloomington: Indiana University Press, 2006.
Bataille, Georges. "Informe." *Documents* 1, no. 7 (1929): 382.
Bataille, Georges, ed. *Encyclopaedia Acephalica*. Translated by Iain White. London: Atlas Press, 1995.
Baugh, Edward. "Neville Dawes, 1926–1984." In *Fifty Caribbean Writers*, edited by Daryl Cumber Dance, 141–50. New York: Greenwood Press, 1986
Beckles, Hilary McD. *Great House Rules: Landless Emancipation and Workers' Protest in Barbados, 1838–1938*. Kingston: Ian Randle Publishers, 2004.
Beckles, Hilary McD. *A History of Barbados: From Amerindian Settlement to Caribbean Single Market*. Cambridge: Cambridge University Press, 2006.
Bedasse, Monique. *Jah Kingdom: Rastafarians, Tanzania, and Pan-Africanism in the Age of Decolonization*. Chapel Hill: University of North Carolina Press, 2017.
Bekele, Frances L. "The History of Cocoa Production in Trinidad and Tobago." In *Re-vitalisation of the Trinidad and Tobago Cocoa Industry: Proceedings of the APASTT Seminar*, edited by L. A. Wilson, 4–12. St. Augustine, Trinidad and Tobago: Association of Professional Agricultural Scientists of Trinidad and Tobago, 2004.
Bernault, Florence. *Démocraties ambiguës en Afrique Centrale: Congo-Brazzaville, Gabon, 1940–1965*. Paris: Karthala, 1996.
Bernault, Florence, ed. *Enfermement, prison, et châtiments en Afrique du 19e siècle à nos jours*. Paris: Karthala, 1999.
Birmingham, David, and Phyllis Martin, eds. *History of Central Africa*, vol. 2. London: Longman Group, 1983.
Blackett, R. J. M. "Return to the Motherland: Robert Campbell, a Jamaican in Early Colonial Lagos." *Phylon* 40, no. 4 (1979): 375–86.

Blanche, Jean-Claude. "6000 'engagés volontaires' en Afrique et en Guadeloupe, 1858–1861." PhD diss., Université de Paris 1, 1994.
Blyden, Edward Wilmot. "The Call of Providence to Descendants of Africa in America." In *Black Spokesman: Selected Published Writings of Edward Wilmot Blyden*, edited by H. R. Lynch, 25–34. London: Frank Cass, 1971.
Blyden, Nemata. *West Indians in West Africa, 1808–1880: The African Diaspora in Reverse*. Rochester, NY: Rochester University Press, 2000.
Bocquet, Léon. "Préface." In *Le petit roi de Chimérie*, by René Maran, 7–63. Paris: Albin Michel, 1924.
Bois, Yve-Alain, and Rosalind E. Krauss. *Formless: A User's Guide*. New York: Zone Books, 1999.
Boittin, Jennifer. *Colonial Metropolis: The Urban Grounds of Anti-imperialism and Feminism in Interwar Paris*. Lincoln: University of Nebraska Press, 2010.
Borquaye, Stephen. *The Saga of Accra Hearts of Oak Sporting Club*. Accra: New Times Press, 1968.
Bouquiaux, Luc, Jean-Marie Jobozo, and Marcel Diki-Kidiri. *Dictionnaire sango-français*. Paris: Société d'Études Linguistiques et Anthropologiques de France, 1978.
Boyle, Sheila Tully, and Andrew Bunie. *Paul Robeson: The Years of Promise and Achievement*. Amherst: University of Massachusetts Press, 2001.
Brand, Dionne. *A Map to the Door of No Return: Notes to Belonging*. Toronto: Vintage Canada, 2001.
Brathwaite, Kamau. "The African Presence in Caribbean Literature." *Daedalus* 103, no. 2 (1974): 73–109.
Brathwaite, Kamau. "Caliban's Garden." *Wasafiri* 16 (Autumn 1992): 2–6.
Brathwaite, Kamau. "Caribbean Man in Space and Time." *Savacou* 11–12 (September 1975): 1–11.
Brathwaite, Kamau. *Contradictory Omens: Cultural Diversity and Integration in the Caribbean*. Mona: Savacou Publications, 1974.
Brathwaite, Kamau. *The Development of Creole Society in Jamaica, 1770–1820*. Oxford: Oxford University Press, 1971.
Brathwaite, Kamau. *History of the Voice: The Development of Nation Language in Anglophone Caribbean Poetry*. London: New Beacon Books, 1984.
Brathwaite, Kamau. "Islands." In *The Arrivants: A New World Trilogy*, 204–5. Oxford: Oxford University Press, 1973.
Brathwaite, Kamau. *Middle Passages*. New York: New Directions Books, 1992.
Brathwaite, Kamau. "Timehri." *Savacou* 2 (1970): 35–45.
Brereton, Bridget. *Race Relations in Colonial Trinidad, 1870–1900*. Cambridge: Cambridge University Press, 1979.
Brereton, Bridget. "Society and Culture in the Caribbean: The British and French West Indies, 1870–1900." In *The Modern Caribbean*, edited by Franklin W. Knight and Colin A. Palmer, 85–110. Chapel Hill: University of North Carolina Press, 1989.
Brown, Carolyn. *"We Were All Slaves": African Miners, Culture, and Resistance at the Enugu Government Colliery*. Portsmouth, NH: Heinemann, 2003.
Brown, Emmanuel Joseph Peter. *A Gold Coast and Asianti Reader*. London: Crown Agents for the Colonies, 1929.

Brunschwig, Henri. *Noirs et blancs dans l'Afrique noire française, ou comment le colonisé devient colonisateur, 1870–1914*. Paris: Flammarion, 1983.
Caine, W. Ralph Hall. *The Cruise of the Port Kingston*. London: Collier, 1908.
Campt, Tina M. *Listening to Images*. Durham, NC: Duke University Press, 2017.
Calloc'h, J. *Vocabulaire français-sango et sango-français, langue commerciale de l'Oubangui-Chari, précédé d'un abrégé grammatical*. Paris: P. Geuthner, 1911.
Capdepuy, Arlette. *Félix Eboué: De Cayenne au Panthéon (1884–1944)*. Paris: Karthala, 2015.
Carr, Andrew. "A Rada Community in Trinidad." *Caribbean Quarterly* 3, no. 1 (1953): 36–54.
Carew, Jan. *The Wild Coast*. London: Secker and Warburg, 1958.
Ceriana Mayneri, Andrea. *Sorcellerie et prophétisme en Centrafrique: L'imaginaire de la dépossession en pays Banda*. Paris: Karthala, 2014.
Césaire, Aimé. "Cahier d'un retour au pays natal." *Volontés* 20 (August 1939): 23–51.
Césaire, Aimé. *Cahier d'un retour au pays natal*. New York: Brentanos, 1947.
Césaire, Aimé. *Cahier d'un retour au pays natal*. Paris: Bordas, 1947.
Césaire, Aimé. *Cahier d'un retour au pays natal*. Paris: Présence Africaine, 1956.
Césaire, Aimé. *Cahier d'un retour au pays natal*. Paris: Présence Africaine, 1983.
Césaire, Aimé. "Letter to Maurice Thorez." Translated by Chike Jeffers. *Social Text* 28, no. 2 (2010): 145–52.
Césaire, Aimé. *Nègre je suis, nègre je resterai: Entretiens avec Françoise Vergès*. Paris: Albin Michel, 2005.
Chaduteau, Georges-Antoine. *Sango, langue nationale de Centrafrique: Dictionnaire français-sango, lexique sango-français, grammaire pratique du sango*. Sancerre, France: Dictionnaires d'Aujourd'hui, 2006.
Chakrabarty, Dipesh. *Provincializing Europe: Postcolonial Thought and Historical Difference*. Princeton, NJ: Princeton University Press, 2000.
Cheyfitz, Eric. *The Poetics of Imperialism: Translation and Colonization from the Tempest to Tarzan*. Philadelphia: University of Pennsylvania Press, 1991.
Christaller, Johann Gottlieb. *A Dictionary of the Asante and Fante Language Called Tshi (Chwee, Twi)*. Basel: L. Reinhardt, 1881.
Clegg, Claude A. *The Price of Liberty: African Americans and the Making of Liberia*. Chapel Hill: University of North Carolina Press, 2004.
Clifford, Lady Elizabeth. *Our Days on the Gold Coast, in Ashanti, in the Northern Territories, and in the British Sphere of Occupation in Togoland*. Accra: Charles Fairweather and Government Printing Office, 1918.
Cloarec-Heiss, France. *Dynamique et équilibre d'une syntaxe: Le banda-linda de Centrafrique*. Cambridge: Cambridge University Press, 1986.
Condé, Maryse. *La vie sans fards*. Paris: Jean-Claude Lattès, 2012.
Condé, Maryse. *What Is Africa to Me? Fragments of a True-to-Life Autobiography*. Translated by Richard Philcox. London: Seagull Books, 2017.
Conklin, Alice L. *In the Museum of Man: Race, Anthropology, and Empire in France, 1850–1950*. Ithaca, NY: Cornell University Press, 2013.
Conklin, Alice L. *A Mission to Civilize: The Republican Idea of Empire in France and West Africa, 1895–1930*. Stanford, CA: Stanford University Press, 1997.
Cooper, Frederick. *Citizenship between Empire and Nation: Remaking France and French Africa, 1945–1960*. Princeton, NJ: Princeton University Press, 2014.

Cooper, Frederick. *Colonialism in Question: Theory, Knowledge, History*. Berkeley: University of California Press, 2005.

Cooper, Frederick. "Conflict and Connection: Rethinking Colonial African History." *American Historical Review* 99, no. 5 (1994): 1516–45.

Cooper, Frederick. *Decolonization and African Society: The Labor Question in French and British Africa*. Cambridge: Cambridge University Press, 1996.

Cooper, Frederick, and Ann Laura Stoler, eds. *Tensions of Empire: Colonial Cultures in a Bourgeois World*. Berkeley: University of California Press, 1997.

Coquery-Vidrovitch, Catherine. *Le Congo au temps des grandes compagnies concessionaires, 1898–1930*. Paris: Mouton, 1972.

Cordell, Dennis. *Dar al-Kuti and the Last Years of the Trans-Saharan Slave Trade*. Madison: University of Wisconsin Press.

Curtin, Philip. *The Image of Africa: British Ideas and Action, 1780–1850*. Madison: University of Wisconsin Press, 1964.

Darby, Paul. "'Let Us Rally around the Flag': Football, Nation-Building, and Pan-Africanism in Kwame Nkrumah's Ghana." *Journal of African History* 54, no. 2 (2013): 221–46.

Daughton, J. P. *In the Forest of No Joy: The Congo-Océan Railroad and the Tragedy of French Colonialism*. New York: W. W. Norton, 2021.

Davies, H. O. *Memoirs*. Ibadan: Evans Brothers, 1989.

Dawes, Neville, and Kwame Dawes. *Fugue and Other Writings*. Leeds, UK: Peepal Tree, 2012.

de Dampierre, Éric. *Un ancien royaume bandia du Haut-Oubangui*. Paris: Librairie Plon, 1967.

de Graft-Johnson, Joseph William. *Towards Nationhood in West Africa*. London: Headley Brothers, 1928.

de Luna, Kathryn M. "Sounding the African Atlantic." *William and Mary Quarterly* 78, no. 4 (2021): 581–616.

Dennis, John A. "The René Maran Story: The Life and Times of a Black Frenchman, Colonial Administrator, Novelist, and Social Critic, 1887–1960." PhD diss., Stanford University, 1987.

Dewitte, Philippe. *Les mouvements nègres en France, 1919–1939*. Paris: L'Harmattan, 1985.

Diallo, Mamadou Bani. "La fonction initiatique du voyage dans l'oeuvre littéraire de Fily Dabo Sissoko." In *Les discours de voyages: Afrique-Antilles*, edited by Romuald Fonkoua, 217–25. Paris: Karthala, 1998.

Dickson, Kwamina B. *A Historical Geography of Ghana*. Cambridge: Cambridge University Press, 1971.

Doortmont, Michel, ed. *The Pen-Pictures of Modern Africans and African Celebrities by Charles Francis Hutchison*. Leiden: E. J. Brill, 2005.

Douglas, Rachel. *Making The Black Jacobins: C. L. R. James and the Drama of History*. Durham, NC: Duke University Press, 2019.

Drake, St. Clair. *The Redemption of Africa and Black Religion*. Atlanta: Third World Press, 1970.

Dubois, Laurent. *A Colony of Citizens: Revolution and Slave Emancipation in the French Caribbean, 1787–1804*. Chapel Hill: University of North Carolina Press, 2004.

Duffield, Ian. "Dusé Mohamed Ali and the Development of Pan-Africanism, 1866–1945." PhD diss., Edinburgh University, October 1971.

Duhamel, Georges. *Géographie cordiale de l'Europe*. Paris: Mercure de France, 1931.

Dumett, Raymond E. "The Social Impact of the European Liquor Trade on the Akan of Ghana (Gold Coast and Asante), 1875–1910." *Journal of Interdisciplinary History* 5, no. 1 (1974): 69–101.

Dyde, Brian. *The Empty Sleeve: The Story of the West India Regiments of the British Army*. Hertfordshire, UK: Hansib Publications, 1997.

Eboué, Félix. *Langues sango, banda, baya, mandjia: Notes grammaticales, mots groupés d'après le sens, phrase usualles, vocabulaire*. Paris: Larose, 1918.

Eboué, Félix. *La nouvelle politique indigène pour l'Afrique Équatoriale Française*. Paris: Office Français d'Édition, 1941.

Eboué, Félix. *Les peuples de l'Oubangui-Chari*. New York: AMS Press, [1933] 1977.

Eboué, Félix, and Narcisse Simonin. "Les Bayas de l'Ouham Pende." *Bulletin de la Société des Recherches Congolaises* 9 (1928): 32–38.

Ebroin, Ary. *Quimbois, magie noire et sorcellerie aux Antilles*. Paris: Jacques Grancher, 1977.

Edwards, Brent Hayes. "Aimé Césaire and the Syntax of Influence." *Research in African Literatures* 36, no. 2 (2005): 1–18.

Edwards, Brent Hayes. "The Ethnics of Surrealism." *Transition* 78 (1998): 84–135.

Edwards, Brent Hayes. *The Practice of Diaspora: Literature, Translation, and the Rise of Black Internationalism*. Cambridge, MA: Harvard University Press, 2003.

Edwards, Brent Hayes. "The Taste of the Archive." *Callaloo* 35, no. 4 (2021): 944–72.

Ellis, Major A. B. *The History of the First West India Regiment*. London: Chapman and Hall, 1885.

Esedebe, P. O. *Pan-Africanism: The Idea and Movement, 1776–1991*. Washington, DC: Howard University Press, 1994.

Eshleman, Clayton, and Annette Smith, trans. *Aimé Césaire: The Collected Poetry*. Berkeley: University of California Press, 1983.

Fabre, Michel. "René Maran, the New Negro and Négritude." *Phylon* 36, no. 3 (1975): 340–51.

Fallope, Josette. *Esclaves et citoyens: Les noirs à la Guadeloupe au XIXe siècle dans les processus de résistance et d'intégration: 1802–1910*. Basse-Terre: Société d'Histoire de la Guadeloupe, 1992.

Falola, Toyin. *Colonialism and Violence in Nigeria*. Bloomington: Indiana University Press, 2009.

Falola, Toyin, and Matt D. Childs, eds. *The Yoruba Diaspora in the Atlantic World*. Bloomington: Indiana University Press, 2005.

Fanon, Frantz. "Antillais et Africains." *Esprit* 223, no. 2 (February 1955): 261–69.

Fanon, Frantz. *Black Skin White Masks*. Translated by Richard Philcox. New York: Grove Press, [1952] 2007.

Fanon, Frantz. *The Wretched of the Earth*. Translated by Richard Philcox. New York: Grove Press, [1964] 2004.

Feierman, Steven. "Colonizers, Scholars, and the Creation of Invisible Histories." In *Beyond the Cultural Turn: New Directions in the Study of Society and Culture*, edited by Victoria E. Bonnell and Lynn Hunt, 182–216. Berkeley: University of California Press, 1999.

Feierman, Steven. *Peasant Intellectuals: Anthropology and History in Tanzania*. Madison: University of Wisconsin Press, 1990.

Feierman, Steven. "Struggles for Control: The Social Roots of Health and Healing in Modern Africa." *African Studies Review* 28, nos. 2–3 (1985): 73–147.

Feierman, Steven, and John M. Janzen, eds. *The Social Basis of Health and Healing in Africa*. Berkeley: University of California Press, 1992.

Ferdinand, Malcolm. *A Decolonial Ecology: Thinking from the Caribbean World*. Cambridge: Polity Press, 2022.

Ferreira, Jo-Anne S. "Caribbean Languages and Caribbean Linguistics." In *Caribbean Heritage*, edited by Basil Reid, 135–47. Kingston: University of the West Indies Press, 2012.

Ferrell, Lacy. "Fighting for the Future: A History of Education in Colonial Ghana, c. 1900–1940." PhD diss., University of Wisconsin-Madison, 2013.

Flores-Villalobos, Joan. "'Freak Letters': Tracing Gender, Race, and Diaspora in the Panama Canal Archive." *Small Axe* 23, no. 2 (2019): 34–56.

Flores-Villalobos, Joan. *The Silver Women: How Black Women's Labor Made the Panama Canal*. Philadelphia: University of Pennsylvania Press, 2023.

Fonkoua, Romuald, ed. *Correspondance Maran-Gahisto*. Paris: Présence Africaine, 2021.

Foster, Philip. *Education and Social Change in Ghana*. Chicago: University of Chicago Press, 1965.

Frobenius, Leo. "Dessins rupestres du sud de la Rhodésie." *Documents* 2, no. 4 (1930): 185–88.

Gahisto, Paul Manoel. "La genèse de Batouala." In *Hommage à René Maran*, 93–155. Paris: Présence Africaine, 1965.

Gaines, Kevin. *American Africans in Ghana: Black Expatriates in the Civil Rights Era*. Chapel Hill: University of North Carolina Press, 2006.

Garane, Jeanne. "The Invisibility of the African Interpreter." *Translation: A Transdisciplinary Journal* (2015). https://sc.edu/study/colleges_schools/artsandsciences/dllc/documents/faculty_pubs/garane/invisibility_of_the_african_interpreter.pdf.

Geissler, Paul Wenzel, and Guillaume Lachenal. "Brief Instructions for Archaeologists of African Futures." In *Traces of the Future: An Archaeology of Medical Science in Twenty-first-Century Africa*, edited by Paul Wenzel Geissler, Guillaume Lachenal, John Manton, and Noémi Tousignant, 14–30. Chicago: University of Chicago Press, 2016.

Getz, Trevor R. *Slavery and Reform in West Africa: Toward Emancipation in Nineteenth-Century Senegal and the Gold Coast*. Athens: Ohio University Press, 2004.

Gil, Alexander. "Bridging the Middle Passage: The Textual (R)evolution of Césaire's Cahier d'un Retour au Pays Natal." *Canadian Review of Comparative Literature* 38, no. 1 (2011): 40–56.

Giles-Vernick, Tamara. *Cutting the Vines of the Past: Environmental Histories of the Central African Rainforest*. Charlottesville: University of Virginia Press, 2002.

Giles-Vernick, Tamara. "Na lege ti guiriri (On the Road of History): Mapping Out the Past and Present in M'Bres Region, Central African Republic." *Ethnohistory* 43, no. 2 (1996): 245–75.

Giovannetti-Torres, Jorge L. *Black British Migrants in Cuba: Race, Labor, and Empire in the Twentieth-Century Caribbean, 1898–1948*. Cambridge: Cambridge University Press, 2018.

Giraud, Gaston. *Vocabulaire des dialectes sango, bakongo et a'zandé*. Paris: A. Challamel, 1908.

Glissant, Édouard. *Caribbean Discourse: Selected Essays*. Translated by Michael Dash. Charlottesville: University Press of Virginia, 1989.

Glissant, Édouard. *Poetics of Relation*. Translated by Betsy Wing. Ann Arbor: University of Michigan Press, [1990] 1997.

Goebel, Michael. *Anti-imperial Metropolis: Interwar Paris and the Seeds of Third World Nationalism*. Cambridge: Cambridge University Press, 2015.

Gomez, Michael. *African Dominion: A New History of Empire in Early and Medieval West Africa*. Princeton, NJ: Princeton University Press, 2018.

Gomez, Michael. *Exchanging Our Country Marks: The Transformation of African Identities in the Colonial and Antebellum South*. Chapel Hill: University of North Carolina Press, 1998.

Gondola, Didier. *Tropical Cowboys: Westerns, Violence, and Masculinity in Kinshasa*. Bloomington: Indiana University Press, 2016.

Goumba, Abel. *Les mémoires et les réflexions politiques du résistant anti-colonial, démocrate et militant panafricaniste, Abel Goumba*. Paris: Ccinia, 2006.

Graham, C. K. *The History of Education in Ghana: From the Earliest Times to the Declaration of Independence*. London: Frank Cass, 1971.

Grayzel, Susan R. *At Home and Under Fire: Air Raids and Culture in Britain from the Great War to the Blitz*. Cambridge: Cambridge University Press, 2012.

Green, Jeffrey. "Barbour-James, John Alexander." In *Dictionary of Caribbean and Afro-Latin American Biography, Volume 1*, edited by Franklin W. Knight and Henry Louis Gates Jr., 218–19. New York: Oxford University Press, 2016.

Green, Jeffrey. *Black Edwardians: Black People in Britain, 1901–1914*. London: Frank Cass, 1998.

Green, Jeffrey. "John Alexander Barbour-James (1867–1954)." *Journal of Ethnic and Migration Studies* 13, no. 2 (2010): 250 56.

Greene, Sandra E. *Gender, Ethnicity, and Social Change in the Upper Slave Coast: A History of the Anlo-Ewe*. London: Heinemann, 1995.

Greene, Sandra E. *Sacred Sites and the Colonial Encounter: A History of Meaning and Memory in Ghana*. Bloomington: Indiana University Press, 2002.

Greene, Sandra E. *West African Narratives of Slavery: Texts from Late Nineteenth- and Early Twentieth-Century Ghana*. Bloomington: Indiana University Press, 2011.

Guha, Ranajit. "Not at Home in Empire." *Critical Inquiry* 23, no. 3 (Spring 1997): 482–93.

Guha, Ranajit. "The Prose of Counter-Insurgency." In *Selected Subaltern Studies*, edited by Ranajit Guha and Gayatri Chakravorty Spivak, 45–86. Oxford: Oxford University Press, 1988.

Guyer, Jane, and Samuel M. Eno Belinga. "Wealth in People as Wealth in Knowledge." *Journal of African History* 36, no. 1 (1995): 91–120.

Hall, Stuart. "Negotiating Caribbean Identities." *New Left Review* 1, no. 209 (1995): 3–14.

Hamilton, Carolyn, Verne Harris, Jane Taylor, Michele Pickover, Graeme Reid, and Razia Saleh, eds. *Refiguring the Archive*. Dordrecht: Kluwer Academic Publishers, 2002.

Hanciles, Jehu J. "Dandeson Coates Crowther and the Niger Delta Pastorate: Blazing Torch or Flickering Flame?" *International Bulletin of Missionary Research* 18, no. 4 (1994): 166–72.

Hanretta, Sean. *Islam and Social Change in French West Africa: History of an Emancipatory Community*. Cambridge: Cambridge University Press, 2009.
Harding, Colin. *In Remotest Barotseland*. London: Hurst and Blackett, 1905.
Harms, Robert. *River of Wealth, River of Sorrow: The Central Zaire Basin in the Era of the Slave and Ivory Trade, 1500–1891*. New Haven, CT: Yale University Press, 1981.
Hélénon, Véronique. *French Caribbeans in Africa: Diasporic Connections and Colonial Administration, 1880–1939*. New York: Palgrave Macmillan, 2011.
Heuman, Gad. *"The Killing Time": The Morant Bay Rebellion in Jamaica*. Knoxville: University of Tennessee Press, 1994.
Heuman, Gad. "Peasants, Immigrants, and Workers: The British and French Caribbean after Emancipation." In *The Caribbean: A History of the Region and Its Peoples*, edited by Stephan Palmié and Francisco A. Scarano, 347–60. Chicago: University of Chicago Press, 2011.
Hill, Robert A., ed. *The Marcus Garvey and Universal Negro Improvement Association Papers, Volume VII: November 1927–August 1940*. Berkeley: University of California Press, 1983.
Hill, Robert A., ed. *The Marcus Garvey and Universal Negro Improvement Association Papers, Volume X: Africa for the Africans, 1923–1945*. Berkeley: University of California Press, 2006.
Hollier, Denis. "La valeur d'usage de l'impossible." In *Documents*, vii–xxxiv. Paris: Jean Michael Place, 1991.
Holm, John A. *Pidgins and Creoles, Volume 1: Theory and Structure*. Cambridge: Cambridge University Press, 1988.
Holt, Thomas C. *The Problem of Freedom: Race, Labor, and Politics in Jamaica and Britain, 1832–1938*. Baltimore: Johns Hopkins University Press, 1992.
Hunt, Nancy Rose. *A Colonial Lexicon: Of Birth Ritual, Medicalization, and Mobility in the Congo*. Durham, NC: Duke University Press, 1999.
Hunt, Nancy Rose. "History as Form, with Simmel in Tow." *History and Theory* 57, no. 4 (2018): 126–44.
Hunwick, John. "A Contribution to the Study of Islamic Teaching Traditions in West Africa: The Career of Muhammad Baghayogho, 930/1523–4 to 1002/1594." *Islam et Sociétés au Sud du Sahara* 4 (1990): 149–63.
Hunwick, John, and Nancy Lawler, eds. *The Cloth of Many Colored Silks: Papers on History and Society, Ghanaian and Islamic in Honour of Ivor Wilks*. Evanston, IL: Northwestern University Press, 1996.
Ibarra, Jorge, and K. O. Laurence, eds. *General History of the Caribbean, Volume IV: The Long Nineteenth Century: Nineteenth Century Transformations*. Paris: UNESCO, 2011.
Ibhawoh, Bonny. *Imperial Justice: Africans in Empire's Court*. Oxford: Oxford University Press, 2013.
Ikonné, Chidi. *Links and Bridges: A Comparative Study of the Writings of the New Negro and Negritude Movements*. Ibadan: University Press, 2005.
Izzo, Justin. *Experiments with Empire: Anthropology and Fiction in the French Atlantic*. Durham, NC: Duke University Press, 2019.
Jackson, Julian. *De Gaulle*. Cambridge, MA: Harvard University Press, 2018.
James, C. L. R. *Beyond a Boundary*. Durham, NC: Duke University Press, [1963] 2013.

James, C. L. R. *The Black Jacobins: Toussaint L'Ouverture and the San Domingo Revolution*. London: Secker and Warburg, 1938.

James, C. L. R. *The Life of Captain Cipriani*. Durham, NC: Duke University Press, [1932] 2014.

James, Winston. "Black Experience in Twentieth-Century Britain." In *Black Experience and the Empire*, edited by Philip D. Morgan and Sean Hawkins, 347–86. Oxford: Oxford University Press, 2004.

Janzen, John M. *Lemba, 1650–1930: A Drum of Affliction in Africa and the New World*. New York: Garland, 1982.

Janzen, John M. *The Quest for Therapy in Lower Zaire*. Berkeley: University of California Press, 1978.

Janzen, Philip. "Linga's Dream? Interpreters, Entextualization, and Knowledge Production in Central Africa." *American Historical Review* 127, no. 2 (2022): 755–85.

Janzen, Philip. "Tensions on the Railway: West Indians, Colonial Hierarchies, and the Language of Racial Unity in West Africa." *Journal of African History* 64, no. 3 (2023): 388–405.

Jarrett-Macauley, Delia. *The Life of Una Marson, 1905–65*. Manchester, UK: Manchester University Press, 1998.

Jean-Baptiste, Rachel. *Conjugal Rights: Marriage, Sexuality, and Urban Life in Colonial Libreville, Gabon*. Athens: Ohio University Press, 2013.

Jean-Baptiste, Rachel. *Multiracial Identities in Colonial French Africa: Race, Childhood, and Citizenship*. Cambridge: Cambridge University Press, 2023.

Jean-Louis, Henri. *Visions of Africa: Ten Years of Voyages of a West Indian Lawyer, Poet through the Western and Equatorial Black Continent*. Port of Spain: Guardian Commercial Printery, 1938.

Jenkins, David. *Black Zion: The Return of Afro-Americans and West Indians to Africa*. London: Wildwood House, 1975.

Jézéquel, Jean-Hervé. "'Collecting Customary Law': Educated Africans, Ethnographic Writings, and Colonial Justice in French West Africa." In *Intermediaries, Interpreters, and Clerks: African Employees in the Making of Colonial Africa*, edited by Benjamin N. Lawrance, Emily L. Osborn, and Richard L. Roberts, 139–58. Madison: University of Wisconsin Press, 2006.

Jones, Hilary. *The Métis of Senegal: Urban Life and Politics in French West Africa*. Bloomington: Indiana University Press, 2013.

Joseph, O'Neil. "History and Public Memory in Tobago: Opportunities and Obstacles." *History* 107, no. 375 (2022): 249–69.

Joseph-Gabriel, Annette K. *Reimagining Liberation: How Black Women Transformed Citizenship in the French Empire*. Urbana: University of Illinois Press, 2020.

Josephs, Kelly Baker. "Caribbean Studies in Digital Space and Time." *Small Axe* 25, no. 3 (2021): 105–15.

Kalck, Pierre. *Central African Republic: A Failure in De-colonisation*. Translated by Barbara Thomson. New York: Praeger, 1971.

Kale, Madhavi. *Fragments of Empire: Capital, Slavery, and Indian Indentured Labor in the British Caribbean*. Philadelphia: University of Pennsylvania Press, 1998.

Kane, Cheikh Hamidou. *Ambiguous Adventure*. Translated by Katherine Woods. London: Heinemann, 1972.

Kazanjian, David. *The Brink of Freedom: Improvising Life in the Nineteenth-Century Atlantic World*. Durham, NC: Duke University Press, 2016.

Keller, Kathleen. *Colonial Suspects: Suspicion, Imperial Rule, and Colonial Society in Interwar French West Africa*. Lincoln: University of Nebraska Press, 2018.

Killingray, David, and James Matthews. "Beasts of Burden: British West African Carriers in the First World War." *Canadian Journal of African Studies* 13, nos. 1–2 (1979): 5–23.

Knight, Franklin W. *The Caribbean: The Genesis of a Fragmented Nationalism*, 3d ed. Oxford: Oxford University Press, 2012.

Knight, Franklin W., and Colin A. Palmer, eds. *The Modern Caribbean*. Chapel Hill: University of North Carolina Press, 1989.

Kopytoff, Igor, and Suzanne Miers. *Slavery in Africa: Historical and Anthropological Perspectives*. Madison: University of Wisconsin Press, 1977.

Labrune-Badiane, Céline, and Étienne Smith. *Les hussards noirs de la colonie: Instituteurs africains et "petites patries" en AOF (1913–1960)*. Paris: Karthala, 2018.

Lachenal, Guillaume. *The Doctor Who Would Be King*. Translated by Cheryl Smeall. Durham, NC: Duke University Press, 2022.

Lamming, George. *In the Castle of My Skin*. Ann Arbor: University of Michigan Press, [1970] 1991.

Lamming, George. *The Pleasures of Exile*. Ann Arbor: University of Michigan Press, [1960] 1992.

Langley, J. A. *Pan-Africanism and Nationalism in West Africa, 1900–1945: A Study in Ideology and Social Classes*. Oxford: Oxford University Press, 1973.

Lara, Oruno D. *Le commandant Mortenol: Un officier guadeloupéen dans la Royale*. Epinay, France: Centre de Recherches Caraïbes-Amériques, 1985.

Lara, Oruno D. *La naissance du panafricanisme: Les racines caraïbes, américaines et africaines du mouvement au XIXe siècle*. Paris: Maisonneuve and Larose, 2000.

Larcher, Silyane. *L'autre citoyen: l'idéal républicain et les Antilles après l'esclavage*. Paris: Armand Colin, 2014.

Law, Robin, ed. *From Slave Trade to "Legitimate" Commerce: The Commercial Transition in Nineteenth-Century West Africa*. Cambridge: Cambridge University Press, 1995.

Lawrance, Benjamin N., Emily L. Osborn, and Richard L. Roberts, eds. *Intermediaries, Interpreters, and Clerks: African Employees in the Making of Colonial Africa*. Madison: University of Wisconsin Press, 2006.

Leiris, Michael. "De Bataille l'impossible à l'impossible *Documents*." *Critique* 195–96 (1963): 685–93.

"Lettre inédite de René Maran à André Fraisse, December 21, 1952." *Francofonía* 14 (2005): 11–13.

Lightfoot, Natasha J. *Troubling Freedom: Antigua and the Aftermath of British Emancipation*. Durham, NC: Duke University Press, 2015.

Lindsay, Lisa A. *Atlantic Bonds: A Nineteenth-Century Odyssey from America to Africa*. Chapel Hill: University of North Carolina Press, 2017.

Lindsay, Lisa A. *Working with Gender: Wage Labour and Social Change in Southwestern Nigeria*. Portsmouth, NH: Heinemann, 2003.

Louis, Patrice. *Conversation avec Aimé Césaire*. Paris: Arléa, 2007.
Lovejoy, Paul. *Transformations in Slavery: A History of Slavery in Africa*, 3d ed. Cambridge: Cambridge University Press, 2012.
Lowe, Lisa. *The Intimacies of Four Continents*. Durham, NC: Duke University Press, 2015.
Macaulay, Thomas Babington. "Machiavelli." In *English Essays: From Sir Philip Sidney to Macaulay*, edited by Charles W. Eliot, 380–421. New York: Collier and Son, 1909.
Macdonald, Roderick J., ed. *The Keys: The Official Organ of the League of Coloured Peoples*. Millwood, NY: Kraus-Thomson Organization, 1976.
Macharia, Keguro. "On Being Area-Studied: A Litany of Complaint." *GLQ* 22, no. 2 (April 1, 2016): 183–90.
MacNeill Stewart, Kenneth. "Ode to Independence." In *Ghana: One Year Old, a First Independence Anniversary*. Accra: Guinea Press, 1958.
Maddox, Tyesha. *A Home Away from Home: Mutual Aid, Political Activism, and Caribbean American Identity*. Philadelphia: University of Pennsylvania Press, 2024.
Mahabir, Noor Kumar, ed. *The Still Cry: Personal Accounts of East Indians in Trinidad and Tobago during Indentureship (1845–1917)*. Port of Spain: Calaloux Publications, 1985.
Makalani, Minkah. *In the Cause of Freedom: Radical Black Internationalism from Harlem to London, 1917–1939*. Chapel Hill: University of North Carolina Press, 2011.
Mallet, Robert. *Mussolini in Ethiopia, 1919–1935*. Cambridge: Cambridge University Press, 2015.
Mam Lam Fouck, Serge. *La Guyane au temps de l'esclavage, de l'or et de la francisation, 1802–1946*. Matoury, Guyane: Ibis Rouge, 1999.
Mamattah, Charles M. K. *The Ewes of West Africa: The Anlo-Ewes and Their Immediate Neighbours*. Accra: Volta Research Publications, 1978.
Manchuelle, François. "The 'Regeneration of Africa': An Important and Ambiguous Concept in 18th and 19th Century French Thinking about Africa." *Cahiers d'Études Africaines* 36, no. 144 (1996): 559–88.
Mann, Gregory. "Locating Colonial Histories: Between France and West Africa." *American Historical Review* 110, no. 2 (2005): 409–34.
Mann, Gregory. *Native Sons: West African Veterans and France in the Twentieth Century*. Durham, NC: Duke University Press 2006.
Maran, René. *Batouala: Véritable roman nègre*. Paris: Albin Michel, [1921] 1938.
Maran, René. *Félix Eboué: Grand commis et loyal serviteur, 1884–1944*. Paris: L'Harmattan, [1957] 2007.
Martin, Phyllis. *Leisure and Society in Colonial Brazzaville*. Cambridge: Cambridge University Press, 1995.
Massing, Andreas W. "Baghayogho: A Soninke Muslim Diaspora in the Mande World." *Cahiers d'Études Africaines* 44, no. 176 (2004): 887–922.
Matera, Marc. *Black London: The Imperial Metropolis and Decolonization in the Twentieth Century*. Oakland: University of California Press, 2015.
Matory, J. Lorand. *Black Atlantic Religion: Tradition, Transnationalism, and Matriarchy in the Afro-Brazilian Candomblé*. Princeton, NJ: Princeton University Press, 2005.
Matory, J. Lorand. "The English Professors of Brazil: On the Diasporic Roots of the Yoruba Nation." *Comparative Studies in Society and History* 41, no. 1 (1999): 72–103.

Mayer, Ruth. *Artificial Africas: Colonial Images in the Times of Globalization*. Hanover, NH: University Press of New England, 2002.

Maximin, Daniel. *Les fruits du cyclone: Une géopoétique de la Caraïbe*. Paris: Éditions du Seuil, 2006.

McCaskie, T. C. *Asante Identities: History and Modernity in an African Village, 1850–1950*. Bloomington: Indiana University Press, 2000.

McCaskie, T. C. "'Water Wars' in Kumasi, Ghana." In *African Cities: Competing Claims on Urban Spaces*, edited by Francesca Locatelli and Paul Nugent, 135–55. Boston: E. J. Brill, 2009.

McKinsey, Martin. "Missing Sounds and Mutable Meanings: Names in Derek Walcott's Omeros." *Callaloo* 31, no. 3 (2008): 891–902.

McKittrick, Katherine. *Dear Science and Other Stories*. Durham, NC: Duke University Press, 2021.

McKittrick, Katherine. *Demonic Grounds: Black Women and the Cartographies of Struggle*. Minneapolis: University of Minnesota Press, 2006.

Mignolo, Walter. *Local Histories, Global Designs*. Princeton, NJ: Princeton University Press, 2000.

Mills, John James. *J. J. Mills: His Own Account of His Life and Times*. Kingston: William Collins and Sangster, 1969.

Ministère de la Culture du Mali. *Tradition et modernité dans l'oeuvre littéraire de Fily Dabo Sissoko*. Bamako: Jamana, 2001.

Moses, Wilson Jeremiah. *Alexander Crummell: A Study of Civilization and Discontent*. Oxford: Oxford University Press, 1989.

Moyd, Michelle R. *Violent Intermediaries: African Soldiers, Conquest, and Everyday Colonialism in German East Africa*. Athens: Ohio University Press, 2014.

Mudimbe, V. Y. *The Invention of Africa: Gnosis, Philosophy, and the Order of Knowledge*. Bloomington: University of Indiana Press, 1988.

Mukoma wa Ngugi. "Blackness, Africans, and African Americans: Complex Solidarities and Beauty." Lecture, University of Nebraska-Lincoln, September 11, 2019. https://mediahub.unl.edu/media/11493.

Newell, Stephanie. *The Power to Name: A History of Anonymity in Colonial West Africa*. Athens: Ohio University Press, 2013.

Nicol, Abioseh. "West Indians in West Africa." *Sierra Leone Studies*, no. 13 (June 1960): 14–23.

Nicolas, Armand. *L'insurrection du sud à la Martinique: Septembre 1870*. Fort-de-France, Martinique: Imprimeur Populaire, 1970.

Niranjana, Tejaswini. *Siting Translation: History, Post-structuralism, and the Colonial Context*. Berkeley: University of California Press, 1992.

Nobili, Mauro, and Mohamed Shahid Mathee. "Towards a New Study of the So-called Tārīkh al-Fattāsh." *History in Africa* 42 (2015): 37–73.

Nzabakomada-Yakoma, Raphaël. *L'Afrique Centrale insurgée: La guerre du Kongo-Wara, 1928–1930*. Paris: L'Harmattan, 1986.

Ochonu, Moses E. *Colonialism by Proxy: Hausa Imperial Agents and Middle Belt Consciousness in Nigeria*. Bloomington: Indiana University Press, 2014.

Odamtten, Harry N. K. *Edward W. Blyden's Intellectual Transformations: Afropublicanism, Pan-Africanism, Islam, and the Indigenous West African Church*. East Lansing: Michigan State University Press, 2019.

Odotei, Irene K. "The Ga and Their Neighbors, 1600–1742." PhD diss., University of Ghana, 1972.

Okonkwo, Rina. "Amos Stanley Wynter Shackleford: Bread King and Nationalist." In *Heroes of West African Nationalism*, by Rina Okonkwo, 45–58. Enugu, Nigeria: Delta, 1985.

Okonkwo, Rina. "The Garvey Movement in British West Africa." *Journal of African History* 21, no. 1 (1980): 105–17.

Okonkwo, Rina. "A Jamaican Export to Nigeria! The Life of Amos Stanley Wynter Shackleford." *Caribbean Quarterly* 30, no. 2 (June 1984): 48–59.

Okuda, Alison. "Caribbean and African Exchanges: The Post-Colonial Transformation of Ghanaian Music, Identity, and Social Structure." PhD diss., New York University, 2016.

Omolewa, Michael. "'Educating the 'Native': A Study of the Education Adaption Strategy in British Colonial Africa, 1910–1936." *Journal of African American History* 91, no. 3 (Summer 2006): 267–87.

Onana, Charles. *René Maran: Le premier Goncourt noir, 1887–1960*. Paris: Duboiris, 2007.

Otim, Patrick William. *Acholi Intellectuals: Knowledge, Power, and the Making of Colonial Northern Uganda, 1850–1960*. Athens: Ohio University Press, 2024.

Palmer, Colin A. *Inward Yearnings: Jamaica's Journey to Nationhood*. Kingston: University of the West Indies Press, 2016.

Palmié, Stephan, and Francisco A. Scarano, eds. *The Caribbean: A History of the Region and Its Peoples*. Chicago: University of Chicago Press, 2011.

Parker, John. *Making the Town: Ga State and Society in Early Colonial Accra*. Portsmouth, NH: Heinemann, 2000.

Paton, Diana. *The Cultural Politics of Obeah: Religion, Colonialism, and Modernity in the Caribbean World*. Cambridge: Cambridge University Press, 2015.

Paton, Diana, and Matthew J. Smith, eds. *The Jamaica Reader*. Durham, NC: Duke University Press, 2021.

Pels, Peter, and Oscar Salemink, eds. *Colonial Subjects: Essays on the Practical History of Anthropology*. Ann Arbor: University of Michigan Press, 1999.

Perbi, Akosua Adoma. *A History of Indigenous Slavery in Ghana: From the Fifteenth to the Nineteenth Century*. Accra: Sub-Saharan Publishers, 2004.

Peterson, Derek R., Emma Hunter, and Stephanie Newell, eds. *African Print Cultures: Newspapers and Their Publics in the Twentieth Century*. Ann Arbor: University of Michigan Press, 2016.

Pieterse, Jan Nederveen. *White on Black: Images of Africa and Blacks in Western Popular Culture*. New Haven, CT: Yale University Press, 1992.

Prais, Jinny. "Imperial Travelers: The Formation of West African Urban Culture, Identity, and Citizenship in London and Accra, 1925–1935." PhD diss., University of Michigan, 2008.

Pratt, Mary Louise. *Imperial Eyes: Travel Writing and Transculturation*. London: Routledge, 1992.

Putnam, Lara. "Circum-Atlantic Print Circuits and Internationalism from the Peripheries in the Interwar Era." In *Print Culture Histories beyond the Metropolis*, edited by James J. Connolly, Patrick Collier, Frank Felsenstein, Kenneth R. Hall, and Robert G. Hall, 215–39. Toronto: University of Toronto Press, 2016.

Putnam, Lara. *The Company They Kept: Migrants and the Politics of Gender in Caribbean Costa Rica, 1870–1960*. Chapel Hill: University of North Carolina Press, 2002.

Putnam, Lara. *Radical Moves: Caribbean Migrants and the Politics of Race in the Jazz Age*. Chapel Hill: University of North Carolina Press, 2013.

Putnam, Lara. "To Study the Fragments/Whole: Microhistory and the Atlantic World." *Journal of Social History* 39, no. 3 (Spring 2006): 615–30.

Putnam, Lara. "The Transnational and the Text-Searchable: Digital Sources and the Shadows They Cast." *American Historical Review* 121, no. 2 (2016): 377–402.

Ray, Carina E. *Crossing the Color Line: Race, Sex, and the Contested Politics of Colonialism in Ghana*. Athens: Ohio University Press, 2015.

Reindorf, Carl C. *History of the Gold Coast and Asante*. Basel: Basel Mission Book Depot, 1895.

Renauld, George. *Félix Eboué et Eugénie Eboué-Tell: Défenseurs des peuples noirs*. Paris: Detrad aVs, 2007.

Renwick, Vivian. "Forty Years On . . ." *Nigeria: A Quarterly Magazine of General Interest* 43–44 (1954): 192–236.

Rey, Terry. "Kongolese Catholic Influences on Haitian Popular Catholicism: A Sociohistorical Exploration." In *Central Africans and Cultural Transformations in the American Diaspora*, edited by Linda M. Heywood, 265–86. Cambridge: Cambridge University Press, 2002.

Rhys, Jean. *Voyage in the Dark*. New York: W. W. Norton, [1934] 1982.

Robinson, Douglas. *Translation and Empire: Postcolonial Theories Explained*. London: Routledge, [1997] 2016.

Rodney, Walter. *A History of the Guyanese Working People, 1881–1905*. Baltimore: Johns Hopkins University Press, 1981.

Rodney, Walter. *How Europe Underdeveloped Africa*. Washington, DC: Howard University Press, 1982.

Rouse-Jones, Margaret, and Estelle M. Appiah. "Interview with Dr. Ralph Hoyte." Oral history interview, June 28, 2005, file no. OP117. Oral and Pictorial Records Programme, University of the West Indies, St. Augustine, Trinidad.

Rouse-Jones, Margaret, and Estelle M. Appiah. *Returned Exile: George James Christian of Dominica and the Gold Coast, 1869–1940*. Kingston: University of the West Indies Press, 2016.

Rubiales, Lourdes. "Désillusion et frustration: L'administration coloniale contre René Maran." *Cahiers de la Société Internationale d'Étude des Littératures de l'Ere Coloniale* 6 (2010): 218–37.

Rubiales, Lourdes. "Notes sur la réception du Goncourt 1921 en France." *Francofonia* 14 (2005): 123–45.

Saada, Emmanuelle. *Les enfants de la colonie: Les métis de l'empire français entre sujétion et citoyenneté*. Paris: La Découverte, 2007.

Sackeyfio, Naaborko. "The Politics of Land and Urban Space in Colonial Accra." *History in Africa* 39 (2012): 293–329.

Sacks, Ruth. "Lived Remainders: The Contemporary Lives of Iron Hotels in the Congo." *Architectural Theory Review* 22, no. 1 (2018): 64–82.

Said, Edward. *Orientalism*. New York: Vintage, 1979.

Samson, Anne. "Unravelling the Past: World War I in Africa." *Journal of Asian and African Studies* 57, no. 1 (2022): 60–77.

Sanneh, Lamin. *Abolitionists Abroad: American Blacks and the Making of Modern West Africa*. Cambridge, MA: Harvard University Press, 1999.

Sautter, Gilles. "Notes sur la construction du chemin de fer Congo-Océan (1921–1934)." *Cahiers d'Études Africaines* 7, no. 26 (1967): 219–99.

Scarano, Francisco. "Labor and Society in the Nineteenth Century." In *The Modern Caribbean*, edited by Franklin W. Knight and Colin A. Palmer, 51–84. Chapel Hill: University of North Carolina Press, 1989.

Scheel, Charles W. "Jean-Louis Baghio'o père et fils: Deux écrivains antillais du vingtième siècle entre quatre continents." *Revue de Littérature Comparée* 537, no. 1 (2016): 63–77.

Scheel, Charles W. "René Maran: Genèses de la première édition (1921) de Batouala, véritable roman nègre, et de sa préface." *Continents Manuscrits* 17 (2021): 1–18.

Scheel, Charles W., ed. *Victor Jean-Louis Baghio'o par lui-meme: Lettres, journaux, essais, et récits inédits*. Paris: L'Harmattan, 2016.

Schoenbrun, David L. "Conjuring the Modern in Africa: Durability and Rupture in Histories of Public Healing between the Great Lakes of East Africa." *American Historical Review* 111, no. 5 (2006): 1403-1439.

Schuler, Monica. *Alas, Alas, Kongo: A Social History of Indentured African Immigration to Jamaica, 1841–1865*. Baltimore: Johns Hopkins University Press, 1980.

Scott, David. "The Re-enchantment of Humanism: An Interview with Sylvia Wynter." *Small Axe* 8 (2000): 119–207.

Sekyi, Kobina. *The Blinkards*. London: Heinemann, [1915] 1974.

Selvon, Samuel. *The Lonely Londoners*. London: Penguin Classics, [1959] 2021.

Senah, Emmanuel Kwaku. "Rada." In *The Encyclopedia of Caribbean Religions, Volume 2: M–Z*, edited by Patrick Taylor and Frederick I. Case, 742–48. Chicago: University of Illinois Press, 2013.

Sharpe, Jenny. *Immaterial Archives: An African Diaspora Poetics of Loss*. Evanston, IL: Northwestern University Press, 2020.

Shepperson, George. "Notes on Negro American Influences on the Emergence of African Nationalism." *Journal of African History* 1, no. 2 (1960): 299–312.

Sibeud, Emmanuelle. *Une science impériale pour l'Afrique? La construction des savoirs africanistes en France 1878–1930*. Paris: Éditions de l'École des Hautes Études en Sciences Sociales, 2002.

Sidbury, James. *Becoming African in America: Race and Nation in the Early Black Atlantic*. Oxford: Oxford University Press, 2007.

Sidibe, Modibo Halassi. *Fily Dabo Sissoko, un grand sage africain*. Bamako: Cité du Niger, 2007.

Sissoko, Fily Dabo. "Enquête sur l'enfant noir de l'AOF: L'enfant bambara." *Bulletin de l'Enseignement de l'Afrique Occidentale Française* 76 (1931): 3–24.

Sissoko, Fily Dabo. "La géomancie." *Bulletin de Recherches Soudanaises* 8–9 (November–December 1936): 1–21 [248–68].

Sissoko, Fily Dabo. *Une page est tournée*. Dakar: A. Diop, 1959.

Sissoko, Fily Dabo. "La politesse et les civilités des noirs." *Extrait du Bulletin de Recherches Soudanaises* 4 (October 1936): 1–14 [178–92].

Sissoko, Fily Dabo. *La savane rouge*. Avignon, France: Presses Universelles, 1962.

Smith, Faith. *Strolling in the Ruins: The Caribbean's Non-sovereign Modern in the Early Twentieth Century*. Durham, NC: Duke University Press, 2023.

Smith, Matthew J. "A Tale of Two Tragedies: Forgetting and Remembering Kingston (1907) and Port-au-Prince (2010)." *Kartib-Nordic Journal for Caribbean Studies* 4, no. 1 (2019): 1–14.

Smith, Theophus H. *Conjuring Culture: Biblical Formations of Black America*. Oxford: Oxford University Press, 1995.

Steemers, Vivian. "Appropriation of a Controversial Novel: Transnational Reception of René Maran's Batouala." *Research in African Literatures* 50, no. 2 (2019): 219–37.

Steiner-Khamsi, Gita, and Hubert O. Quist. "The Politics of Educational Borrowing: Re-opening the Case of Achimota of British Ghana." *Comparative Education Review* 44, no. 3 (August 2000): 272–99.

Stephens, Michelle Ann. *Black Empire: The Masculine Global Imaginary of Caribbean Intellectuals in the United States, 1914–1962*. Durham, NC: Duke University Press, 2005.

Stewart, Dianne. *Three Eyes for the Journey: African Dimensions of the Jamaican Religious Experience*. Oxford: Oxford University Press, 2005.

Stoler, Ann Laura. *Along the Archival Grain: Epistemic Anxieties and Colonial Common Sense*. Princeton, NJ: Princeton University Press, 2008.

Stoler, Ann Laura, and Frederick Cooper. "Between Metropole and Colony: Rethinking a Research Agenda." In *Tensions of Empire: Colonial Cultures in a Bourgeois World*, edited by Frederick Cooper and Ann Laura Stoler, 1–56. Berkeley: University of California Press, 1997.

Stovall, Tyler. *Paris Noir: African Americans in the City of Light*. New York: Houghton Mifflin, 1996.

Sweet, James H. "The Evolution of Ritual in the African Diaspora: Central African Kilundu in Brazil, St. Domingue, and the United States, Seventeenth–Nineteenth Centuries." In *Diasporic Africa: A Reader*, edited by Michael Gomez, 64–80. New York: New York University Press, 2006.

Sweet, James H. "Mistaken Identities? Olaudah Equiano, Domingos Álvares, and the Methodological Challenges of Studying the African Diaspora." *American Historical Review* 114, no. 2 (April 2009): 279–306.

Sylvestre, Emile, and Eustache Lotaut, eds. *Annuaire de la vie martiniquaise, 1936*. Fort-de-France, Martinique: Imprimerie du Gouvernement, 1936.

Taber, Charles R. *A Dictionary of Sango*. Hartford, CT: Hartford Seminary Foundation, 1965.

Tasie, G. O. M. *Christian Missionary Enterprise in the Niger Delta, 1864–1918*. Leiden: E. J. Brill, 1978.

Teelucksingh, Jerome. *Labour and the Decolonization Struggle in Trinidad and Tobago.* London: Palgrave Macmillan, 2015.
Terretta, Meredith. "Anticolonial Lawyering, Postwar Human Rights, and Decolonization across Imperial Boundaries in Africa." *Canadian Journal of History* 52, no. 3 (2017): 448–78.
Thomas, J. J. *The Theory and Practice of Creole Grammar.* Port of Spain: Chronicle Publishing Office, 1869.
Thomas, Roy Darrow, ed. *The Trinidad Labour Riots of 1937: Perspectives 50 Years Later.* St. Augustine, Trinidad: University of the West Indies Press, 1987.
Tisserant, Charles. *Dictionnaire Banda-Français.* Paris: Institut d'Ethnologie, 1931.
Tisserant, Charles. *Sango, langue véhiculaire de l'Oubangui-Chari.* Issy-les-Moulineaux. France: Presses Missionnaires, 1950.
Treves, Frederick. *The Cradle of the Deep: An Account of a Voyage to the West Indies.* New York: E. P. Dutton, 1908.
Trouillot, Michel-Rolph. *Silencing the Past: Power and the Production of History.* Boston: Beacon Press, 1995.
Tuffrau, Paul. "Hommage." In *Hommage à René Maran*, 253–62. Paris: Présence Africaine, 1965.
Vansina, Jan. *Paths in the Rainforests: Toward a History of Political Tradition in Equatorial Africa.* Madison: University of Wisconsin Press, 1990.
Venkatachalam, Meera. *Slavery, Memory, and Religion in Southeastern Ghana, c. 1850–Present.* Cambridge: Cambridge University Press, 2015.
Venuti, Lawrence. *The Translator's Invisibility: A History of Translation*, 2d ed. London: Routledge, [1995] 2008.
Vickery, Kenneth P. *Black and White in Southern Zambia: The Tonga Plateau.* New York: Greenwood Press, 1986.
Vinson, Robert Trent. *The Americans Are Coming! Dreams of African American Liberation in Segregationist South Africa.* Athens: Ohio University Press, 2012.
Walcott, Derek. "The Antilles: Fragments of an Epic Memory" (1992). In *What the Twilight Says: Essays*, by Derek Walcott, 65–84. New York: Farrar, Straus and Giroux, 1998.
Walcott, Derek. *Omeros.* New York: Farrar, Straus and Giroux, 1990.
Wariboko, Waibinte. *Ruined by "Race": Afro-Caribbean Missionaries and the Evangelization of Southern Nigeria, 1895–1925.* Trenton, NJ: Africa World Press, 2007.
Warner, Keith Q., ed. *Critical Perspectives on Léon-Gontran Damas.* Washington, DC: Three Continents Press, 1988.
Warner-Lewis, Maureen. *Central Africa in the Caribbean: Transcending Time, Transforming Culture.* Kingston: University of the West Indies Press, 2003.
Warner-Lewis, Maureen. *Guinea's Other Suns: The African Dynamic in Trinidad Culture.* Kingston: University of the West Indies Press, 2015.
Warner-Lewis, Maureen. *Trinidad Yoruba: From Mother Tongue to Memory.* Tuscaloosa: University of Alabama Press, 1996.
Watson, Ruth, "Literacy as a Style of Life: Garveyism and Gentlemen in Colonial Ibadan." *African Studies* 73, no. 1 (2014): 1–21.
Weinstein, Brian. *Eboué.* Oxford: Oxford University Press, 1972.
Weinstein, Brian. "Eboué and the Chiefs." *Journal of African History* 11, no. 1 (1970): 107–26.

White, Bob W. "Talk about School: Education and the Colonial Project in French and British Africa (1860–1960)." *Comparative Education* 32, no. 1 (March 1996): 9–25.
White, Owen. *Children of the French Empire: Miscegenation and Colonial Society in French West Africa, 1895–1960*. Oxford: Oxford University Press, 1999.
White, Walter. *A Rising Wind*. New York: Doubleday, 1945.
Whitehouse, Bruce. *Migrants and Strangers in an African City: Exile, Dignity, Belonging*. Bloomington: Indiana University Press, 2012.
Wilder, Gary. "Colonial Ethnology and Political Rationality in French West Africa." *History and Anthropology* 14, no. 3 (2003): 219–52.
Wilder, Gary. *Freedom Time: Negritude, Decolonization, and the Future of the World*. Durham, NC: Duke University Press, 2015.
Wilder, Gary. *The French Imperial Nation-State: Negritude and Colonial Humanism between the Two World Wars*. Chicago: University of Chicago Press, 2005.
Wilder, Gary. "Untimely Vision: Aimé Césaire, Decolonization, Utopia." *Public Culture* 21, no. 1 (2009): 101–40.
Williams, Gavin. "Garveyism, Akinpelu Obiesesan and His Contemporaries: Ibadan, 1920–1922." In *Legitimacy and the State in Twentieth-Century Africa*, edited by Terence Ranger and Olufemi Vaughan, 112–32. Hampshire, UK: Macmillan, 1993.
Winer, Lise, ed. *Dictionary of the English/Creole of Trinidad and Tobago on Historical Principles*. Montreal: McGill-Queen's University Press, 2008.
Wrangham, Elizabeth. "An African Road Revolution: The Gold Coast in the Period of the Great War." *Journal of Imperial and Commonwealth History* 32, no. 1 (2004): 1–18.
Wynter, Sylvia. "Novel and History, Plot and Plantation." *Savacou* 5 (1971): 95–102.
Yankholmes, Aaron Kofi Badu, Kwaku Adutwum Boakye, and Henry Nii Adziri Wellington. "'Awusai Atso': Community Attachment to and Use of Transatlantic Slave Trade Resources in Danish-Osu, Ghana." *Journal of Heritage Tourism* 5, no. 1 (2010): 49–67.
Yates, Walter Ladell. "The History of the African Methodist Episcopal Zion Church in West Africa, Liberia, Gold Coast (Ghana) and Nigeria, 1900–1939." PhD diss., Hartford Seminary Foundation, Hartford, CT, 1967.
Yeboah, Tony. "Phoenix Rise: A History of the Burnt City of Kumase, 1874–1960." *Journal of West African History* 5, no. 1 (2019): 51–82.
Zachernuk, Philip S. *Colonial Subjects: An African Intelligentsia and Atlantic Ideas*. Charlottesville: University of Virginia Press, 2000.
Zimmermann, Johannes. *A Grammatical Sketch and Vocabulary of the Akra- or Gã-Language*, 2 vols. Stuttgart: J. F. Steinkopf, 1858.

Index

Page locators in italics indicate figures.

Accra (Ghana), *37*; Achimota College, 145; Angelou in, 98–99; Hearts of Oak Sporting Club, 153; Lakote Aduaoshi's settlement of, 42–44, *43*; plague of 1908, 36; print culture, 13, 100–102. *See also* MacNeill Stewart, Kenneth

Achimota College (Accra), 145

administrators, Caribbean: Africa, ideas about, 22–26; and African languages, 41–45, 47, 74–75, 77, 81–88, 109–16; African views of, 31–32, 35–36, 46–47, 75–76, 89, 114, 138, 142, 154–55; attachment to British and French empires, 19–20, 31–32, 35, 48–50, 105–6, 136, 142, 177, 180; awareness of implications of imperialism, 41, 48–50, 71, 75, 98, 143, 178, 179; "Caribbean" identities, 71; children of, 16, 75–79, 91, 99–103, 114–16, 152; in colonial archives, 5–6, 50–51, 53–62, 65–68, 157–61, 180–81; and colonial imperatives, 26–28, 33–35, 45–46, 50 76, 89; deaths of, 55–58, 59, 69–70, 100, 106, 130–31, 175–76, 180, 198n57, 220n106; doubly marginalized, 4, 31–32, 35, 38, 47, 48, 177; economic reasons for migration, 17–19, 29; educational reasons for migration, 20–22; and "Europeanness," 39–40, 48–50, 146; families of, 53–61, 75–79, 89, 99–100, *117*, 131, 135, 140–41, 147–48; and "imaginary" grievances, 45, 48–49, 59; mobility of, 14, 20, 70, 162; positions held by in Caribbean, 22, 35, 75, 122–24, 128, 135; racism encountered by, 32, 35, 37–41, 46–49, 59, 71, 74, 78, 95, 134, 140, 178, 180; role of in violence, 34, 45–46, 50, 109; salaries, 26, 36–37, 64, 139, 200n24, 214n26, 215n34; sense of paternalistic kinship with Africans, 17, 24, 29, 50, 111, 127; sense of superiority, 32, 50, 115, 130–31, 134, 142, 180; stranded in metropole, 56, 62, 64, 78

Afolabe (character in *Omeros*), 14, 186n58

Africa: connections with Caribbean, 14, 86–88, 100, 102, 122–23, 125, 129, 149, 152–53, 171; cultures and histories of, 4, 106, 110–14, 124–27, 128, 131, 149, 159, 178; emigration initiatives, 27–28; hierarchies of colonies in, 32, 38–40, 47–49, 114–15, 145–46; intellectual traditions in, 73, 86, 88, 99, 106–7, 111, 131; migration within, 33, 35–36; as "mysterious" continent, 22–26, 100–101, 131; tropical illnesses, 26, 57, 59, 75–76, 87–88, 190n60, 199n9; Republic of, 155–57, 164, 174–76

"Africa for Africans" slogan, 36, 169, 192n27

African Affairs, 101, 204n102

African cultures: celebrated in London, 148–49; destructive effects of colonial ideologies on, 33, 42–44, 109–10, 178; ethnographic study of, 106–7, 109, 110–22, 124, 126–27, 131, 177; form and fragmentation imposed on, 131; influence of in Caribbean, 22–26, 86–88, 189n48

African Methodist Episcopal (AME) Zion Church, 13, 94–97, 99, 142; "racial consciousness" and, 95–98; transatlantic links, 95–98; Zion Secondary School (Anloga), 96–97
African Morning Post, 101
African Progress Union (APU), 93, 148–49, 150, 202n73
The African Times and Orient Review, 69, 129, 147
Afrique Équatoriale Française (AEF), 41, 105–6, 115, 125, 128, 158–59, 164, 205n10, 206n28, 212n133
Afrique Occidentale Française (AOF), 55, 123–24, 158–60
Afro-Atlantic dialogue, 153, 220n107
Afro-Brazilians, 153
Agbebi, Mojola, 101
Aggrey, James Kwegyir, 94–96, 145, 214n18, 216–17n55
agricultural production: in Caribbean, 17–19, 152; in Central Africa 109, 119–20; in West Africa, 122, 134
Alexis, Edwina Violetta, *52*, 53–54, 56, 59, 61–62, 72, 177
Alexis, Mark, 53–54, 61–62, 177; "imaginary" illness of, 59; transfer requests of, 56, 59, 196n19
Alfassa, Matteo, 124
Algerian War, 106, 157, 173–74
Ali, Dusé Mohamed, 69, 93, 129, 147–48, 150, 217n69
All God's Children Need Traveling Shoes (Angelou), 73, 90–99, 202n66
Ambiguous Adventure (Kane), 172–73, 223n66
Ambleston, John, 68–69, 146–47
American Colonization Society, 27
Amissah, George, 138, 140
ancestors, Africans as, 31–32, 85, 179; in Caribbean, 23–25, 102, 170–71, 179, 186n58
Angelou, Maya, 73, 90–99, 202n66
Anglican Church, 16, 27, 69, 75, 140, 147
Anlo-Ewe people, 89–90, 94–97
Anlo Progress Union, 93, 95
anticolonial movements, 5, 98, 157; Cameroon, 157, 160
"Antillais et Africains" (Fanon), 130, 179, 212n131
Appiah, James W., 89, 98, 201n55

Archer, John Richard, 148
archives, 3–7, 197n34; "archival recovery," 68, 161; colonial archives, 3–6, 50–51, 61–62, 68, 72, 153; forms of, 3–6, 50–51, 67–68, 134; power to fragment, 4, 6, 11, 41, 51, 61–62, 68, 153, 180–81; imperial bureaucracies reflected in, 53–72; limits of, 5–6; photographs in, *52*, 53–54, 67; "reading across," 6, 184n19; scattered geographically, 134; scopic metaphors and, 13, 61–62; unformed, 11, 14
Archives Nationales d'Outre-Mer (Aix-en-Provence), 41, 158–61
Archives Territoriales de Martinique, 161
Arthur, John, 88–89, 198n55
Arthur, Joseph, 69
Asante state, 35–36, 79–80, 89
Assan, J. A., 81, 86–87
assimilation, 111, 165–68; critiques of, 124, 126, 165–68, 170; education as tool for, 20–22; through slavery in West Africa, 35
Atorkor narrative, 97, 203n87
Attoh-Ahuma, Samuel, 138, 142, 215n42
Azikiwe, Nnamdi, 101

Bâ, Magatte, 160
Baba, Ahmad, 171
Bada Marcelline, 114–15, 116, 117, 131
Baghayogho, Mohammed, 171, 189n53, 223n59
Baghio'o, Henri Jean-Louis. *See* Jean-Louis, Henri
Baghio'o, Mohamed, 25, 157, 170–71, 174
Baghio'oh, Jean-Louis dit, 170–71
"The Ballad of Africanus" (MacNeill Stewart), 100–101
Banda folktales, 13, 118–21, *119*, *120*, 208n68
Banda language, 106, 109, 111–15, 118–21, *119*, *120*, 208n72
Bandia (Ngbandi lineage), 110, 206n21
Bandung Conference (April 1955), 172, 175
Barbados, 19, 85, 135; imperial culture of, 73–74, 136; 1937 rebellion, 19, 135, 213n9
Barbour-James, Caroline, 17, 145, 187n9, 217n57
Barbour-James, Edith (née Goring), 13, 134–39, 144–51, *148*, 177; and League of Coloured Peoples, 150–51
Barbour-James, John, 19, 72, 135, 144, *148*; African appointment sought by, 15–17, 22, 26; and African Progress Union, 93, 148–49,

150; McNeil-Stewart, friendship with, 76, 93, 98, 199n17; racism encountered by, 145–46, 217n63
Basel Mission, 42
Bataille, Georges, 9–10
Batouala: Véritable roman nègre (Maran), 47, 194n70
Beaudu, William, 55, 57–58, 60–61, 62, 177
Beccaria, Arthur, 160
belonging, geographies of, 4, 11, 14, 51, 99, 122, 181; kinship and social networks, 70, 96–98, 102–3; new forms, 89–91, 153; and "racial consciousness" discourse, 95–96; re-creating home, 70–72. *See also* networks
biblical references, 143, 190n71
Bibliothèque Nationale (Paris), 161
bilingualism, 120–21, 158. *See also* languages; translation
biomedicine, incursions of, 45–46, 114
"Black Atlantic" histories, 5
black internationalism, 5, 120–21. *See also* Pan-Africanism
The Black Jacobins: Toussaint Louverture and the San Domingo Revolution (James), 151
Black Stars football team (Ghana), 154
Bland, Edward, 31
Blum, Edgard, 55, 58
Blum, Léon, 166
Blyden, Edward W., 28, 36, 143
Boer War, 17
Bonneveau, Jean, 46
Borquaye, Stephen, 153–54
bounjouvouko (African clerk), meaning of, 47, 74, 114
Bouverat, Lucie, 55, 57–58, 60–61, 177
Brand, Dionne, 53, 200n23
Branker, W. A., 69
Brathwaite, Kamau, 10–11, 102, 179–81, 224n5
Brazil, 153
Brazzaville Conference (1944), 125–26, 130, 212n133
Bremen missionaries, 90, 94–95
British Empire, 3, 5–6, 17, 141, 151–52, 153; "Black London," 5, 149–51; educational model, 20, 75, 133–34; shift in administrators' thinking about, 38, 49, 88–89, 151, 153; shift in Hoyte's thinking about, 38, 49; undermined by networks, 151; and World War I, 88–89. *See also* empire; Empire Day

British Guiana, 15–17, *16*, 69, 71, 72, 76, 128–30, 139, 143, 148. *See also* Barbour-James, John; Britton, Joseph
Britton, Joseph, 13, 134–40, 142–45, 177, 180; and European sense of superiority, 139–40, 214nn24–26; fragmentation in sermon of, 143, 216n44; influence of, 144–45; links with League of Coloured Peoples, 149; loyalty to British Empire, 142; as preacher, 143, 216n44, 216n45; racial uplift, language of, 138, 153–54; retirement, 137–39, 144
"Brittonite Club," 144–45, 216nn51–52
Brown, E. J. P., 138, 214n18
Bryan, Herbert, 135–36
Buckle, Desmond, 138, 150–51, 219n94
Buckle, Vidal, 138, 151
Buckmire, Elias, 74
Bulletin de Recherches Soudanaises, 124
bureaucracies, imperial: indifference of, 45, 48–49, 55, 57, 59, 61–65, 100, 177; and transfer requests to, 15–17, 26, 53–61, 74, 196n19
Bustamante, Alexander, 140–41
Butler, Tubal Uriah, 168

Cahier d'un retour au pays natal (Césaire), 8–10, 123, 185nn41–42, 209n85
"Caliban's Garden" (Brathwaite), 10
Cameroon, 70, 83, 90, 128, 157, 160, 161, 173
Campbell, Robert, 198n51
Candace, Gratien, 47
Cape Coast (Gold Coast), 94, 135–38, *137*, 139–40 142–43; Cape Coast Castle, 136, 143; Christ Church, 142–43, *144*; Fante society, 137, 142; as slave-trading post, 143; *See also* Gold Coast
Cardew, Frederic, 27–28
Caribbean: African cultural influence in, 22–26, 189n47; archives in, 161; confederation concept, 166–70, 175; departmentalization, 10, 170, 172; education in, 20–22, *21*; fragmentation and form in, 7–12; imperial culture in, 19–20, 38, 50; languages of, 85–88; legacies of slavery in, 17–19; "Les Antilles aux Antillais," 169, 170; social divisions, 22; as space of relation, 7–11, 185n29; tobacco production, *18*; tricentenary of French Empire in, 71, 122, 165; uprisings, 19, 135

INDEX 249

"Caribbean Man in Space and Time" (Brathwaite), 11
Caribbean Sea, 7, 10, 149, 152, 181
Casely Hayford, Joseph, 93, 100–101, 137, 138, 148, 202n73, 214n20
centers and peripheries, 5–6, 162–63, 165, 180
Césaire, Aimé, 8–11, 22, 166, 181, 209–10n86; and departmentalization, 170, 223n56
Chad, 47, 105, 125, 127–28, 164; and World War II, 166–67
The Chicago Defender, 129–30
chicotte (whip), 120
chiefs, colonial-appointed, 13, 193n54, 206n28; terms for, 110–11, 114, 206n23, 206n30
Christian, George James, 71, 76, 151, 219n95
Church Missionary Society, 3, 141, 215n38
citizenship, 5, 115, 140
civilizing mission (*mission civilisatrice*), 27, 29, 34, 38, 111
Clarke, James, 152
Clifford, Elizabeth, 136, 214n13
Clifford, Hugh, 48–49, 136
cocoa industry, 77
Code de l'Indigénat, 34, 207n39
colonial categories: contradictions of, 12; "false universalism" of, 50; petitions used to challenge inconsistencies of, 32–33, 38–40, 47–49, 192n33
colonialism: critiques of, 123–25, 142, 165, 172–73; dichotomized language of, 40; education, 20–22, *21*, 133–34; imperatives of, 26–28, 46, 109, 134; imperial and diasporic visions entangled, 17; military campaigns, 26, 33, 189n56, 189n57; prisons, 34, 68, 76, 80, 109, 112–13, 207n39; and World War I, 88–89. *See also* archives; British Empire; France
Colonial Office (London), 16–17, 56, 147; archive, 62–68; Nigeria Register of Correspondence, *66*
colonial studies, 50
Comité de Défense de la Race Nègre (CDRN), 158–59
Compagnie Nouvelle du Kouango Français, 119
concessionary companies, 33, 41, 119–20
Condé, Mamadou, 130
Condé, Maryse, 105, 130–31, 180
Congo-Océan Railway, 109, 119, 205n14

Coppet, Marcel de, 31
cosmopolitanism, constrained, 177
creole languages, 13, 25, 85–88, 201n43
creolization, 10–11
Crowther, Dandeson Coates, 3, 5, 141–42, 146, 152
Crowther, Samuel Ajayi, 3, 142, 195n81

The Daily Chronicle, 140
The Daily Gleaner, 3
Damas, Léon-Gontran, 20
Danquah, J. B., 101, 204n100
Danquah, Moses, 102
Davies, Hezekiah Oladipo, 149–50, *151*, 218n87, 219n92
Dawes, Kwame, 204n111, 220n104
Dawes, Levi, 103, 152, 180, 220n104
Dawes, Neville, 102–3, 180, 204n111
decolonization: geography of, 167–68, 172, 177; Jean-Louis's poetry about, 13–14, 155–57
de Gaulle, Charles, 105–6, *107*, 125
Delafosse, Maurice, 109, 126, 223n66
Delany, Martin, 36
Delgrès, Louis, 170, 176
Delmont, Alcide, 160
departmentalization, 10, 170, 172, 223n56
d'Esnambuc, Pierre Bélain, 165
Dewitte, Philippe, 157
diasporic exchanges, 4, 5, 99, 106, 120–21, 132, 153, 178, 180
diasporic imaginations, 22–23
"Dictionnaire Critique" (*Documents*), 9, 185n36
Diki-Kidiri, Marcel, 205n20, 207n44, 207n46
Dirat, Auguste, 158, 160
diseases, tropical, 26, 76, 81, 87–88, 190n60, 199n9, 217n63; of administrators as "imaginary," 59, 62; malaria, 59; yellow fever, 57, 75–76, 199n9
Documents (journal), 9–10
Doumatchi, Paul, 118, 122–23, 131
Doungouyolo (village chief), 45–46, 193n54
Duhamel, Georges, 123, 209n83, 209n84

Eboué, Félix, 47, 71, *107*, *108*; African heritage of, 24–25; African intellectuals, relationships with, 106–7, 110, 116, 118–22, 123–26, 209n77, 210n93; *annuaire* about life in Martinique,

122–24, 209n82; at Bambari, 117–18; and Césaire, 123, 209–10n86, 212n133; erotic and domestic relations, 114–17, *117*; ethnographic and linguistic research, 106–7, 109–22, 126–27, 131–32, 177; ethnographic fictions, 13, 107, 131, 213n140; and Fanon, 130, 212n131; and Free French, 105–7, 125, 126, 129; governorships, 122–25, 128; intimate geographies of, 107, 122–23, 126–31; loyalty to France, 105–6, 127, 130; Maran, friendship with, 47, 107–8, 115, 127–28, 211n118; "native bourgeoisie," call for, 130, 206n28; as Pan-African symbol, 13, 107, 127–30; in Panthéon, 106, 167, 205n2; personal archive of, 106–7, 131–32; postage stamp of, *129*; promotions denied to, 115–16; racism encountered by, 114–16, 122, 125, 210n102; *Writings:* dictionary, 109–16; *La nouvelle politique indigène*, 111, 206n28, 211n114; *Les peuples de l'Oubangui-Chari*, 106

Eboué, Henri, 114–16, 208n60, 209n80, 209n86
Eboué, Marie-Gabrielle, 25
Eboué, Robert, 115–16, *117*, 208n60, 209n80
Eboué-Tell, Eugénie, 116–18, *117*, 208n63, 211n115
Ebute Metta (Lagos), 58, 63, 68, 147
École Coloniale (Paris), 74, 108
education: and AME Zion Church, 94–96; "book depots," 215n383; in Caribbean, 20–22, *21*, 88, 133; European models for, 23, 29, 86; government schools in West Africa, 133–39, 141, 144–47; headmasters, 133, 139, 153, 213n3, 214n25; missionary schools, 133; networks in, 134, 138–39; salaries of educators, 139, 214n26, 215n34; "unanticipated results" of, 134
Edwards, Brent Hayes, 121, 184n18, 209n76
edwó (yam), 87, 88; as *eddoe*, 87, 88
El Hadj Omar, 126
emigration initiatives, 27–28
empire: "Black Empire," 164, 174–75; criticisms of, 46–47, 62, 88–89, 95, 119–120, 164–70, 174–76; epistemologies of, 6, 14, 184n22; fragmentation by, 3–7, 10; imperial culture, 19–22, 50; imperial geographies, 3–6, 11, 14, 49–50, 68, 70, 115, 125, 131–32, 153, 160, 162, 168, 170, 176–77, 185n29; imperial identity, 14, 29, 71, 105–6, 142, 177; languages of, 75–79, 88, 98; mobility within, 14, 70, 125;

networks of, 75, 84–85. *See also* archives; British Empire; French Empire
Empire Day, 20, 86, 136–37, *137*
errance (errantry), 177
Eshleman, Clayton, 8–9
ethnographic and linguistic research, 106–7, 109, 116–22, 124–26, 131–32, 177
"Europeanness," 20–22, 39–40, 48–50, 146
Excelsior football club (Accra), 153–54

Fairley, Milton, 74
Fanon, Frantz, 15, 130, 179, 180, 212n131
Fante language, 13, 75, 77, 81–89, 94, 98, 177
Feierman, Steven, 113
Ferjus, Raymond, 108, *108*
Fiawoo, F. K., 96–97, 99
fictions, ethnographic, 13, 107, 131, 213n140
folktales, 116–122, *119*, *120*; Tere, figure of, 118, 208n68
Fondation Charles de Gaulle (Paris), 106
football clubs, 153–54, 220n109
Ford, Miss F. L., 54–55, 57, 62, 177
form, 186n52; of colonial archives, 50–51, 67–68; narrative, 12–14, 50; new forms of belonging, 89–91 103; new forms of identity, 177–78. *See also* fragmentation
Fort-de-France (Martinique), *23*, 122–23, 165
Fort Lamy (N'Djamena, Chad), 106, 125
fragmentation: of African intellectual and linguistic traditions, 73, 86, 88, 99, 106, 111, 131; of archives, 4, 6, 11, 51, 61–62, 68, 153, 180–81; in Britton's sermon, 143, 216n44; by bureaucracies, 161, 177; by "disciplinarity," 6; by education, 20–22, 23; by European empires, 3–7, 10; geographical, 7–12; in Jean-Louis's poetry, 162; of memories, 134–35; new forms found in, 62, 98, 131, 135, 143, 153, 177, 180–81; "orchestrated fragments," 13, 186n55. *See also* form; geographies
Fraisse, André, 40–41, 46
France, 5–6, 32, 47, 184n16, 223n66; Dien Bien Phu, defeat at, 172; Free French, 105–7, 125, 126, 128–29; German occupation of, 105; Jean-Louis's views of, 13–14, 160, 164–67, 174; June 18 *appel*, 105–106; *loi-cadre*, 173; Panthéon, 106–7, 167, 205n2; "Paris Noir," 5, 158; Vichy government, 105, 129. *See also* French Empire

INDEX   251

French Caribbeans in Africa (Hélénon), 157
French Congo, 13–14, 108
French Empire, 4, 5–6, 40–41, 90–91, 105–7, 125–27, 166, 169; attachments to, 19–20, 31–32, 40, 122, 180; and Cameroon as "mandate," 157, 160; citizenship in, 115–16; concessionary companies, 33, 41, 119; racial hypocrisies of challenged, 115, 116, 119–20; tricentenary of French Caribbean, 71, 122, 165. *See also* Afrique Équatoriale Française (AEF); Afrique Occidentale Française (AOF); empire; France
French Guiana, 20, 24–25, 32, 111, 116, 130, 188n40. *See also* Eboué, Félix
Frobenius, Leo, 10
Front de Libération Nationale, 173
fufu, 87

Ga language and history, 41–45, 74, 193n48
Gang Gang Sarah story, 77
Garvey, Marcus, 154; influence in Nigeria, 142, 146–47; as mentee of Dusé Mohamed Ali, 69, 93; political leader in Jamaica, 140, 215n32; influence on Jean-Louis, 163–64, 168–70, 174; UNIA, leader of, 147, 170, 192n27
"*géographie cordiale*" (intimate geography), 13, 122–23, 125, 177
Géographie cordiale de l'Europe (Duhamel), 123, 209nn83–84
geographies: as "alterable terrain," 14; cartography between Africa and the Caribbean, 122–23; colony-metropole nexus, 5; fractured by European empires, 3–4, 7, 10; intimate geographies, 107, 122–23, 125–27, 130–31. *See also* belonging, geographies of; fragmentation
George V, 140, 198n55, 215n28
Ghana, 5, 73; Accra print culture, 13, 100–101; after World War I, 90–91; Angelou in, 73, 90–99, 202n66; Boy Scouts, 73, 74, 102; Brathwaite in, 179–80; Condé in, 130–31; football club, 153–54; independence, 73, 102–3, 157, 175; migration to Nkrumah's, 102, 130–31. *See also* Gold Coast
Glissant, Édouard, 7, 23, 162–63, 177, 186n54
Gold Coast, 13, 32, 35–38, 179–80, 216n53; AME Zion Church in, 94–97; Anlo settlements, 89–90; Asante state, 36, 89; cocoa industry, 77; connections with Caribbean and United States, 142; Keta, 89–90, 97–98; Kumasi, 79–81, *80*, *82*, *84*, *87*, 88–89; segregation areas, 36, 145–46, 217n63; Sekondi, 75–77, 145–46, 199n9, 217n63; Swedru, 77. *See also* Cape Coast (Gold Coast); Ghana
The Gold Coast Leader, 36, 45, 75–77, 137, 140, 202n73
The Gold Coast Observer, 100
The Gold Coast Pioneer, 101
Goring, Edith. *See* Barbour-James, Edith (née Goring)
Gothon-Lunion, Joseph, 158–59, 174
Gouandjia, Albert, 118, 121–22, 123, 131, 208n72
Government Boys' School (Cape Coast), 136–38, 144–45, 153
Government Girls' School (Cape Coast), 135–36, 147
Government High School (Bonny, Nigeria), 141, 147, 149
A Grammatical Sketch and Vocabulary of the Akra-or Gã-Language (Zimmermann), 42–44, *43*
Greene, Sandra, 96, 203n85, 203n89
Grenada, 19, 74, 149
Guadeloupe, 19, 71 188n40, 212n135; departmentalization of, 170; Eboué as acting governor of, 124, 128; Eugénie Eboué-Tell as senator of, 211n115; indentured laborers in, 19, 187nn16–17; Kikongo communities, 24, 189n47; as *pays natal*, 55, 57–58, 60, 61; reenslavement, fight against, 170–72; Sainte-Anne, 157, 170, 175. *See also* Bouverat, Lucie; Condé, Maryse, Jean-Louis, Henri
Guha, Ranajit, 196–97n30

Hall, Stuart, 21
Hannibal, 175
Harcourt, Lewis, 31
Harding, Colin, 91, 92, 202n67
Hardy, Georges, 126
Harrow Workhouse, 62–64, 66
Hay, Malcolm, 145–46
healing and social reproduction, 112–14
Hearts of Oak Sporting Club (Accra), 153
Hélénon, Véronique, 157, 158, 188n40
Hitler, Adolf, 130, 173

Hoare, Samuel, 219n90
Hotel Alimentation du Bas-Congo (ABC), 38–40, *39*
Houdas, Octave, 171, 223n66
housing and accommodations, 38–40, 78, 145–47, 217n63, 217nn65–66
How Britain Rules Africa (Padmore), 151
Hoyte, Cunliffe Malcolm, 12, 25, 32, 35–38, 50–51, 177, 180; as "Dhani," 25; "European" claims of, 48–49; Ga language exams taken by, 41, 42–45, 192n41, 193n47; petitions of, 12, 38–40, 47–49, 192n33, 194n77; racism encountered by, 37–38, 48–49; in West Indian networks, 102, 189n52, 204n109
Hoyte, Ralph, Jr., 25
Hunt, Nancy Rose, 186n52

identity: "Caribbean," 71; imperial, 14, 22, 29, 50 71, 105–6, 125, 142, 177; new forms of, 177–78; racial, 95–96, 115, 125
Ikoli, Ernest, 147, 149, 150, 217n66, 218n73, 219n90
indentured laborers, 7, 19, 24, 86, 187nn16–17, 188n40; from China, 19, 187n17
informe (unformed). *See* form; unformed (*informe*)
Ingham, Ernest, 139, 143; and providential design, 27–28
"*instituteurs-ethnographes*," 123
intellectuals: African, 4, 88, 89–98, 100–101, 106–7, 118–27, 131–32; Caribbean, 6–8, 25, 133, 213n3; exchanges of, 118–22, 123–27, 132, French, 9, 28; networks of, 95, 98, 127, 160. *See also* Pan-Africanism
intellectual trajectories, 4, 13, 17, 98, 106–7, 131, 157, 162
Internationale Communiste, 159
interpreters, 13, 26, 74, 81, 118, 121–22, 193n56
"intimate geography" (*géographie cordiale*). *See* geographies
Islam, 71, 122, 124, 126, 128, 171–72, 173, 223n66
Italy-Ethiopia crisis of 1935, 150, 219n90

Jamaica, 19–20, 135; earthquake (1907), 1–3, *2*, 7, 141, 142; indentured laborers in, 19, 187n16; infant mortality in, 19; race and identity in, 20, 21, 23; rebellion in, 19, 135.

See also Shackleford, Amos; Veitch, Lebert Josiah
Jamaica Labour Party, 140–41
James, C. L. R., 20, 23, 102, 133, 151, 184n16, 188n38, 213n1, 213n3, 219n97
James, Gwendolyn, 152
James, Winston, 38
Jamot, Eugène, 45, 46
Jean-Baptiste, Rachel, 115, 207n49
Jean-Louis, Henri, 13–14, 155–78, *176*, 221–22n24, 222n52; African heritage, 25–26; African Republic concept, 157, 164, 174, 175–76; assimilation, views of, 165–68; as "Baghio'o," 157, 161, 170–72, 174; "Black Empire" concept, 164, 174; centers and peripheries in thinking of, 162–63, 165; as character in *Ambiguous Adventure*, 172–73, 223n66; confederation concept, 166–70, 175, 223n62; constrained cosmopolitanism of, 177; criticisms of imperialism, 164–65; empire, critiques of, 168–69, 172–73, 175–76; and errantry, 177; fragmentary archive of, 157, 161, 177; France, views of, 13–14, 160, 164–67, 174; Garvey's influence on, 163–64, 168, 174; great-uncle "Jean-Louis dit Baghio'o," 170–71; international socialist confederation concept, 174–75; as lawyer, 157–58, 160, 163, 173–74; and LDRN, 158–60; Mohamed Baghio'o claimed as ancestor, 25, 157, 170–71; networks in West and Central Africa, 158–60, 162; in Paris, 155–56, 157–60, 172–73; and *Revue*, 159, 160; *Visions of Africa*, 168
Jean-Louis, Laurence, 164, 175
Jean-Louis, Victor, 161, 189n53
Jean-Louis, Wyck, 161
Josephs, Kelly Baker, 11

kanga (slave), 111–13; Eboué's possible confusion with *kânga* (attach) 112–13
Kane, Cheikh Hamidou, 172–73, 223n66
Keïta, Modibo, 126
kenkey (maize dough), 77; as *conkee*, 87, 200n28
Kenyatta, Jomo, 150, 151, 184n16, 218n87
The Keys, 151
King, R. O. C., 140
King's College (Lagos), 146, 149, 151, 218n73, 219n92

kinship: language of, 75, 96–99, 102–3; national, 102; paternalistic, 17, 24, 29, 50, 111, 127; *pays natal* as source of, 61
Kipling, Rudyard, 38
knowledge production: academic, 6, 50–51, 67–68; colonial, 4, 14, 22, 121; "*instituteurs-ethnographes*," 123
kokobey (leprosy), 87–88; as *cocobay*, 87–88
Koulouba (Soudan Français), 122–23
Kouyaté, Tiemoko Garan, 158–59, 161
Kruger, Paul, 108, 205n9
Kryenhoff, Donald, 69–70, 198n57
Kuofie, H. O., 138, 214n17
Kweku Dua (or Duah), 89

labor, forced: in German Togoland, 202n65; in Gold Coast, 35–36; in Oubangui-Chari; 33, 46, 109, 112, 119–20, 122, 191n10, 205n14. *See also* slavery
Lagos, 63–64, 68–69, 146–47, 149–51, 218n74; death of Frank Reid in, 55–57, 58, 60
The Lagos Standard, 3, 69
Lakote Aduaoshi, 42, *43*, 44
Lamming, George, 7–8, 15, 71, 213n7; in Accra, 73–74, 102
Langford, S. J., 66–67
languages, 4, 13, 73–75; Akan, 13, 85–86; Banda, 106, 109, 111–15, 118–21, *119*, *120*, 208n72; Bantu, 112; creole, 85–86, 88; Eboué's dictionary, 109–16; of empire, 38, 40, 75–77, 88, 92, 98; Ewe, 13, 75, 89, 91, 92, 93, 98; Fante, 13, 73, 75, 77, 81–89, 94, 98, 177; financial incentives for learning, 74, 77; Ga, 41–44; intonation in, 111–12; of kinship, 75, 96–98, 102–3; learned by administrators, 74–75, 132, 177–78, 180; Lingala, 110; linguistic fragmentation, 74, 88; and meaning, 74, 88, 99; Ngbandi, 110, 206n21; "origins" and "survivals" ascribed to linguistic connections, 88; of Pan-Africanism, 98; of racial uplift, 93–98, 101, 139; Sango, 47, 74, 106, 109–15, 118, 207n35, 207n46; of Trinidad, 73, 86–88; Twi, 13, 75, 81, 85, 87–88, 89, 193n49, 201n41; Zande, 110. *See also* translation
Lara, Oruno, 157
La Revue du monde noir (journal), 120–21, 127, 158, 160
Las Palmas (Canary Islands), 99

Laval, Pierre, 122
La vie sans fards (Condé), 130, 212n34
League of Coloured Peoples (LCP), 138, 149, 150–51
League of Nations, 157, 160, 166, 219n90
Leiris, Michael, 9
Lémery, Henry, 160
Lenin, Vladimir, 174
Lewis, George Stanley, 151, 204n109
Lewis, W. Arthur, 102, 151, 204n109
Liberia, 28, 94, 128, 164
Ligue de Défense de la Race Nègre (LDRN), 158–60
Ligue des Droits de l'Homme, 160, 166; archives of, 221n6
Literary and Recreation Club of Kumasi, 88–89
Livingstone College (North Carolina), 94, 95, 215n43
Locke, Alain, 128
The Lonely Londoners (Selvon), 78–79, 200n32
Lugard, Frederick, 68
Lynch, Hylton Wright, 141

Macaulay, Herbert, 147, 152, 195n81, 218nn74–75, 219n103
Macaulay, Thomas Babington, 49, 195n81
Machiavelli, Niccolò, 49
MacNeill Stewart, Kenneth, 13, 75, 78, 99–103, 180, 204n100; *Writings*: "The Ballad of Africanus," 100–101; *The Gold Coast Answers*, 100; *If I Had Wings*, 100; "Ode to Independence," 102; "Ode to Stools and Stool Worship," 101–2
Manga Bell, Richard Duala, 157, 160, 166
Maran, Herménégilde, 32, 108, 191n4
Maran, René, 12, *34*, 74, 177, 191n4; Africans, view of, 31–32; as "*bounjouvouko*," 47, 114; and CDRN, 159; double-edged mistreatment of, 45–47, 50; Eboué, friendship with, 47, 107–8, 115, 127–28, 211n118; preface to *Batouala*, 47, 194n70; languages, familiarity with, 115, 195n68; loyalty to France, 35; as police commissioner, 33–34; racism encountered by, 32, 35, 38–41, 46–47, 194n72; role in consolidating colonial power, 33–35; violence against Africans, 45–46
Marson, Una, 150, 151, 204n102

Martin, René, 173
Martinique, 6, 19, 24, 70–71, 130, 209–10nn85–86; archives in, 161–62, 221–22n24; "African" as term of insult in, 23; departmentalization of, 10, 170; Eboué as interim governor of, 122–23, 128; Eboué's *annuaire* about life in, 122–24, 209n82; Fort-de-France, *23*, 122–23, 165; indentured laborers in, 19, 187n16; as *pays natal*, 55, 60; three-hundred year celebration, 165. *See also* Beaudu, William; Fanon, Frantz; Césaire, Aimé
Matory, J. Lorand, 153
Maximin, Daniel, 8, 185n29
Maxwell, John, 76, 145–46, 217n63
mbrosā (rum), 84–85, 201n41
mbunzu vuko (African clerk), meanings and translations of, 114–15, 207n48. *See also bounjouvouko* (African clerk)
McKittrick, Katherine, 14, 51, 184n22, 186n54
McNeil-Stewart, David, 13, 45, 74–103, 177, 180, 201n40; Barbour-James, friendship with, 76, 93, 149; British Empire, view of, 75, 88–89, 98; changed approach of, 92–93; death of, 100; intellectual trajectory of, 98; languages learned by, 74–75, 77, 81–85, 89, 200n26; and new forms of belonging, 89–91, 103, 177; and political figures, 89, 90–95, 201n55; racism encountered by, 95; as sanitary inspector, 75–76, 80, 82–83, 89, 92–93, 199n16; unpopularity of, 45, 75–76, 88
McNeil-Stewart, Gladys, 75, 78, 91, 100
McNeil-Stewart, Octavia, 75, 77, 78–79, 99–100
Merwart, Emile, 108
métis children, 115
Mico College (Jamaica), 141
middle class, 21–22
Mills, John James, 141, 149, 215n33
Milner, Alfred, 17
Ministère des Colonies (Paris), 32, 34, 62, 122, 161; transfer requests made to, 55, 58, 60
missionaries, 3, 27; in Caribbean, 18, 20, 75; in West Africa, 42, 94–95, 133, 141–42
Moody, Harold, 149, 150
Muss, Leonard, 76

Nanka-Bruce, Frederick, 138, 139
Nardal, Andrée, 211n117

Nardal, Paulette, 120–21, 127, 160, 211n117
narrative form, 4, 6, 12–14, 50–51, 68, 72, 134–35, 157, 162; in *The Lonely Londoners*, 78
National Archives of the United Kingdom, 62, 65–67
National Association for the Advancement of Colored People (NAACP), 128, 130
National Congress of British West Africa, 138, 204n98
"native bourgeoisie," 130, 206n28, 212n132
Ndorkutsu, Togbi, 97
networks, 5, 187n10; in Accra, 98, 102–3, 180; Afro-Atlantic dialogue, 153; and bilingualism, 120–21; British Empire undermined by, 151; between Caribbean, Oubangui-Chari, and Soudan Français, 107; between Caribbean and West Africa, 127–30, 134, 147–51, 156, 180; in education, 134, 138–39; of empire, 33, 36, 75, 84–85; extra-imperial, 6, 13, 68–70, 76, 121, 123, 125; family, 56, 62, 116–17, 126, 131; fragmented by archives, 72, 180; Garveyite, 146, 147; as "*géographie cordiale*," 13, 123, 125, 177; in interwar Paris, 127–28, 158–59; of Jean-Louis, 159–62, 176–77; and language of kinship, 70, 96–98, 102–3; lectures on Africa in Caribbean, 152, 220nn104–5; and *pays natal*, 55–61; of railway workers, 68–70. *See also* belonging, geographies of
ngbâa (slave), 111; Eboué's possible confusion with *mba*, 111–12. *See also kanga* (slave)
Niambia (Soudan Français), 123
Niger, Paul, 180
Niger Delta Pastorate, 3, 141–42
Nigeria, 3–4, 22, 47, 62–70, *63*, 103, 141–42, 152; Aro, British war against, 26; Garveyite networks in, 146–147; Nigerian Youth Movement, 149, 150. *See also* Lagos; Saro returnees; Simmons, Francis
The Nigerian Daily Telegraph, 150
The Nigerian Daily Times, 150
The Nigerian Pioneer, 142
Nigerian Railway, 54, 56, 58, 63–64, 68–69, 70, 197n47, 198n55
Ninine, Jules, 70
Nkrumah, Kwame, 98, 101, 154, 184n16, 216n53, 218n87; Ghana's independence and, 102, 103, 130–31, 180

Nurse, Malcolm. *See* Padmore, George
nyomo (wages or debt), 44, 193n48
nyon (slave), 44, 193nn48–49
Nzakara territory, 110, 206n21

oburoni (European or foreigner), 85
Ogunbiyi, Thomas Adesina, 69
ɔkɔŋkɔnsání (hypocrite), 88; as *konkonsa*, 88
Omar, Mohammad (B. Basil Marshall), 128–29, 212n126
Opportunity, 128
Order of the British Empire, 141
Oubangui-Chari, 12, 32, 33, 107–9; Banda folktales, 13, 118–21, *119*, *120*, 208n68; forced labor in, 45–47, 119–20, 191n10, 205n14; history of slavery in, 111–13; intellectual traditions in, 106; Nzakara in, 110, 206n21; political institutions of, 110–11, 206n23; postings to considered demotions, 108, 115–16, 205n10; sleeping sickness in, 45; upheaval in, 33. *See also* Eboué, Félix; Maran, René; Sango language; Banda language
Our Days on the Gold Coast (Clifford), 136

Paddington Board of Guardians, 62, 65, 66–67
Padmore, George, 102, 129–30, 133, 151, 188n31, 189n52, 213n2
Pan-African Conferences, 76, 93, 147, 149, 218n72
Pan-Africanism, 76, 93, 98, 101, 103, 147; "AFRIKA," 128–29; Eboué as symbol of, 13, 107, 127–30; in African Progress Union, 148–49, 150, 202n73; in Anlo Progress Union, 93, 95; in Jean-Louis's poetry, 157, 163–64, 168, 172, 173–75; in League of Coloured Peoples, 138, 149, 150–51; World Cup boycott (1966), 154. *See also* intellectuals
Paris Noir, 5, 158
Payne, Clement, 135
pays natal (native land), 70–72; healing and support in, 55, 57–58, 60–61; transfer requests to, 53–61, 74, 196n19. See also *Cahier d'un retour au pays natal* (Césaire)
People's Political Party (Jamaica), 140
Périscope Africain, 160
petitions, 12, 32–33, 38–40, 47–49, 192n33; to League of Nations, 157, 160, 166; for unpaid sums, 56, 59, 89–90, 93; by West Indian networks, 68–69
Pitt, Walter J., 139–40, 214n26
plantation, 11, 17–19, 22, 77, 85; alienation of, 7; as unit of study, 7, 11
plot (provision grounds), 7, 11
Poetics of Relation (Glissant), 162–63, 177–78
Pomeyie, Samuel Athanasius, 90–92, 94, 98, 99; and Anlo Progress Union, 93; and "racial consciousness," 95–96, 97
Port of Spain (Trinidad), 54, 59, 80–81, *81*, *83*, *85*; African presence in, 22–24, 86, 188n40
Poujade, Juste, 71, 109
Présence Africaine, 10
providential design, 27–28, 143, 190n70
Putnam, Lara, 67, 197n34, 197n44

Quénum, Maximilien, 210n93

"racial consciousness," language of, 95–98, 100–101
racial hierarchies, 32, 114–15, 118, 126, 146
racial uplift, language of, 75, 93–95, 98, 138, 139, 153–54
racism, 3, 70, 78, 94, 134; and accommodations, 37–41, 145–47, 217n63; challenges to colonial and racial categories, 39–40; and coronation of George V, 139–40; encountered by Caribbean administrators, 32, 35, 37–41, 46–49, 59, 74, 78, 115–16, 178; opposition to, 95–96
Radas (Dahomey), 24, 86
railway workers, 28, 36, 62–65, *63*, 74, 197n47, 198n55; networks of, 64, 68–70, 146–47
Rassemblement du Peuple Français, 106
Raymore, Stephen, 63, 68–69, 217n67
regroupement policy, 33
Reid, Frank, 54–60, 61, 62, 65, 177, 197n47
Reindorf, Carl C., 44
René-Boisneuf, Achille, 47
Renwick, Vivian, 22–24, 70–71, 86
Revert, Eugène, 209–10n86
Rhys, Jean, 78
Rights of Passage (Brathwaite), 181
Roberts, Percy, 71, 76
Robeson, Eslanda Goode, 132
Robeson, Paul, 151
Rodger, John, 35, 191n22
Rodney, Walter, 21, 212n133

Roger, Jacques-François, 28
Royal African Society, 101

Sajous, Léo, 120–21, 127–28, 158, 160
Sango language, 47, 74, 106, 109–15, 118, 206–7n35
sanitary inspectors, 35, 36, 45, 80, 191n22, 199n14; Hoyte as, 25, 35–38, 44–45, 48; McNeil-Stewart as, 75–77, 80, 82–83, 88, 89, 92–93, 100, 199n16
Saro returnees, 3, 69, 142, 147, 183n4, 198n50
Scheel, Charles W., 161, 221–22n24
Schoelcher, Victor, 125, 169, 205n2
Section Française de l'Internationale Ouvrière (SFIO), 160, 166
Sekondi (Gold Coast), 36, 75–77, 79, 98; Government Rest House (Sekondi), 145–46; port of, 100n12; segregation areas, 145–46, 217n63; Sekondi International Club, 76; yellow fever in, 199n9
Sekyi, William Essuman Gwira (Kobina Sekyi), 100–101, 204n98
Selvon, Sam, 78–79, 200n32
Sénégal, 14, 22, 57–58, 115, 130, 172–73
Senghor, Lamine, 158–59
Senghor, Léopold, 166
Service de Liaison avec des Originaires des Territoires de la France Outre-Mer (SLOTFOM), 158, 160–61, 162, 184n16
Shackleford, Amos, 69–70, 146–47, 152, 217n67, 220n103
Sharpe, Jenny, 68
Sierra Leone, 27, 71, 90, 93, 128; emigration initiatives, 27–28; "liberated Africans" in, 183n4, 187n17, 198n50
Silvandre, Jean, 71, 198n63
Simmons, Francis, 13, 62–70, 161, 177, 197n37, 197n42
Simmons, William, 76
Simonin, Narcisse, 110
Sissoko, Fily Dabo, 13, 123–26, 131, 210n94, 210n96; *Writings*: "La Politesse et les Civilités des Noirs," 124; *La savane rouge*, 126, 211n112; "Les Noirs et la culture," 211n105
Slater, Alexander, 47–48
slave raiding, 33, 112
slavery, 4, 25; in Central Africa, 111–13; economies reoriented around, 35–36; forced labor as, 33, 35–36, 45–46, 189n56; in Gold Coast, 35–36, 44, 96–98; legacies in Caribbean, 17–19, 143, 187n13; reenslavement in Guadeloupe, 170–72; in Soudan Français, 122. *See also* labor, forced; transatlantic slave trade
Small, John Bryan, 94, 99
Smith, Annette, 8–9
Smith, Faith, 187n10
Sokambi, Raymond, 110, 114, 116, 117, 131
Soloman, John, 70–71
Soudan Club (Bamako), 71
Soudan Français (Mali), 71, 107, 122–26, 180
Soumaoro Kanté, 126
Spio-Garbrah, Britton, 145, 216n53
Spio-Garbrah, Josiah, 138, 144–45, 214n18, 216n53
Sri II, 90–93, 98, 202n61, 202n65
S. Thomas & Co., 69, 147
Stoler, Ann, 61
Sturge Town, 141, 149, 152, 220n104
Sundiata, 124, 126
Swanzy, Henry, 204n102
Swedru (Gold Coast), 77, 89, 98
Swettenham, Alexander, 16–17

Taffin, Dominique, 161
Tall, Tidiani, 126
Tarikh al-fattash, 173, 223n66
Tarikh es-Soudan, 171
Thomas, Peter J. C., 69–70, 147, 150, 151, 218nn72–73
Thomas, Stella, 149–50, 151
Thomas, Stephen, 149–50
Tijani, Amodu, 93, 147, 218nn74–75
Timbuktu, 25, 170–74
Tirolien, Guy, 180
Tisserant, Charles, 115
Tobago, 77, 200n23
Togo, borders of, 83, 89, 90–91, 202n61, 202n65
Toko Atolia (Fiawoo), 96
toubab (European or foreigner), 130, 131, 212n137
"Toussaint L'Ouverture" (play, James), 151
transatlantic slave trade, 3, 35, 36, 44, 99; and Anlo people, 89; Atorkor kidnapping narrative, 97, 203n87; "liberated Africans," 183n4, 187n17, 195n81; providential design, 27–28, 143, 190n70; role of rum in, 85. *See also* slavery

translation, 5, 13, 41–45, *43*, 81–84, 143, 171; and diaspora, 121, 209n76; in Eboué's dictionary, 110–16; of folktales, 118–21, *119*, *120*; of *informe*, 8–9, 11

Trinidad, 19–20, 59, 70, 75, 77, 99–100, 133; Africans living in, 22–24, 25, 188n40; Belmont area, Port of Spain, 13, 25, 35, 75, 80–81, *81*, 86, 189n52; Dangbwe settlement, 24; indentured laborers in, 19, 187n16, Jean-Louis in, 168–69; languages of, 73, 86–88, 177; Water Riots (1903), 19. *See also* Alexis, Edwina Violetta; Alexis, Mark; Hoyte, Cunliffe Malcolm; McNeil-Stewart, David; Simmons, Francis

Tuffrau, Paul, 35

unformed (*informe*): conceptual language of, 11, 12; futurity in, 9, 11; translations and meanings of, 8–10; unformed map, concept of, 14, 181

United Gold Coast Convention, 101

Universal Negro Improvement Association (UNIA), 147, 169–70, 192n27

Veitch, Felix Gordon, 140–41, 146, 152

Veitch, Lebert Josiah, 13, 134, 140–42, 152, 177, 219n92, 220n104; and Garveyite networks, 142, 146–47, 217n63, 217nn65–66; and Jamaica earthquake, 3–4, 141, 142; and "Nigerian reunion dinner," 152; racism encountered by, 146–47; as remembered by students, 215n33, 219n92; in United Kingdom, 149–51

Vendôme, Henri, 71, 109

Vietnam, 172

Volontés (journal), 10

Voyage in the Dark (Rhys), 78

Walcott, Derek, 14, 73, 88

Waller, F. H., 55–56, 57, 58–59, 197n47

Weinstein, Brian, 24–25, 210n102, 212n131

West African Pensions Law, 48

West African Students' Union (WASU), 150

West Africa Times (*The Times of West Africa*), 101

West Indian Federation, 168, 170

White, Walter, 128, 130

Wilberforce, Samuel Isaac, 138, 139

Wilks, Ivor, 216n53

Winer, Lise, 200n28

wolo (paper or document), 42, 44

World Cup (1966), 154

World War I, 48, 83, 88–89, 90–91, 95, 160; African soldiers and, 83; stranded in London due to, 56, 78–79

World War II, 99, 105, 115, 125, 130 152; African soldiers and, 166–67, 211n115

Wynter, Sylvia, 7, 11

yevu (*yevuwo*) ("cunning dog," European), 89, 96, 203n85

Zimmermann, Johannes, 42–44, *43*, 193n47

zo vuko (Black person), meanings and translations of, 114, 115

www.ingramcontent.com/pod-product-compliance
Lightning Source LLC
Chambersburg PA
CBHW021852230426

43671CB00006B/362